D1345363

Consumer Psychology of Tourism, Hospitality and Leisure

This volume is dedicated in loving memory of Martin Oppermann by his colleagues, friends and admirers. In his brief life he made lasting contributions of knowledge in the field of tourism and leisure studies.

Thank you, Martin, for your inspiration, dedication and sharing.

Consumer Psychology of Tourism, Hospitality and Leisure

Edited by

**A.G. Woodside,
G.I. Crouch,
J.A. Mazanec,
M. Oppermann,
M.Y. Sakai**

CABI *Publishing*

CABI Publishing is a division of CAB International

CABI Publishing
CAB International
Wallingford
Oxon OX10 8DE
UK

CABI Publishing
875 Massachusetts Avenue
7th Floor
Cambridge, MA 02139
USA

Tel: +44 (0)1491 832111
Fax: +44 (0)1491 833508
Email: cabi@cabi.org
Web site: www.cabi-publishing.org

Tel: +1 617 395 4056
Fax: +1 617 354 6875
Email: cabi-nao@cabi.org

A catalogue record for this book is available from the British Library, London, UK

Library of Congress Cataloging-in-Publication Data
Consumer psychology of tourism, hospitality and leisure / edited by
    A. G. Woodside ... [et al.].
        p. cm.
    Includes bibliographical references.
    ISBN 0-85199-322-2 (alk. paper)
    1.   Tourism—Psychological aspects. 2. Travelers—Psychology.
    3. Hospitality industry. 4. Consumer behavior. I. Woodside, Arch G.
  G155.A1c65 1999
  338.4'791'0019—dc21

99-31570
CIP

ISBN-13: 978-0-85199-322-5
ISBN-10: 0- 85199-322-2

First published 2000
Reprinted 2001, 2002
Transferred to print on demand 2005

Printed and bound in the UK by Antony Rowe Limited, Eastbourne.

Contents

Contributors

Vinod B. Agarwal,
Department of Economics, Old Dominion University, 49th Street/Hampton Blvd, Norfolk, VA 23529-0221, USA

Irena Ateljevic,
School of Business and Management, Victoria University of Wellington, PO Box 600, Wellington, New Zealand

Seyhmus Baloglu,
Department of Tourism & Convention Administration, University of Nevada Las Vegas, Las Vegas, NV 89154-6023, USA

Christo Boshoff,
Department of Business Management, University of Port Elizabeth, PO Box 1600, Port Elizabeth 6000, South Africa

G.I. Crouch,
School of Tourism and Hospitality, Faculty of Law and Management, La Trobe University, Bundoora, Victoria 3083, Australia

Alain Decrop,
Department of Business Administration, University of Namur, Rempart de la Vierge 8, 5000 Namur, Belgium

S. Dolnicar,
Institute for Tourism and Leisure Studies of the Vienna University of Economics and Business Administration, Augasse 2-6, 1090 Vienna, Austria

Teresa J. Domzal,
School of Management, George Mason University, UKM-42600 Bangi, Malaysia

Yüksel Ekinci,
School of Management Studies, University of Surrey, Guildford GU2 5XH, UK

Mary Fish,
Department of Economics, University of Alabama, 1405 High Forest Drive, Tuscaloosa, AL 35406, USA

Elspeth Frew,
School of Tourism and Hospitality Studies, La Trobe University, Bundoora, VIC 3083, Australia

David Gilbert,
School of Management Studies, University of Surrey, Guildford GU2 5XH, UK

Jürgen Gnoth,
Department of Marketing, University of Otago, PO Box 56, Dunedin, New Zealand

K. Grabler,
Institute for Tourism and Leisure Studies of the Vienna University of Economics and Business Administration, Augasse 2-6,1090 Vienna, Austria

Simon Hudson,
School of Service Management, University of Brighton, 49 Darley Road, Eastbourne BN20 7UR, UK

Kenneth F. Hyde,
School of Marketing and Advertising, Manukau Institute of Technology, Private Bag 94006, Manukau City, Auckland, New Zealand

Jerome B. Kernan,
School of Management, George Mason University, UKM-42600 Bangi, Malaysia

Ruediger Lengmueller,
Department of Marketing, University of Otago, PO Box 56, Dunedin, New Zealand

J.A. Mazanec,
Institute for Tourism and Leisure Studies of the Vienna University of Economics and Business Administration, Augasse 2-6, 1090 Vienna, Austria

Scott McCabe,
Derbyshire Business School, University of Derby, Kedleston Road, Derby DE22 1GB, UK

Robyn L. McGuiggan,
School of Marketing, University of Technology Sydney, PO Box 222, Lindfield, NSW 2070, Australia

Martin Oppermann (deceased),
School of Tourism & Hotel Management, Griffith University, PMB50 Gold Coast Mail Centre, QLD 9726, Australia

Michael Riley,
School of Management Studies, University of Surrey, Guildford GU2 5XH, UK

Wesley S. Roehl,
Department of Tourism & Convention Administration, University of Nevada Las Vegas, Las Vegas, NV 89154-6023, USA

Gary Russell,
School of Hotel and Restaurant Studies, Auckland Institute of Technology, Private Bag 92006, Auckland 1020, New Zealand

M.Y. Sakai,
University of Hawaii, Hilo, 200 West Kawili Street, Hilo, Hawaii 96720-4091, USA

Peter Schofield,
Department of Business Studies, University of Salford, The Crescent, Salford M5 4WT, UK

Robin Shaw,
School of Tourism and Marketing, Victoria University of Technology, PO Box 14428 MCMC, Melbourne, VIC 8001, Australia

Craig Walters,
School of Hotel and Restaurant Studies, Auckland Institute of Technology, Private Bag 92006, Auckland 1020, New Zealand

Karin Weber,
Department of Tourism & Convention Administration, University of Nevada Las Vegas, Las Vegas, NV 89154-6023, USA

A.G. Woodside,
The A.B. Freeman School of Business, Tulane University, New Orleans, LA 70118, USA

Yi Xia,
Department of Economics, University of Alabama, 1405 High Forest Drive, Tuscaloosa, AL 35406, USA

Gilbert R. Yochum,
Department of Economics, Old Dominion University, 49th Street/Hampton Blvd, Norfolk, VA 23529-0221, USA

Andreas Zins,
Institute for Tourism and Leisure Studies of the Vienna University of Economics and Business Administration, Augasse 2-6, 1090 Vienna, Austria

Preface

Only a few scholars recognized consumer psychology of tourism, hospitality, and leisure (CPTHL) as a field of scientific study in the 1960s. CPTHL entered a rapid growth stage in the 1970s and 1980s; this rapid growth included the publication of hundreds of scientific reports in several newly founded journals devoted to CPTHL. The 1990s witnessed continued rapid growth with the start-up of several book series devoted to CPTHL. Because CPTHL as a field of behavioural science is still very young, continued rapid growth can be expected during the next decade. This rapid growth is likely to include the start-up of new organizations devoted to the scientific study of CPTHL, as well as additional degree-granting programmes at research universities and colleges. Thus, CPTHL is coming of age.

This book is one result of the first symposium of a new, loosely structured organization, the Society of Consumer Psychology of Tourism, Hospitality, and Leisure (CPTHL). This first symposium was held over 3 days in August 1998 at Hilo, Hawaii. It was sponsored jointly by the Society of Consumer Psychology, the American Marketing Association's Special Interest Group for Tourism, Hospitality, and Leisure, and the University of Hawaii at Hilo. The second symposium will be held in Vienna in 2000 and the third will be held in Melbourne in 2002.

Twenty papers were selected (from 60 submitted) and presented at the first symposium covering the topics of why, how, where, and who travels and visits, as well as who does not participant in discretionary travel and why. In the months following the first symposium, each presenter revised his or her paper based on criticisms and suggestions received during the presentations. The results from these revisions are now in your hands.

The present book focuses on improving our 'mental models' (Senge 1990) of why discretionary travel and leisure occurs. A mental model is a set of related assumptions of reality. Senge (1990) and Weick (1979) provide strong evidence that our mental models are highly inaccurate, shallow, and lack insights necessary for understanding the complex processes that we are studying. Steps toward overcoming our inherently, and usually unrecognized, poor mental models, include the following actions:

- Ask ourselves and (non-) travellers seemingly naïve questions, for example, 'what events triggered the trip you are now making?'

- Convert our implicit mental models into written, explicit, statements
- Do formal (post)positivistic testing of our mental models–get some useful data (positivistic testing is moving from theory-to-data to test the theory; post-positivistic testing is moving from data-to-theory to build mental models)
- Create and use tools for revising and deepening our mental models
- Ask others for help–seek sage advice from trusted, knowledgeable others
- Use 'what if' scenarios, run simulations, revise, and run some more simulations of our mental models
- Repeat the first six steps in a never-ending cycle.

The present book is an outcome of following the first five steps. The upcoming symposia in Vienna and Melbourne illustrate the implementation of the seventh step. Please join us in Vienna and/or Melbourne.

References

Senge, P. (1990) *The Fifth Discipline*. New York: Doubleday.
Weick, K.E. (1979) *The Social Psychology of Organizing*. New York: McGraw-Hill.

Chapter one
Introduction: Theory and Research on the Consumer Psychology of Tourism, Hospitality and Leisure

Arch G. Woodside
The A.B. Freeman School of Business, Tulane University, New Orleans, LA 70118, USA

Introduction

The field of consumer psychology of tourism, hospitality and leisure (CPTHL) focuses on describing, understanding, predicting and/or influencing the discretionary travel and time-use motivations, beliefs, attitudes, intentions and behaviours of individuals, households and organizations. As a field of study, CPTHL represents widespread and complex phenomena that deserve (and are now receiving) substantial attention by scholars.

Since the early 1970s, CPTHL has gained ground in being recognized as a unique field of study embracing researchers trained in divergent disciplines, including sociology, geography, transportation, marketing, psychology, social psychology, accommodations management, leisure science, strategic management and economics. The bond among these researchers is their shared motivation to create knowledge useful for theory and applications in CPTHL.

No one year triggered the establishment of the scientific field of CPTHL. However, several factors contributed to its transformation from a research interest to a recognized branch of social science. In part, these factors include the following three propositions: (1) scholars working in CPTHL refuse to be restricted to the literature from any one discipline; (2) several household and organizational behaviours related to travel and leisure activities are highly associated; and (3) the economic, social and psychological impacts of travel and leisure are very substantial for many individuals, cities, states and nations.

Evidence of CPTHL as a separate scientific field includes the robust health of several scholarly journals, and a substantial increase in the number of undergraduate and postgraduate university degree programmes in CPTHL. The journals include: *Annals of Tourism Research, Journal of Travel Research, Tourism Management, Journal of Leisure Science, Journal of Tourism Studies, Journal of Travel and Tourism Marketing, Cornell Hotel and Restaurant Administration*

Quarterly, FIU Hospitality Review, Journal of Tourism, International Journal of Management and Tourism, and *Journal of Hospitality and Leisure Marketing.* The degree programmes include those of the School of Hotel and Restaurant Administration, Cornell University, USA; the Institute for Tourism and Leisure Studies of the Vienna University of Economics, Austria; and the School of Tourism and Hotel Management, Griffith University, Australia.

The present book presents detailed evidence of relationships among travel and leisure knowledge, attitudes, decisions, and behaviours of individuals and organizations. For example, travel and leisure activities are linked with destination choices, mode of travel choices, accommodation decisions, shopping decisions, restaurant choices and travel route decisions; these choices and behaviours are grounded in specific cultural, motivational, social and marketing influences. Consequently, an eclectic systems perspective is useful for achieving deep understanding and description of travel and leisure behaviour. Chapter 10, by Kenneth Hyde, provides theoretical structure and empirical evidence to support this view. Descriptions of such travel and leisure behavioural systems are available elsewhere (see Arnould and Price, 1993; Woodside and MacDonald, 1994; Arnould *et al.*, 1999; Holyfield, 1999).

Whether or not the travel and leisure industry is the world's largest when measured in expenditures is arguable. However, few would disagree that the field of travel and leisure, as economic and social activities, influences the quality of life of substantial shares of the populations of many regions, cities and nations. Internationally, the World Trade Organization (1999) estimates that nearly 600 million international travellers spent more than US$425 billion in 1997; international tourist arrivals grow by an average of 4.3 per cent annually; and receipts climb by 6.7 per cent annually. Thus, as we enter the 21st century, international leisure travel is experiencing rapid increases in numbers of persons and economic impacts for many nations and regions.

Within the USA, striking estimates indicate the large economic impacts of leisure travel: the combined US within- and between-state leisure travel is about the same size as international travel. In the state of Illinois alone, in 1997 non-residents were estimated to have spent US$20 billion on transportation, lodging, food service, entertainment and recreation and general retail trade in 1997: 'a $1.2 billion or 6.5 per cent increase from 1996. Those expenditures supported nearly 266,000 jobs for Illinoisans across the state. Tourism is one of Illinois' largest industries, and its outstanding growth through the 1990s has helped boost related economic development in communities throughout the state' (Edgar, 1998, p. 1). 'In addition, travel-generated payroll [in Illinois] increased 4.7 per cent from 1996 to more than $5.5 billion, and tax revenue generated by tourism rose to more than $3.2 billion in 1997, an increase of 6.2 per cent from the previous year' (Edgar, 1988, p. 2).

Counting within-state (or within-region), between-state and international travel for nations of the economically developed world, the travel industry can be estimated realistically to include total expenditures four times the estimate of international travel expenditure, or US$2 trillion. These expenditures do not include near-home travel for sports, leisure and other discretionary purposes (e.g. visiting nearby friends and family), travelling to and from destinations less than 150 km from home.

Understanding Who Travels Where, How, and Why

Households and organizations may be usefully categorized into four behavioural segments:

- A: local-area-only travellers (non-travellers)
- B: near-home travellers (i.e. travel only within the state or region, or no further than the next state or region)
- C: distant domestic travellers who also sometimes travel near home
- D: international travellers who also sometimes travel domestically.

A research finding that may be surprising is that segment A has the largest share of US households – in the USA about 45 per cent of households report no travel away from home annually (see the annual Simmons Market Research Bureau studies, e.g. 1993). While estimates are unavailable, many of these households are unlikely to travel away from home for several years, and possibly for several decades. A substantial share of Americans do not participate in any travel away from their home areas in any one year and, in many cases, for many years.

Most Swedish households are members of segments B and C. Given the many nearby international destinations, this research finding may be surprising. What may be even more surprising is the finding that for most discretionary trips by Swedish households, only one type of trip having only one destination is considered. Making travel plans automatically, without strategic thought about where to go and what to do, is the dominant paradigm in Sweden – 'when asked about what to do in case of the trip being cancelled, the most commonly reported alternative was to stay at home. This is in itself a further indication that mostly no destination alternatives were considered' (Lindh, 1998, p. v).

In the US fewer than 20 per cent of households take more than two-thirds of the total trips taken away from home. Fewer than 5 per cent of households take about 50 per cent of the international trips and 70 per cent of the total airline trips. See annual Simmons' reports for further details.

Figure 1.1 is a composite, meta-analysis view that summarizes shares of households with their shares of travel expenditures among G7 (economically rich) nations. This figure shows non-users of travel accounting for roughly 5 per cent of total travel expenditure because of unplanned trips.

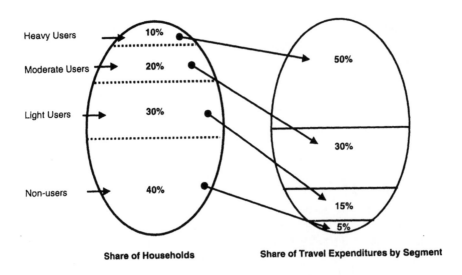

Figure 1.1 National households and approximate shares of discretionary travel.
Dotted lines indicate small amount of shifting among user segments reflecting the
attainment of new 'travel horizons' (see Oppermann, Chapter 2) by some households, but most adults in households remain in one of the four user segments for
most adult years.

Figure 1.1 does not distinguish between work-related and leisure-related travel.
Certainly, substantial numbers of trips by heavy and moderate users are work-
related. However, work-related and leisure-related trips are likely to be overlapping categories rather than completely dichotomous. Should we attempt to
decompose trip expenditures when, for example, a senior corporate executive
invites her husband and teenager to join her on a 5-day business trip to London
from their home in Pittsburgh so that they can all visit some museums and theatre
productions in London; or do we count the entire trip as business-related or leisure-related? The point here is not to resolve this issue, but rather to emphasize
the problem of restricting discretionary travel research to strictly leisure-only
trips.

For development of theories of CPTHL and practical insights, a few conclusions from behaviour-based research findings are worth noting. Firstly, travel is
not a pervasive activity for most households in all economically developed
nations. A large population segment is not oriented toward travel.

Secondly, travel and non-travel are often driven by habit, not conscious decision-making: behaviour-based learning is a major influence on household travel
propensity. Many households do not make decisions about what destinations to
visit and what to do and see in these destination areas; motivations, demographics

and lifestyles are associated strongly with segmenting households by travel and non-travel behaviour (Mayo and Jarvis, 1981), as well as strategic thinking about travel alternatives (Lindh, 1998).

Thirdly, discretionary travel and leisure involve a blend of thinking and behaviour processes about several related decisions and actions: whether or not to make a trip; when to travel; to consider only one destination or several alternatives; the composition of the travel party; the mode of travel to reach the destination area; the route to take to the destination area; accommodation; routes to take in the destination area; number of destinations to visit on the trip; attractions and activities during the trip; gift-buying occurring during the trip; whether or not to use professional travel advice in planning/buying; and which brands to buy and stores to shop in, related to airlines, car rental firms, hotels, restaurants, gift shops, and so on. Figure 1.2 illustrates most of these issues: consumers may be segmented into groups according to how they go about solving the issues shown in this figure.

A general systems theory of the consumer psychology of travel behaviour

Figure 1.3 summarizes a general systems framework useful for understanding how consumers go about solving the issues shown in Fig. 1.2, and includes four sets of related variables. Each of the following chapters in this book concerns one or more of the relationships summarized in Fig. 1.3.

Some propositions follow from Fig. 1.3.

Proposition 1

Travel- and leisure-orienting (TLO) foundation variables are the primary explanatory variables for consumers' travel horizons. For example, both heavy travellers and non-travellers have unique core value systems, lifestyles, travel-related motivations, and income and education distributions. Each segment makes use of different external sources of information and marketing influences. Martin Oppermann expands proposition 1 in Chapter 2 of this volume.

Proposition 2

Consumers use a blend of unconscious (i.e. automatic; see Bargh, 1994) and conscious (i.e. controlled or strategic) thinking processes regarding different travel-related issues. For some segments of consumers, travellers think about thinking, that is, they have meta-cognitions about how they should go about searching and deciding a travel-related issue, for example, deciding on what type of decision rule to apply in making a destination choice. Some evidence exists that many travel-related decisions are made automatically (see Lindh, 1998), or in a blend of automatic and controlled thinking processes.

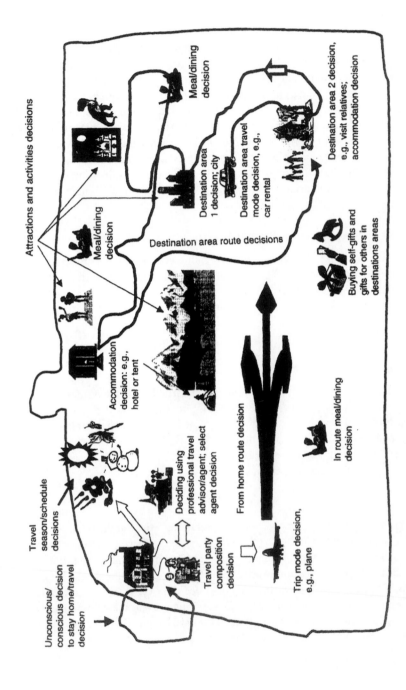

Figure 1.2 The field of consumer psychology of travel, hospitality and leisure.

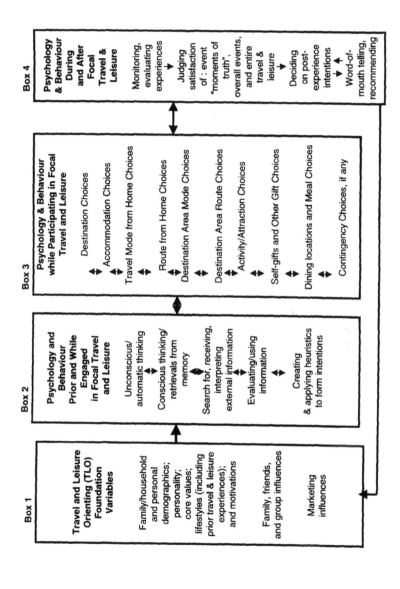

Figure 1.3 General systems framework of customer decision-making and behaviour.

Box 1

Travel and Leisure Orienting (TLO) Foundation Variables

Family/household and personal demographics; personality; core values; lifestyles (including prior travel & leisure experiences); and motivations

Family, friends, and group influences

Marketing influences

Box 2

Psychology and Behaviour Prior and While Engaged in Focal Travel and Leisure

Unconscious/automatic thinking

Conscious thinking/retrievals from memory

Search for, receiving, interpreting external information

Evaluating/using information

Creating & applying heuristics to form intentions

Box 3

Psychology & Behaviour while Participating in Focal Travel and Leisure

Destination Choices

Accommodation Choices

Travel Mode from Home Choices

Route from Home Choices

Destination Area Mode Choices

Destination Area Route Choices

Activity/Attraction Choices

Self-gifts and Other Gift Choices

Dining locations and Meal Choices

Contingency Choices, if any

Box 4

Psychology & Behaviour During and After Focal Travel & Leisure

Monitoring, evaluating experiences

Judging satisfaction of : event "moments of truth", overall events, and entire travel & leisure

Deciding on post-experience intentions

Word-of-mouth telling, recommending

Proposition 3

Consumers' handling of information, both internal from memory and external from friends, family and marketing sources, affects their travel decisions. How consumers go about combining external information with travel-related information retrieved from memory before and during their trips is a core issue in CPTHL (see Box 2 in Fig. 1.3).

Proposition 4

Thinking by travellers includes bits and pieces of automatic, controlled and partially controlled thinking processes (Bargh, 1994). See Exhibit 1.1, and 'unconscious/automatic thinking' and 'conscious thinking' in Box 2 of Fig. 1.3. Exhibit 1.1 on thinking processes describes the core issues: meta-thoughts (i.e. thoughts on how to think); heuristics (i.e. decision rules) applied; and decision goals for each of three types of thinking processes. Note in Exhibit 1.1 that the question is raised in controlled thinking of how the traveller compares 'non-comparable alternatives', such as buying new furniture versus going on a round-the-world cruise. Learning answers to how (non) travellers frame and answer such questions would be useful for understanding the product features and decision rules they use when making travel-related decisions.

Proposition 5

Discretionary travel includes several focal behaviours that may or may not include destination choices. For some trips the activity, not the destination, dominates plans and behaviour of visitors, for example the golfing excursions. Each of the choice topics in Box 3 of Fig. 1.3 may serve as the major catalyst for trip planning and behaviour. Thus destination choice sometimes depends on the desire to engage in certain trip-related activities (e.g. downhill skiing), and *vice versa*. Making self-gift choices may trigger destination choices, and *vice versa*. Destination area route choices are likely to influence dining location choices and accommodation choices, and *vice versa*. For a specific accommodation, or fine-dining enterprise, detailed information on the influences on travellers' decision/behaviour paths (to and within Box 3 of Fig. 1.3) would be useful for planning effective tourism marketing strategies. Learning such detailed information helps answer the following question for the tourism-related strategist: 'What are the nuances in thinking and prior behaviour that trigger the traveller to become my customer?'

Focus	Thinking Process		
	Automatic	Partially Controlled	Controlled
Core Issue	Timing: Is now the time to buy?	Brand choice: What alternative destinations, travel modes, routes, or accommodations, should I consider buying?	Product choice: Should I travel, buy a new personal computer, or go to graduate school?
Meta-thoughts, if any	Can I delay action?	Any different features to consider?	How can I compare these "non-comparable" alternatives?
Heuristic applied	Follow my established routine behaviour	Combination of non-compensatory followed by compensatory	Reflective thinking: can I afford to go? Can I afford not to go? What do I really want from life?
Decision Goals	Take go/no go action with minimal effort	Manage complexity: make satisfactory choice while avoiding high effort	Best-for-me product choice

Exhibit 1.1 Thinking processes and travel and leisure decision-making.

Proposition 6

Monitoring (i.e. sense-making perceptions about what is/has happened) and evaluating the worth of experiences completed are outcome variables that affect overall satisfaction and post-experience intentions toward similar travel-related behaviour (see Box 4 of Fig. 1.3). Thus consumer perceptions and judgements regarding specific events experienced during travel influence global quality assessments of the trip experience. The global quality assessment affects global satisfaction with the trip; global satisfaction affects post-experience intentions toward performing similar trips, as well as the word-of-mouth stories told by the traveller to friends and family members. Learning such detailed information helps to answer the following questions for the tourism-related strategist: 'Was my customer satisfied with the tourism-related product/service experience received from my business? Is the customer likely to return and buy again from my business?' Two big mistakes often made by the tourism strategist in relation to Box 4 include (1) not asking customers such questions; and (2) using biased, leading questions when collecting such information. Asking biased and leading questions includes all questioning procedures where the respondents know that the study is being sponsored by the firms serving the customers. Thus, while the fine-dining waiter asking the customer if the meal is satisfactory during the customer's dining experience is good business practice, it is unlikely to provide useful information on whether customers are actually satisfied with their meal or whether or not they are likely to return.

Proposition 7

These perceptions, quality judgements, global satisfactions and intentions often become clear to travellers only upon their telling of their trip experiences to friends and family members; thus the making of word-of-mouth recommendations to friends influences travellers' decisions on their post-experience intentions (see the bottom of Box 4 of Fig. 1.3). To paraphrase Weick (1995), consumers become aware of what they think after they hear what they have to say about their trip experience. The important point here is that word-of-mouth telling often occurs before the consumer is able to reach quality judgements and report intentions that reflect likely future behaviour.

Only a brief introduction of a general systems framework of CPTHL is presented here. Figure 1.3 is intended to represent a mental map useful for broadening and deepening understanding when reading the chapters in this volume. Detailed development of a general systems framework of CPTHL is available elsewhere (see Woodside and MacDonald, 1994).

An Introduction to Exploring Some Core Propositions of CPTHL

This section presents a brief introduction to each of the following chapters. The objective is to stimulate your interest in reading each chapter, as well as offering a quick tour of the views on CPTHL provided by the contributors to this volume.

Chapter 2: The Psychology and Geography Interface in Tourism Research

Oppermann proposes that destination choice is the core issue in the interface between geography and psychology in tourism. Chapter 2 includes a detailed review of theory and research related to this interface issue. Oppermann links the concept of 'travel horizons' with destination choices to provide a tentative tourist typology of destination-related (dis)loyalty behaviour.

Chapter 3: Perceptual Charting for Analysing Destination Images

How do you perceive Budapest, Prague and Vienna in terms of being 'authentic', 'romantic', and 'friendly'? How might travellers' answers to such questions be used to construct perceptual maps that summarize each destination's image? In Chapter 3, Dolnicar, Grabler and Mazanec review multivariate methods to segment travellers by their answers to such questions. The authors describe the marketing usefulness of such research studies in creating unique destination brand images to attract customer segments. Chapter 3 is intended for readers technically trained in tourism research using multidimensional scaling.

Chapter 4: Path Analysis of Visitation Intentions

Path analysis includes combining a series of multiple regression models to examine the direct and indirect effects predicted on one or more dependent variables. Figure 1.4 shows examples of a general path analysis model and an applied path analysis model. An assumption central to path analysis is that some variables are both independent and dependent constructs; such variables are referred to as endogenous variables in a path analysis model. For example, Boxes C and D in the two models shown in Fig. 1.4 are both independent and dependent variables in the models. A second assumption in path analysis is that some relationships between variables are 'direct effects' and some are 'indirect effects'. For example, Box B, demographic variable, has a direct effect on level of Box D, travel-related intentions, and an indirect effect via Box C, product-specific lifestyle. See Woodside and Pitts (1976) for further details and an application to tourism psychology.

In Chapter 4, Baloglu describes path analysis models to predict and explain consumers' visitation intentions. Such research provides deep insights into the direct and indirect effects of consumer motivations, destination images, and information sources on intentions. If you would like to develop skills in path analysis, the best (technical and user-friendly source) I have found is Pedhazur's 1982 book (see References to Chapter 4).

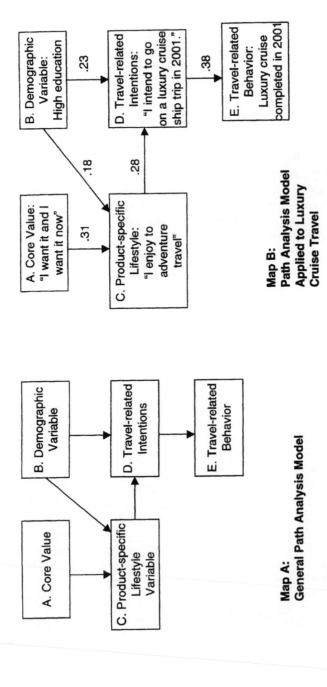

Map B:
Path Analysis Model
Applied to Luxury
Cruise Travel

Map A:
General Path Analysis Model

Figure 1.4 Basic path analysis models applied to tourism psychology. In Map B, the core value shown in Box A is found to have an indirect influence on travel-related intentions, Box D, via its influence on product-specific lifestyle, Box C. The numbers shown on the arrows are measures of influence (i.e. standardized, partial, regression coefficients). For example, in Map B for each one standard unit increase in Box A, Box C increases by 0.31 standard units and Box D increases by 0.09 units (0.31x0.28=0.09). Note in Map B that Box B has both a direct and an indirect influence on Box D.

Chapter 5: Postmodern Research on Action Leisure as Self-Identity

'Action leisure' is a broad concept that ranges from 'adventure tourism' to individual and team-sports participation. Kernan and Domzal provide an introduction to the action leisure literature. The authors develop the central proposition that action leisure participation is motivating as a self-identity process: intense experiences provide perspective and meaning to life; such experiences 'crystallize selfhood'.

Chapter 6: Applying Holland's Personality Theory in Consumer Psychology

Individuals can be segmented usefully by their personal orientations to life. In Chapter 6, Frew and Shaw apply one personality typology (developed by Holland) in consumer psychology. Holland described six personality types: realistic, investigative, artistic, social, enterprising, and conventional. The central proposition offered by Frew and Shaw is that groups of visitors to specific tourist attractions have similar personality types. Designing tourism destinations and services to match specific personality types is a useful insight that follows from Frew and Shaw's proposition. Thus Chapter 6 offers insights on the wisdom of matching specific tourism products with specific personality segments, instead of working under the less useful assumption that 'destination X has something for everyone'.

Chapter 7: Consumer's Risk and Gambling

Casinos attract tourists. In Chapter 7, Weber and Roehl describe an exploratory study designed to increase our understanding of gambling behaviour. The authors test the relationships among risk taking, optimum stimulation level and gambling behaviour among young gamblers. Their review of related literature is particularly useful for tourism researchers interested in understanding gambling–tourism links.

Chapter 8: Examining Tourism Constraints to Learn Why People Do Not Travel

While the study reported by Hudson and Gilbert in Chapter 8 is limited to skiing and non-skiing behaviour, their contribution is particularly valuable reading for deepening our knowledge as to why people engage or do not engage in specific tourism-related activities. Hudson and Gilbert theoretically and empirically examine consumers' psychological constraints to tourism behaviours. The authors raise several uncomfortable questions in the field of CPTHL. Given the substantial numbers of non-users and light users of specific tourism products, comparing the unconscious and conscious beliefs, attitudes and thinking processes of people who do and do not participate in tourism behaviours is a valuable perspective.

Chapter 9: Emotions, Moods and Motivations to Travel

Specific emotions and moods trigger tourism behaviours. This assumption is explored deeply by Gnoth, Zins, Lengmueller and Boshoff in Chapter 9. These authors suggest that CPTHL be grounded in poles of static versus dynamic orientations to life. The theory and empirical research described in Chapter 9 complements and extends the work by Hudson and Gilbert in Chapter 8.

Chapter 10: Advances in Modelling CPTHL

In Chapter 10, Hyde expands on the theory of multiple decision-making by leisure travellers. He combines inductive and deductive empirical research to develop a grounded theory of the sequences in travellers' decisions. He emphasizes that an integral feature of independent travel is the enjoyment gained from not planning the details of the vacation trip. Consequently, many tourism strategists need to plan with great care to ensure that their travel-related services are in the seemingly unplanned paths taken by travellers. For example, Hyde's findings point to the usefulness of suggesting partial plans to visitors, such as the strategy of providing visitors with detailed maps of heritage routes around the destination region.

Chapter 11: Tourist Motivation, Values and Perceptions

In Chapter 11, Ateljevic demonstrates the point that perceptions, motivations and values of international visitors depend on the visitors' own-country experiences. For example, most Japanese, Korean and Taiwanese visitors to New Zealand refer to open spaces, freedom and room to move as motivations for visiting New Zealand – motivations Australians do not refer to as reasons for their visits to this destination. However, certain motivations that help trigger visits are universal; for example, New Zealand's extreme natural beauty. A big mistake of tourism strategists is making the often-mistaken assumption that 'I know what motivates our visitors and what perceptions are motivating triggers for their visits'. Ateljevic provides a detailed description on leisure travel research that helps reduce the tendency of knowing what isn't so. Gaining deep knowledge about visitors' motivations, values and perceptions points the way for designing tourism services and positioning strategies that are desired by visitors.

Chapter 12: Understanding the Leisure Day Visit

Leisure day visits are valuable from two perspectives: (1) increasing the quality of life of such visitors; and (2) success versus failure for many tourism service providers. Tourism researchers often overlook these two perspectives. However, the following proposition is likely to be accurate for most tourism service providers: repeat visits by a few segments of leisure travellers, living within a 3-hour trip radius, are crucial for survival and success of the service enterprise. McCabe offers a useful theory and a detailed blueprint of research methods for learning the

motivations of leisure day visitors, and provides a deep understanding of what
motivations underpin leisure day visits. The research methodology used is simple,
powerful and very useful.

Chapter 13: Learning the Nuances in Leisure Travellers' Decision Processes

In Chapter 13, Decrop demonstrates empirically that prior leisure travel experience is a key personal factor influencing the nature of both vacation sub-decisions
and during-travel decision-making processes. Decrop's contribution on
'grounded theory' perspectives of leisure travel is particularly valuable.

Chapter 14: Examining 16 Personality Types of Leisure Travellers

In Chapter 14, McGuiggan offers a positivistic examination of the Myers–Briggs
Type Indicator (MBTI) of personalities to explain leisure choices. McGuiggan
finds strong empirical support for the idea that some categories of leisure activity
and choice preferences are strongly related to personality types. The MBTI
includes 16 personality types formed from two levels of four dimensions:

- psychological energy: extraversion versus introversion
- perception style: sensing versus intuition
- making judgements: thinking versus feeling
- orientation to the outer world: judging versus perceiving.

Chapter 15: Further Sense-making on Day-trip Behaviour

In Chapter 15, Schofield reports on four waves of interviews of the same respondents, to learn their expectations, experiences and satisfactions with their leisure
day trips. Chapter 15 illustrates the great value of using a combination of data-col-
lection methods. Scholfield's contribution is particularly valuable for tourism
researchers preferring to combine open-ended with closed-ended questioning in
tourism research studies.

Chapter 16: Designing and Applying Gutmann Scales in Leisure Travel Research

In Chapter 16, Ekinci and Riley provide a technical report on the value of designing and using Gutmann-scaled items for questioning users of tourism-related services. They confirm prior research findings that multiple service quality
dimensions exist in the customer's mind. Having a multiple dimension perspective of customers' beliefs about the service quality they have experienced is likely
to be more useful than a single dimension perspective.

Chapter 17: Determining Expenditure by Tourists

Agarwal and Yochum advance our knowledge of how to estimate the economic impact of visits to a local regional area. Details on how to conduct representative, large-sample-size surveys of visitors are described. While the independent variables hypothesized to influence tourists' expenditure may appear intuitive, the real issue is how substantial these influences are in relation to one another. Agarwal and Yochum provide benchmark data analysis useful beyond the empirical study they report. Exhibit 17.1 is a survey instrument useful for studying when planning similar economic impact studies.

Chapter 18: Tourism Demand Elasticities in European Countries

In Chapter 18, Fish and Xia report that travellers from the USA view the UK, Germany and Italy as complementary destinations, but France appears to be a substitute for travel to the UK. The success versus failure of designing combinations of destination trips for distant visitors is likely to depend on these visitors' perceptions of what destination combinations are most appealing. Fish and Xia offer a unique research method to estimate the complementarity and substitutability of alternative destinations. Their methodology is useful for Asia, Australia, Africa, and travels in the Americas, as well as Europe.

Chapter 19: Shams in Heritage-Tourism Interpretations

In Chapter 19, Russell and Walters describe how Pacific cultural customs have a strong spiritual significance that is often at odds with western conservation and natural resource-management policies. They provide results from studies on New Zealand and Fiji useful for understanding how to displace shams in heritage-tourism interpretations and end cultural 'trivialization'.

Chapter 20: Meta-Evaluation of Tourism Marketing Programmes

How do governments go about evaluating the effectiveness and efficiency of their departments' tourism marketing programmes? Are such evaluations accurate assessments? In Chapter 20, Woodside and Sakai review and apply the literature of programme evaluation to government tourism-marketing evaluations. Their findings are discouraging, but they suggest several possible avenues for improving the state of the art on tourism programme evaluation.

Conclusions

Scholars devoted to increasing knowledge of CPTHL are now working on several theoretical and empirical approaches to provide deep understanding of the motivations, decision-making, behaviours, and outcomes of leisure activities. Particular note should be made of the interdisciplinary perspectives these scholars bring to the field of CPTHL. Researchers in the field of CPTHL are particularly prone to accept both qualitative and a quantitative approaches to the study of leisure behaviours. The present volume provides evidence supporting this assumption. Email: jozef.manzec@wu-wien.ac.at and a.woodside@unsw.edu.au

You are invited!

You are invited to join the authors of this volume in contributing to the field of CPTHL. Plans are in place to host further symposia, with the second scheduled for Vienna in 2000, and the third for Melbourne in 2001. Search on the World Wide Web, including checking the websites of Josef Mazanec and Geoffrey Crouch, for further details. Please plan on attending and contributing your thoughts and research reports at one of these future meetings.

References

Arnould, E.J. and Price, L.L. (1993) 'River magic': hedonic consumption and the extended service encounter. *Journal of Consumer Research* 20, 24–25.

Arnould, E.J., Price, L.L. and Otnes, C. (1999) Making magic consumption: a study of white-water river rafting. *Journal of Contemporary Ethnography* 28, 33–68.

Bargh, J.A. (1994) The four horsemen of automaticity: awareness, intention, efficiency, and control in social cognition. In: R.S. Wyer and T.K. Srull (eds) *Handbook of Social Cognition (1)*. New York: Lawrence Erlbaum.

Edgar, J. (1998) Governor announces Illinois tourism revenues reached record level of $19.5 billion for 1997. Press Releases, Chicago, July 8, 1–3.

Holyfield, L. (1999) Manufacturing adventure: the buying and selling of emotions. *Journal of Contemporary Ethnography* 28, 3–32.

Lindh, C. (1998) *Decision Processes in Discretionary Long-Range Travel*. Stockholm: Royal Institute of Technology.

Mayo, E.J. and Jarvis, L.P. (1981) *The Psychology of Leisure Travel*. Boston: CBI Publishing.

Simmons Market Research Bureau (1993) *Study of Media and Markets, New York*.

Woodside, A.G. and MacDonald, R. (1994) A general systems framework of customer choice processes of tourism services. In: R. Gasser and K. Weiermair (eds) *Spoilt for Choice*. Vienna: Kultur Verlag, pp. 30–59.

Woodside, A.G. and Pitts, R.E. (1976) Effects of consumer life styles, demographics, and travel activities on foreign and domestic travel behavior. *Journal of Travel Research* 14, 13–15.

World Trade Organization (1999) *World Trade Organization Estimates*. www.ecotourism.org.

Chapter two
Where Psychology and Geography Interface in Tourism Research and Theory

Martin Oppermann

School of Tourism & Hotel Management, Griffith University, PMB50 Gold Coast Mail Centre, Queensland 9726, Australia

Introduction

At first, the title of this paper appears very implausible. After all, what has psychology to do with geography, and *vice versa*? Psychology is the discipline concerned with the nature, function and phenomena of the human mind, whereas geography deals largely with spatial issues and expressions on the earth, whether physical or human in nature. Yet both disciplines do interface, and this paper will discuss and review the literature concerning this interface in tourism. At the interface of both disciplines' inquiry into tourism, both spatial and a psychological components will need to be present, and this excludes many of the major research interests in both disciplines, such as tourists' motivations in psychology, and the spatial distribution of tourism resources and infrastructure in geography. For obvious reasons, the interface requires a human element, the tourist. From a geographical perspective, the spatial behaviour and perceptions of tourists could be part of the interface: issues that deal with where and when tourists travel, how they perceive distances and different places, etc. From a psychology perspective, psychological aspects of tourists and their behaviour could be part of the interface: issues that deal with what makes a tourist behave a certain way, choose a destination, adopt a certain travel style, perceive a place, etc. This already indicates several areas of overlap between both disciplines, most notably in the areas of destination choice, perceptual differences, and travel styles. Other areas that are also part of this interface are cognitive maps, destination loyalty, destination horizon, travel maturity and travel career, and life-long travel patterns (travel lifecourse analysis). This is not to say that in all cases both disciplines have actually shown an active interest in these specific research fields. Indeed, in some, psychological research is conspicuously absent. Figure 2.1 provides an overview of the interrelations of the three major aspects that will be discussed in this paper: destination choice, travel experience, and destination loyalty. One may view these areas as forming part of a causal circle,

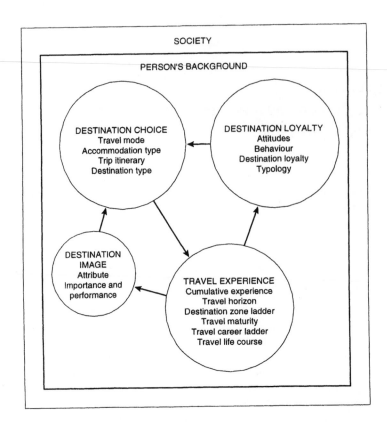

Figure 2.1 Interactions between choice and experience.

with destination choice impacting on travel experience, which in turn results in a person becoming destination loyal or not, and finally the person's loyalty or disloyalty contributes to the choice of the next destination. Destination image is another related causal circle, with the travel experience impacting on the destination image, which in turn affects destination choice. All of these are embedded in the person's specific background and the society he/she lives in.

The remainder of this chapter will review the literature in these areas. If a bias towards the geographical literature is evident, this might be a reflection of this author's own background, but it might also be due to the much greater tradition and research volume, both in terms of publications and researchers. Geography was one of the very first disciplines with an academic interest in tourism, going back to the end of the 19th century in Europe and to the 1930s in North America. Psychology, on the other hand, picked up an interest in tourism only after World War II. The listings of the tourism journals' Editorial Boards are also quite revealing, with a large number of Editorial Board members being geographers, at least by training if not by current affiliation, with generally very few psychologists. Also, some of the literature discussed below is written not by either geographers or psychologists, but by researchers from other disciplines. However, since this paper does not endeavour to review all the research by the two disciplines mentioned, but rather to concentrate on specific topics where the two disciplines interface, the affiliation and academic background of the contributors is immaterial. Besides, many tourism researchers' research interests evolve over time and may develop away from their original background and training.

Destination Choice

Destination choice can be seen as the central core of the interface between geography and psychology in tourism. Psychologists are interested in why and how tourists make certain selections, whereas geographers are interested in the outcome of these choices and their spatial implications. However, in order to understand the outcomes geographers have also shown interest in the actual decision process.

Over the years a number of different, yet often very similar destination-decision models have been proposed (e.g. Woodside and Lysonski, 1989; Chon, 1990; Um and Crompton, 1990; Crompton, 1992; Mansfeld, 1992; Crompton and Ankomah, 1993; Woodside and MacDonald, 1994). Common features of these models are their often explicit integration of previous experience as a decision-making variable, and the notion of a multi-stage process.

Woodside and Lysonski's (1989) model of traveller destination choice specifically included previous destination experience in the traveller's variables that influence destination awareness as well as traveller destination preferences. Hence previous experience, in addition to some other traveller-related variables (i.e. life cycle, income, age, lifestyle, value system), has a dual influencing role in the destination choice process. They also specifically hypothesized that 'previous travel to a destination relates positively to inclusion of the destination in a consumer's consideration set versus other mental categories [inert, inept and unavailable sets] of vacation destinations' (Woodside and Lysonski, 1989, p. 10). Further, they supported their hypothesis with findings from automobile brand choice, where it was found that positively reinforced past automobile brand choices decrease prepurchase information-seeking by consumers. Translated to the tourism destination choice arena, if tourists were happy with the previous (or even immediately past) destination choice, they may not even look for information on other destinations for their next destination selection.

Chon's (1990) model of destination image and buyer behaviour is a multi-stage process in which the buyer forms a primary image, makes a tentative decision to travel, and chooses between different destinations based on information search and accumulated images of destinations. It also includes a feedback loop, from the actual travel and the consequent evaluation of the destination back into the accumulated images. However, his model largely suggests that the feedback is restricted to the image formation rather than the actual decision process. He also did not elaborate on the ramifications of multiple repeat travel and/or other possible repeat destination choice processes.

Crompton (1992) also deliberated on the structure of destination choice sets. His model refers largely to the progressively smaller number of destinations included in the various stages of the decision process, with no explicit reference to the importance of previous experience of a destination. Empirical work conducted by a number of authors (e.g. Woodside and Sherrell, 1977) suggests that for any given vacation, 'potential tourists are likely to consider no more than an average of four destinations in their late consideration set' (Crompton, 1992, p. 427). Thus one can only surmise the importance of previous experience in the radical reduction from the set of all potential destinations, through the awareness and initial consideration set. In a related study, Crompton and Ankomah (1993) discussed choice-set propositions in destination decisions. They argued the importance of the early consideration set for the final destination selection. However, they did not refer at all to the influence of previous experience on the likelihood of destinations being included in the early consideration set. Yet the existence of tourists who choose the same destination year after year (Schmidhauser, 1976/77) indicates that for some tourists the early consideration set may even be smaller than for others, and may consist of just one destination, namely the previous year's.

Mansfeld (1992) suggested a conceptual model of tourist destination choice. He also included a feedback loop, from actual travel and the consequent choice evaluation to the travel motivation as well as collection of travel information. Just as in Chon's model, the feedback from previous travel appears to be directed more at the motivation/information stage of the destination selection process, rather than the actual destination choice.

Woodside and MacDonald's (1994) 'general systems framework of customer choice decisions of tourism services' is a very complex model, and specifically moves beyond destination choice as such by also including choices for activities, accommodation, meals, attractions, souvenirs, etc. With respect to its geographic dimension it also moves beyond the destination choice as such, and integrates issues such as route choices and destination choices within the destination area. Thus Woodside and MacDonald recognized that indeed many tourists do not simply choose one destination, but rather that their choice of a destination area is likely to be the made according to the total number of opportunities available within the general destination area. Hence, while all other destination models referred to above inherently assume a single destination, Woodside and MacDonald's model explicitly assumes a multi-destination trip. This line of thinking about tourists and their choices ties in a lot better with recent advances and discussion of tourists' itineraries.

Destination itineraries

As shown by those studies that inquire into tourists' travel patterns, tourist trips are not solely composed of single-destination trips, but may take a whole variety of different forms involving several destinations in one country and/or numerous countries. Depending on the location and size of the destination country, its tourist attraction base, and the composition of its visitors (e.g. short-, medium- or long-haul markets), single or multi-destination itineraries within the country may be dominant. Multi-destination trips are the primary type of travelling in New Zealand, being a long-haul destination for most of its visitors and offering a whole range of different scenic attractions (Oppermann, 1993). In the Bahamas, on the other hand, being located close to the USA and not having such a diverse resource base, the majority of tourists stay largely on one island, if not in the resort itself (Debbage, 1988; Ungefehr, 1988).

The intranational travel pattern may be differentiated into a number of categories. In studying travel patterns of visitors to Yellowstone National Park, Mings and McHugh (1992) identified four distinct route types, namely direct route, partial orbit, full orbit, and fly–drive trips. The direct route itinerary leads the visitor directly to and from the main destination. This is commonly considered a single-destination trip. The partial orbiters set out on a more or less direct route to the destination area; however, upon reaching the area (in a wider sense) they tour the countryside, visit several destinations, and stay at different places. Towards the end of the trip the 'orbit' is closed and the return path is to a considerable extent the same as the one taken when setting out. This is very similar to the fly–drive itinerary, only the plane is taken for the initial and return leg. The full orbit trip involves visiting a number of different places, never travelling on the same travel leg twice.

In a separate, more theoretical study, Lue *et al.* (1993) proposed five spatial patterns of pleasure vacation trips, namely single destination, *en route*, base camp, regional tour, and trip chaining. The single destination corresponds to Mings and McHugh's direct route trip; the regional tour pattern is evident in the partial orbit and fly–drive trips; and the trip chaining pattern is equivalent to the full orbit itinerary. Although Lue *et al.* (1993) grouped the base camp pattern into the multi-destination category, it is more an extended single-destination pattern because the visitors stay only in the 'base camp', undertaking day excursions from that base. This is quite common for a single-destination pattern, especially when the stay is longer than just a few days. The *en route* pattern represents an itinerary where the visitors have one main destination, but do visit other places *en route* to that main destination.

Both the approaches of Mings and McHugh (1992) and Lue *et al.* (1993) were developed in a largely US (domestic) tourism context. On an international level, however, the addition of at least two more multi-destination travel patterns are needed (Oppermann, 1995b). Oppermann's model of trip itineraries (Fig. 2.1) shows two types of single-destination and five types of multi-destination travel patterns, whereby S1, S2, and M1 to M3 correspond to patterns identified by Mings and McHugh (1992) and by Lue *et al.* (1993). M4 or the 'open-jaw loop' is a type of long-haul travel in more and more demand. Arrival and departure points in the destination area (region) are not identical. This type of travelling is popular where a number of destinations are to be visited that are far apart, making the return to the arrival point too bothersome. The multi-destination area loop (M5) is an extension or combination of the destination area (M3) and open-jaw loop (M4). The tourist visits completely different regions and travels to a number of places within each region.

While one may view destination itineraries and their spatial implications simply as something of interest to tourism geographers, this would ignore the psychological dimension underlying the choice of specific itineraries and modes of travel. Arguably, there is a considerable difference between an S1-type tourist and an M5-type; or even between S1- and S2-types. The psychological profile of the traveller is likely to become more allocentric as more destinations are integrated into the circuit, whereas single-destination travellers are likely to be more on the psychocentric end of the scale. Unfortunately, this is a research avenue not yet used, although current work (Tomljenovic, personal communication) hopefully will shed some light on this area. A rough indicator of the different behaviour of tourists, which could also be seen as an indicator of psychographic openness to exposure to a different country, is Oppermann's (1992) Travel Behaviour Index. Using characteristics such as number of different overnight destinations, accommodation and transportation types, length of stay, and travel organization, a composite index has been established which touches on some of the issues a psychographic profile of single/multi-destination travellers should integrate.

Destination image

Just like destination choice, destination image has received a tremendous amount of attention in the tourism literature, often closely linked to the former. The literature on this topic has been extensively reviewed by Echtner and Ritchie (1991, 1993) and Gartner (1993), and it shall suffice here to refer to their works where image formation itself is concerned. More recent works, by Fesenmaier and MacKay (1996), Dann (1996), Baloglu and Brinberg (1997) and MacKay and Fesenmaier (1997), are noteworthy additions to the literature.

Psychology and geography are directly linked in destination image by cognitive maps, and perceptual differences of destination regions and/or between different origin regions. Research in both is very limited although potentially rich in insights. Goodrich (1978) looked into the perception of Mexico as a destination region by residents in the USA, and was able to plot isolines of perception similarity in the latter. Unfortunately this line of research has never been taken up by others. Cognitive maps of destination regions and cities (Walmsley and Jenkins, 1992a, b, 1993; Jenkins and Walmsley, 1993; Mazanec, 1995).

The Travel Experience Spectrum

Travel experience can only be gained through participation in the activity, therefore any discussion of travel experience has to be linked to actual (past) behaviour. Travel experience can also refer to a wide range of different issues, such as destinations, types of vacation, types of accommodation and transportation used, and types of attractions visited or activities undertaken.

Only few authors have tackled the issues related to cumulative travel experience and its implications for travel behaviour, destination choice and travel style choice. A specific notion within the travel experience spectrum is the travel career ladder (Pearce, 1993). Pearce suggests that travel behaviour reflects a hierarchy of travel motives: as with a career at work, people start at different levels and are likely to change levels during their lifetime. Pearce explicitly recognized that tourists do not always seek the same type of fulfilment from travel, and that people can descend as well as ascend on the ladder. To what extent tourists do so from one trip to the next, or whether this only occurs over longer time periods, is not quite as clear.

The concept of travel experience is also reflected in the notion of maturity of markets (Hamilton, 1988). The argument here is that tourists from new markets (such as the then emerging Japanese and later Taiwanese and South Korean, and today's Chinese overseas travellers) travel differently from the old markets (tourists from Europe and North America) simply because the former lack the experience of travelling overseas. This concept inherently assumes that once tourists have gained more experience, their travel behaviour will become similar to that of the old market. In a sense, this is the concept of 'development' applied to tourist behaviour: travel experience is gained on an unidimensional path which every market follows. This assumption, however, has not so far proven valid. Oppermann (1997b) showed that today's travel behaviour of Japanese tourists in New Zealand is vastly different from that of older markets, and even that of Japanese repeat visitors is nowhere close to the behaviour of Western visitors.

In contrast to many other social sciences disciplines, life-course analysis has rarely been applied in tourism. Exceptions are the works of Becker (1992) and Oppermann (1994, 1995a, c, d). Becker used senior cohorts and examined how their travel behaviour had changed over their life course: contrasting three different cohorts, he was able to show how behaviour had changed between successive generations. Taking this avenue one step further, Oppermann (1995a) used a wide age spectrum and was able to support Becker's notion that successive generations exhibit different travel behaviour. Oppermann also showed how the different generations have gained vastly different travel experiences in their youth, and how that affects their destination decisions.

In an earlier work, Schmidhauser (1976/77) had already used cumulative travel experience. He used the expression of maximum attained travel horizon in order to express how 'far' respondents had travelled at one point in the past. This evidently refers to one past trip which was undertaken to the 'furthest' destination zone; it specifically does not imply that the same respondent is travelling so far every year or on each trip. However, the notion of travel horizon indicates a certain travel experience or exposure to a different country (culture) by the individual. Thus the higher the travel horizon, or the further one has travelled, the more exposed one has been to a different environment, and the higher the risk-taking has been.

Oppermann (1998) visualized the travel horizon as shown in Fig. 2.2. The various curves indicate possible different 'travel horizon careers', ranging from curve A (non-traveller) to curve B (domestic traveller), and from curve C (explorer) to curve D (adventurer). These travel horizon careers refer to the maximum travel horizon attained, and do not make any reference to trip intensity, trip frequency or destination zone visits.

Since the concept of travel horizons is based on the maximum achieved distance zone in the past, the 'progress' of an individual on the travel horizon ladder is unidimensional – a descent is not possible. This leaves open the issue of how relevant a past trip, especially in the distant past, is to today's travel. For example, if an Australian resident travelled to Africa some 20 years ago but has not left Australia since, that respondent would be recorded as having a high travel horizon; in that case, the maximum travel horizon achieved bears little prognostication value as to whether the respondent will embark on an overseas trip or not. This is important to realize, as Oppermann's (1995a) study illustrates. A small proportion of respondents seemed to travel very little or had descended from an earlier higher travel horizon level, presumably due to life-cycle influences (i.e. old age). Hence it may be necessary to qualify the usage of travel horizons to a medium-term past and not necessarily over the whole lifespan.

In testing Schmidhauser's (1976/77) concept of the travel horizon, Oppermann (1998) showed that it is indeed a useful concept, but that it works better if modified to a 'destination-zone horizon ladder' on which tourists can ascend as well as descend over their life course. Oppermann showed that descents were almost as frequent as ascents. Furthermore, he was able to illustrate the predictive utility of the concept, with a significant number of tourists revisiting the same destination zone as they had visited in the immediate past. This leads to the issue of destination loyalty.

Destination Loyalty

Destination loyalty is another prime example of where geography and psychology meet in tourism research, as loyalty is generally considered to include both behavioural and attitudinal components. A recent review of the literature on destination loyalty suggests that this topic has effectively not been researched at all, although some research has been conducted on tourism services loyalty (Oppermann, 1999).

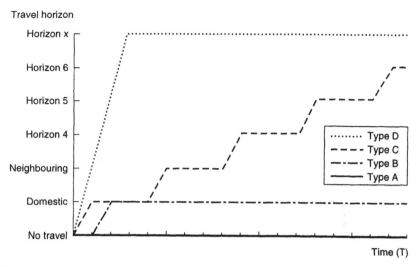

Figure 2.2 Travel horizon attained.

There are three approaches to loyalty measurement: behavioural, attitudinal, and composite (combination of both). Jacoby and Chestnut's (1978) review suggests that a large number of approaches have been used in defining brand loyalty – they present 53 different operational definitions. They also indicate two general philosophies as to why repeat purchasing takes place: stochastic and deterministic. Stochastic theory is quite commonly applied in studies of buyer behaviour. Stochastic models essentially rely on the assumption that there are strong random components underlying changes in market structure. This stochastic argument is especially powerful when applied to buyer behaviour in aggregate, where a multitude of different factors influence decisions. 'Even if behaviour is caused but the bulk of the explanation lies in a multitude of variables which occur with unpredictable frequency, then, in practice, the process is stochastic' (Bass, 1974, p. 2). The second viewpoint, determinism, assumes the existence of one or a limited number of causes. 'Repeated purchase of the same brand by the same consumer does not just happen; rather, it is the direct consequence of something underlying the consumer's behaviour' (Jacoby and Chestnut, 1978, p. 4).

Repeat visitation and destination loyalty

On a very general level, one can distinguish two categories of tourist: first-time visitors, and repeat visitors. However, there are vast differences in repeat visitors: on one side of the spectrum, they could return year after year to the same destination, possibly even several times a year; at the other extreme, they could have visited only once before, many years ago. Thus, whereas the category of first-time visitors is homogeneous, repeat visitors are not.

Although the number of studies investigating the repeat visitation phenomenon has grown in recent years (e.g. Gitelson and Crompton, 1984; Gyte and Phelps, 1989; Mazursky, 1989; Fakeye and Crompton, 1991; Oppermann, 1997a, b), the vast majority have taken the superficial route of only identifying repeat and first-time visitors, rather than discriminating among the various repeat visitors. To this author's knowledge, no study has looked at differences in tourist behaviour or other characteristics of the various repeat visitor types. Furthermore, the linkage between previous experience and destination choice has not been investigated, although several authors have indicated a relationship between both. Wall and Nuryanti (1997) suggested that the ratio of repeat visitors is related to the 'age' of the destination, with newer destinations having fewer repeat visitors than older ones.

Schmidhauser suggested that 'the tourist demand of an individual in a given year is not independent of his (her) travel experience gained in previous years' (Schmidhauser, 1976/77, p. 86). Further he argued that:

'The high repeat visitor proportion in many holiday destinations, for example indicates that many tourists are faithful to a destination when they had a positive experience with it; on the other hand, there are immensely curious tourists who choose year after year a different destination and for whom a decision for a certain destination in one year is at the same time a decision against that destination in the following year'. (Schmidhauser 1976/77, p. 86)

Thus Schmidhauser indicates the existence of at least two different types of tourist, based on their destination choice history: continuous repeaters and continuous switchers, or in Brown's (1952) terminology, undivided loyalty and no loyalty. Obviously, these two types of destination choice history patterns might be considered the end points of a spectrum, with a number of other types in between.

Woodside and MacDonald (1994) argued that 'intentions toward returning to a destination visited previously affect traveler decision-choices' (Woodside and MacDonald, 1994, p. 34). In addition, they identified two travel segments which were characterized by the following statements:

- 'the reason we come here is because we always come here, we are familiar with the place, this is where we come to relax'
- 'the reason we are not going there is because we've been there, we've seen it, we've done [destination name]'.

They also suggested that 'learning the share of travelers holding each of these views, as well as the causes for these beliefs, is an important research objective for destination marketing' (Woodside and MacDonald, 1994, p. 34). Thus Woodside and MacDonald imply that there are specific attitudes underlying the behavioural dimension. Another author who noted both behavioural and attitudinal aspects was Ryan (1995). He mentioned that multiple repeat vacationers also express a high level of identification with the destination. However, this area has not been further investigated at the destination level, and other commentators have commented that despite advances in attitude measurement, a methodologically robust measure has yet to be developed (Pritchard *et al.*, 1992).

Loyalty studies in tourism-related fields

Over the past decade, a number of studies on loyalty have been published in tourism-related fields such as leisure, recreation and hospitality (Howard *et al.*, 1988; Backman and Crompton, 1991a, b; Heung *et al.*, 1996; Evans *et al.*, 1997; Pritchard and Howard, 1997). It is perhaps logical that such studies appeared first in these areas, as the topic of investigation tended to be activities and/or purchase behaviour of specific products which are more frequent than vacation trips, such as playing tennis or golf, or hotel visitation. Most of the studies in the leisure/recreation area have adopted a composite measure of assessing loyalty, most notably an adoption of Day's (1969) loyalty index. However, Day's original index was not directly used in any of these cases, although the authors usually left the impression that it had been (e.g. Backman and Crompton, 1991a, b; Pritchard and Howard, 1997). They measured attitude toward the activity (e.g. golf, tennis) in retrospect, rather than as 'initial attitude'. Thus the question arises as to whether the measured attitude was already a function of their purchasing behaviour (Beatty and Kahle, 1988). Also, as Day (1969) earlier pointed out, measuring attitude at one point in time only, but using an interval estimate for the behavioural component, may result in an inherent bias. Furthermore, none of the studies seemed to apply a weighting to either attitude or behavioural measure, as proposed by Day.

Several authors indicate that participation in leisure activities may represent habitual behaviour and may not be the result of active decision-making (Howard *et al.*, 1988; Backman and Crompton, 1991a). This would support Beatty and Kahle's (1988) argument that, while at the beginning there might have been an active decision, over time and through continued purchase, behaviour might become a habit. Further, Backman and Crompton found that frequency of participation was inversely related to the attitudinal dimension, which suggests that 'individuals may have a positive attitude toward the activity despite low frequency of participation' (Backman and Crompton, 1991a, p. 217). Thus there is an inconsistency between attitude and behaviour which may be caused by intervening variables or situational constraints, such as time, money, and lack of opportunity (Backman and Crompton, 1991a).

Backman and Crompton (1991b) suggested a loyalty typology which evolved from a simple matrix of behaviour and attitudes. High-loyalty are participants who exhibit a strong psychological attachment as well as a high use intensity. Spurious loyal are those with a high use intensity but a low psychological attachment. Latent loyal are participants who exhibit a low use intensity but a strong psychological attachment. Finally, low-loyalty refers to those who score low on both dimensions. The authors classified respondents into the four categories by using a median response split for both behavioural and attitudinal measures.

While such an approach is useful in the absence of any other indicator, it lacks face validity, in that it means approximately 50% are defined *a priori* as either loyal or not loyal along each of the two dimensions. And arguably there are vast differences between people who, for example, participate in one activity exclusively and those who participate in two to an equal extent.

Heung *et al.* (1996) investigated loyalty in the context of hotel choice. They adopted Kotler's (1991) four brand loyalty categories – hard-core, soft-core, shifting loyal, and switchers – and categorized travellers to Hong Kong comparing the four segments. Their results indicate that older and frequent users were more loyal, with hardly any differences found for other variables.

The above studies tended to be retrospective rather than predictive, and none of them attempted to make an assessment of the predictive validity of their classification for future purchases – an issue generally of major concern for tourism destination and operators.

Oppermann's (1997c) study into destination loyalty of New Zealand residents is one of the few which applied the loyalty concept to a destination level. However, he used only the behavioural aspect rather than a combination of both attitude and behaviour. Nonetheless, based on retrospective 10-year-interval data, he was able to show that those respondents who had frequently travelled to Australia during 1985–94 also travelled significantly more often to Australia in 1995. Thus Oppermann's research suggests that past behaviour is a good predictor for future behaviour. For destination marketing organizations this is a very important result, as it will allow them to better predict the purchase probability of their markets.

Issues and obstacles to loyalty measurement in tourism

One problem inherent in the analysis of purchase sequences is the issue of length of time used for each purchase period. While in the tourism industry one may automatically assume that period to be one year, this assumption ignores the issues of multiple travel within one year, and of those travelling only every other or every third year. For example, while the latter might choose the same destination on every trip, because these trips are three years apart with two 'no-trip' purchases in between, these persons might not be considered to be as loyal to the destination as those who return every year. The occurrence of multiple travel within a given time frame raises the issue of whether each trip should be valued the same, or whether a distinction needs to be made between primary, secondary, tertiary etc. trips. For example, a person might have chosen destination X for a long time as the primary destination, but at one stage has switched to choosing it simply as the secondary or tertiary destination, and may travel to other places for the primary vacation trip. While still travelling to destination X every year, the importance of that trip has changed, which might need to be reflected in the loyalty assessment.

An even more perplexing issue is that of multi-purpose trips. Generally, destination-choice models make the inherent presumption that travel is for vacations and pleasure. While straightforward business travel can and should be excluded, since there is often no destination choice as such, the mixing of business with pleasure activities and/or visiting friends/relatives makes the issue of destination choice and loyalty much more complex. Furthermore, issues concerning the decision-maker also play a prominent role in tourism. Studies have indicated that the decision might be reached differently depending on the family composition and/ or the status of each family member (Smith, 1979; Nichols and Snepenger, 1988; Madrigal *et al.*, 1992; Madrigal, 1993; Thornton *et al.*, 1997).

Another issue is at which level destination loyalty should be measured. Goodall suggests that 'whilst there is a degree of repeat visiting to countries, there is evidence that tourists display a greater originality when it comes to choosing resorts within these countries' (Goodall, 1988, p. 9).

Furthermore, and in contrast to many packaged -goods products, the number of destination choices available to tourism consumers is very large. Whereas in most packaged goods the number of brands is somewhere between 10 and 30, there are virtually hundreds and thousands of destinations, and even that would be defining them at a fairly general level. Thus the danger of simply looking at the destination in question and subsuming all others under the 'other' category is even higher than in the packaged-goods industries, where Blattberg and Sen (1976) have shown the danger of using such an approach.

In contrast to most frequently consumed products, which generally have been the focus of the brand loyalty literature, vacation travel is a rare purchase, one which might be purchased only once a year or even less frequently. Thus data on purchase behaviour, following Blattberg and Sen's (1974, 1976) histories of those having made 30 or more purchases, would mean collecting data on travel choice for a time interval of, say, at least 10 years, up to a standard of perhaps 30 years, and even longer for those who travel infrequently. However, such data are not generally available. While the behavioural component might be collected through retrospective surveys, attitudes cannot be measured retrospectively, and any measurement of attitudes today which will be related to future purchases will require at least several years. Furthermore, several studies in the leisure context have indicated that attitudes are not positively related to actual behaviour, and thus are of little predictive value, the main reason being that while people might have a positive attitude toward a certain activity, there are situational constraints which may prevent people from participating in such activities. Arguably, situational constraints such as time, cost and opportunity are even higher in tourism destination choice, since vacation travel tends to be a rather high-value item. Thus one can presume that destination choice is a conscious decision, rather than simply habitual behaviour avoiding information search and evaluation of alternatives due to time constraints, as can be the case in the packaged-goods industries. Actual travel behaviour can be expected to much more closely reflect actual positive attitudes towards a destination than purchase behaviour in low-cost product categories. Since most people take only one or perhaps just a few vacation trips in a given year, the total amount of information search investment is also not so large as to be a major concern. Without doubt, some people do not place any priority on such search and rather allow their travel agent to decide on the specific destination. This is another problem issue in tourism destination loyalty, as not only there are likely to be several decision-makers among the end consumers, but possibly also several 'gatekeepers' in the distribution channels who influence and possibly redirect destination choice (Michie and Sullivan, 1990). This can be expected to have a greater influence at the specific 'resort' level, rather than at the country level.

Since measuring attitudes over a longer time period is currently outside our reach, and in many cases probably not really practical for many destinations, it seems pragmatic to move a step backwards to behavioural measures only. The earlier discussion on repeat visitation suggests that there are different types of tourists based on their single/repeat purchase characteristics. In addition, further categories can be gleaned from the general brand-loyalty literature. The following proposed tourist typology is based on travel-choice behaviour, and as it stands is tentative, derived from a literature review and deductive reasoning rather than through analysis of data.

A Tentative Tourist Typology

Figure 2.3 provides an overview of the typology structure. It can be understood as a typology tree with several levels which are based on different criteria. The first level is the number of previous visits to the destination in question, divided into: none, one, multiple. The second level is a combination of different measures related to people's attitude/behaviour toward travel in general and the destination in question. The third level, where applicable, provides a further segmentation into the probability of those segments visiting the destination in the future. In total, seven different types might be identified.

Non-purchasers

The non-purchasers are those who have never visited the destination in their whole life. They can be further distinguished by the reasons why they have not visited it. Some have never travelled at all and are thus non-purchasers of any destination. Others may be unaware of the destination. Another group of people may be aware of it but do not hold a favourable perceptions toward it. Yet others may have a positive perception about the destination and may even have included it in one of their destination choice sets, but a lack of resources or other reasons have prevented them from actually visiting the destination. Thus this group are potential visitors and may be worthwhile targets for the destination marketing organization.

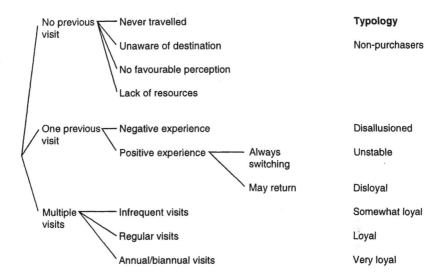

Figure 2.3 Tentative tourist loyalty typology.

Disillusioned

This segment consists of previous one-time visitors who did not have a satisfactory experience and for that reason will never return to the destination. This negative experience may have been related to any aspect of their vacation, for example their accommodation, but has been 'transferred' to their experience with the whole destination. Any marketing efforts are likely to be wasted on this segment.

Instable

These people are always visiting a different destination in constant striving for novelty and new experiences. Even when they had a very positive experience, they will not return to the destination, as there are other places to be visited and 'conquered'. It is with this category of travellers that typical post-visit satisfaction surveys fail, especially when researchers assume that positive satisfaction leads to return visitation. The only interesting aspect about this segment for destination marketing organizations is that it is likely to contain a large number of opinion leaders and destination fashion trendsetters. Thus it would be of value to identify them as such, before they have actually visited one's own destination, and to attract them for their first and only visit.

Disloyal

The disloyal travellers are characterized by a lesser quest for the novel and, in contrast to the instable travellers, may return in future to the destination. However, the longer the time lag between their visit and the survey date, the lower the likelihood that they will actually do so, since more and more other destinations have been visited in the meantime, providing many other impressions and opportunities.

Somewhat loyal, loyal and very loyal

These three categories are differentiated by frequency and intensity of previous visits, rather than by their attitudes or beliefs. The very loyal traveller is returning to the destination every year or perhaps every second year. They are the regulars who do not need any target marketing; they will return anyway. This type of traveller is characterized by a high degree of 'inertia' and a high destination attachment. This somewhat less the case for the loyal traveller who visits the destination regularly but not every year. Perhaps visiting the destination every third or fourth year, this traveller appreciated the destination but also wants to experience other places. However, because of their liking and positive attachment to it, they will always find a reason to return. The somewhat loyal category is of travellers who have visited the destination at least twice before, but hardly more than that. They obviously were re-attracted to the destination, but that has not translated into regular visitation behaviour. However, because they have visited it on more than one occasion, they might be a good segment to target for a future visit.

Conclusions

This paper provides an overview of the literature at the interface of psychology and geography research into tourism. While by no means all possible topics are covered, it illustrates that two very diverse fields do have some areas of inquiry in common. The interactions between the various thematic areas at the interface are illustrated in Fig. 2.1, and hopefully will provide some incentive for future enquiries into these areas. The topic of destination loyalty is specifically targeted in this paper, and a destination loyalty typology developed. This typology can be a useful instrument for destination marketing and management organizations, because the different types of tourist require different marketing and encounter strategies. In summary, much research has yet to be done in the specific areas of travel experience and destination loyalty, and even destination choice has yet to be fully understood.

References

Backmann, S.J. and Crompton, J.L. (1991a) The usefulness of selected variables for predicting activity loyalty. *Leisure Sciences* 13, 205–220.

Backmann, S.J. and Crompton, J.L. (1991b) Differentiating between high, spurious, latent, and low loyalty participants in two leisure activities. *Journal of Park and Recreation Administration* 9, 1–17.

Baloglu, S. and Brinberg, D. (1997) Affective images of tourism destinations. *Journal of Travel Research* 35, 11–15.

Bass, F.M. (1974) The theory of stochastic preference and brand switching. *Journal of Marketing Research* 111, 1–27.

Beatty, S.E. and Kahle, L.R. (1988) Alternative hierarchies of the attitude–behavior relationship, the impact of brand commitment and habit. *Journal of the Academy of Marketing Science* 16, 1–10.

Becker, C. (1992) Lebenslanges urlaubsreisenerhalten – erste ergebnisse einer pilstudie [Lifelong holiday behavior – first results of a pilot study]. *Materialien zur Fremdenverkehrsgeographie* 25, 70–82.

Blattberg, R.C. and Sen, S.K. (1974) Market segmentation using models of multidimensional purchasing behavior. *Journal of Marketing* 38, 17–28.

Blattberg, R.C. and Sen, S.K. (1976) Market segments and stochastic brand choice models. *Journal of Marketing Research* 13, 34–35.

Brown, G.H. (1952) Brand loyalty – fact or fiction. *Advertising Age* 23, 53–55.

Chon, K.S. (1990) The role of destination image in tourism, a review and discussion. *Tourist Review* 45, 2–9.

Crompton, J.L. (1992) Structure of vacation destination choice sets. *Annals of Tourism Research* 19, 420–434.

Crompton, J.L. and Ankomah (1993) Choice set of propositions in destination decisions. *Annals of Tourism Research* 20, 461–476.

Dann, G. (1996) Tourists' images of a destination – an alternative analysis. *Journal of Travel and Tourism Marketing* 5, 41–55.

Day, G.S. (1969) A two-dimensional concept of brand loyalty. *Journal of Advertising Research* 9, 29–35.

Debbage, K.G. (1988) Activity spaces in new environments. Tourist movements in a resort setting in the Bahamas. PhD thesis.

Echtner, C.M. and Ritchie, J.R.B. (1991) The meaning and measurement of destination image. *Journal of Tourism Studies* 2, 2–12.

Echtner, C.M. and Ritchie, J.R.B. (1993) The measurement of destination image, an empirical assessment. *Journal of Travel Research* 31, 3–13.

Evans, M., Patterson, M., O'Malley, L. and Mitchell, S. (1997) Consumer reactions to database-based supermarket loyalty schemes. *Journal of Database Marketing* 4, 307–320.

Fakeye, P.C. and Crompton, J.L. (1991) Image differences between prospective, first-time, and repeat visitors to the lower rio grande valley. *Journal of Travel Research* 30, 10–16.

Fesenmaier, D.R. and MacKay, K. (1996) Deconstructing destination image construction. *Tourist Review* 51, 37–43.

Gartner, W.C. (1993) Image formation process. *Journal of Travel and Tourism Marketing* 2, 191–216.

Gitelson, R.J. and Crompton, J.L. (1984) Insights into the repeat vacation phenomenon. *Annals of Tourism Research* 11, 199–217.

Goodall, B. (1988) How tourists choose their holidays, an analytical framework. In: B. Goodall and G. Ashworth (eds) *Marketing in the Tourism Industry*. London: Croom Helm, pp. 1–17.

Goodrich, J.N. (1978) The relationship between preferences for and perceptions of vacation destinations, application of a choice model. *Journal of Travel Research* 17, 8–13.

Gyte, D.M. and Phelps, A. (1989) Patterns of destination repeat business, British tourists in Mallorca, Spain. *Journal of Travel Research* 28, 24–28.

Hamilton, J. (1988) *Trends in Visitor Demand Patterns in New Zealand, Past and Future.* Wellington: New Zealand Tourism Department.

Heung, V.C.S., Mok, C. and Kwan, A. (1996) Brand loyality in hotels, an exploratory study of overseas visitors to Hong Kong. *Australian Journal of Hospitality Management* 3, 1–11.

Howard, D.R., Edington, C.R. and Selin, S.W. (1988) Determinant of program loyalty. *Journal of Park and Recreational Administration* 6, 41–51.

Jacoby, J. and Chestnut, R.W. (1978) *Brand Loyality Measurement and Management.* New York: Wiley.

Jenkins, J.M. and Walmsley, D.J. (1993) Mental map of tourists, a study of Coffs Harbour, New South Wales. *GeoJournal* 29, 233–241.

Kotler, P. (1991) *Marketing Management.* New York: Prentice-Hall.

Lue, C.C., Crompton, J.L. and Fesenmaier, D.R. (1993) Conceptualization of multidestination pleasure trips. *Annals of Tourism Research* 20, 289–301.

MacKay, K. and Fesenmaier. D.R. (1997) Pictorial element of destination in image formation. *Annals of Tourism Research* 24, 537–565.

Madrigal, R. (1993) Parents' perceptions of family members' relative influence in vacation decision making. *Journal of Travel and Tourism Marketing* 2, 39– 57.

Madrigal, R., Havitz, M.E. and Howard, D.R. (1992) Married couples' involvement with family vacations. *Leisure Sciences* 14, 287–301.

Mansfeld, Y. (1992) From motivation to actual travel. *Annals of Tourism Research* 19, 399–419.

Mazanec, J.A. (1995) Competition among European tourist cities, a comparative analysis with multidimensional scaling and self-organizing maps. *Tourism Economics* 1, 283– 302.

Mazursky, D. (1989) Past experience and future tourism decisions. *Annals of Tourism Research* 16, 333–334.

Michie, D.A. and Sullivan, G.L. (1990) The role(s) of the international travel agent in the travel decision process of client families. *Journal of Travel Research* 30, 38–46.

Mings, R.C. and McHugh, K.E. (1992) The spatial configuration of travel to Yellowstone National Park. *Journal of Travel Research* 30, 38–46.

Nichols, C.M. and Snepenger, D.J. (1988) Family decision making and tourism behavior and attitudes. *Journal of Travel Research* 26, 2–6.

Oppermann, M. (1992) Travel dispersal index. *Journal of Tourism Studies* 3, 44–49.

Oppermann, M. (1993) German tourists in New Zealand. *New Zealand Geographer* 49, 31–34.

Oppermann, M. (1994) Travel life cycles – a multitemporal perspective of changing travel patterns. In: R.V. Glasser and K. Weiermair (eds) *Spoilt for Choice. Decision Making Processes and Preference Changes for Tourists – Intertemporal and Intercountry Perspectives.* Vienna: Kultur Verlag, pp. 81–97.

Oppermann, M. (1995a) Travel life cycle. *Annals of Tourism Research* 22, 535–552.

Oppermann, M. (1995b) A model of travel itineraries. *Journal of Travel Research* 33, 57– 61.

Oppermann, M. (1995c) Family life cycle and cohort effects, a study of travel patterns. *Journal of Travel and Tourism Marketing* 4, 23–44.

Oppermann, M. (1995d) Travel life cycles – a multitemporal perspective of changing travel patterns. *Journal of Travel and Tourism Marketing* 4, 101–109.

Oppermann, M. (1997a) First-time and repeat visitors to New Zealand. *Tourism Management* 18, 177–181.

Oppermann, M. (1997b) Comparative study of Asian and Western first-time and repeat visitors to New Zealand – dispersal or concentration? In: *Proceedings of Trails Conference*. Dunedin: University of Otago.

Oppermann, M. (1997c) Tourism destination loyalty – an analysis of New Zealand residents' destination choice. In: Proceedings of Trails Conference. Dunedin: University of Otago.

Oppermann, M. (1998) Travel horizon – a valuable analysis tool? *Tourism Management* 19, 321–329.

Oppermann, M. (1999) Predicting destination loyalty. Journal of Vacation Marketing (in press).

Pearce, P. (1993) Fundamentals of tourist motivation. In: D.G. Pearce and R.W. Butler (eds) *Tourism Research, Critiques and Challenges*. London: Routledge, pp. 113–134.

Pritchard, M. and Howard, D.R. (1997) The loyal traveler, examining a typology of service patronage. *Journal of Travel Research* 35, 2–10.

Pritchard, M., Howard, D.R. and Havitz, M.E.(1992) Loyalty measurement, a critical examination and theoretical extension. *Leisure Sciences* 14, 155–164.

Ryan, C. (1995) Learning from tourists' conversations, the over-55s in Majorca. *Tourism Management* 16, 207–216.

Schmidhauser, H. (1976/77) Neue Erkenntnisse über Gesetzmäßigkeiten bei der Wahl des Reiseziels [New insights into regularities in destination choice]. *Jahrbuch für Fremdenverkehr* 24/25, 86–102.

Smith, V.L. (1979) Women, the taste-makers in tourism. *Annals of Tourism Research* 6, 49–60.

Thornton, P.R., Shaw, G. and Williams, A.M. (1997) Tourist group holiday decision-making and behaviour, the influence of children. *Tourist Management* 18, 287–297.

Um, S. and Crompton, J.L. (1990) Attitude determinants in tourism destination choice. *Annals of Tourism Research* 17, 432–448.

Ungefehr, F. (1988) *Tourism und Offshore-Banking auf den Bahamas. Internationale Dienstleistungen als dominanter Wirtschaftsfaktor in einem kleinen Entwicklungsland*. Frankfurt/Main: Peter Lang.

Wall, G. and Nuryanti, W. (1997) Marketing challenges and opportunities facing Indonesian tourism. *Journal of Travel and Tourism Marketing* 6, 69–84.

Walmsley, D.J. and Jenkins, J.M. (1992a) Tourism cognitive mapping of unfamiliar environments. *Annals of Tourism Research* 31, 24–29.

Walmsley, D.J. and Jenkins, J.M. (1992b) Cognitive distance, a neglected issue in travel behavior. *Journal of Travel Research* 31, 24–29.

Walmsley, D.J. and Jenkins, J.M. (1993) Appraising images of tourist areas, application of personal constructs. *Australian Geographer* 24, 1–13.

Woodside, A.G. and Lysonski, S. (1989) A general model of traveler destination choice. *Journal of Travel Research* 27, 8–14.

Woodside, A.G. and MacDonald, R. (1994) General systems framework of customer choice processes for tourism services. In: R.V. Gasser and K. Weiermair (eds) *Spoilt for Choice. Decision Making Processes and Preference Changes of Tourists – Intertemporal and Intercountry Perspectives*. Vienna: Kultur Verlag, pp. 30–59.

Woodside, A.G. and Sherrell, D. (1977) Traveler evoked, inept, and inert sets of vacation destinations. *Journal of Travel Research* 16, 14–18.

Chapter three
A Tale of Three Cities: Perceptual Charting for Analysing Destination Images

Sara Dolnicar, Klaus Grabler and Josef A. Mazanec
Institute for Tourism and Leisure Studies of the Vienna University of Economics and Business Administration, Augasse 2-6, 1090 Vienna, Austria

Introduction

Heterogeneity of perceptions is a neglected issue in market-segmentation studies. Parametric approaches toward modelling segmented perception-preference structures, such as combined multidimensional scaling (MDS) and latent class procedures, have been introduced only recently. A completely different non-parametric method is based on topology-sensitive vector quantization (VQ) for consumers-by-brands-by-attributes data. It maps the segment-specific perceptual structures into bar charts with multiple brand positions exhibiting perceptual distinctiveness or similarity. An extensive literature review is followed by an introduction to the VQ methodology, and a sample study on three urban destinations competing in the world travel markets. City images serve as the underlying behavioural constructs. Preferential data are based on respondents' 'comes-closest-to-ideal-city' judgements and incorporated into the perceptual positions of city profiles. Perceptual charting works on two levels of aggregation: named prototypes and perceptual substructures. The results demonstrate how this method prevents the analyst from drawing erroneous conclusions due to uncontrolled aggregation.

Visualizing Market Structure and Detecting Perceptual Positions

Market structuring and positioning analysis are routine marketing research exercises. Although they use very similar methodology, authors tend to keep them separate. Market structure analysis (as introduced by Myers and Tauber, 1977) aims at uncovering the competitive relationships between the brands in a product class. Positioning analysis aims at detecting the perceptual differences between the brands of a product class and the way they are linked to consumer preferences. These results assist in clarifying the competitive strengths and weaknesses of the individual product brands as seen by buyers (Urban and Hauser, 1993).

Positioning analysis has always been considered as a preparatory step towards new product planning or towards differentiating, diversifying, or simply improving existing brands. Normative model-building, therefore, is common for product positioning (Albers and Brockhoff, 1977; Green et al., 1981; Hauser and Clausing, 1988). Market structure results are often presented in a descriptive manner not necessarily intended to assist in manipulating brand attributes. Then microdata collected from individual respondents are not mandatory for market structuring. Aggregate data on market shares, elasticities (Cooper, 1988) and competitors' market operation also do a good job. Positioning, on the other hand, cannot proceed without perceptions (similarity or profile data) and stated or revealed preference data. Market structure analysis may be based on choice data from consumer panels. In this case the brand positions in an attribute space are not directly measured, but are inferred from the utility models underlying brand choice (Elrod, 1988; Erdem, 1996). The measurement results are called market or choice maps, in contrast to the perceptual maps derived from explicit brand attribute profiles, proximities or preference data.

The data techniques to be discussed in the forthcoming sections deal with descriptive market structuring and with the non-normative part of positioning models. The common assumption is that the raw data arrive in a three-way format. This means that three directions of variation are involved: subjects (respondents), objects (brands), and their attributes. The number of brand attributes is not restricted. Data reduction, therefore, is an implicit objective as the measurement of attitudes toward product brands and, particularly, of highly emotional brand images requires a substantial amount of redundancy in the data-gathering instruments. To bridge the gap between the fuzzy language of consumers and the more concise jargon of marketing managers, the symptomatic patterns of brand–attribute associations should be automatically respected by the data processing methodology. Given a battery of numerous image or attitudinal items, the respondents' willingness to collaborate must not be challenged by cumbersome rating scales. The data techniques should be capable of processing binary data. As a third requirement, the methodology should accept an arbitrarily small number of brands if the typical size of the consumers' choice set does not exceed, say, three or four alternatives. Classical MDS procedures would not then be applicable because of too few restrictions in the proximity data.

A pictorial display of the results that does not sacrifice crucial information is desirable. A more fundamental criterion to value the merits of market structuring and positioning procedures will be whether the technique preserves the consumer segment information by avoiding rigorous homogeneity assumptions and rude aggregation steps during data processing.

Reduction Techniques for Condensing Three-Way Data: Maps, Trees and Charts

The typical data techniques that have been used for perceptual mapping and market structure analysis are principal components or discriminant analysis (Green et al.,

1988); multidimensional scaling (MDS) and unfolding (Kruskal, 1964; Young, 1987; Malhotra *et al.*, 1988); correspondence analysis (Greenacre, 1984; Carroll *et al.*, 1986; Hoffman and Franke, 1986; Kaciak and Louviere, 1990); and conjoint analysis (Green and Carmone, 1969; Green and Rao, 1971, 1972; Green, 1975; for review see Green and Krieger, 1993). Probabilistic MDS models such as PROSCAL also allow for significance testing; they seem to exceed deterministic methods regarding the accuracy of the stimulus configurations (MacKay and Zinnes, 1986; MacKay, 1989) and appear to be robust even for very small samples (Büyükkurt and Büyükkurt, 1990).

If positioning and market structure analyses are applied to disaggregate data, it is a common goal to extract group-specific results. For conjoint data it has been a popular approach to segment consumers according to their individual part-worth estimates for product attribute levels. Kamakura (1988) suggests a single-step procedure to account for the predictive validity of the part worths at segment level. Proximity or profile data usually arrive in a three-way format. Preference data for unfolding analysis may be restricted to a two-way format. More modes (buying or consumption situations) may be added to proximity or profile data (see Young, 1987 for a taxonomy of data). Two ways are required either for the (dis)similarities between product brands, or for the multi-attribute brand profiles. The third way covers the variation over consumers (Dillon *et al.*, 1989). Most frequently, a three-way profile data matrix is rearranged by stacking the brand-by-attributes submatrices of all respondents into an elongated two-dimensional array. Standardization across the brands for each separate respondent is required to suppress spurious results caused by confounding two sources of variance, i.e. the attribute ratings over respondents with brand variation within each respondent (Dillon *et al.*, 1989). Brand positions are then derived by averaging the component scores over respondents (Roberts and Lilien, 1993, p. 48).

The classical models for three-way data compute a set of parameters for individual respondents such as the INDSCAL weights to capture individual differences (Carroll and Chang, 1970; see also the General Euclidean Model in Young, 1987, pp. 118–153). INDSCAL also has a three-way clustering counterpart known as INDCLUS, which processes brands-by-brands-by-subjects data and sorts brands into clusters. It extracts information on individual respondents by estimating a weight parameter that might be used for segmentation purposes (Carroll and Arabie, 1983; Arabie *et al.*, 1987). Like the more familiar distance-oriented MDS models, INDCLUS and its recent extensions for overlapping and higher-way data (Carroll and Chaturvedi, 1995) need proximity data as input. One would have to transform profile data into (dis)similarities at a loss of information.

Sato *et al.* (1997) introduced several fuzzy clustering procedures for three-way data. One of these procedures is appropriate for analysing objects-by-attributes matrices for repeated measurements (called a time or 'situations' dimension by the authors). Due to the fuzzification, a Pareto optimal multi-criteria clustering solution can be computed fairly easily. The degree of belongingness of an object to each cluster, however, is regarded to be independent from the 'situations'. This would not apply to brands-by-attributes-by-respondents data, irrespective of whether one lets the brands or the respondents represent the time dimension.

The classical three-mode component and factor models according to Tucker (1964) or less general derivats such as CANDECOMP (Carroll and Chang, 1970) and PARAFAC (Harshman and Lundy, 1984) generate component/factor loadings for all three sources of variation (attributes, brands, respondents: Snyder *et al.*, 1984; Kroonenberg, 1984; Kiers, 1991). Cooper (1988) demonstrates how three-mode factoring can be adapted to analyse the competitive patterns hidden in 52 weekly measurements of (asymmetric) cross-elasticities. This example illustrates the advantages of the visual representation for all three sources of variation in the data as long as the number of subjects remains small. For a larger data set, however, an additional clustering step must be applied.

Correspondence analysis (CA) is another tool to tackle market structuring and positioning problems. Given categorical data, the simple CA processes a bivariate contingency table of brands by attributes aggregated over subjects (Hoffman and Franke, 1986). But the CA handles disaggregate data in stacked format as well. More flexibility is found in multiple correspondence analysis (MCA) which covers the multivariate case and a variety of data arrays collected in conjoint experiments (Kaciak and Louviere, 1990). None of these traditional methods provides for an implicit clustering of respondents while analysing a brands-by-attributes-by-subjects database. It is more desirable to accomplish the clustering of respondents and the mapping of brands simultaneously than to run through two subsequent processing steps.

The GENFOLD2 model performs an internal unfolding analysis. In addition to constructing the joint space of brands and subjects' ideal points, it incorporates background characteristics of the respondents and explicit product attributes or marketing mix variables (DeSarbo and Rao, 1986). These additional characteristics assist in identifying segments of consumers with similar brand preferences. DeSarbo *et al.* (1991) propose a simultaneous MDS and clustering algorithm for dominance or profile data. MULTICLUS produces maximum-likelihood estimates for the stimulus coordinates and segment-specific ideal vectors from two-way data. Jedidi and DeSarbo (1991) also develop a stochastic model for the joint space analysis of binary data collected in a three-way and three-mode format. This method centres on modelling preferences via brand positions and subjects' ideal points/vectors under various consumption situations reflected by dimension weights. The brands' as well as the subjects' coordinates may be constrained to form linear functions of some product attributes or personal characteristics. A review of the recent attempts to arrive at segment-specific brand positions by linking latent class to classical MDS concepts is presented by DeSarbo *et al.* (1994). It confirms that these models are confined to proximity, dominance and choice data, and are unsuited for profile data based on a redundant set of attributes.

In their paper on joint positioning/segmentation analysis, DeSarbo and Jedidi (1995) process profile data and manage to solve one variant of the 'missing data' problem. If a consumer's consideration set of purchase alternatives is taken as a basis to define market segments, an additive utility function defines the brands' positions in a T-dimensional attribute space and the dimension weights specific for each market segment. A brand cannot enter a consumer's consideration set unless its utility exceeds a segment-specific threshold value. Assuming a normal distribution for the segment-conditional and consequently for the unconditional utility variable, the utility/preference measurement still faces the problem of numerous missing observations where a brand is not an element of a consumer's consideration set. Distinguishing the latent utility variable from its observable counterpart (a censored variable) salvages the tractability of the model by preparing it for maximum likelihood estimation. The DeSarbo–Jedidi (1995) proposal is an elegant example of how the combined segmentation/positioning problem may be tackled with a parametric model. However, it must be noted that the dimensionality (the optimal value for T) as well as the number of segments (i.e. the utility threshold) are model constants and thus predetermined by the analyst. One ought to look for approaches for an arbitrary number of attributes which are condensed and reduced during analysis.

The portrayal of consumers' evaluations of competing brands does not necessarily entail a spatial model. Ramaswamy and DeSarbo (1990) illustrate the usage of hierarchical tree structures. The tree reveals the preference structure in an ordinal or neighbourhood sense. Another related concept is simultaneous market structuring and segmentation by applying a clusterwise regression of perceived brand attributes on preferences. Wedel and Steenkamp (1991) propose a fuzzy version of clusterwise regression allowing brands to compete with each other in more than one product class and consumers to belong to more than one benefit segment. Chintagunta (1994) proposes a joint segmentation and positioning model based on indirect utility estimates from preference data. The dimension weights vary over households but the brand 'locations' in the latent attribute space do not, meaning that perceptions are 'household invariant'. The state of the art in segmentation analysis is reflected in Wedel and Kamakura (1998). The authors emphasize the latest developments in the field of mixture (regression and MDS/unfolding) models. All of these models assume that a specific density function underlies the observations collected from each subpopulation. Artificial neural networks are mentioned to be a 'particularly interesting technique' (p. 24) but do not gain further attention.

Since the second half of the 1980s, neurocomputing techniques for unsupervised learning have been added to the marketing research toolkit (Krycha and Wagner, 1999). In particular, the LBG- and other K-means-related adaptive vector quantization (VQ) methods are attractive for marketing analysts (Linde *et al.*, 1980). They can operate online and thus may be used to classify customers by processing samples of unlimited size (such as a steady influx of scanner data).

This gives them an advantage over other K-means extensions such as the overlapping K-centroids approach proposed by Chaturvedi *et al.* (1997).

The neurocomputing tools offer more than that. It has been claimed that self-organizing maps (SOMs) assist in solving clustering problems while preserving topological properties of the data (Kohonen, 1982, 1984, 1990, 1997; for review see Nour and Madey, 1996; for marketing research applications see Mazanec 1995a, b, 1999). The SOM does not produce a spatial configuration like MDS. Instead, the brand positions are topologically ordered telling the analyst about the order of perceptual similarity. Neighbouring positions of first order (with no other positions in between) are more similar to each other than second-order neighbours (one hop over an adjacent position). The quality of the topology preservation may be rated by examining the number of neighbourhood violations which arise from forcing the brand prototypes from a high-dimensional data space into a two-dimensional output space. (This is implemented in the SOMnia program available via the WWW page http://leisure.wu-wien.ac.at/software/.) A more sophisticated indicator, the 'topographic product' as a measure for neighbourhood preservation, was introduced by Bauer and Pawelzik (1992). Like many other neural networks, SOMs operate on disaggregate data by learning from examples, one at a time (e.g. data vectors from individual respondents). As no prior aggregation is required during the training of a SOM network, any subset of data vectors can be processed in subsequent recall runs. Only then, during the recall run, the SOM classifies each data vector exposed as an input according to its similarity to the winner among the prototypes. This postponement of the aggregation step enables SOM networks to cope with the three-way data encountered in market structure and combined segmentation/positioning studies. SOMs have been employed for clustering purposes and compared to hierarchical procedures (Mangiameli *et al.*, 1996) which does not make sense for the experienced user of partitioning and hierarchical methods. It is also unfeasible to compare the SOM to a (batch or adaptive) K-means procedure (Flexer, 1996). The 'fringe benefit' of getting a topological ordering requires a compromise as the prototypes in the SOM cannot fully coincide with the centroids at the same time. As an analyst, one has to decide on either improving the topology preservation or making the prototypes perfect centroids.

SOM models are deterministic and reconstruct a joint representation for product and subject positions in an exploratory manner. The positions of brand profiles correspond to the prototypes in the SOM. The values (weights) in the prototype vectors self-organize in a way that neighbouring positions in the SOM respond to neighbouring data points in the input space. So far, the necessary and sufficient conditions for 'guaranteed' self-organization have been established only for the one-dimensional case (Ritter and Schulten, 1988; Ritter *et al.*, 1991; Thiran and Hasler, 1994; Flanagan, 1996). The SOM is criticised for two main reasons. (i) The SOM update rule – for continuous variables – is not a gradient-descent process and thus hinders the mathematical analysis of the asymptotic behaviour of an explicit objective (energy) function. (2) SOMs impose a rigid framework (a pre-determined grid) of neighbourhood relations that the update algorithm has to respect during the training. It may be desirable not to impose rigorous neighbour-hood connections but either to have them learned and unlearned during the train-ing, or to introduce them after the quantization step. A procedure of this type was developed by Martinetz and Schulten (1994).

Topology-representing network

This model was introduced under the name topology-representing network (TRN: Martinetz and Schulten, 1994). It employs the 'neural-gas' algorithm of Martinetz *et al.* (1993) to perform a topology-sensitive vector quantization. (A Windows95/ NT implementation with special features for processing three-way data, TRN32 by J. Mazanec, © 1997, may be obtained from the website http://leisure.wu-wien.ac.at/software/.) The training rule adjusts not only the winning prototype but also the adjacent prototypes according to the rank order of distances to the 'win-ner'. Thus the neural-gas method exploits a higher amount of information stored in a system of prototypes. As in SOMs, the 'similarity' between data points and their prototypes (cluster centres) is also measured by the Euclidean distance d between the ith prototype's coordinates or weights' vector w_i and a data vector x with values $x_{1,...,m}$ arriving as input:

$$d_i = \| x - \mathbf{w}_i \| = [(\Sigma_{k=1, ..., m} = (x_k - \mathbf{w}_{ik})^2]^{1/2} \qquad \text{(Equation 1)}$$

where $x = (x_{1,...,}x_m)$ and $w_i = (w_{i,1,...,}w_{i,m})$. During the training the system of proto-types is repeatedly exposed to input vectors randomly selected from the data set. Starting from an initial weight distribution of small random coordinates, it learns to adapt its weight structure according to the distribution pattern of the input data. Each of the prototypes learns to take responsibility for a homogeneous set of data vectors. The weight update follows the learning rule (Martinetz *et al.*, 1993):

$$\Delta w_i = \varepsilon \cdot h_\lambda [k_i(x, w_i)] \cdot (x - w_i) \qquad i = 1, ..., N \qquad \text{(Equation 2)}$$

where $0 < \varepsilon < 1$ is a learning constant. $k = 0, 1, ... , N-1$ and $k_i(x, w)$ indicates the rank number k associated with each prototype. Thus rank 0 is attached to the winning prototype i', rank 1 to the second-closest node i'' (the co-winner), etc. As in the SOM, the prototypes compete with each other and only the winner i' with

$$\| x - \mathbf{w}_{i'} \| < \| x - \mathbf{w}_i \|, \forall i \qquad \text{(Equation 3)}$$

gets full update. The units in its neighbourhood are allowed to improve their fit by a weight update with

$$h_\lambda[k_i(x, w_i)]=\exp[-k_i(x, w_i)/\lambda] \qquad \text{(Equation 4)}$$

where λ is a decay constant that decreases during the training. For $\lambda=0$ the process is equivalent to the online version of the popular K-means clustering. The update rules outlined above have been shown to optimize an explicit cost function where the co-updating of adjacent prototypes resembles a 'fuzzy' assignment of data points to the best, second-best, third-best prototype. The neural-gas algorithm was shown to exceed K-means as well as the SOM and the maximum-entropy clustering procedure (Martinetz et al., 1993).

Up to this point the training process does not enforce a topographic mapping of the data points into a set of prototypes subject to a learned adjacency structure. This step was added by Martinetz and Schulten (1994). Adjacency is conceived as a dichotomous concept in the topology representing network. Two prototypes are neighbours or not. The adjacency learning and unlearning process is based on the similarity of the winning prototype and its 'toughest' competitor. Each data point arouses a winner–co-winner pair for which it either confirms or establishes the adjacency relation. Adjacency connections for pairs of data points that are not confirmed for a number of successive updates die out, but may emerge again later on in the training. The age and lifetime parameters are subject to exponential decay during training. In a simulation experiment, the authors demonstrate that the TRN is capable of preserving rather complicated topological structures. It seems to render a perfect topological mapping as long as the grid of prototypes is dense enough to approximate a manifold of lower dimensionality embedded in the high-dimensional data space.

Topological models such as the SOM and the TRN do not enforce a disjunctive partitioning of brands or consumers. They do not classify either brands or consumers, but brand profiles as perceived by individual consumers. Therefore the resulting brand prototypes may represent different real brands for different subjects. Brands as well as consumers usually occupy more than one position in a topological graph with varying frequency. These frequencies report on the distinctiveness or fuzziness of the brand perceptions. The choice or preference information is easily incorporated into this framework as each brand profile position reflects an observed number of past purchases or buying intentions. The results are conveniently visualized by a series of bar charts or by a combined pie–bubble–bar chart; hence the term perceptual charting.

Exploiting the adjacency structure

The TRN generates a system of prototypes in conjunction with the accompanying information on the mutual similarity of the prototypes. The frequency of winner–co-winner pairs as aroused by the data points (the 'statistical neighbourhood') serves as the proximity measure. Two prototypes which are more frequently activated as the first and the second winners by the data vectors are expected to be more similar to each other than prototypes less frequently tied in a winner–co-winner relationship. The strength of adjacency or similarity is usually strong for a limited number of prototypes, thus producing prototype substructures. Strong similarity is visualized as a connecting path in the adjacency graph.

From the positioning/segmentation point of view, the adjacency graph fulfils a double function. (i) It indicates groups of neighbouring brand profiles (and respondents having these profiles on their minds); this means that market structuring occurs on a second level of aggregation in addition to the first level of the prototypes. (ii) It indicates which (brand) prototypes may be merged if the analyst seeks a representation with larger perceptual segments; this may happen if the competing brands do not differ markedly in their prototype affiliation, or the perceptual prototypes do not vary in terms of consumer preferences.

A Sample Application of Perceptual Charting

The sample application is a typical positioning study. It exploits data from the Austrian national guest survey conducted at 3-year intervals. The aim of this survey is to monitor travel trends and the service quality offered by the Austrian tourism industry. The master sample comprises 10,000 respondents annually, with about 7000 interviewed during the summer season, 632 in the capital city Vienna. This subsample of 632 cases is used to analyse the images of three Central European cities which compete in the international travel markets. Budapest, Prague, and Vienna are hypothesized to share a number of attributes in travellers' perceptions. The perceptions, however, are expected to vary by perceptual segments.

Each respondent judges the three cities in terms of image attributes such as 'authentic', 'calm', 'romantic', 'friendly', etc. Each of the 20 attributes may be considered appropriate or inappropriate for a destination . The disaggregate image profiles of binary data are subject to vector quantization. In this stage the three-way data are stacked into an elongated two-dimensional data matrix. During the data reduction step the block structure (due to repeated measurements) in the data [(632 cases × three cities) × 20 vars] is ignored. Given the large number of data vectors (1896 city profiles) it is evident that a partitioning procedure will have to be applied rather than a hierarchical clustering method. The first decision of the analyst thus regards the number of image prototypes hidden among the city profiles. The literature on cluster analysis has developed numerous criteria for characterizing the homogeneity of a cluster solution. For example, Milligan and Cooper (1985) list and evaluate 30 'stopping rules'. None of these measures, in particular when one faces binary data, assists in determining the number of clusters by taking account of the contextual interpretation.

In the neural network literature the issue of determining the network size (e.g. the number of nodes in a SOM network) in a principled manner is known as structural adaptation. If the prototypes (or 'reference vectors' in neural network jargon) are expected to approximate the unknown probability distribution function of the data, the number-of-prototypes problem may be transformed into an entropy maximization task. Yanez-Suarez and Azimi-Sadjadi (1997) propose a structural adaptation algorithm for SOM networks, where nodes are added to the high-density regions of the data space as long as the relative entropy increases after each training update. However, this procedure contrasts with the ease-of-interpretation objective, as more prototypes deployed in the high-density regions tend to become more similar to one other; the uniqueness of the prototype system may decrease for the same reason.

One attempt at including the ease-of-interpretation point of view was made by Kaufman and Rousseeuw (1990). They state that little effort has been made to elaborate graphical displays for partitioning results, except such approaches as taxonometric maps, cluster silhouettes, distance graphs or validity profiles (Kaufman and Rousseeuw, 1990, pp. 119–123). However, a graphic display such as the silhouette, and a strength-of-structure index such as the silhouette coefficient (Kaufman and Rousseeuw, 1990, pp. 83–88), do not impose a penalty on an ever-increasing number of clusters. The simple structure index (SSI) proposed here incorporates three elements influencing the practical relevance and interpretability of a partition: (1) the maximum difference of each variable found in a pair of prototypes; (2) the number of data points represented by this most contrasting pair of prototypes; and (3) the difference between the mean of variable values in each prototype and the overall mean of variable values for all prototypes. Element (1) recognizes that a contextual interpretation is based on those variables of a prototype which exhibit values markedly different from at least one other prototype. Element (2) is a weighting factor which penalizes the differences found in (1) which arise for small clusters; it is the geometric mean of the two cluster sizes involved in each computation of (1). Element (3) is a second weighting factor pertaining to the information value conveyed by a variable in the system of prototypes; it grows larger if the average prototype deviates more distinctly from the overall mean in the whole data set; it is small if there is either little variation in a variable over the prototypes, or the positive deviations tend to offset the negative ones. The third factor assumes that a variable becomes more relevant for the contextual interpretation if its extreme values are exclusively owned by few prototypes. Elements (1), (2) and (3) are multiplicatively combined and divided by the maximum product attainable. The SSI thus ranges between zero and unity. The experience gained for binary data shows that the SSI initially increases with the number of clusters but starts levelling off after a fairly small number is exceeded. As very few solutions with high simple structure indices are recommended for 'manual' inspection by the analyst, the SSI reduces the interpretation effort substantially.

According to Fig. 3.1 the (weighted) SSI recommends two cluster solutions to be examined in more detail. Six or ten prototypes promise to offer ease of interpretation. In order to decide between these two recommendations another relevant criterion – the reproducibility of the solution by repetitive quantization runs – was considered. 'Reproducibility' is operationalized as the quantization method's capability of placing pairs of data points consistently into prototypes. A measure called percentage uncertainty reduction (%UR) indicates to what degree the analyst can trust in finding each of two data points in the same cluster after taking several consecutive quantization runs. Each run starts with a different system of randomly initialized prototypes. Some pairs may be found to be recaptured perfectly, others may produce a varying amount of misplacements. The percentage of error-free reproduction of pair placements over all replications may be regarded separately. In this demonstration study, 15 TRN solutions were generated for the six- and the ten-prototype cases, respectively. The relative frequencies of the membership of pairs of data points in one cluster (prototype) were counted. In case of absolutely identical cluster solutions over 15 replications with a different initialization, the pairs of data points are members of the same cluster either 15 times or never, indicating that they consistently belong to the same prototype or not. In the worst solution of maximum uncertainty the pairs are members of the same prototype in only seven or eight of the 15 replications. The overall %UR was 87.7 for the six-, and 89.8 for the ten-prototype solution. Examining the distribution of relative frequencies of misplaced pairs for the six- and ten-cluster solutions showed that 80 per cent of the pairs in the ten-prototype solution had either 15 or no matches (thus being in the zero-error category). The frequency distribution for the six-prototype replication runs was clearly inferior (with 71.8 per cent of the pairs of data points in the zero error category). The six-prototype alternative was thus discarded.

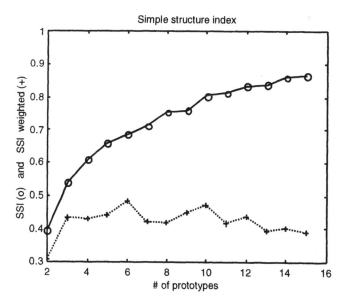

Figure 3.1 Simple structure index (circles); weighted SSI (crosses).

Having opted for the 10-prototype solution, the data matrix of perceptual judgements by 632 tourists for Vienna, Prague and Budapest was used to train a TRN.
After the training of the prototypes, a recall run through the 1896 data vectors was
performed. During the recall the prototypes are no longer subject to a training
update, but the first and the second winning prototype for each data point is determined. The pairs of prototypes differ in their relative frequency of being tied in a
winner–co-winner relationship (called the 'statistical neighbourhood'), giving an
appropriate measure for the similarity between prototypes. The statistical neighbourhood is usually strong for a limited number of prototype pairs and then levels
off. It helps to delineate the perceptual structures on a macro level:

Pairs of prototypes	Statistical neighbourhood %
#9–#10	22.47
#1–#7	10.55
#8–#10	7.02
#5–#8	6.17
#4–#5	5.06
#1–#3	3.96
#3–#6	3.32
#5–#6	2.85
#2–#6	2.79

A cut-off value of 3.0 for the statistical neighbourhood measure leads to three
groups of prototypes. One group consists of five prototypes (#4, #5, #8, #10, #9);
one of four types (#6, #3, #1, #7); and the remaining node (#2) represents a unit
of its own. A smaller cut-off point of 2.8 causes an additional link in the neighbourhood graph as #5 and #6 are connected; the resulting structure is degenerate,
because #2 (representing 8 per cent of all data points) remains unconnected while
all the rest forms one undifferentiated substructure. The prototypes and their proximities are of double interest. The statistical neighbourhood between the prototypes may be regarded as a measure of intensity of competition due to perceptual
similarity. At the same time each prototype represents a distinct attribute profile,
as shown in Fig. 3.2. For prototype #3, for example, the respondents judged the
city under consideration to be modern, expensive, safe and well-known.

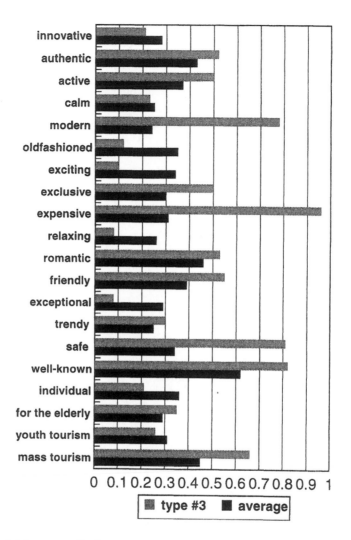

Figure 3.2 Image profile for prototype 3.

It is convenient to portray the prototypes in two dimensions. By means of Sammon mapping as in the TRN program (Sammon, 1969) or by using standard MDS software, the 20-dimensional prototypes are mapped onto a two-dimensional plane. However, it is important to emphasize that the chart conveys topological rather than spatial information. The distances between the prototypes are meaningless and are not exploited for drawing conclusions. (therefore no stress value is given). However, arranging the prototypes pictorially by a Sammon or

52   S. Dolnicar, K. Grabler and J.A. Mazanec

MDS projection may assist the reader familiar with perceptual mapping to become accustomed to the more elementary perceptual charting display. Figure 3.3 shows a combined perceptual bubble-pie chart for all three cities. The size of the bubbles indicates the number of city profiles located in this position. It represents the singularity or the generality of a perceptual position: the larger the bubble, the more frequent is the bundle of attributes indicating a higher risk of being substituted. The three cities share each bubble position as portrayed by its pie structure. For example, Prague and Budapest are highly concentrated in positions #8, #9 and #10. Vienna most strongly coincides with the Type #1 and #3 positions. One cautious remark regarding the conclusions about competitive threat is in order here. Interpreting the aggregate frequencies as given in Fig. 3.3 may be misleading. The respondents placing several cities into a perceptual position may belong to different subsamples which are partially or even completely non-overlapping. However, competition is likely to occur where a number of identical respondents perceive two or more cities in the same position or in the same substructure of prototypes.

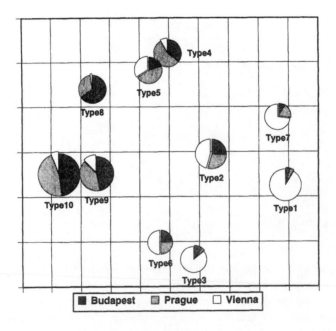

Figure 3.3 Three cities occupying ten perceptual positions.

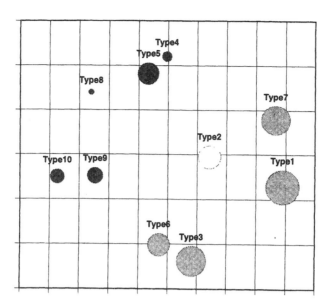

Figure 3.4 Image positions for Vienna.

The prototypes system resulting from the vector quantization may be employed to derive individual charts for each city. Figure 3.4 shows the proto-types configuration for Vienna, where the bubble size denotes the number of respondents placing Vienna in the respective position. In addition to what was presented in Fig. 3.3, the substructures of similar prototypes are identified by their grey-scale shading. The charting thus incorporates the statistical neighbourhood results, i.e. three substructures, where prototype #2 stands aloof, prototypes #1, #3, #6 and #7 are grouped together, and the remaining types form the third substructure.

The perceptual chart in Fig. 3.4 gives information about the image positions and the corresponding segment sizes. It is based on a recall run on the perceptual profiles for Vienna. Obviously, there are popular image positions of Vienna in substructure 1 (prototypes #1, #3, #6 and #7). These perceptual segments account for 68 per cent of all respondents. The substructure profiles indicate that this sub-graph of the perceptual chart implies strong agreement of the respondents with the majority image items. Position #1 (23 per cent of respondents placing Vienna there) is characterized by above-average ratings on all attributes except 'calm', similar to position #7 (17 per cent), where only the attributes 'modern' and 'trendy' are not in compliance with Vienna. Position #3 (18 per cent) stands for the modern and expensive Vienna image; the segment underlying position #6 (10 per cent) believes that Vienna is 'calm', 'relaxing', and 'friendly'. Few perceptual segments place Vienna in structure 3 (consisting of types #4, #5, #8, #9 and #10). These five tourist groups account for only 21 per cent of the respondents. Position

#10 indicates that no attribute matches with the Viennese image; position #9 is very similar to this view, except for the above-average rating on the 'well-known' item. Position #8 is based on 'old-fashioned' as a stand-alone item, whereas 'authentical' is the attribute a respondent of type #5 would assign. Finally, position #4 is related to the images of 'mass tourism' and 'youth tourism'. The remaining 11 per cent of respondents place Vienna on position #2, meaning that this city is an 'active' and 'exciting' destination with plenty of opportunities for 'individuality'.

Regarding the different image positions for Vienna, it is desirable for the destination manager to learn about the preferences attached to the prototype positions. The survey contains information on which of the three cities comes closest to the subjective 'ideal' urban destination. Adding this piece of knowledge to the chart yields a joint representation of perceptions and preferences. The height of the bars in Fig. 3.5 denotes the amount of preference. Only those respondents positioning Vienna in a prototype coinciding with their 'ideal' profile are considered. By using the percentages over all cities, one may analyse the preference information for city positions in general. Unlike branded products, however, a city cannot be built from scratch to please a tourist segment. So this sample application rests on the assumption that tourists bear in mind different ideal positions for different cities. Thus the chart in Fig. 3.5 includes only the preferences stated for Vienna. A chi-square test against a uniform distribution clearly supports the preferential differences between perceptual positions ($P<0.01$).

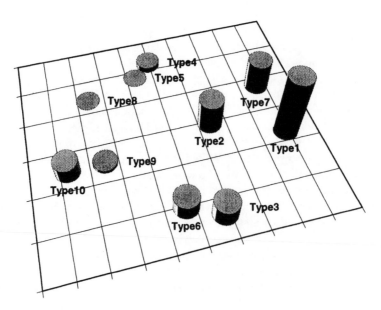

Figure 3.5 Height of preference for Vienna.

There is no doubt that respondents placing Vienna in position #1 are most satisfied with the destination image. Thirty-five per cent of the image profiles coinciding with a 'closest to ideal' statement can be found in this segment. It seems that the image of Vienna offering nearly everything – except calmness – is fairly desirable, followed by positions #7 and #2 with equal preferential strength (17 per cent). These findings demonstrate the importance of the preference information on a single-segment level. Seventeen per cent believe that Vienna is 'exciting' and 'active' and would like it to stay this way, while another 17 per cent tend to avoid a 'modern' and 'trendy' destination, valuing the attribute 'old-fashioned'. Obviously, there is some amount of contradiction in the ideal positions of these two segments. The destination manager has to take this into consideration when deciding on how to channel marketing efforts. The charting exercise proves the usefulness of processing the perceptual and preference information on a disaggregate level.

So far the sample application has dealt only with segmenting the image of one choice alternative (Vienna) into several perceptual groups exhibiting different preferences. Perceptual charting, however, aims at detecting the positions of competitors and the degree of competition. In the TRN solution, therefore, the information on competitive relationships resides in the distribution of individual cities over the ten prototypes. Competitive threat is likely to occur if a number of respondents perceive two or more cities in the same position or in the same prototype substructure. Thus a cross-tabulation of the classification of cities into prototypes is required. The number of respondents classifying a pair of cities into the same prototypes serves a measure of competitive threat. The 'identically classified' index (ICI) for the three cities clearly identifies Budapest and Prague as the toughest competitors (43.8 per cent). It reveals an almost identical degree of competition for Vienna versus Prague (10.8 per cent) and Vienna versus Budapest (10.1 per cent). The ICI is a measure for the overall intensity of competition between pairs of cities. A micro-analysis of competition may differentiate by perceptual positions. To identify those prototype positions where intense competitive relationships prevail, a series of cross-tabulations of city pairs in terms of identical versus non-identical positions is appropriate. For the 2×2 tables a measure of association such as the phi coefficient may then be interpreted as a competitive intensity measure. Owing to the small sample size, the Exact Tests option of SPSS was used ($P<0.05$):

Vienna in position #	Vienna competing with	
	Budapest	Prague
1	0.10	0.06
2	0.15	0.11
3	0.04 (n.s.)	0.11
4	0.08 (n.s.)	0.05 (n.s.)
5	0.01 (n.s.)	0.01 (n.s.)
6	0.11	0.01 (n.s.)
7	0.11	0.08 (n.s.)
8	0.05 (n.s.)	0.08 (n.s.)
9	0.10	0.15
10	0.16	0.18

Obviously, the intensity of competition varies among different perceptual positions and is particularly strong in positions #10 (which is indicative of a single-response pattern) and #2. Different competitive relationships emerge for different city pairs. Generally, the intensity of competition between Vienna and Prague or Budapest appears to be rather low (which is partly attributable to the sampling of guests staying in Vienna). Nevertheless, the phi values for Budapest versus Prague demonstrate their usefulness as a measure for competitive intensity. Excluding position #3, which reveals no significant relationship, the phi values for these two cities range from 0.137 (in #8) to 0.549 (in #10).

Given a number of 10 prototypes, the analyst may prefer a condensed version. Exploiting the statistical neighbourhood, the same analysis can be run on a macro level, taking the three perceptual substructures as competitive clusters. The ICI there confirms the strong competitive relationship between Budapest and Prague (77.4 per cent) and the comparable results for Vienna versus Budapest (25.9 per cent) and Vienna versus Prague (29 per cent). On the substructure level the phi value again serves as the competitive intensity measure. The intensity of competition becomes uniform on this higher aggregation level. This means that a cluster solution with only three prototypes – something that seems appropriate in a tale of three cities – would have failed to extract accurate market-structure results. The adjacency-of-prototypes component of the vector quantization method gives more flexibility than conventional methodology in operating over aggregation levels.

Substructure	Vienna competing with	
	Budapest	Prague
1 (#1, 3, 6, 7)	0.11	0.14
2 (#2)	0.11	0.12
3 (#4, 5, 8, 9, 10)	0.12	0.14

Managerial Implications

Perceptual charting teaches the managers in a city tourism organization three lessons. (i) The individual city charts (such as Fig. 3.4 for Vienna) inform them about segment-specific image positions of the destination they are responsible for and about the size of each underlying perceptual segment. The attribute pattern corresponding to each prototype shows the perceptual characteristics of the positions, e.g. the image a particular segment has of this city. (ii) By relying on past choice behaviour or by direct questioning, the height of preference for each destination-position is added (Fig. 3.5 in the Vienna example). It indicates the segment-specific preference attainable in each position. (iii) The contingency tables of image profiles classified into prototypes for one city versus another highlight the segment-wise competitive relations among cities.

The results under (i) assist in spotting perceptual strengths and weaknesses. The uniqueness of attributes is easily verified. The variability of the images also becomes apparent. A brand evenly scattered over many prototypes lacks distinctiveness. In the city case study, Vienna is strongly represented and highly valued in those perceptual positions where the respondents tended to attribute many characteristics to the city. (This may be partly due to the fact that the respondents were interviewed during their stay in Vienna.) The perceptual profiles of this destination are concentrated on few positions rather than being scattered all over the chart.

The findings under (ii) are linked to setting positioning objectives. In the absence of interaction effects between a brand name and the preference for a perceptual profile attached to it, the height of preference (number of actual choices, stated first rank) may be accumulated over brands. The manager then obtains brand-independent information on which positions are more or less desirable. Unlike the city case study, these cumulative results are also relevant for placing new product profiles under a new brand name. Objectives for product positioning are set in terms of a target frequency distribution rather than spatial coordinates. In the city case study, the interaction is apparent between the destination name, the perceptual profiles, and the preferences. The profiles must not be merged. Drawing conclusions for one city, the city tourism organization of Vienna ought to convince the members of segment #6 not satisfied with this position of the additional strengths of Vienna that these tourists had underestimated in the past. This would shift tourists from segment #6 to the more preferred position #1. As in any psychographic segmentation, more information on demographics and socio-economic characteristics is needed to implement such a strategy.

The competitive pressure expected from the rivalling brands follows from the cross-classifications under (iii). In the city case study, position #7 represents a high preference profile for Vienna, where fairly strong competition with Budapest can be detected. Marketing managers may want to put more emphasis on the attributes appreciated by this group. Clear distinction from Budapest is necessary, whereas competitive action to appear more distinct from Prague is not urgent.

The entire planning process benefits from the disaggregate findings, as the perceptual positions, the preference information, and the competitive relations are analysed from a strictly segment-specific point of view. It requires no parametric assumptions regarding the generation of perceptual response and the formation of preferences. For marketing applications, a parsimonious model in terms of the number of perceptual positions is desirable. In addition to the similarity of profiles, the information on preferences or brand choice may assist in selecting the appropriate number. Ideally, positions with similar perceptual profiles and the same height of preference should be grouped together. In the city case study, the 10-prototype solution was compared with a reduced substructure solution that originated from the statistical neighbourhood. Whereas the large number of 10 positions bothers the destination manager and makes decisions more complex, the substructures – in this application – blur the information about individual differences. Chi-square tests against a uniform distribution of preferences within both substructures containing more than one prototype confirm significant differences in substructure 1. Given the diverse competitive relationships among prototypes even within the same substructures an automatic grouping of prototypes into substructures is not advocated. A more refined methodology for identifying the most parsimonious model is needed. Further development of the two-stage procedure combining data reduction via adaptive partitioning with subsequent nonparametric testing is under way.

References

Albers, S. and Brockhoff, K. (1977) A procedure for new product positioning in an attribute space. *European Journal of Operations Research* 1, 230–283.

Arabie, P., Carroll, J.D. and DeSarbo, W.S. (1987) *Three-Way Scaling and Clustering*. Newbury Park: Sage.

Bauer, H.U. and Pawelzik, K.R. (1992) Quantifying the neighborhood preservation of self-organizing feature maps. *IEEE Transactions on Neural Networks* 3, 570–579.

Büyükkurt, B.K. and Büyükkurt, M.D. (1990) Robustness and small-sample properties of the estimators of probabilistic multidimensional scaling (PROSCAL). *Journal of Marketing Research* 27, 139–149.

Carroll, J.D. and Arabie, P. (1983) INDCLUS: an individual differences generalization of the ADCLUS model and the MAPCLUS algorithm. *Psychometrika* 48, 157–169.

Carroll, J.D. and Chang, J.J. (1970) Analysis of individual differences in multidimensional scaling via an N-way generalization of Eckart–Young decomposition. *Psychometrika* 35, 283–319.

Carroll, J.D. and Chaturvedi, A. (1995) A general approach to clustering and multidimensional scaling of two-way, three-way, or higher-way data. In R.D. Luce, M.D. Zmura, D.D. Hoffman, G. Iversen and A.K. Romney (eds) *Geometric Representations of Perceptual Phenomena: Papers in Honor of Tarow Indow's 70th Birthday*. Hillsdale: Lawrence Erlbaum, pp. 295–318.

Carroll, J.D., Green, P.E. and Schaffer, C.M. (1986) Interpoint distance comparisons in correspondence analysis. *Journal of Marketing Research* 23, 271–280.

Chaturvedi, A., Carroll, J.D., Green, P.E. and Rotondo, J.A. (1997) A feature-based approach to market segmentation via overlapping K-centroids clustering. *Journal of Marketing Research* 34, 370–377.

Chintagunta, P.K. (1994) Heterogeneous logit model implications for brand positioning. *Journal of Marketing Research* 31, 304–311.

Cooper, L.G. (1988) Competitive maps: the structure underlying asymmetric cross elasticities. *Management Science* 34, 707–723.

DeSarbo, W.S. and Jedidi, K. (1995) The spatial representation of heterogeneous consideration sets. *Marketing Science* 14, 326–342.

DeSarbo, W. and Rao, V.R. (1986) A constrained unfolding methodology for product positioning. *Marketing Science* 5, 1–19.

DeSarbo, W.S., Howard, D.J. and Jedidi, K. (1991) Multiclus: a new method for simultaneously performing multidimensional scaling and cluster analysis. *Psychometrika* 56, 121–136.

DeSarbo, W.S., Manrai, A.K. and Manrai, L.A. (1994) Latent class multidimensional scaling: a review of recent developments in the marketing and psychometric literature. In: R.P. Bagozzi (ed.) *Advanced Methods of Marketing Research*. Cambridge: Blackwell, pp. 190–222.

Dillon, W.R., Frederick, D.G. and Tangpanichdee, V. (1985) Decision issues in building perceptual product spaces with multi-attribute rating data. *Journal of Consumer Research* 12, 47–63.

Dillon, W.R., Mulani, N. and Frederick, D.G. (1989) On the use of component scores in the presence of group structure. *Journal of Consumer Research* 16, 106–112.

Elrod.T. (1988) Choice map: inferring a product market map from observed choice behavior. *Marketing Science* 7, 21–40.

Erdem, T. (1996) A dynamic analysis of market structure based on panel data. *Marketing Science* 15, 359–370.

Flanagan, J.A. (1996) Self-organisation in Kohonens SOM. *Neural Networks* 9, 1185–1197.

Flexer, A. (1996) *Limitations of Self-Organizing Maps for Vector Quantization and Multidimensional Scaling*, Technical Report No. 23. Austrian Research Institute for Artificial Intelligence.

Green, P.E. (1975) Marketing applications of MDS: assessment and outlook. *Journal of Marketing* 39, 24–31.

Green, P.E. and Carmone, F.J. (1969) Multidimensional scaling: an introduction and comparison of nonmetric unfolding techniques. *Journal of Marketing Research* 6, 330–341.

Green, P.E. and Krieger, A.M. (1993) Conjoint analysis with product-positioning applications. In: J. Eliashberg and G.L. Lilien (eds) *Marketing*. Amsterdam: North-Holland, pp. 467–515.

Green, P.E. and Rao, V.R. (1971) Conjoint measurement for quantifying judgmental data. *Journal of Marketing Research* 8, 355–363.

Green, P.E. and Rao, V.R. (1972) Applied multidimensional scaling: a comparison of approaches and algorithms. New York: Holt, Rinehart & Winston.

Green P.E., Carroll, J.D. and Goldberg, S.M. (1981) A general approach to product design optimization via conjoint analysis. *Journal of Marketing* 45, 17–37.

Green, P.E., Tull, D.S. and Albaum, G. (1988) *Research for Marketing Decisions*, 5th edn. Englewood Cliffs, New Jersey: Prentice-Hall.

Greenacre, M. (1984) *Theory and Applications of Correspondence Analysis*. London: Academic Press.

Harshman, R.A. and Lundy, M.E. (1984) The PARAFAC model for three–way factor analysis and multidimensional scaling. In: H.G. Law, C.W. Snyder Jr, J.A. Hattie and R.P. McDonald (eds) *Research Methods for Multimode Data Analysis*. New York: Praeger.

Hauser, J.R. and Clausing, D. (1988) The house of quality. *Harvard Business Review* 3, 63–73.

Hoffman, D.L. and Franke, G.R. (1986) Correspondence analysis: graphical representation of categorical data in marketing research. *Journal of Marketing Research* 23, 213–227.

Jedidi, K. and DeSarbo, W.S. (1991) A stochastic multidimensional scaling procedure for the spatial representation of three-mode, three-way pick any/J data. *Psychometrika* 56, 471–494.

Kaciak, E. and Louviere, J. (1990) Multiple correspondence analysis of multiple choice experiment data. *Journal of Marketing Research* 27, 455–465.

Kamakura, W.A. (1988) A least squares procedure for benefit segmentation with conjoint experiments. *Journal of Marketing Research* 25, 157–167.

Kaufman, L. and Rousseeuw, P.J. (1990) *Finding Groups in Data, An Introduction to Cluster Analysis*. New York: Wiley.

Kiers, H.A.L. (1991) Hierarchical relations among three-way methods. *Psychometrika* 56, 449–470.

Kohonen, T. (1982) Self-organized formation of topologically corrrect feature maps. *Biological Cybernetics* 43, 59–69. [Reprinted 1988 in J.A. Andersen and E. Rosenfeld (eds) *Neurocomputing: Foundations of Research*. Cambridge, Massachussetts: MIT Press, pp. 511–521.]

Kohonen, T. (1984) *Self-Organization and Associative Memory*. New York: Springer. [3rd edn 1988.]

Kohonen, T. (1990) The self-organizing map. *Proceedings of the IEEE* 78, 1464–1480. [Reprinted 1992 in P. Mehra and B.W. Wah (eds) *Artificial Neural Networks: Concepts and Theory*. Los Alamitos: IEEE Computer Society Press, pp. 359–375.]

Kohonen, T. (1997) *Self-Organizing Maps*, 2nd edn. Springer Series in Information Sciences. Berlin/Heidelberg: Springer Verlag.

Kroonenberg, P.M. (1984) Three-mode principal component analysis: illustrated with an example from attachment theory. In: H.G. Law, C.W. Snyder Jr, J.A. Hattie and R.P. McDonald (eds) *Research Methods for Multimode Data Analysis*. New York: Praeger.

Kruskal, J.B. (1964) Nonmetric multidimensional scaling. *Psychometrika* 29, 1–27, 115–199.

Krycha, K.A. and Wagner, U. (1999) Applications of artificial neural networks in management science – a survey. *Journal of Retailing and Consumer Services*, Special Issue on Neural Networks, in press.

Linde, Y., Buzo, A. and Gray, R.M. (1980) An algorithm for vector quantizer design. *IEEE Transactions on Communications, COM*-28, 84–95.

MacKay, D.B. (1989) Probabilistic multidimensional scaling: an anisotropic model for distance judgments. *Journal of Mathematical Psychology* 33, 187–205.

MacKay, D.B. and Zinnes, J.L. (1986) A probabilistic model for the multidimensional scaling of proximity and preference data. *Marketing Science* 5, 325–344.

Malhotra, N.K., Jain, A.K. and Pinson, C. (1988) the robustness of MDS configurations in the case of incomplete data. *Journal of Marketing Research* 25, 95–102.

Mangiameli, P., Chen, S.H. and West, D. (1996) A comparison of SOM neural network and hierarchical clustering methods. *European Journal of Operational Research* 93, 402–417.

Martinetz, T. and Schulten, K. (1994) Topology representing networks. *Neural Networks* 7, 507–522.

Martinetz, T., Berkovich, St G. and Schulten, K. (1993) 'Neural gas' network for vector quantization and its application to time-series prediction. *IEEE Transactions of Neural Networks* 4, 558–569.

Mazanec, J.A. (1995a) Competition among European tourist cities: a comparative analysis with multidimensional scaling and self–organizing maps. *Tourism Economics* 1, 283–302.

Mazanec, J.A. (1995b) Positioning analysis with self-organizing maps, an exploratory study on luxury hotels. *Cornell HRA Quarterly* 36, 80–95.

Mazanec, J.A. (1999) Simultaneous positioning and segmentation analysis with topologically ordered feature maps: a tour operator example. *Journal of Retailing and Consumer Services*, Special Issue on Neural Networks, in press.

Milligan, G.W. and Cooper, M.C. (1985) An examination of procedures for determining the number of clusters in a data set. *Psychometrika* 50, 159–179.

Myers, J.H. and Tauber, E. (1977) *Market Structure Analysis*. Chicago: AMA.

Nour, M.A. and Madey, G.R. (1996) Heuristic and optimization approaches to extending the Kohonen self organizing algorithm. *European Journal of Operational Research* 93, 428–448.

Ramaswamy, V. and DeSarbo, W. (1990) SCULPTRE: a new methodology for deriving and analyzing hierarchical product-market structures from panel data. *Journal of Marketing* 27, 418–427.

Ritter, H. and Schulten, K. (1988) Convergence properties of Kohonen's topology conserving maps: fluctuations, stability, and dimension selection. *Biological Cybernetics* 60, 59–71.

Ritter, H., Martinetz, T. and Schulten, K. (1991) Neural computation and self-organizing maps. Reading: Addison-Wesley.

Roberts, J.H. and Lilien, G.L. (1993) Explanatory and predictive models of consumer behavior. In: J. Eliashberg and G.L. Lilien (eds) *Marketing*. Amsterdam: North-Holland, pp. 27–82.

Sammon, J.W. Jr (1969) A nonlinear mapping for data structure analysis. *IEEE Transactions on Computers*, C–18, 401–409.

Sato, M., Sato,Y. and Jain, L.C. (1997) *Fuzzy Clustering Models and Applications.* Heidelberg: Physica.

Snyder, C.W. Jr, Law, H.G. and Hattie, J.A. (1984) Overview of multimode analytic models. in H.G. Law, C.W. Snyder Jr, J.A. Hattie and R.P. McDonald (eds) *Research Methods for Multimode Data Analysis.* New York: Praeger, pp. 2–35.

Thiran, P. and Hasler, M. (1994) Self-organization of a one-dimensional Kohonen network with quantized weights and inputs. *Neural Networks* 7, 1427–1439.

Tucker, L.R. (1964) The extension of factor analysis to three-dimensional matrices. In: N. Frederiksen and H. Gulliksen (eds) *Contributions to Mathematical Psychology.* New York: Holt, Rinehart & Winston, pp. 129–140.

Urban, G.L. and Hauser, J.R. (1993) *Design and Marketing of New Products,* 2nd edn. Englewood Cliffs, New Jersey: Prentice Hall.

Wedel, M. and Kamakura, W.A. (1998) *Market Segmentation, Conceptual and Methodological Foundations.* Boston: Kluwer Academic.

Wedel, M. and Steenkamp, J.B. (1991) A clusterwise regression method for simultaneous fuzzy market structuring and benefit segmentation. *Journal of Marketing Research* 28, 385–396.

Yanez-Suarez, O. and Azimi-Sadjadi, M.R. (1997) entropy-driven structural adaptation in sample-space self-organizing feature maps for pattern classification. In: *Proceedings of the 1997 IEEE International Conference on Neural Networks,* Vol. 1, pp. 287–291.

Young, F.W. (1987) Theory. In: F.W. Young and R.M. Hamer (eds) *Multidimensional Scaling: History, Theory, and Applications.* Hillsdale: Lawrence Erlbaum, pp. 42–158.

Chapter four

A Path-Analytical Model of Visitation Intention Involving Information Sources, Socio-Psychological Motivations and Destination Images

Seyhmus Baloglu
Department of Tourism and Convention Administration, University of Nevada Las Vegas, Las Vegas, NV 89154-6023, USA

Introduction

Understanding travellers' decision-making and destination selection process is a focal point of great interest to both tourism researchers and practitioners in developing effective tourism marketing and communication strategies. In consumer behaviour and destination selection models, the ultimate goal is to better predict or explain the behaviour of interest by relating it to demographic, psychological and stimulus variables (Howard and Sheth, 1969; Fishbein and Ajzen, 1975; Woodside and Lysonski, 1989; Um and Crompton, 1992). The concept of behavioural intention has been suggested as a central factor which correlates highly with actual or observed behaviour. Therefore a better prediction or explanation of intention may lead to a better understanding of overt behaviour (Reibstein, 1978; Long and Evans, 1983; Ajzen and Driver, 1992). Several models of consumer behaviour built upon the theory of reasoned action emphasize intention as an immediate antecedent to actual behaviour (Howard and Sheth, 1969; Fishbein and Ajzen, 1975; Engel *et al.*, 1978).

Numerous studies have demonstrated that information sources (awareness and familiarity), socio-psychological motivations, some demographic variables, and image or attitude toward destinations influence travellers' or consumers' preferences and intentions (Mayo, 1973; Goodrich, 1978; Scott *et al.*, 1978; Woodside, 1982; Milman and Pizam, 1995; Court and Lupton, 1997). Image has been proven a crucial and major concept in predicting consumer behaviour (Mayo, 1973; Goodrich, 1978; Scott *et al*, 1978; Bagozzi, 1982). However, so far the variables influencing visitation intention have been studied on a piecemeal basis rather than simultaneously in an integrative process. The purpose of this study is to develop and test a model of travellers' intention formation, with particular reference to image, for destinations never visited before. The study examines the organization

of informational, motivational and mental constructs on visitation intention in a
path analytic framework.

Conceptual Framework and Proposed Model

Identification of model variables, and theoretical linkages among model variables,
build on works from several fields such as consumer behaviour and marketing,
travel and tourism, environmental psychology, and geography. The conceptual
models found in the literature deal mainly with the role of psychological and stimulus variables in consumer behaviour, tourist destination selection, spatial behaviour of people, man–environment interaction, image formation, and the
dimensions or different levels of evaluations embedded in image structure. Based
on a thorough literature review, information sources, socio-psychological variables and perceptual/cognitive and affective evaluations were selected for this
study as influences on visitation intention. Numerous scholars across disciplines
and fields have consistently and repeatedly cited these elements as influential variables on image and destination choice before visiting a destination (Gunn, 1972;
Kassarjian and Robertson, 1973; Burgess, 1978; Carman, 1978; Mayo and Jarvis,
1981; Friedmann, 1986; Friedmann and Lessig, 1986; Woodside and Lysonski,
1989; Goodall, 1990; Stabler, 1990; Um and Crompton, 1990; Fakeye and
Crompton, 1991; Mansfeld, 1992; Gartner, 1993; Court and Lupton, 1997; Vogt
et al., 1998).

This paper firstly presents the proposed model, and then provides a discussion
of previous conceptual and empirical works to delineate the relationship among
model variables. The proposed model and hypothesized relationships (straight
arrows) are illustrated in Fig. 4.1. The model posits that perceptual/cognitive evaluations of tourism destinations are determined by variety (amount) of information,
type of information sources used, and socio-psychological travel motivations. The
perceptual/cognitive evaluations and socio-psychological travel motivations then
together form affective evaluations of destinations, where the effects of percep-
tual/cognitive evaluations on affect are hypothesized to be positive. In turn, visitation intention is a positive function of perceptual/cognitive and affective images
(evaluations). The path analysis was conducted on the full model with all possible
connections (involving the dotted arrows), which is further discussed under Data
Analysis.

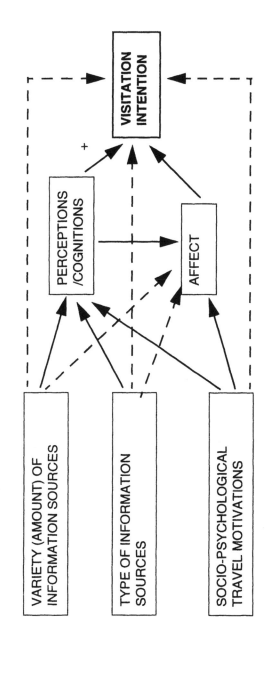

Figure 4.1 The proposed test model of visitation intention formation before actual visit. Straight arrows indicate hypothesized relationships. The path coefficients from primary cause variables – variety (amount) of information source, and socio-psychological travel motivations – to endogenous variables – perception/cognition and affect – were hypothesized as non-directional (positive or negative).

Literature Review

Image and behaviour

Previous studies in consumer behaviour and tourism have demonstrated that there is a positive correlation between image and behavioural intention (Mayo, 1973; Goodrich, 1978; Scott *et al.*, 1978; Long and Evans, 1983; Reibstein *et al.*, 1980; Bagozzi, 1982; Court and Lupton, 1997). Destination image studies in tourism and travel have centred on the relationship between destination image and preference or purchase intentions. Mayo (1973) and Hunt (1975) were the first tourism scholars to point out that a more favourable image of a destination would result in increased visitation to that destination. Goodrich (1978) demonstrated a positive correlation between preference and perceptions. Likewise, Scott *et al.* (1978) found that the preference for states was highly related to varying perceptions of state attributes. Court and Lupton (1997) examined the factors contributing to behavioural intention and found that perceptual/cognitive evaluations significantly influence travellers' intent to visit a destination.

Reibstein *et al.* (1980) examined the direction of causality between perceptions (beliefs), affect and behaviour regarding the choices of transportation modes. The analysis revealed that the relationship between perceptions and behaviour is mediated by affect. Bagozzi (1982) examined the causal relations among cognition, affect, intention and behaviour, and demonstrated that, although the affect mediates the relationship between cognition and behavioural intention, cognition can also directly influence behavioural intention. All these studies have demonstrated that image (cognitive and affective) is an important construct to predict consumers' or travellers' behaviour.

Image components

The image construct has often been suggested as including two distinct but interrelated components: perceptual/cognitive and affective. Perceptual or cognitive evaluation refers to beliefs and knowledge about an object, whereas affective evaluation refers to feelings about the object (Burgess, 1978; Holbrook, 1978; Ward and Russel, 1981; Zimmer and Golden, 1988; Walmsley and Jenkins, 1993; Gartner, 1993; Baloglu and Brinberg, 1997). Zimmer and Golden (1988) and Keaveney and Hunt (1992), based on their literature review of store image, have concluded that research into retail store image focused on the attribute component (a subset) of store image. The authors have proposed that consumer images may also include an affective or emotional component toward the store and, therefore, should be conceptualized that way to 'capture the richness of store image'. Burgess (1978) studied 32 urban–rural locations and concluded that many places have both denotative (cognitive) and connotative (affective) meanings for individuals. Many findings in environmental psychology also support the notion that environments and places have both perceptual/cognitive and affective images (Lynch, 1960; Burgess, 1978; Russel and Pratt, 1980; Russel *et al.*, 1981; Hanyu, 1993).

Similarly, studies on image of place in the geographic literature often distinguish between two type of images: cognitive (designative) and affective (appraisive) (Walmsley and Lewis, 1984; Walmsley and Jenkins, 1993; Stern and Krakover, 1993).

These two components are interrelated in the sense that affective evaluations are formed as a function of the cognitive evaluations (Lynch, 1960; Burgess, 1978; Holbrook, 1978; Reibstein *et al.*, 1980; Russel and Pratt, 1980; Anand *et al.*, 1988; Gartner, 1993; Stern and Krakover, 1993). This relationship has also been emphasized in various travel decision-making models (Mayo and Jarvis, 1981; Woodside and Lysonski, 1989). Woodside and Lysonski (1989) and Gartner (1993) proposed that the cognitive component of image, the sum of beliefs and knowledge of attributes of the object or product, and affective component of image are distinct but hierarchically related because some minimal knowledge is necessary for formation of the affect.

Stimulus and personal influences on image

Numerous researchers across fields and disciplines suggest that image is mainly formed by two major forces: stimulus factors and personal factors. In other words, image depends on both characteristics of physical stimuli and conditions within the individual (Krech *et al.*, 1962; Kassarjian and Robertson, 1973; Crompton, 1979a; Mayo and Jarvis, 1981; Walmsley and Lewis, 1984; Moutinho, 1987; Kotler, 1988; Stabler, 1990). Amadeo and Golledge (1975, p. 381) have indicated that 'the extent of our information about a system ... the specific needs and values of the individuals ... will influence our cognitions of the spatial properties of such a system'.

Friedmann (1986) and Friedmann and Lessig (1986) equated image (perceptions and affective reactions) with psychological meaning of products and, deriving from the literature in perceptual psychology and consumer behaviour, proposed a model of the development of the psychological meaning of products. The authors identified three major categories of intervening or determining variables that have an influence in the development of the products' psychological meaning: individual characteristics, social characteristics, and situational characteristics (i.e. level of familiarity or previous experience with the product).

Stimulus and consumer elements have been adopted and included in travel destination selection models. Mayo and Jarvis (1981) adopted Krech *et al.*'s (1962) conceptualization and divided the factors that influence perception into two categories: stimulus factors such as the characteristics of the physical object; and personal factors such as values, motivations, past experience, expectations, personality and sociodemographic variables of the individual. "What an individual perceives in many situations is determined not only by the intrinsic nature of the stimulus object ... but also by his or her own system of values and needs determined by the social context" (Moutinho, 1987, p. 11). Um and Crompton's (1990) model of pleasure travel destination choice identified two major factors that influence the images of tourism destinations: external and internal inputs. External inputs include various information sources and actual visitation to the destination, while internal inputs comprise socio-psychological characteristics of travellers. Likewise, Woodside and Lysonski's (1989) model of traveller destination choice emphasized marketing variables (tourism information sources) and traveller variables (previous destination experience, income, age and value system) as determinants of destination image. Based on consumer behaviour and economic theory (supply and demand interaction), Stabler (1990) presented image as a function of demand (consumer) and supply (stimulus) factors. Consumer factors include socio-economic characteristics, motivations, perceptions and psychological characteristics, whereas supply factors include promotional, non-promotional and social sources of information, and the previous destination experience. Stabler (1990) states that 'transmission of information from supply [destination] through the marketing of tourism and the media, previous experience and opinions of other consumers, combined with motivations and socio-economic characteristics form perceptions, the images of tourism and tourist destinations' (p. 140).

Sources of information

Travellers' images of tourism destinations are to a great extent influenced by the sources of information (stimulus variables) they are exposed to. Gunn (1972, pp. 20–55) conceptualizes the evolution of image in travellers' behavioural processes, and suggests that the initial image formation is largely a function of information sources before visiting the destination. In this process, Gunn emphasizes two major sources of information through which an image of a destination is developed: 'organic' and 'induced'. Organic image-formation sources include non-tourism information such as news stories, documentary, magazine articles, and books and movies. Induced image-formation sources, on the other hand, consist of marketing efforts by the destination such as brochures, advertising and promotional campaigns. The role of information sources in forming destination images is also emphasized in Fakeye and Crompton's (1991) model of image formation. Adapting from Gunn's (1972) notion of organic and induced images, their model suggests that the type of information sources used will result in differentiated destination images. According to Woodside and Lysonski's (1989) traveller destination-choice model, marketing variables or information sources are presented as a force which influences the formation of perceptions or cognitive evaluations of tourism destinations but not the affective component of image. Similarly, Um and Crompton's (1990) cognitive model of pleasure travel destination choice posits that the perceptual/cognitive evaluation of destination attributes (belief) is formed by external factors which include various information sources such as symbolic stimuli (promotional efforts of a destination through media) and social stimuli (friends' and relatives' recommendations or word-of-mouth). A critical review of theoretical aspects of the destination-choice process conducted by Mansfeld (1992) reveals problems for further theoretical refinement of the tourist destination-choice process. One major problem identified is the role of information sources in image creation and actual destination choice. Mansfeld (1992) also argues that, since it is assumed that various information sources have a differential effect on tourists' images of destinations, it is important to understand their marginal contribution to the development of images.

Burgess (1978) states that without direct personal experience, images of a place are formed by information from the media and other secondary or external sources. Burgess hypothesizes that the type, quality and quantity of information available to individuals determines the type of image they are likely to develop. Although quite a few classifications of travel information sources exist in the literature, a more detailed classification has been offered by Gartner (1993), who develops a theoretical basis for the touristic image-formation process and presents a typology of the image formation agents (information sources) that act independently or in some combination to form a destination image unique to the individual. Modifying Gunn's (1972) organic-induced image typology, Gartner (1993) places various information sources on a continuum, non-promotional sources at one end and friends' or relatives' recommendation at the other, and suggests that different image formation agents would affect the development or formation of images differently. Defining the cognitive component of image as the sum of beliefs and knowledge of the attributes of an object, Gartner (1993) also notes that the type and amount of external stimuli (information sources) received will influence the formation of the cognitive component of image but not the affective component. In this sense, the development of the perceptual/cognitive component of destination image is presented as a function of the amount (variety) and type of information sources to which travellers are exposed. Fishbein and Ajzen (1975, pp. 387–410) recognize information sources as a major force or change agent directly influencing the formation of beliefs about an object. The authors also suggest that information from outside sources has a causal effect on the perceptual and cognitive component but not on the affective component of attitude. Likewise, Mayo and Jarvis (1981, p. 190) propose a travel decision-making model where they posit that information sources form beliefs and opinions about a destination which, in turn, lead to feelings (affect).

Baloglu (1997) provides some, but inconclusive, empirical support for the idea that different information users would have different images of a tourist destination. Holbrook (1978) contends that marketing research has narrowly focused on the static structure of attitude, ignoring its informational determinants. He found that information sources do influence the cognitive component of image, but not the affective image, and that cognition plays an intervening role between information sources and the affective component of image. Some recent studies suggest that travel information sources also influence destination choice and behavioural intention (Court and Lupton, 1997; Vogt *et al.*, 1998). Vogt *et al.* (1998) investigate travellers' information search strategies for destinations before visitation, and find significant relationships between some information sources (print and broadcast media sources) and intent to visit the selected destination. Similarly, Court and Lupton (1997) find that travellers' exposure to tourism information significantly influences their intention to visit a destination.

Socio-psychological travel motivations

In the travel and tourism field, motivations for travel are accepted as a central concept in understanding travel behaviour and the destination-choice process (Uysal and Hagan, 1993; Weaver *et al.*, 1994) because they are the impelling and compelling force behind all behaviours (Crompton, 1979b; Iso-Ahola, 1982). Motivations are usually defined as socio-psychological forces that predispose an individual to travel and participate in a touristic activity (Crandall, 1980; Iso-Ahola, 1982; Beard and Raghep, 1983).

Travel motivations as personal factors are included in destination choice and image formation models as a major influence guiding the development of destination images (Stabler, 1990; Um and Crompton, 1990). Stabler (1990) presents socio-psychological travel motivations such as physical, status, social contact, cultural, intellectual, escape and relaxation as the most important construct impinging on the destination images. In the destination-choice process, images of destinations are formed in relation to travel motivations in a conscious or unconscious way (Moutinho, 1987). Mayo and Jarvis (1981) indicate that travellers' psychological motivations influence their images of destinations. Although several empirical studies provide some support for the relationship between socio-psychological motivations and destination image (Crompton *et al.*, 1992; Hu and Ritchie, 1993), Pearce (1995) suggests that the relationship between tourist motivations and destination image should be explored to better understand travel behaviour and to enhance motivation theory.

Whether socio-psychological motivations influence affective or cognitive component of image remains a controversial issue among scholars. Several tourism scholars suggest that motivations are related to the affective component of image, and an individual's affective image toward a destination is, to a great extent, influenced by his/her motivations or benefits sought from the travel experience (Gartner, 1993; Dann, 1996). However, the travel destination-selection models of Woodside and Lysonski (1989) and Um and Crompton (1990) portray travel motivations as a major variable influencing destination awareness and perceptual/cognitive evaluations.

Methodology

Sample

The relevant population for this study consisted of adult individuals (18 years old or over) who had the willingness and ability to take a vacation in a foreign country. People who engage in information search about tourism destinations can be considered potential tourists, and represent the population of interest to this study.

Therefore the sample population for this study was chosen from a list maintained by the Turkish National Tourism Office in New York. The list consisted of 4600 people who requested information about Turkey between the periods of November 1994 and October 1995. A self-administered questionnaire was mailed to a random sample of 1530 individuals from that list in spring 1996. A total of 484 (31.6%) questionnaires were returned. After eliminating unusable responses, 448 questionnaires (29.6% usable response rate) were coded for data analysis.

To address the issues of non-response bias, a random sample of 100 individuals were telephoned. Data were collected from 39 individuals on demographics, previous experience and selected image items. An apparent bias could not be detected because, after a series of chi-square and *t*-tests, no significant differences were found between respondents and non-respondents with respect to selected variables.

Data were collected for four Mediterranean tourism destination countries: Turkey, Egypt, Greece and Italy. Table 4.1 shows the breakdown of visitors and non-visitors for each destination. The model was tested on the combined data set (pooled data) regardless of destinations. Therefore data coding was carried out according to a pooled cross-sectional design where dummy variables were used for tourism destinations (Kliman, 1981; Dielman, 1988). This allows the researcher to build or test a single model for the entire group of tourism destinations rather than a separate model for each destination (Dielman, 1988). One advantage of a pooled cross-sectional design is that it increases sample size by the number of testing units (tourism destinations). The sample responses of the pooled data increased to 1792 (448×4). Because the purpose of this study was to test a model for destinations not previously visited, previous actual visitation to selected destinations was used to screen the respondents. A subsample (*n*=356) was identified from the entire sample of 448 respondents. The subsample included those who did not visit at least one of the tourism destinations included in the study. The pooled data, on the other hand, included 716 responses from this subsample on which the model was tested (Table 4.1).

Measurement

Exogenous variables

Type of information sources Four information-source categories were used to measure the importance of type of information in forming impressions about selected tourism destinations. The categories were derived from the literature and were used instead of individual items to avoid memory bias, and to a great extent captured organic–induced (Gunn, 1972; Phelps, 1986; Fakeye and Crompton, 1991); symbolic–social (Howard and Sheth, 1969; Um and Crompton, 1990); interpersonal–impersonal (Hsiesh and O'Leary, 1993); formal (commercial)–informal (social) (Gitelson and Crompton, 1983; Mansfeld, 1992; Mill and Morrison, 1992) categories, and Gartner's (1993) typology of information sources.

Table 4.1 Previous experience with tourism destinations

Country	Visited	
	Yes (*n*=1067)	No (*n*=716)
Turkey	308	138
	(28.9%)*	(19.3%)
	(69.1%)†	(30.9%)
Egypt	124	321
	(11.6%)	(44.8%)
	(27.7%)	(72.3%)
Greece	286	160
	(26.8%)	(22.3%)
	(63.8%)	(36.2%)
Italy	349	97
	(32.7%)	(13.5%)
	(77.9%)	(22.1%)

*Column percentages
†Row percentages

Four information source categories include (1) professional advice (tour opera-tors, travel agents and airlines); (2) word-of-mouth (friends, relatives, social clubs); (3) advertisement (print or broadcast media); and (4) non-tourism (books/movies/news). Respondents were asked to rate each information category as to its importance in forming their impressions about each tourism destination country on a four-point scale where 1 = not at all important; 2 = not very important; 3 = somewhat important; and 4 = very important. An option of 'did not use' was pro-vided to respondents and added to this scale on the assumption that travellers are not likely to use unimportant information sources. This resulted in a five-point scale with 1 being 'did not use' and 5 being 'very important'.

Variety (amount) of information sources The variety (amount) of information sources used was measured by a variable indicating the number of institutions, services and materials through which the respondents have seen or heard about destinations (Stern and Krakover, 1993). Nine different information sources were compiled from the literature and survey instruments used by Tourism Canada

(1989) and NFO (1993). They included travel agents, brochures/travel guides, friends/family members, airlines, tour operator/company, advertisements, books/ movies, articles/news, and direct mail from destination. The variety of information score was calculated as the sum of the number of information sources used.

Socio-psychological travel motivations A thorough literature review on socio-psychological travel motivations revealed that no single established scale exists to measure tourists' overseas or international travel motivations. Therefore, socio-psychological travel motivations were derived from various studies (Crompton, 1979b; Dann, 1981; Iso-Ahola, 1982; Beard and Raghep, 1983; Shoemaker, 1989; Tourism Canada, 1989; Lounsbury and Franz, 1990; McIntosh and Goeldner, 1990; Fisher and Price, 1991; Loker and Purdue, 1992; Uysal and Hagan, 1993). After identified items were pre-tested on 45 students and faculty, they were measured by 17 items in the questionnaire. Respondents were asked to evaluate each reason on scale of 1, not at all important; 2, not very important; 3, somewhat important; and 4, very important.

Endogenous variables

Perceptual/cognitive evaluations Fifteen perceptual/cognitive evaluation items were generated from the literature review and a content analysis of four destinations' guidebooks and brochures, so that attributes selected could be applied to all the destinations included in this study. In particular, studies were selected that dealt with destination image in an international context (Gearing *et al.*, 1974; Haahti, 1986; Tourism Canada, 1989; Echtner and Ritchie, 1993; Hu and Ritchie, 1993). The pre-test on a sample of 60 students resulted in 14 items. A grid-response format, where columns indicate destinations and rows represent attributes, is used for measuring perceptual/cognitive evaluation items. Respondents were asked to rate each country as a summer vacation destination on each of 14 attributes on a five-point scale with 1 = offers very little, 2 = offers somewhat little, 3 = neither little nor much, 4 = offers somewhat much, and 5 = offers very much.

Affective evaluations Affective evaluations of destinations were measured using four bipolar scales (arousing–sleepy, pleasant–unpleasant, exciting–gloomy and relaxing–distressing). The reliability and validity of the scales have been proven over different languages, samples, cultures and environment types (Russel *et al.*, 1981, 1989; Ward and Russel, 1981; Russel and Snodgrass, 1987; Hanyu, 1993; Walmsley and Jenkins, 1993; Baloglu and Brinberg, 1997). A seven-point scale is used for all four bipolar scales where the positive poles were assigned to lower values. A composite score of four bipolar scales, providing overall affective evaluation of a given destination (Russel and Snodgrass, 1987), was computed for the analysis. Internal consistency among four items was estimated by Cronbach Alpha which indicated a coefficient of 0.88.

Visitation intention Respondents were asked to rate their visitation intentions for four tourism destinations in the next 5 years. A four-point rating scale, adapted from Milman and Pizam (1995), was used with 1 = very likely; 2 = somewhat likely; 3 = somewhat unlikely; and 4 = very unlikely. This variable was recoded as 1 = very unlikely and 4 = very likely.

Data analysis

The data analysis consisted of three stages. Firstly, principal axis factor analysis and varimax rotation procedure were performed on socio-psychological travel motivations and perceptual/cognitive image items in the pooled data set. The latent root criterion of 1.0 was utilized for factor extraction and factor loadings of 0.40 were utilized for item inclusion (Nunnally, 1978; Hair *et al.*, 1992). Secondly, descriptive statistics, correlations and reliabilities for multi-item variables were computed. Finally, path analysis was employed to test the hypothesized model and calculate direct, indirect and total effect of variables on one another. The data were also examined for several assumptions of multiple regression and path analysis such as normality, linearity, homoskedasticity and multicollinearity. Descriptive statistics, frequencies and correlations were initially used. Residual plots, normal probability plots and tolerances were examined when conducting path analysis, and no significant violation of assumptions was detected.

Path analysis was employed to test the proposed model since it allows the simultaneous evaluation of variables in a causal process. In path analysis, a distinction is made between exogenous and endogenous variables (Pedhazur, 1982; Asher, 1983). Exogenous variables are those not influenced by other variables in the model. It is assumed that their variability is influenced by causes outside the model; therefore the relationship between exogenous variables remains unanalysed in the model. Endogenous variables, on the other hand, are those whose variability is influenced by exogenous and/or endogenous variables in the model. In the proposed path model, the variety (amount) of information sources, the type of information sources used, and socio-psychological travel motivations are exogenous variables. The perceptual/cognitive evaluations, affective evaluation, and visitation intention are endogenous variables.

One advantage of path analysis lies in its explanatory information when the correlations between variables are decomposed into simple (direct) and compound (indirect) effects (Holbrook, 1981; Asher, 1983; Davis, 1985; Duncan, 1985; Wolfle and Ethington, 1985). Direct effects in recursive path models are estimated by partial regression coefficients, referred to as direct path coefficients. The indirect effect of each variable is the sum of the products of direct path coefficients from an exogenous variable through intervening variables to an endogenous variable. The total effect of a variable is the sum of the direct effects measured by the simple path and indirect effects measured by the compound path. This decomposition provides a basis for substantively interpreting the causal effects and identifying the operating casual system, and providing a means to test the overall pattern of the model.

In this study, path coefficients were estimated by ordinary least squares (OLS), partial standardized regression coefficients, between the cause (exogenous) variables and the effect (endogenous) variables on which they have impact (Pedhazur, 1982; Asher, 1983; Davis, 1985). A path coefficient was considered significant at the 0.05 or better probability level. The path analysis was conducted on the full model with all possible connections (involving the dotted arrows), which was followed by deleting non-significant paths. This procedure helps researchers to develop a more parsimonious causal model which is expected to correspond closely to the proposed model, reveal the overall pattern of the model, and validate the intervening variables by examining direct and indirect effects of one variable on the other (Holbrook, 1981; Sirgy and Samli, 1985). Based on the full model, each endogenous variable was regressed on the preceding variables in the model.

Results

The demographic profile of 356 respondents showed that the gender of respondents was almost evenly distributed, with 47.5% male and 52.5% female. In terms of age, education and income, respondents appeared to be homogeneous. The majority of the respondents were within older age brackets, with 35.1% between 50 and 64, followed by 30.6% at 65 years old or older. Only 11.7% belonged to the 18–34 age group. Most of the respondents were married (62.7%). The respondents were highly educated, 44.4% attended college and 47.5% attended graduate school. Almost 70% of the respondents reported a yearly income of $50,000 or more, while only 8.2% indicated a yearly income under $25,000.

The factor analysis of the 14 perceptual/cognitive items from the questionnaire produced three factors and explained 61.5% of the variance (Table 4.2). The factors were labelled as 'quality of experience', 'attractions' and 'value/environment'. The 17 motivation items from the factor analysis resulted in five factor groupings and explained 62.4% of the variance (Table 4.3). Factors were labelled as 'relaxation/escape', 'excitement/adventure', 'knowledge', 'social', and 'prestige'. Factor scores were derived by averaging responses to items within each factor. The descriptive statistics, correlations and reliabilities for multi-item variables are illustrated in Table 4.4.

S. Baloglu

Table 4.2 Factor analysis of perceptual/cognitive items

Factor	Factor loadings	Eigen-value	Variance explained (%)
I. Quality of experience		5.87	41.9
Standard hygiene and cleanliness	0.84		
Quality of infrastructure	0.81		
Personal safety	0.76		
Good nightlife and entertainment	0.70		
Suitable accommodations	0.69		
Appealing local food (cuisine)	0.66		
Great beaches/water sports	0.65		
Interesting and friendly people	0.52		
II. Attractions		1.67	11.9
Interesting cultural attractions	0.86		
Interesting historical attractions	0.85		
Beautiful scenery/natural attractions	0.56		
III. Value/environment		1.07	7.6
Good value for money	0.82		
Unpolluted/unspoiled environment	0.54		
Good climate	0.50		
Total			61.5

Table 4.3 Factor analysis of travel motivation items

Factor	Factor loadings	Eigen-value	Variance explained (%)
I. Relaxation/escape		4.12	24.3
Relieving stress and tension	0.85		
Getting away from demands of everyday life	0.81		
Relaxing physically and mentally	0.75		
Getting away from crowds	0.62		
Escaping from the routine	0.62		
II. Excitement/adventure		2.23	13.1
Doing exciting things	0.82		
Finding thrills and excitement	0.82		
Being adventurous	0.63		
Having fun, being entertained	0.57		
III. Knowledge		1.67	9.8
Learning new things, increasing my knowledge	0.79		
Experiencing different cultures and ways of life	0.73		
Enriching myself intellectually	0.66		
Experiencing new/different places	0.58		
IV. Social		1.50	8.8
Meeting people with similar interests	0.83		
Developing close friendships	0.76		
V. Prestige		1.09	6.4
Going places my friends have not been	0.87		
Telling my friends about the trip	0.71		
Total			62.4

S. Baloglu

Table 4.4 Correlation matrix and descriptive statistics for model variables

Variable	VIS	TIS1	TIS2	TIS3	TIS4	MOT1	MOT2	MOT3	MOT4	MOT5	COG1	COG2	COG3	AFF	VI
Variety (amount) of information (VIS)	1.00														
Professional advice (TIS1)	0.244**	1.00													
Word-of-mouth (TIS2)	0.086	0.033	1.00												
Advertisement (TIS3)	0.388**	0.239**	-0.061	1.00											
Books/movies/news (TIS4)	0.197**	-0.124*	0.117*	0.141**	1.00										
Escape/relaxation (MOT1)	0.003	-0.090	0.108*	0.120*	0.027	1.00									
Excitement (MOT2)	0.069	-0.025	0.224**	-0.021	0.152*	0.251**	1.00								
Knowledge (MOT3)	0.211**	-0.084	0.028	0.013	0.301**	-0.009	0.051	1.00							
Social (MOT4)	0.109*	-0.039	0.143**	-0.044	0.137**	0.136**	0.239**	0.202**	1.00						
Prestige (MOT5)	0.026	0.032	0.118*	0.086	0.018	0.332**	0.226**	0.073	0.178**	1.00					
Quality of experience (COG1)	0.324**	0.045	0.148**	0.122*	0.092	0.186**	0.163**	0.164*	0.102*	0.153**	1.00				
Attractions (COG2)	0.325**	0.021	-0.007	0.078	0.191**	0.064	0.028	0.232**	0.022	-0.054	0.444**	1.00			

Table 4.4 (Continued) Correlation matrix and descriptive statistics for model variables

Variable	VIS	TIS1	TIS2	TIS3	TIS4	MOT1	MOT2	MOT3	MOT4	MOT5	COG1	COG2	COG3	AFF	VI
Value/environment (COG3)	0.225**	0.039	0.081	0.169*	0.114*	0.255**	0.084	0.163**	0.044	0.102*	0.623**	0.383**	1.00		
Affect (AFF)	0.209**	0.045	0.108*	0.058	0.124*	0.175**	0.177**	0.209**	0.149**	0.108*	0.639**	0.409**	0.612**	1.00	
Visitation intention (VI)	0.385**	0.193**	0.068	0.202**	0.083	−0.097	0.044	0.145**	0.050	−0.094	0.461**	0.448**	0.364**	0.428**	1.00
Mean	2.01	1.56	1.49	1.27	1.35	0.70	0.64	0.30	0.75	0.76	0.80	0.57	0.80	1.44	
S.D.	3.17	3.70	3.19	3.58	2.87	2.92	3.81	2.34	2.02	3.34	4.59	5.24	2.95		1.05
Scale	0–9	1–5	1–5	1–5	1–5	1–4	1–4	1–4	1–4	1–4	1–5	1–5	1–5	1–7	1–4
Reliability (Cronbach Alpha)							0.80	0.73	0.64	0.64	0.61	0.89	0.72	0.56	0.88

Note: missing values were deleted listwise (N=408).
*Significant at 0.05 level; **significant at 0.01 level.

Path analysis

The results of path analysis are shown in Fig. 4.2. Perception of quality of experience (COG1) was significantly and positively influenced by variety (amount) of information sources used (VIS) (0.262), word-of-mouth (TIS2) (0.099), relaxation/escape (MOT1) (0.124), and knowledge (MOT3) (0.108). Perception of attractions (COG2) was significantly and positively affected by variety (amount) of information used (VIS) (0.287), non-tourism information sources (0.099), relaxation/escape (MOT1) (0.098), and knowledge (MOT3) (0.108). There were significant and positive effects of variety (amount) of information sources (VIS) (0.132), advertisement (0.108), relaxation/escape (MOT1) (0.218), and knowledge (MOT3) (0.135) on value/environment (COG3).

Affect was found to be significantly and positively influenced by only quality of experience (COG1) (0.368), attractions (COG2) (0.115), and value/environment (COG3) (0.335). Visitation intention was significantly and positively influenced by variety (amount) of information sources (VIS) (0.140), professional advice (TIS1) (0.094), advertisement (TIS3) (0.105), quality of experience (COG1) (0.196), attractions (COG2) (0.227), and affect (0.175). However, sociopsychological motivations of relaxation/escape (MOT1) (−0.172) and prestige (MOT5) (−0.108) significantly and negatively influenced visitation intention.

The explanatory power of the model was examined by explained variabilities in endogenous variables (Fig. 4.2). Variety (amount) of information sources, type of information sources, and socio-psychological travel motivations explained 14.8% of the variability in quality of experience (COG1), 15.3% of the variability in attractions, and 15.3% of the variability in value/environment. Perceptual/cognitive evaluations explained 51.6% of the variability in affect. Finally, variety (amount) of information sources, type of information sources, socio-psychological travel motivations, perceptual/cognitive evaluations and affective evaluations explained 40.6% of the variability in visitation intention. A large portion of this variability resulted from perceptual/cognitive and affective evaluations.

Decomposition of causal effects

Direct, indirect and total causal effects of exogenous variables on endogenous variables were examined to delineate the overall pattern of the model and validate the role of intervening variables in the model (Table 4.5). Although affect was only directly influenced by perceptual/cognitive evaluations, variety (amount) of information sources (VIS) (0.174), relaxation/escape (MOT1) (0.130), and knowledge (MOT3) (0.104) had significant and positive indirect effects through perceptual/cognitive evaluations on affect. Based on magnitude of the path coefficients, the indirect effects of variety (amount) of information sources used and relaxation/escape were found to be stronger than the direct effects of attractions. Several information source types also influenced affect indirectly; however, they were weak.

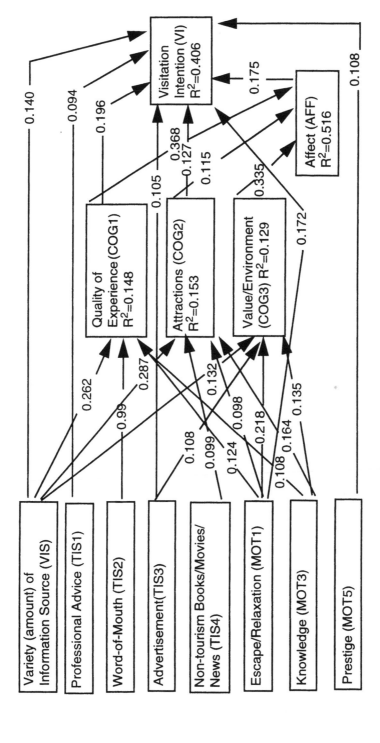

Figure 4.2 Path analysis of visitation intention formation before actual visit, showing significant path coefficients at 0.05 or better probability level.

Table 4.5 Direct, indirect and total effects

Exogenous variables	Endogenous variables								
	COG1	COG2	COG3	AFF DE	AFF IE	AFF TE	VI DE	VI IE	VI TE
Variety of information sources (VIS)	0.262	0.287	0.132	–	0.174	0.174	0.140	0.147	0.287
Professional advice (TIS1)	–	–	–	–	–	–	0.094	–	0.094
Word-of-mouth (TIS2)	0.099	–	–	–	0.036	0.036	–	0.026	0.026
Advertisement (TIS3)	–	–	0.108	–	0.036	0.036	0.105	0.006	0.111
Non-tourism (TIS4)	–	0.099	–	–	0.011	0.011	–	0.024	0.024
Relaxation/Escape (MOT1)	0.124	0.098	0.218	–	0.130	0.130	-0.172	0.069	-0.103
Excitement (MOT2)	–	–	–	–	–	–	–	–	–
Knowledge (MOT3)	0.108	0.164	0.135	–	0.104	0.104	–	0.077	0.018
Social (MOT4)	–	–	–	–	–	–	–	–	–
Prestige (MOT5)	–	–	–	–	–	–	-0.108	–	-0.108
Quality of experience (COG1)	–	–	–	–	0.368	0.368	0.196	0.064	0.260
Attractions (COG2)	–	–	–	0.115	–	0.115	0.227	0.020	0.247
Value/environment (COG3)	–	–	–	0.335	–	0.335	–	0.059	0.059
Affect (AFF)	–	–	–	–	–	–	0.175	–	0.175

Note: table shows only those effects significant at 0.05 or better probability level.
DE, direct effect; IE, indirect effect; TE, total effect (DE+IE).

Variables such as variety (amount) of information sources (VIS), advertisement (TIS3), relaxation/escape (MOT1), quality of experience (COG1), and attractions (COG2) influenced visitation intentions both directly and indirectly. The total effects of these variables increased from their direct effects as they pass through perceptual/cognitive and affect variables in the casual system. In general, the direct effects of these variables accounted for the greater proportion in their total effects on visitation intention, except for variety (amount) of information sources. The effect of variety (amount) of information sources on visitation intention increased significantly after adding direct (0.140) and indirect effects (0.147), which doubled the size of the total effect (0.287). After taking indirect effects into consideration, the total effect of quality of experience (COG1) (0.260) appeared to be more influential on visitation intention than that of attractions (COG2) (0.247). The negative direct effect of relaxation/escape (MOT1) (−0.172) was suppressed by its positive indirect effect (0.069), reducing negative total effect (−0.103) on visitation intention. Socio-psychological variables such as escape/relaxation (MOT1) and prestige (MOT5) appeared to be suppressor variables in the path model. Suppressors in a causal system result in an inconsistent system. Technically, in inconsistent systems the partial coefficient between two variables (when intervening variables are controlled) may become larger than the bivariate coefficient (correlation) between the two. However, this does not undermine the substantive effects of the suppressor variables in a system (for further explanation, see Davis, 1985, pp. 32–33, 57–58).

Discussion

This study empirically demonstrates that visitation intention is determined by interrelated stimuli (information sources), and psychological (socio-psychological travel motivations) and image (perceptual/cognitive and affective) variables. Perceptual/cognitive evaluations are determined by variety (amount) of information sources, type of information sources (word-of-mouth, advertisement and non-promotional), and socio-psychological travel motivations (relaxation/escape and knowledge). The variety (amount) of information sources used was found to be a stronger predictor of perceptual/cognitive image than type of information sources and motivations, particularly for perceptions of attractions and quality of experience. An interesting finding is that type of information sources had differential effects on perceptual/cognitive evaluations of destinations, because different types of information sources influenced perception of certain destination offerings. Word-of-mouth acted on perception of quality of experience, while advertisement influenced perception of value/environment. Non-promotional sources such as books, movies and news, on the other hand, formed the perceptions of destination attractions. In this regard, word-of-mouth affected the perception-intangible or psychological (evaluative) destination attributes, whereas advertisement and non-promotional sources contributed to formation of tangible or physical destination attributes. Relaxation/escape and knowledge motivations consistently and positively affected all three perceptual/cognitive image dimensions. Relaxation/escape was found to be more influential on value/environment, while knowledge was influential on attractions.

Affective image (feelings) about a destination was influenced by perceptual/cognitive evaluations only. This indicates that perceptual/cognitive evaluations serve as intervening variables and mediate the relationship between stimuli (variety and type of information sources) and consumer characteristics (travel motivation) variables, and affect towards destinations.

Visitation intention was determined not only by perceptual/cognitive and affective images, but also by variety (amount) of information, type of information source, and socio-psychological motivations. Interestingly, professional advice from tour operators and travel agents influenced the visitation intention, but not destination images. It is important to note that, while statistically significant, the estimated direct effects of variety (amount) of information, professional advice, relaxation/escape, and knowledge on visitation intention were not quite substantive compared to those of perceptual/cognitive and affective images. Based on the magnitudes of path coefficients, the perceptual/cognitive and affective evaluations were much more influential than these variables in predicting visitation intention. In a path model, if the chain model correctly represents the 'true' causal flow, then correlation between variables is expected to approach zero as the distance between them in the causal chain increases (Davis, 1985). The general pattern of the model met that requirement, validating the intervening role of perceptual/cognitive and affective evaluations. However, it should be noted that both perceptual/cognitive and affective evaluations influence intentions, where perceptual/cognitive evaluations are found to be more influential on visitation intention than affect before visiting a tourist destination. Perceptual/cognitive evaluations influenced visitation intention directly and indirectly through affect, rather than through affect only.

Limitations and Future Research

This study has several limitations. The findings are limited to unidirectional influences among the variables in the model (recursive causal modelling) because reciprocal (two-way) relationships among the variables were not studied (nonrecursive causal modelling). For example, it is possible that behavioural intention and variety (amount) of information used, and image components, would influence each other reciprocally. Future research can develop and test a model with bidirectional influences between variables. LISREL would be a more appropriate technique for such a study. Findings are also limited to the set of tourist destination countries included in the study. Future research should be carried out to validate the findings of this study. The relationships among the model variables can be extended to other international tourism destinations, or local destinations, to further assess the external validity of the findings.

This study did not control whether the destinations selected are in awareness or evoked sets of respondents. Gartner (1993), when discussing image-formation agents, noted that socio-psychological motivations in formation of affective images become operational for destinations in the choice (evoked) set. This suggests that the determinants of image may vary with destinations in the awareness and evoked sets. A test of the model for the destinations in different stages can clarify this point. The findings are also limited to the variables selected for the study. There may be other factors influencing the development of destination image and behavioural intention. Future research would expand the model by integrating other variables.

Finally, the fact that some sample members are over-represented in the pooled data set is a limitation of this study. A respondent who has not been to one tourism destination country was counted once, while a respondent who has not been to any of four tourism destination countries was counted four times. An ideal case would be a subsample who had not been to any four destinations, which was not possible in this study as very few cases met this criterion.

Conclusion and Implications

Unlike most related work in travel and tourism, this study investigates the process of formation of behavioural intention in an integrative path analytic framework, by analysing informational, motivational and mental constructs on visitation intention simultaneously in a path analytic framework. From a theoretical standpoint, the results of the present study advance our understanding of destination selection process by demonstrating the process involved in formation of visitation intention for tourism destinations. The formation of visitation intention is dependent on the different roles played by the informational, motivational and image elements in the process, image being a major antecedent concept to predicting travel behaviour among the constructs included in this study. Variety (amount) and type of information sources, and socio-psychological motivations, form the perceptions of destinations which, in turn, determine travellers' affection (feelings) about destinations. Finally, the travellers' affective and perceptual/cognitive evaluations, to a great extent, form the visitation intention for tourism destinations.

From a practical standpoint, this study provides important implications for developing marketing and communication strategies. It provides a set of variables that should be taken into consideration to entice first-time visitors to a destination. This study found that visitation intention could best be predicted by both perceptual/cognitive and affective evaluations (images). Considering the effects of motivations on visitation intention, tourism destinations should stress both destination attributes and benefits to enhance their destination images, as well as increase the likelihood to visit their destinations. To influence image, on the other hand, both informational and motivational determinants should be taken into consideration. This study demonstrates that different types of information sources have varying degrees of effect on perceptual/cognitive evaluations. This would assist tourism destinations in selecting the right mix of image-formation agents to influence the desired component of destination offerings. Among different types of information sources, travel professionals such as tour operators and travel agents should be given special attention mostly because of their promotional and transactional (distribution channel) role in influencing visitation intention. Because of the positive contribution of the variety (amount) of information sources used in perceptual/ cognitive evaluations and visitation intention, tourism destinations should not only promote their destinations through as many information channels as possible, but also encourage travellers to use a variety of information sources. Destinations should also tailor their efforts to specific travel motivation segments in image and positioning development efforts.

From a methodological standpoint, this study used a pooled cross-sectional design, a useful method to develop a single model for different testing units (i.e. tourist destinations), rather than a separate model for each tourist destination. Also, since destination selection is a process, linear structural modelling provides a useful technique for understanding this process.

References

Ajzen, I. and Driver, B.L. (1992) Application of the theory of planned behavior to leisure choice. *Journal of Leisure Research* 24, 207–224.

Amadeo, D. and Golledge, R.G. (1975) *An Introduction to Scientific Reasoning in Geography*. New York: Wiley.

Anand, P., Holbrook, M.B. and Stephens, D. (1988) The formation of affective judgments: the cognitive–affective model versus the independence hypothesis. *Journal of Consumer Research* 15, 386–391.

Asher, H.B. (1983) *Causal Modeling*. Quantitative applications in the social sciences series (3). Newbury Park, California: Sage.

Bagozzi, R.P. (1982) A field investigation of causal relations among cognitions, affect, intentions and behavior. *Journal of Marketing Research* 19, 562–584.

Baloglu, S. (1997) The relationship between destination images and sociodemographic and trip characteristics of international travelers. *Journal of Vacation Marketing* 3, 221–233.

Baloglu, S. and Brinberg, D. (1997) Affective images of tourism destinations. *Journal of Travel Research* 35, 11–15.

Beard, J.G. and Raghep, M.G. (1983) Measuring leisure motivation. *Journal of Leisure Research* 15, 219–228.

Burgess, J.A. (1978) *Image and Identity*. Occasional Papers in Geography No. 23, University of Hull Publications/W.S. Maney and Son.

Carman, J.M. (1978) Values and consumption patterns: a closed loop. *Advances in Consumer Research* 5, 403–407.

Court, B. and Lupton, R.A. (1997) Customer portfolio development: modeling destination adopters, inactives and rejecters. *Journal of Travel Research*, 36, 35–43.

Crandall, R. (1980) Motivations for leisure. *Journal of Leisure Research* 12, 45–53.

Crompton, J.L. (1979a) An assessment of the image of Mexico as a vacation destination and the influence of geographical location upon that image. *Journal of Travel Research* 17, 18–23.

Crompton, J.L. (1979b) Motivations for pleasure vacation. *Annals of Tourism Research* 6, 408–424.

Crompton, J.L., Fakeye, P.C. and Lue, C.C. (1992) Positioning: the example of the lower Rio Grande Valley in the winter long stay destination market. *Journal of Travel Research* 31, 20–26.

Dann, G.M.S. (1981) Tourism motivation: an appraisal. *Annals of Tourism Research* 8, 187–219.

Dann, G.M.S. (1996) Tourist images of a destination: an alternative analysis. In: D.R. Fesenmaier, J.T. O'Leary and M. Uysal (eds.) *Recent Advances in Tourism Marketing Research.* New York: Haworth Press, pp. 41–55.

Davis, J.A. (1985) *The Logic of Causal Order.* Quantitative applications in the social sciences series (55). Newbury Park, California: Sage.

Dielman, T.E. (1988) *Pooled Cross-Sectional and Time Series Data Analysis.* New York: Marcel Dekker.

Duncan, O.D. (1985) Path analysis: sociological examples. In: H.M. Blalock (ed.) *Causal Models in the Social Sciences.* New York: Aldine, pp. 55–79.

Echtner, C.M. and Ritchie, J.R.B. (1993) The measurement of destination image: An empirical assessment. *Journal of Travel Research* 31, 3–13.

Engel, J.F., Kollat, D.T. and Blackwell, R.D. (1978) *Consumer Behavior.* New York: Holt, Rinehart and Winston.

Fakeye, P.C. and Crompton, J.L. (1991) Image differences between prospective, first-time and repeat visitors to the lower Rio Grande Valley. *Journal of Travel Research* 30, 10–16.

Fishbein, M. and Ajzen, I. (1975) Belief, attitude, intention and behavior: an introduction to theory and research. Massachusetts: Addison-Wesley.

Fisher, R. and Price, L. (1991) International pleasure travel motivations and post-vacation cultural attitude change. *Journal of Leisure Research* 23, 193–208.

Friedmann, R. (1986) Psychological meaning of products: identification and marketing implications. *Psychology and Marketing* 3, 1–15.

Friedmann, R. and Lessig, V.P. (1986) A framework of psychological meaning of products. *Advances in Consumer Research* 13, 338–342.

Gartner, W.C. (1993) Image formation process. In: M. Uysal and D.R. Fesenmaier (eds.) *Communication and Channel Systems in Tourism Marketing.* New York: Haworth Press, pp. 191–215.

Gearing, C., Swart, W. and Var, T. (1974) Establishing a measure of touristic attractiveness. *Journal of Travel Research* 12, 1–8.

Gitelson, R.J. and Crompton, J.L. (1983) The planning horizons and sources of information used by pleasure vacationers. *Journal of Travel Research* 23, 2–7.

Goodall, B. (1990) How tourists choose their holidays: an analytical framework. In: B.Goodall and G. Ashworth (eds) *Marketing in the Tourism Industry: The Promotion of Destination Regions.* London: Routledge, pp. 1–17.

Goodrich, J.N. (1978) The relationship between preferences for and perceptions of vacation destinations. *Journal of Travel Research* 17, 8–13.

Gunn, C. (1972) *Vacationscape: Designing Tourist Regions.* Austin: Bureau of Business Research, University of Texas.

Haahti, A.J. (1986) Finland's competitive position as a destination. *Annals of Tourism Research* 13, 11–35.

Hair, J.F., Anderson, R.E., Tatham, R.L. and Black, W.C. (1992) *Multivariate Data Analysis with Readings*. New York: Macmillan.

Hanyu, K. (1993) The affective meaning of Tokyo: verbal and nonverbal approaches. *Journal of Environmental Psychology* 13, 161–172.

Holbrook, M.B. (1978) Beyond attitude structure: Toward the informational determinants of attitude. *Journal of Marketing Research* 15, 545–56.

Holbrook, M.B. (1981) Integrating compositional and decompositional analyses to represent the intervening role of perceptions in evaluative judgements. *Journal of Marketing Research* 18, 13–28.

Howard, J.A. and Sheth, J.L. (1969) *The Theory of Buyer Behavior*. New York: Wiley.

Hsiesh, S. and O'Leary, J.T. (1993) Communication channels to segment pleasure travelers. In: M. Uysal and D.R. Fesenmaier (eds) *Communication and Channel Systems in Tourism Marketing*. New York: Haworth Press, pp. 57–75).

Hu, Y. and Ritchie, J.R.B. (1993) Measuring destination attractiveness: a contextual approach. *Journal of Travel Research* 32, 25–34.

Hunt, J.D. (1975) Image as a factor in tourism development. *Journal of Travel Research* 17, 1–7.

Iso-Ahola, S.E. (1982) Toward a social psychological theory of tourism motivation: a rejoinder. *Annals of Tourism Research* 9, 256–262.

Keaveney, S.M. and Hunt, K.A. (1992) Conceptualization and operationalization of retail store image:a case of rival middle level theories. *Journal of Academy of Marketing Science* 20(2), 165–175.

Kassarjian, H.H. and Robertson, T.S. (1973) *Perspectives in Consumer Behavior*. Illinois: Scott, Foresman & Co.

Kliman, M.L. (1981) A quantitative analysis of Canadian overseas tourism. *Transportation Research* 15A. 487–497.

Kotler, P. (1988) *Marketing Management: Analysis, Planning, Implementation and Control* (6th edn). New Jersey: Prentice Hall.

Krech, D., Crutchfield, R.S. and Ballachey, E.L. (1962) *Individual in Society*. New York: McGraw Hill.

Loker, L. and Perdue, R. (1992) A benefit-based segmentation of a nonresident summer travel market. *Journal of Travel Research* 31, 30–35.

Long, S.B. and Evans, R.H. (1983) Linking product characteristics to behavioral intention: contrasting findings with regression, path analysis and LISREL. In: *AMA Winter Educators' Conference: Research Methods and Causal Modeling in Marketing*, pp. 227–234.

Lounsbury, J.W. and Franz, C.P.G. (1990) Vacation discrepancy: a leisure motivation approach. *Psychological Reports* 66, 699–702.

Lynch, K. (1960) *The Image of the City*. Cambridge, MA: Massachusetts Institute of Technology.

Mansfeld, Y. (1992) From motivation to actual travel. *Annals of Tourism Research* 19, 399–419.

Mayo, E.J. (1973) Regional images and regional travel destination. In: *Proceedings of the Fourth Annual Conference of TTRA*. Salt Lake City, Utah: Travel and Tourism Research Association, pp. 211–217.

Mayo, E.J. and Jarvis, L.P. (1981) *The Psychology of Leisure Travel*. Boston: CBI.

McIntosh, W.R. and Goeldner, C.R. (1990) *Tourism: Principles, Practices, Philosophies* (6th edn). New York: Wiley.

Mill, R.C. and Morrison, A.M. (1992) *The Tourism System: An Introductory Text.* New Jersey: Prentice Hall.

Milman, A. and Pizam, A. (1995) The role of awareness and familiarity with a destination: the Central Florida case. *Journal of Travel Research* 33, 21–27.

Moutinho, L. (1987) Consumer behavior in tourism. *European Journal of Marketing* 21, 5–44.

NFO (1993) *Virginia Image and Perceptions.* Greensboro, NC: NFO Research.

Nunnally, J.C. (1978) *Psychometric Theory.* New York: McGraw-Hill.

Pearce, P.L. (1995) Pleasure travel motivation. In: R.W. McIntosh, C.R. Goeldner and J.R. Brent Ritchie (eds) *Tourism: Principles, Practices, Philosophies* (7th edn). New York: Wiley pp. 167–178.

Pedhazur, E.J. (1982) *Multiple Regression in Behavioral Research* (2nd edn). Orlando, Florida: Harcourt Brace Jovanovich.

Phelps, A. (1986) Holiday destination image: the problem of assessment. *Tourism Management* 7, 168–180.

Reibstein, D.J. (1978) The prediction of individual probabilities of brand choice. *Journal of Consumer Research* 5, 163–168.

Reibstein, D.J., Lovelock, C.H. and Dobson, R.P. (1980) The direction of causality between perceptions, affect and behavior: an application to travel behavior. *Journal of Consumer Research* 6, 370–376.

Russel, J.A. and Pratt, G. (1980) A description of affective quality attributed to environment. *Journal of Personality and Social Psychology* 38, 311–322.

Russel, J.A. and Snodgrass, J. (1987) Emotion and environment. In: D. Stockols and I. Altman (eds) *Handbook of Environmental Psychology.* New York: Wiley, pp. 245–280.

Russel, J.A., Ward, L.M. and Pratt, G. (1981) Affective quality attributed to environments: a factor analytic study. *Environment and Behavior* 13, 259–288.

Russel, J.A., Lewicka, M. and Niit, T. (1989) A cross-cultural study of a circumplex model of affect. *Journal of Personality and Social Psychology* 57, 848–856.

Scott, D.R., Schewe, C.D. and Frederick, D.G. (1978) A multi-brand/multi-attribute model of tourist state choice. *Journal of Travel Research* 17, 23–29.

Shoemaker, S. (1989) Segmentation of the senior pleasure travel market. *Journal of Travel Research* 27, 14–21.

Sirgy, M.J. and Samli, A.C. (1985) A path analytic model of store loyalty involving self-concept, store image, geographic loyalty and socioeconomic status. *Journal of Academy of Marketing Science* 13, 265–291.

Stabler, M.J. (1990) The image of destination regions: theoretical and empirical aspects. In: B. Goodall and G. Ashworth (eds) *Marketing in the Tourism Industry: The Promotion of Destination Regions.* London: Routledge, pp. 133–161.

Stern, E. and Krakover, S. (1993) The formation of a composite urban image. *Geographical Analysis* 25, 130–146.

Tourism Canada (1989) *Pleasure Travel Markets to North America.* Montreal: Market Facts of Canada.

Um, S. and Crompton, J.L. (1990) Attitude determinants in tourism destination choice. *Annals of Tourism Research* 17, 432–448.

Uysal, M. and Hagan, L.A.R. (1993) Motivation of pleasure travel and tourism. In: M. Khan, M. Olsen and T. Var (eds) *VNR's Encyclopedia of Hospitality and Tourism.* New York: Van Nostrand Reinhold, pp. 798–810.

Vogt, C.A., Stewart, S.I. and Fesenmaier, D.R. (1998) Communication strategies to reach first-time visitors. *Journal of Travel and Tourism Marketing* 7, 69–89.

Walmsley, D.J. and Jenkins, J.M. (1993) Appraisive images of tourist areas: application of personal construct. *Australian Geographer* 24, 1–13.

Walmsley, D.J. and Lewis, G.J. (1984) *Human Geography: Behavioral Approaches.* New York: Longman.

Ward, L.M. and Russel, J.A. (1981) The psychological representation of molar physical environments. *Journal of Experimental Psychology: General* 110, 121–52.

Weaver, P.A., McCleary, K.W., Lepisto, L. and Damonte, L.T. (1994) The relationship of destination selection attributes to psychological, behavioral and demographic variables. *Journal of Hospitality and Leisure Marketing* 2, 93–109.

Wolfle, L.M. and Ethington, C.A. (1985) GEMINI: program for analysis of structural equations with standard errors of indirect effects. *Behavior Research Methods, Instruments and Computers* 17, 581–84.

Woodside, A.G. (1982) Positioning a province using travel research. *Journal of Travel Research* 20, 2–6.

Woodside, A.G. and Lysonski, S. (1989) A general model of traveler destination choice. *Journal of Travel Research* 27, 8–14.

Zimmer, M.R. and Golden, L.L. (1988) Impressions of retail stores: a content analysis of consumer images. *Journal of Retailing* 64, 265–93.

Chapter five
Playing on the Post-modern Edge: Action Leisure as Self-Identity

Jerome B. Kernan and Teresa J. Domzal
School of Management, George Mason University, UKM-42600 Bangi, Malaysia

Introduction

To study leisure (or its disciplinary affiliates – tourism, hospitality, and recreation) is to court a certain amount of contempt, based on the idea that it is a frivolous topic, undeserving of serious study. This objection can be overcome on at least two fronts. Firstly, the economic activity which supports people's non-work behaviours is extensive by any standard. Indeed, this 'industry' frequently is stated to be the world's largest. Secondly, these behaviours are increasingly being associated with life satisfaction, or the degree to which people associate them with their perceived quality of life (Kernan and Unger, 1987). One of the ways in which the latter occurs is the focus of this paper – the use of a particular category of leisure, involving much risk and action, to establish and maintain one's sense of self-identity. The argument we make is that people express who/what they are, to themselves and to others, by engaging in action-leisure activities. These are of a defining nature – they portray their practitioners as they prefer to be, and to be portrayed – and in that sense they contribute to their practitioners' contentment with life.

Action leisure is more than a curiosity, for several reasons. Firstly, it is rich in theory – anthropological, psychological, and sociological (Arnould and Price, 1993; Celsi *et al.*, 1993) – so there is much to be learned from its study. Secondly, it is a popular phenomenon. Some 31 million Americans took 'adventure vacations' between 1992 and 1997, according to the Travel Industry Association of America. Thirdly, action leisure appeals largely (but by no means exclusively) to younger and middle-aged people, so we might anticipate it to have a reasonably enduring popularity. And fourthly, it has a significant number of commercial trappings, such as the numerous products and venues needed to sustain the various activities; apparent institutionalization in the form of facilities such as the X Games on ESPN; and activity-specific media, such as *blue*, a magazine devoted to 'the new adventure life style'.

We begin by situating action leisure in the larger context of tourism, hospitality, recreation and leisure, indicating how the various behavioural sciences have considered these phenomena historically, with particular emphasis on the changes which the age of post-modernism appears to be introducing into their study. We then emphasize the idea of leisure as life and show how two of its main constructs – the 'gaze' (Urry, 1990) and an 'inversion' (Crick, 1989) – have taken on dynamic properties in consequence of the cultural change recently experienced throughout western civilization, and how this change has affected the rules for establishing, maintaining and enhancing one's identity in a socially constructed world.

Leisure reflects life

To anyone who has never considered leisure systematically, the proposition that it affords a means for understanding life probably seems preposterous. After all, leisure (including phenomena commonly associated with it, such as tourism, hospitality and recreation) represents the antithesis of ordinary life, a characteristic which makes it so desirable. Everyday living is routine and dull, while leisure is different and exciting. Day-to-day life consists of work, and leisure is full of play. The everyday is familiar, while leisure often seeks out the unfamiliar. We mind our manners at work, yet often let ourselves go during leisure pursuits. And as everyone has come to understand, ordinary living is real and necessary, while leisure is escapist and superfluous. We could go on, but the distinction is clear – ordinary life is sensible, leisure is frivolous. Or is it? Indeed, can we understand more about life by studying leisure because it seems to represent the opposite?

Leisure is to quotidian life as a negative is to its photographic print – the negative represents a reversed version of the 'real' print. One might argue that it is easier to understand reality by observing a print, rather than a negative, yet prints are not always available, they fade easily in sunlight, and they often obscure images better portrayed in the contrast of a negative. So it is with leisure and life – if one can observe 'the real thing', well and good, but there are many reasons why and occasions when this is not possible, and leisure affords us a negative – usually called an inversion (Crick, 1989) – for such circumstances. Interpreting leisure as life is no more direct than (and hardly as easy as) reading photographic negatives, so we must know what to look for. People's behaviour is the obvious candidate, and this is read all the time. But beyond that, we look for what is called a gaze (Urry, 1990), which is the way one perceives and appreciates (or anticipates appreciating) the experiences encountered in a leisure activity. The gaze is important because a variety of forces (including the marketing system) combine to produce and modify it: it reflects what people sense, based on what societal forces have encouraged them to sense. To take the case of tourism as leisure, for example, the gaze of Washington, D.C., for a typical visitor among the millions who pour into the area each year, includes all the famous monuments and museums one would imagine, but it rarely includes neighbourhoods such as Anacostia, which the tourist bureau prefers non-residents to avoid. (Washington is not isolated in this regard – all tourist destinations attempt to package themselves in the most attractive and revenue-enhancing way possible.) For reading as leisure, the gaze might include one's favourite chair, good lighting, comfortable clothing, and a preferred author's latest novel.

The student of leisure is interested in what people do during these pursuits, as well as what guides them, that is, in the attendant leisure gaze. Together, these two elements form the inversions of quotidian living (that from which people presumably are getting away, however briefly), which represent the 'data' of leisure as a reflection of life. To study people at play, then, is not to confine one's interest to their ludic pursuits. Such investigations also trace a path of understanding toward people's non-ludic behaviours. One of these in particular – self-identity – is our particular concern in this paper.

It becomes apparent that the leisure gaze is the product of societies, specifically of their respective cultures, as well as of groups within societies. Historically, each society has established (and modified as conditions required) a way for its members to regard leisure, and each one has operated its leisure pursuits (what is considered legitimate leisure and the approved ways of experiencing it) according to a set of corresponding rules. However, the world is shrinking and societal differences are diminishing, so it comes as no great surprise that differences in leisure are also diminishing – we are seeing more and more global examples of leisure. The other (and related) great difference we observe is the passage from modernity to post-modernity as the prevalent cultural condition, and this transformation has had a profound effect on leisure behaviour and the gaze. But we are getting ahead of ourselves. All these changes represent a good deal of psychology, sociology and anthropology – considerations to which we should attend before proceeding further. At this point, suffice to say that while we are interested in leisure pursuits *per se*, we are perhaps more interested in what their intrinsic properties imply in the way of contrasts with non-leisure pursuits. When we play, for example, it is typically for relief from work; when it is cold, we seek vacation venues in warm climates. These implied opposites are clues to people's quotidian lives, so it is often the obverse of a leisure characteristic that captures the analyst's attention. If this seems overly complex, we should recall that much of human behaviour cannot be explained directly by those who engage in it. Inferential thinking is by no means unique to leisure studies.

Leisure is? Choose your favourite facet of the prism

Psychologists, sociologists and anthropologists have investigated the phenomenon (including tourism, hospitality and recreation) fairly extensively. While these disciplines are not in complete agreement on the issues of importance, neither are they at serious odds. Accordingly, we sketch the principal concerns with the leisure phenomenon commonly associated with each of these disciplines, with particular emphasis on the significance of the cultural movement from modernism to post-modernism.

Anthropology of leisure

In the main, anthropology has focused on the tourism and hospitality aspects of leisure, as these reflect three broad topics: economic development, cultural change and semiotic meanings (Crick, 1989). Traditionally, anthropologists have been fascinated by primitive societies and, since much tourism occurs in 'exotic' locations, this is a natural extension of their interest. (Anthropologists were the first to distinguish between travel and tourism, the former referring to something done by individuals with laudable purposes, and the latter to a vague copy thereof by uninformed masses, commonly with little purpose beyond their vulgar, hedonistic amusement – this bias prevails in contemporary anthropological analysis.) Much of the focus is comparative, pitting developed societies against un- or underdeveloped ones. Much study has addressed the economic impact of tourism on host venues, for example, with the general conclusion that any benefits come at a substantial cost to indigenous physical and social resources. (One hears related zero-sum arguments about America's contemporary national park system.) Similarly, whatever cultural change might be engendered by tourism is asymmetrical in favour of the visitors (whose horizons might be broadened), rather than the hosts (who learn nothing, except perhaps disdain for tourists). The semiotic meanings involved are more evenly divided between visitors (who read and interpret the proffered signs/symbols) and hosts (who stage the attractions which are made up of them). From the provider's (host's) perspective, it's a case of imagining what set of symbols might prove sufficient to convince tourists that the site before them is 'authentic', if not real (in the sense of being genuine or historically accurate). For visitors, it's a matter of reading the site for the appropriate gratification – is it pilgrimage, nostalgia, learning, just ludic, what? Hosts must have a pretty good sense of how visitors read their sites, of course, lest these fail to provide the gratifications visitors deem necessary (one wonders whether Las Vegas could survive without neon). There is a vast and substantial industry devoted to semiotic meanings, since these are the essence of the tourist gaze associated with any site (or the gaze of any leisure pursuit, for that matter). What we imagine at the mention of April in Paris, the beaches at Kaanapali, the Indianapolis 500, and so on, is the result of semiology crafted carefully over many years. Yet our imagination can be changed, as witnessed by the general relaxation of formality in both travel and leisure over the past couple of generations. This relaxation reflects post-modernism's celebration of diversity, particularly as it blurs traditional distinctions between high and popular culture. Just as it is currently as appropriate to prefer Mancini to Mahler, it is acceptable to 'do' most any sort of leisure. The traditional polo-to-bowling hierarchy no longer obtains, yet leisure can still mark people in distinctive ways.

Sociology of leisure

Nominally, sociology has addressed all aspects of leisure, but its emphasis has been far from even. Reflecting the traditional agency/structure concerns, a good deal of sociological inquiry about leisure has been couched in questions of social control and class differences. Leisure pursuits have been typed according to class, for example, as often as they have for intrinsic differences. Tourism is frequently argued to be a method of control by visitors from developed nations over hosts in underdeveloped ones. Leisure time is said to represent capitalists' means of keeping the working class at bay. There have been attempts to understand leisure, tourism, hospitality and recreation from an emic perspective (see Cohen, 1984), but as often as not, sociologists have been content to gloss over these findings with etic interpretations (e.g. leisure=recreation or tourism=leisure), with the result that nuances have been lost in the rendering. Of course, individual differences are not the province of sociology and class differences are, so these biases are hardly cause for pillory. But this does mean that we shall not gain an understanding from sociology (with the possible exception of symbolic interactionism) of what leisure 'is' to individuals. Indeed, the macro tradition is so strong here that Rojek (1993) divides the history of leisure's study into three periods: functionalism, politicization and post-modernism. The first of these, the more-or-less traditional way of conceiving leisure, posited it as a means of social control – that which replenishes the energies of the working class and thereby contributes to the stability of society. The second period, politicization, reflected the neo-Marxist idea that leisure represents a form of cultural, indeed moral, regulation and therefore should be a matter of contestation by oppressed groups. Through consciousness-raising and collective mobilization, previously marginalized groups such as women, gays and ethnic minorities hope to uproot the rule of (male-dominated) capital in favour of a more equitable social configuration. Finally, the period of post-modernism began with a rejection of Marxist contentions about ideology as being too simplistic. It moved instead to an argument that, if there is social control, it occurs through hegemony – an organic process which permeates society so effectively that the ruling classes' ideas and institutions become internalized as the natural or normal order of things. Resistance or opposition is managed by allowing (encouraging) diversity, fragmentation and discontinuity rather than disapproving of them. This often involves the mixing of codes (called pastiche), such as high and popular culture, by means of hyperreality (where symbols have no real-world referent). Popular entertainment is replete with examples, such as ET (a completely fictional character), Disney World (where everything is constructed according to what masses of customers might accept as authentic), and so on. By providing something for everyone, no one is likely to complain. And if enough of them do, their complaints represent the market for yet something else which might be provided at a profit.

Psychology of leisure

In their respective ways, both anthropology and sociology tell us something about the arena in which leisure occurs, but neither reveals much about what the experience means to the focal person. For that insight, we must look to psychology.

However, there is so much psychology-of-leisure literature (e.g. Dumazedier, 1974) that we must limit our attention to just two aspects. One of these – easily the most data-rich – concerns the dimensions, gratifications, meanings or motivations perceived by the individual as a part of the leisure experience. The second aspect concerns the relationship between leisure and identity, and why this has become so important in post-modern times.

As might be expected, a good deal of psychological investigation has been devoted to the discovery of what leisure 'is', since how people perceive (or the gratification they expect of) the experience determines their motivations for engaging in it. (Needless to say, it also affects how to market leisure.) Generally, six dimensions, or psychological meanings, have been identified and verified: arousal, intrinsic satisfaction, involvement, mastery, perceived freedom, and spontaneity (Unger and Kernan, 1983; Domzal and Kernan, 1995). Thus, when leisure occurs, the focal person is thought to experience at least one of these dimensions or states of being. A perusal of leisure advertising will indicate the consistent presence of (at least one of) these meanings as copy platforms or appeals. So in general we understand why people seek leisure, what it does for/to them. But it is not so simple as that, for people rarely pick and choose these gratifications in cafeteria style. Instead, they perceive them hierarchically, in the same way that golf is experienced very differently by high and low handicappers. Put another way, people's reasons for seeking leisure evolve through experience, and this leads them to develop likes and dislikes, 'favourite' pastimes.

This is never more clear than in the case of challenging pastimes, those requiring considerable skill and/or replete with danger, which present difficult learning curves to participants. Celsi *et al.* (1993) describe skydiving, while Arnould and Price (1993) do the same for river rafting, but either of these serves as a classic example of 'action leisure'. One can recognize many of leisure's dimensions in these activities, but beyond those, participants exhibit a quest for something higher, almost like Maslow's self-actualization. As skydivers become more accomplished, for example, they move beyond the simple thrill of surviving the activity and begin to take pleasure in their growing achievements, with the ultimate result that they begin to experience communitas and phatic communion with their skydiving colleagues, and this becomes a source of personal identity to them (Celsi *et al.*, 1993). Such immersion in pastime pursuits is important for post-modern reasons, and it can lead to some rather unconventional conceptions of leisure.

A prominent feature of challenging pastimes is venue. This is a place or destination but, more than that, it is ambience. Excitement is a prerequisite, but so is authenticity, and that usually requires a search (often futile) for pristine places, unchanged by western civilization. If these can be found, the idea is to experience them 'as is' – the good with the bad, the safe with the unsafe, the pleasant with the unpleasant – before they are discovered by an enterprising marketer who will sanitize them for commercial purposes, destroying their authenticity in the process.

That is because in the anything-goes tempo of post-modern times, people find comfort, meaning, even identity in things 'real'. As we have more time and money to pursue our leisure, we want it to be something beyond a rejuvenation from work. Besides, work for many of us is boring and sedentary, so perhaps leisure should be exciting and strenuous. Some people think exactly that way, and it is to their ideas that we turn now.

Action leisure: in your face

Accounts of post-industrial society and its effects on the nature of work are common (e.g. Bell, 1976). While all the technological change associated with this phenomenon was occurring, however, some major social inflections happened as well, and together these resulted in a different portrait of the industrialized world. In the USA, for example, older manufacturing industries in the north and midwest gave way to lighter ones in the south and west. The older urban populations which had supported these heavy industries collapsed in the process, and were replaced by less dense, smaller ones, often of a suburban character. An important concomitant was the de-emphasis of 19th century social markers such as ethnicity, religion and class – even race, to some extent. Education became more democratized and occupations lost much of their hierarchical overtones. Even politics became an individual matter (no more ward heelers, etc.). The USA remained 'American', in the sense of abiding by its traditional ethos of individualism, equality, liberty and democracy, but these commitments were now pursued by a socially and politically fragmented population. The old ways of 'being somebody' no longer worked and, for a period during the explosive 1960s and 1970s, it appeared that nothing worked. What we call post-modernism – the celebration of consumer culture – emerged out of all this. There is some argument about the specifics (Cerulo, 1997; Preston, 1997), but not the result.

And why should we care? Largely because the period following World War II also changed the ways in which people framed their self-identities, how they understood who and what they are in a psychological and social context. Identity is biographical, of course, but it also is social. (I 'am' what my characteristics imply, but only to the extent that other people are willing to verify the identity I construct.) Self-identity is very much a matter of consensus. In a world where no-one particularly cares about your religion, your ethnicity, your occupation, your address, or your politics, how do you form an identity? What are you, if none of the foregoing things? Up steps post-modernism, which posits that you can be identified by your 'stuff'. In a world where ascribed identities (Episcopalians are better than Baptists) have become passé, people are turning to acquired ones (people who drive Porsches are more interesting than those who drive Tauruses). No single acquired 'thing' determines one's identity, however, only the constellation of them. Yet, one can – and people do – emphasize differing parts of the self in order to construct a distinctive identity (Kleine *et al.*, 1993), and this can change with time and circumstance. One final point. Leisure is part of the stuff people acquire and, whether it's tangible or intangible, leisure can serve as a marker of a person's identity (Haggard and Williams, 1992; Green and Chalip, 1998). Just as one individual expresses him or herself by driving a Porsche, another might do so by kayaking in the great north-west. Indeed, action leisure seems to exist for self-identity purposes. And while the genre has a nominally rough edge about it, one should not infer that it appeals only (or even principally) to 'a bunch of crazies'. Indeed, it would be no exaggeration to assert that the typical action-leisure enthu-siast is environmentally conscious and without a death wish. That they (and in particular advertisements appealing to them) appear to be so 'in your face' is attributable more to their penchant for the post-modern style of communicating than to any inherent characteristics of theirs or of their leisure pursuit's. This is rough stuff, but not irresponsible stuff. These are people who prefer challenge over apathy, risk to boredom. They seek the essence of freedom, because their fear of danger is less than their fear of living miserably. As Schwarzer (1998) empha-sizes, these are people running toward something as much as away from some-thing.

Blue is cool/blue is hot

Such people are embodied in a magazine called *blue*, which was established in 1998 by Amy Schrier in response to a desultory search for a satisfactory life. *blue*'s editorial philosophy reflects rules, but no structure, in the ordinary sense. Like post-modernism in general, it bespeaks values, but not traditional morality. It points towards extraordinary freedom for the individual, which achievement implicates an almost baffling level of complexity. To the untrained eye, action-leisure enthusiasts may seem to be doing incongruous things, but these are logi-cally related to the achievement of peak experiences, and increasingly difficult to locate in the contemporary world. It therefore becomes necessary on occasion to put up with a fair amount of bad in order to experience the sought-after good, and a magazine like *blue* facilitates enthusiasts' search. In the bargain, they come to know other people who share their enthusiasms and the process of phatic com-munion is set into motion. *blue* features some in-your-face advertising, but this is stylistically, more than philosophically, excessive. (One is reminded of a charita-ble person who uses a lot of vulgar words.) The audience for these ads' are hardly irresponsible hedonists or sociopaths. Indeed, judging by readers' responses to the magazine, they would seem to be rather the opposite. 'How wonderful to find a magazine that celebrates the beauty and possibilities of life while not pursuing selfish hedonism', comments one reader, while another is even more generous: 'You have given us some credit and acknowledged our intelligence with articles about international economics, the environment, politics and other truly important issues'. These reactions, we emphasize, are to a magazine devoted to 'the new adventure lifestyle'.

Blue appears to represent a nexus for people who regard action leisure as a transcendent (or 'sacred') experience. As we write this paper, the magazine is a hot one, gaining in popularity among upscale consumers. It is also a cool publication, in the sense of being extremely sophisticated about action leisure, of running no risk of being seen in the company of guidebooks or travel brochures or enthusiasts' magazines. It is an élitist publication, but not in the sense of staged exclusivity. Rather, it portrays the 'real thing', the natural beauty, power and challenge of nature. Readers expect such magazines to help them devise the most responsible, yet exhilarating, ways of interacting with the natural environment-in ways that are fun, because one should not take oneself too seriously.

Visceral venues, virtual adventures and action artefacts

To summarize our position, we have argued that leisure is more than the study of idle time, that through leisure's inversions ordinary life is reflected. A person who consistently seeks freedom in leisure pursuits tells us implicitly that she/he does not feel free in ordinary life – even though such an admission may never be made explicitly. Through anthropology, sociology and psychology, we know that a certain amount of 'staging' is done by the hospitality industry and marketers of leisure products in order to enhance the typical leisure gaze, and people don't seem to find this too objectionable, as indicated by their playing along with the simulations. Apparently, so long as we perceive some control over how we spend our free time and resources – and the results that accrue – we are content to abide by a market-driven leisure industry.

One – perhaps the – result which can accrue from leisure activity is self-identity. When people strive to be known 'as' or for one or another leisure activity, they are hoping to be identified with it (rather than with their occupation, age, race, etc.) because this activity represents high cathexis for them (while their other markers typically do not). Action-leisure enthusiasts thus like all the energy of such phenomena because these are what produce harmony with nature, communitas, and personal growth or renewal. As Arnould and Price (1993) put it, such intense experiences provide perspective and meaning to life; they crystallize selfhood. This is very important to people, particularly in a post-modern, consumer society, because time – like everything else – is a commodity whose utility can be maximized. When we buy back our own time in the form of convenience products, for example, we are exchanging money for the opportunity to do something of greater value with the bought time. Similarly, when we identify ourselves with leisure pursuits, we are declaring these to portray us with greater verisimilitude than any other marker in which we might invest. Post-modernists such as Baudrillard (1998) see all this in playful terms, arguing that the only real leisure is free time that can be flaunted, so the more outrageous the leisure display, the better. Needless to say, not everyone (e.g. Collins, 1998) agrees with this view.

If one grants the validity of the action-leisure phenomenon, three implications would seem to follow. Firstly, this is an attractive segment of the travel and leisure market, if not one that is easily satisfied. Venues (places and stagings) are critical. Yet suitably allocentric ones are becoming increasingly difficult to find and, when they can be located, there is a problem keeping them in pristine condition (Plog, 1974; Dugard, 1998; Glick, 1998). Nobody finds litter (or worse) attractive, so a delicate balance must be struck between a venue's naturalness, and keeping it that way in the face of inconsiderate visitors. Secondly, the number of products supportable by this industry is legion. One thinks of all the 'stuff' needed to do action leisure, but the genre is much broader than what is implied by equipment and venue ads. Coincidentally, a perusal of ads in *blue* suggests that a post-modern presentation – both the medium and the style – is probably necessary to achieve maximum impact with this segment of the leisure market. Thirdly, there is something to be said for sustaining (reinforcing, as it were) this segment by combining peak leisure experiences with computer software. These are relatively upscale, technologically literate consumers, whose concomitant interest in action leisure and the personal computer would argue that they are a 'natural' for action-leisure software (games, whatever). Indeed, recalling industrial design history, it may well be the case that such availability would prompt enthusiasts to imagine and design novel forms of action leisure. If the PC and the Internet can bring us electronic eros, it does not seem egregious to suppose that technology might engender a bit of virtual adventure as well.

References

Arnould, E.J. and Price, L.L. (1993) River magic: extraordinary experience and the extended service encounter. *Journal of Consumer Research* 20, 24–45.

Baudrillard, J. (1998) *The Consumer Society: Myths and Structures*. London: Sage.

Bell, D. (1976) *The Coming of Post-industrial Society*. New York: Basic Books.

Celsi, R.L., Rose, R.L. and Leigh, T.W. (1993) An exploration of high-risk leisure consumption through skydiving. *Journal of Consumer Research* 20, 1–23.

Cerulo, K.A. (1997) Identity construction: new issues, new directions. *Annual Review of Anthropology* 23, 385–409.

Cohen, E. (1984) The sociology of tourism: approaches, issues and findings. *Annual Review of Sociology* 10, 373–392.

Collins, J. (1998) No (popular) place like home. *Harvard Design Magazine* Winter/Spring, 16–21.

Crick, M. (1989) Representations of international tourism in the social sciences: sun, sex, sights, savings and servility. *Annual Review of Anthropology* 18, 307–344.

Domzal, T.J. and Kernan, J.B. (1995) Leisure advertising: media portrayals of the post-modern *homo ludens*. In M.J. Sirgy and A.C. Samli (eds) *New Dimensions in Marketing/Quality-of-Life Research*. Westport, Connecticut: Quorum Books, pp. 199–226.

Dugard, M. (1998) The adventure race will be televised. *blue* 1, 60–63.

Dumazedier, J. (1974) *The Psychology of Leisure*. New York: Elsevier.

Glick, D. (1998) Climbing and cleaning the peaks. *blue* 1, 38–46.

Green, B.C. and Chalip, L. (1998) Sport tourism as the celebration of subculture. *Annals of Tourism Research* 25, 275–291.

Haggard, I.M. and Williams, D.R. (1992) Identity affirmation through leisure activities: leisure symbols of the self. *Journal of Leisure Research* 24, 1–18.

Kernan, J.B. and Unger, L.S. (1987) Leisure, quality-of-life and marketing. In: A.C. Samli (ed.) *Marketing and the Quality-of-Life Interface.* Westport, Connecticut: Quorum Books, pp. 236–252.

Kleine, R.E., Kleine, S.S. and Kernan, J.B. (1993) Mundane consumption and the self: a social-identity perspective. *Journal of Consumer Psychology* 2, 209–235.

Plog, S.C. (1974) Why destinations rise and fall in popularity. *Cornell Hotel and Restaurant Quarterly* 14, 55–59.

Preston, P.W. (1997) *Political/Cultural Identity.* London: Sage.

Rojek, C. (1993) After popular culture: hyperreality and leisure. *Leisure Studies* 12, 277–289.

Schwarzer, M. (1998) Off-world in the far west. *Harvard Design Magazine* Winter/Spring, 60–65.

Unger, L.S. and Kernan, J.B. (1983) On the meaning of leisure: an investigation of some determinants of the subjective experience. *Journal of Consumer Research* 9, 381–392.

Urry, J. (1990) *The Tourist Gaze.* London: Sage.

Chapter six
Holland's Personality Theory and the Prediction of Tourism Behaviour

Elspeth A. Frew
School of Tourism and Hospitality Studies, La Trobe University, Bundoora, VIC 3083, Australia

Robin N. Shaw
School of Tourism and Marketing, Victoria University of Technology, PO Box 14428 MCMC, Melbourne, VIC 8001, Australia

Introduction

This paper provides a very brief overview of personality theories in general, and then looks in detail at one particular personality theory, Holland's (1973, 1985a) theory of personality type. The paper then considers the relationship between personality and leisure activities with particular reference to the application of Holland's theory to leisure behaviour. A subset of leisure activities is, arguably, tourism, and so the paper considers the relationship between personality and leisure-type tourism behaviour. The paper does not consider business and visiting friends and relatives (VFR) tourists, as these may be seen as non-discretionary travellers in the sense of freely choosing between destinations, and so travel may not be related to personality. Similarly, as this is a theoretical paper considering the ability of Holland's theory to discriminate between tourists, it merely foreshadows any discussion on the broader applied research issue of market segmentation. It also does not include any discussion on the potential association between psychographics, demographics and personality as they relate to tourism behaviour. It should also be noted that the constraints of a paper such as this preclude any detailed expositions of non-core topics such as general theories of personality. Rather, the focus is on the application of one theory of personality to the prediction of tourism behaviour.

For tourist attractions to be successful, they must be able to determine who is visiting, and who is likely to visit the attraction. To determine the types of tourists who are likely to visit, various authors (see e.g. Fodness, 1994) have considered tourist motivation theories. However, no widely accepted theory has been developed which can be successfully applied to tourist motivation and behaviour. This paper proposes that Holland's (1973, 1985a) theory of personality types provides an acceptable theory which can be applied to the tourist industry to contribute to predicting tourism behaviour, including satisfaction with the visit.

Madrigal (1995) suggested that there are five distinct perspectives of personality theories: psychoanalytic and neoanalytic; trait; cognitive; humanistic/existential; and socio-behaviouristic. To briefly describe some of these theories, in the (Freudian) psychoanalytic approach, behaviour is seen primarily to be energized and directed by innate and unconscious forces. Trait theory explains personality as a complex and differentiated structure of traits. A trait is described as a 'mental structure' which accounts for regularity and consistency in behaviour (Cattell, 1950). Cognitive development theory emphasizes learning as a function of development. The theory is that personality develops through 'an invariant sequence of stages which everyone goes through in the same order, though not at the same rate' (Iso-Ahola, 1980, p. 203). The humanistic/existential theory considers the tendency to actualize one's inherent potentialities and to achieve authentic being (Maddi, 1996). The socio-behaviouristic theory suggests that individual differences in behaviour are due to the variety of learning conditions that the individual has encountered, so that the growth of personality is a function of learning (Iso-Ahola, 1980).

Holland's Theory of Personality Types

Holland (1973, 1985a) developed a typology of six different personal orientations to life: Realistic (R), Investigative (I), Artistic (A), Social (S), Enterprising (E), and Conventional (C). He defined each of the six different personality types in terms of its characteristic activities, interests, and competencies. Holland (1973, 1985a) states that the idea for the typology resulted from his frequent observation that several broad classes account for most human interests, traits and behaviours. He suggests that the types developed in his typology are analogous in some ways to the types proposed by earlier researchers, but he believes that his theory is most consistent with Staats' (1981) theory of social behaviourism where the 'six types are models of six common clusters of personality or behavioural repertoires that occur in our society' (Holland, 1985a, p. 18).

In response to reviewers who have suggested that there must exist more than six kinds of vocational interests, Holland notes that the evidence strongly suggests that there are only four to eight independent kinds of vocational interests and only four to eight different kinds of occupations. He suggests that factor analysis demonstrates that a 'limited number of factors account for the individual differences in vocational interests and occupational data' (Holland et al., 1994, p. 52). However, he also admits that the use of six types is a compromise in that 'six main types and their permutations are easy to comprehend, interpret, and use in practice and research' (Holland et al., 1994, p. 52). He also suggests that, although six may not be the correct number, and there is no precise way to determine that number, it is close to the average number obtained by a wide range of diverse methods and data over a long period of time (Holland *et al.*, 1994, p. 52).

To make practical use of his typology, Holland initially devised the Vocational Preference Inventory (VPI) (Holland, 1958, 1973) and then the Self-Directed Search (SDS) (Holland, 1977, 1985b), both of which identify a person's personality and are used as guides to educational and vocational planning. However, the VPI is oriented more to the needs of vocational counsellors engaged in one-to-one counselling, while the SDS relies more on the person's initiative and self-direction, as it is self-scored (Holland, 1985d). The VPI (1985e) is a personality-interest inventory composed entirely of occupational titles. The subjects complete the inventory by indicating the occupations they find interesting and appealing and those which they dislike or find uninteresting (Holland, 1985e). The VPI records 11 different aspects, i.e. the six personality types of Realistic, Investigative, Artistic, Social, Enterprising, and Conventional, and five other dimensions, namely Self-control, Masculinity–Femininity, Status, Acquiescence and Infrequency (which measure atypical vocational preference and help to identify individuals who have been uncooperative or have given random responses) (Holland, 1985d). Holland made the following assumptions in the development of the VPI.

- The choice of an occupation is an expressive act which reflects a person's motivation, knowledge of the occupation in question, insight and understanding of self and abilities (Holland, 1985d).
- People perceive occupational titles in stereotypical ways. Occupational stereotypes or generalizations are stable over long periods of time and are relatively independent of occupational experience or sex of the perceiver (Holland, 1985a).
- Different occupations furnish different kinds of gratification or satisfactions and require different abilities, identifications, values and attitudes. This assertion has extensive empirical support from studies which relate vocational interests to personality variables, psychiatric status, values and attitudes (Holland, 1985d).
- Interest inventories are essentially personality inventories. Interest and personality inventories are identical in principle and provide similar information about the person, although their content is quite diverse. Both kinds of inventories reveal how the person perceives self and milieu (Holland, 1985d).

Holland (1985d, p. 2) points out that these assumptions 'are crucial, for they are fundamental to the reliability and validity of the inventory'.

In the SDS (Holland, 1977, 1985b), individuals answer a series of questions which help them determine which occupations are most suited to their personality type. A three-letter code is produced for each individual, showing the three highest ranked personality types for that individual in order, such as ESC. In the SDS, respondents indicate which activities they would like to do and which they dislike doing or would be indifferent to. Examples of the activities listed under the RIASEC headings include (with Holland's categories in parentheses): 'To use metalworking or machine tools' (R); 'Work on a scientific project' (I); 'Read or write poetry' (A); 'Help others with their personal problems' (S); 'Head a group in accomplishing some goal' (E); and 'Keep detailed records of expenses' (C).

Respondents then indicate which activities they can do well or competently and which activities they have never performed or perform poorly. Examples of competencies include 'I can repair furniture' (R); 'I can interpret simple chemical formulae' (I); 'I can sketch people so that they can be recognized' (A); 'I can plan entertainment for a party' (S); 'I have acted as leader for some group presenting suggestions or complaints to a person or authority' (E); and 'I can file correspondence and other papers' (C). Respondents are also asked to indicate which occupations in the list interest or appeal to them, or those which they dislike or find uninteresting. The occupations listed include carpenter and radio operator (R); zoologist and astronomer (I); journalist, playwright, composer (A); speech therapist, high-school teacher (S); salesperson, hotel manager (E); and bookkeeper and bank teller (C). Respondents are also asked to rate themselves on a list of traits when compared to other persons of their own age. The abilities listed are: mechanical ability and manual skills (R); scientific and maths ability (I); artistic and musical ability (A); teaching and friendliness (S); sales and managerial skills (E); and clerical and office skills (C).

Once the SDS has been completed the respondent adds up the scores for each part of the questionnaire and arrives at a three-letter summary code. Holland's Occupations Finder (1985c), which lists 1156 occupations, is then used to locate the occupations which correspond to the respondent's summary code. If no identical code is found then occupations are sought in the Occupations Finder which are similar to the summary code. As Holland et al. (1994, p. 3) note, 'by indicating the three types a person resembles most, the three-letter Summary Code allows for complexity of personality and reduces some of the problems inherent in categorizing a person as a single type'.

Holland devised a hexagonal model to illustrate the relationship between each personality type and to describe the concepts of consistency and differentiation (Fig. 6.1). Consistency is the degree of relatedness of types within a person. For example, the personality pattern of RI is more consistent than CA or has a high consistency pattern. Other examples of high consistency patterns are RC, IA, AI and SE. Low consistency patterns are RS, IE, AC and SR, and middle consistency are IS, IC, AR and SC. Differentiation is the extent to which a personality pattern is defined. A well differentiated pattern is one which resembles a single type very closely (Kelso, 1986). Undifferentiated or poorly defined personality types are people who resemble several of the six types to about the same degree. Thus, Holland believes that the dominant features of an individual's personality, represented by his or her type, are the major influence on his or her choice of vocation. Holland, in extending the theory, believes that personality types flourish in congruent environments and that because the 'personality types and the environmental models share a common set of constructs, it is possible ... to predict the outcome of pairing people and environments' (1985a, p. 34). Therefore, if a certain personality type is placed in a similar environment then there should be 'a number of desirable outcomes, such as work satisfaction, achievement, and vocational stability' (1985a, p. 35).

Holland *et al.* (1994) reported that Holland's typology and its tools (the classification, the SDS and the VPI) lent themselves to applied and basic research in education, business, psychology and sociology, and highlighted the wide range of research activity which has stemmed from the theory and its typological origins. They indicated also that the SDS, in its published form or with minor changes, has been used successfully with males and females; inner-city, suburban and rural high-school children; college students; young children; and employed and unemployed adults.

Tracey and Rounds (1993) note that Holland's (1973, 1985a) theory of vocational personalities and work environments is widely considered one of the most influential career development theories and occupational taxonomies in vocational psychology. It is estimated by Hyland and Muchinsky (1991) that over the past two decades, approximately 700 studies have been directed toward various aspects of Holland's (1973, 1985a) theory. Taylor *et al.* (1979) note that Holland (1973) has summarized over 100 of these studies, with more than 90 providing some support for his formulations. Although the majority of empirical work has been focused on the use of Holland's theory in education and business, studies have applied Holland's theory to non-vocational aspects of life, to investigate Holland's belief that 'personality pattern determines a person's choice of nonvocational activities and recreations' (1985a, p. 32). It is this relationship which is considered in this paper.

Personality Theory and Leisure Activities

Argyle (1996, p. 4) defined leisure as a 'general category of behaviour which has certain common themes – the enjoyment of freely chosen activities carried out for no material gain'. Similarly, Beard and Ragheb (1983) defined leisure activities as non-work activities where the individual is under no obligation to participate. These activities can be either active or inactive, and may include such things as sports, outdoor activities, social activities, watching television, or reading. Iso-Ahola (1980, p. 201) suggested that 'personal experiences establish and modify one's perceived competence which, within the confines of optimal arousal, determines which leisure activities are chosen (if freedom of choice is given)'.

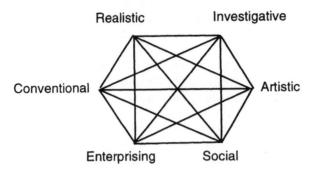

Figure 6.1 Holland's hexagonal model for defining the psychological resemblances among types and environments and their interactions. Source: Holland, 1985a (p. 29).

Madrigal (1995) noted that various authors have related personality to leisure activity decisions. Mannell (1984) suggested that most studies of personality as a predictor of leisure behaviour have used general personality inventories to measure individual differences, but that there is a lack of a theoretical approach that could identify leisure-specific personality differences that may help in understanding leisure behaviour. Nias (1985) also criticized these studies, stating that most of them demonstrated that the relationship between leisure behaviour and personality was not very robust. Similarly, Iso-Ahola (1980) criticized most of these early studies for lacking definitional clarity in variable operationalizations, for failing to rely on theory for the inclusion of specific activities, and for lacking consistency in measuring personality.

Holland's personality theory and avocational behaviour

As outlined above, a secondary assertion by Holland is that 'the character of an environment reflects the nature of its members and that the dominant features of an environment reflect the typical characteristics of its members' (1985a, p. 35), which suggests that the more an environmental pattern resembles a personality pattern, the more a person will find the environment reinforcing and satisfying. Since a congruent environment is made up, in part, of people who have 'similar interests, competencies, values, traits and perceptions' (Holland, 1985a, p. 49), there is a greater likelihood that a person will participate in those situations or have an interest in those environments, rather than in incongruent environments.

Following a literature review, it appears that at least 20 studies have applied Holland's theory to avocational aspects of a person's life. Much of the empirical research which has used Holland's theory as a basis for measurement and interpretation, and has applied the theory to avocational aspects, focused on testing the following:

- the validity of applying Holland's categories to leisure activities (Cairo, 1979; Taylor *et al.*, 1979; Miller, 1991; Long, 1996);
- the relationship between Holland's personality types, vocational and avocational choices, and life satisfaction (Campbell, 1973; Melamed, 1977, 1986; Melamed and Meir, 1981; Graef, 1986; Chesson, 1986; Meir *et al.*, 1990; Parker, 1990; Pusz, 1993; Melamed *et al.*, 1995);
- the relationship between Holland personality types and the specific selection of leisure activities, i.e. non-work, preference behaviours (Miller and Tobacyk, 1987);
- the relationship between occupational preferences (as derived by the SDS), leisure preferences and sensation-seeking (Schenk, 1996);
- the extent to which Holland's leisure or vocational measures of interests are congruent with a respondent's self-estimated personality (Randolph, 1992);
- the differences between leisure participants by Holland personality type (Norman, 1994);
- the stability of avocational interests by Holland personality type (Varca and Shaffer, 1982; Warren *et al.*, 1981).

All the studies except one (Campbell, 1973) demonstrated support for the use of Holland's personality type in predicting leisure activities. As the research by Campbell was carried out in 1973, the study would have used an earlier version of the VPI. Since 1973 the VPI has been substantially improved and updated, and has undergone a number of revisions from 1953, when it was first developed, to 1985. However, Holland (1985d, p. 3) notes that the last three versions have entailed changing only a few items 'as it became increasingly difficult to improve the item pool'. In addition, Holland (1985d) states that the VPI interest scales now demonstrate concurrent or predictive validity equal to, or exceeding, the concurrent or predictive validities of other scales.

Some of the studies which applied Holland's theory to avocational aspects allowed respondents to list their preferred leisure activities without providing any prompts, whereas other studies develop a list of leisure activities and asked the respondents to indicate which wa   favourite. For example, in the study by Taylor *et al.* (1979), a leisure checklist was developed of 36 leisure activities. The respondents were asked to indicate those leisure activities which they enjoyed. The list was made up of leisure activities taken from Holland's SDS (six from each category). In none of these studies were tourism activities explicitly included in the list of activities. It was, therefore, only incidental that tourism activities were included in some of the studies, as they were not asked for explicitly. For example, in the study by Taylor *et al.* (1979) the activities listed in the leisure checklist mainly include activities which occur around the home, such as 'Reading books and magazines on scientific or technical subjects'; 'Writing short stories or poetry'; 'Following politics in the newspapers or on radio or TV'; 'Tidying up sheds, cupboards, drawers, etc.'; 'Making things like model aircraft, dresses, etc., using patterns or instruction kits'; and 'Watching and listening to 'in-depth' reports or documentaries on radio and TV'. However, the list also includes activities which could be defined as tourism activities if people travel away from their place of normal residence to participate in the activity, such as 'Bushwalking, hiking, camping'; 'Attending sports events, pop concerts, films, etc., with a group of friends'; 'Visiting scientific and/or technical displays, fairs or museums'; and 'Visiting art galleries, exhibitions, plays, or concerts'.

Similarly to leisure activities, tourism activities also use discretionary time, but tourism includes 'any activity concerned with the temporary short-term movement of people to destinations outside the places where they normally live and work, and their activities during their stay at these destinations' (Tourism Society, 1979, p. 70). The more participation in an activity involves travelling to a destination or the greater the distance travelled to reach the destination, the more likely the activity will be a tourism-related activity rather than simply a general leisure activity. In the study by Taylor *et al.* (1979), activities such as bushwalking and camping did not require the respondent to indicate the distance travelled to participate in the activity or the travelling time to the destination. Therefore these studies arguably considered Holland and leisure activities, but not Holland and tourism behaviour.

Personality theory and tourism behaviour

Ross (1994, p. 31) suggested that as the study of personality is still evolving, there could be 'no more appropriate or useful study than personality as it illuminates tourist behaviour'. Madrigal (1995) suggested that Plog (1972) was the first to conduct research on personality type as it applies to tourism behaviour. Plog (1974, 1990, 1991) delineated personality types along a continuum ranging from allocentrism to psychocentrism. Ross (1994) noted that allocentric travellers are thought to prefer exotic destinations, unstructured vacations rather than packaged tours, and more involvement with local cultures. Psychocentrics are thought to prefer familiar destinations, package tours, and 'touristy' areas. Leiper (1995) noted that Smith (1991) has argued persuasively that Plog's theory is defective, based on flawed research. Similarly, a study by Nickerson (1989) found that Plog's conceptual travel model was not supported by the data. Hoxter and Lester (1988) also tested Plog's theory, and obtained results opposite to those predicted by Plog. 'Plog asserted that psychocentrics would be nervous and inhibited, whereas the present study has found that psychocentric females may be more likely to be stable extroverts' (Hoxter and Lester, 1988, p. 177). In addition, McDonnell (1994) re-tested Plog's theory and also found that the theory was flawed. Leiper (1995) suggested that Plog's theory is merely a teleology, which is useful as a description but not as an explanation.

Some other authors have related personality to travel decisions. Nickerson and Ellis (1991) used Fiske and Maddi's (1961) activation theory of personality development to develop more types of travellers. They described the personality types in terms of destination preferences, travel companions, interactions with local cultures, degree of activity participation, and other distinguishing characteristics. Ross (1994) suggested that the findings of Nickerson and Ellis's (1991) survey show that personality theories may be useful in explaining tourism phenomena.

Holland's personality theory and tourism behaviour

Following a literature review, the present authors believe that no empirical study has specifically examined the relationship between tourism behaviour *per se* and Holland personality types. The principal objective of this paper, therefore, was to begin the process of addressing this gap in the literature. As mentioned above, since Holland's theory extends into environmental settings, and a person's 'personality pattern determines a person's choice of nonvocational activities and recreations' (1985a, p. 32), a logical extension of this notion would appear to be that, if a tourist attraction is perceived to have created a congruent environment for certain types of people, then people of those types will be interested in that environment and will enjoy visiting the attraction. From a tourism perspective, personality type may be reflected in the choice of holiday destination and the type of activities participated in during the holiday. In addition, tourists' levels of satisfaction with, and enjoyment of, their experience may reflect the consistency and differentiation of their personality type and the congruency of the environment. The following section offers some research propositions which attempt to apply Holland's theory of personality types to tourism behaviour and the level of satisfaction derived from the tourism experience, including satisfaction at tourist sites. Preceding each proposition the reader should add a cautionary 'other things being equal', e.g. age, gender, ethnicity, geography, social class, physical assets or liabilities, educational level attained, and intelligence (Holland, 1985a, p. 12).

Research propositions

Personality

- P1 Groups of visitors to certain types of tourist attraction have similar personality patterns

If personality is reflected in occupational choice, then personality may also be reflected in the type of tourism experience chosen. Tourists select holidays and activities which interest them. Thus the destinations chosen and the types of activities participated in while on holiday may reflect a tourist's personality type. For example, a person who chooses to travel with a small group of people to museums and art galleries may be a social/artistic type. By knowing a person's preferred holiday destination and the types of activities participated in, it is possible to hypothesize on his or her personality type. Holland believes that 'types are attracted to types' (1985a, p. 16). Therefore, it is suggested that groups of people with similar personalities travel together to visit attractions and participate in activities in which they are all interested. Norman (1994) reviewed the six Holland types and six parallel environments and, based on research by Hansom and Campbell (1985) and Walsh and Holland (1992), developed an overview of the types of environments which Holland types would prefer (Table 6.1).

Satisfaction

- P2 The more a person has a personality type which is (a) strongly differentiated or (b) strongly consistent with one of Holland's personality types, the more likely they are to be satisfied with their experience at tourist attractions related to that personality type

As outlined above, Holland's theory includes the concepts of consistency and differentiation. Consistency is the degree of relatedness of types within a person. Differentiation is the extent to which a personality pattern is defined. Holland (1985) believes that the consistency and differentiation of the personality pattern influence the person's stability, satisfaction, achievement, performance and several other aspects of occupational life. If Holland's theory is applied to a tourism situation, then the personality type (i.e. the dominant feature of an individual's personality) may motivate the person to visit the attraction, but the consistency and differentiation of the personality pattern will reflect the level of satisfaction derived from the visit.

- P3 The more similar the personality types of a visitor and a tour guide at a tourist attraction, the more the visitor is likely to respond favourably to that tour guide

Holland notes that 'persons with different personality patterns respond to instructors, teaching methods and styles according to the formulations of the types' (1985a, p. 32). Therefore, an Artistic person would appreciate an Artistic tour guide with an Artistic style leading the group around an attraction such as an art gallery.

Environment

- P4 The more congruent the environment at a tourist attraction, the more a person with a congruent personality will feel comfortable at the attraction and will enjoy the visit

Table 6.1 Activities and environments preferred by Holland types

Type	Preferred activities and environment
Realistic	Like activities and people who represent interest areas such as the outdoors and nature; mechanical, construction and repair activities; and military activities. Preferred environments – the outdoors, and sometimes rural areas.
Investigative	Prefer achievement-oriented environments which stimulate investigative activities and allow a freedom of work styles, and where other Investigative people predominate – places such as universities, research laboratories, and medical and computer-related facilities.
Artistic	Drawn to beauty and aesthetics. Like places where Artistic action is stimulated, and where other Artistic people are. The Artistic environment must be unstructured and flexible, where self-expression is allowed. The Artistic environment fosters Artistic achievements and competencies, such as places where Artistic skills are taught, Artistic items are housed, displayed, performed or created.
Social	Prefer environment to stimulate engagement in Social activities and foster Social competencies, where they can perform their skills and preferred behaviours. Prefer environment to be populated with many other Social people, so they can interact with, or entertain, others. These places may be schools, community agencies, organizations, meetings or special events.
Enterprising	Preferred environments are organizations of people, places where powerful or influential people are, or where they can be involved with entertaining, competition or buying and selling. Such places may be conventions or clubs, large or independently owned businesses, expensive resorts, sporting events, or markets, where the environment rewards display of such Enterprising values and goals as status, power and money.
Conventional	Prefer activities that require attention to detail and accuracy. These include collecting and organizing materials, procedures, making models, charts and graphs, maintaining records and financial ledgers, writing reports, and operating business-type machinery. They are not comfortable with ambiguous situations, preferring to know exactly what is expected.

Source: adapted from Norman (1994).

Holland (1985a) believes that types flourish in congruent environments and suggests that the more an environmental pattern resembles a personality pattern, the more the person will find the environment reinforcing and satisfying. However, it is not only people who make up a congruent environment: it also consists of the natural and built aspects of the site, the people who work there, and the people who visit. If no visitors were to visit the site it would still have a certain environmental pattern. A tourist attraction which is congruent with a person's personality will lead to satisfaction with the visit. Since a congruent environment is made up of people who have 'similar interests, competencies, values, traits and perceptions' (Holland, 1985a, p. 49), then the greater the likelihood is that the person will participate in these situations or have interest in the environment (1985a, p. 57). If a tourist attraction creates a congruent environment by allowing certain types of people to dominate, then more people of that type will be interested in the environment, and will enjoy visiting the attraction.

• P5 The more persons have a consistent personality pattern, the more predictable their behaviour will be in a consistent environment

Holland (1985a) suggests that in a consistent environment, where a person has a consistent personality, it is possible to predict his or her social and avocational behaviour since it will reflect his or her personality pattern. For example, a Realistic person will behave in a particular way in a Realistic environment. Holland also suggests that if a congruent personality type is placed in a congruent situation there will be 'desirable outcomes, such as work satisfaction, achievement, and vocational stability' (1985a, p. 35). Similarly, Holland suggests that the interaction of a differentiated person in a differentiated environment will be the 'most predictable and intense' (1985a, p. 50).

Astin and Holland (1961) devised the Environmental Assessment Technique (EAT) which assesses the occupations or vocational preferences in an environment and then devises a profile of the personality types of the people working in that environment. The EAT could be used to help predict the types of people who would be interested in visiting certain types of tourist attraction. Using the technique, the personality patterns of the workers at the site would be assessed. It would then be possible to suggest the type of visitors (i.e. those with similar personality patterns) who would be interested in visiting the attraction. For example, the EAT may reveal that an operating industrial site creates a Realistic environment where there is the 'systematic manipulation of objects, tools, machines and animals' (Holland, 1985a, p. 36). Realistic types dominate in this Realistic environment, so the people who are motivated to visit the site may also have Realistic personality patterns.

Discussion and Research Agenda

Clearly, primary research is needed to examine the basic hypotheses of a relationship between Holland types and tourist visitation. Further, the above propositions imply that it is important to determine the personality-related characteristics of the environment at a tourist attraction, as it may then become possible to predict the personality patterns of the tourist who would be interested in visiting that attraction. A recent study by Frew and Shaw (1997) considered a range of tourist attractions and the possible code for each of these attractions. To determine the possible codes of the tourist attractions, three 'involved academics' or 'judges', with an understanding of the Holland types, considered the list of named attractions and ranked the three Holland environmental types which most closely characterized each named attraction. This process produced an overall, indicative Holland code for each of the attractions. Although this was an exploratory study, it was pioneering in that it was the first study to apply Holland codes to tourist attractions rather than to non-tourism leisure activities.

To successfully apply Holland's theory to the prediction of tourism behaviour, it is important to be aware of the 'unit of analysis' being considered, i.e. whether the individual or the travel party is being considered. For example, the Holland code of the travel party may fluctuate by occasion, e.g. a travel party may agree to visit an attraction chosen by one person in the group today, on condition that the party will visit another person's choice of attraction tomorrow. This could reflect the dominance of some people in the travel party over others. In relation to families as travelling parties, it may be incorrect to characterize a family by a single family code, as the code may tend to fluctuate depending on the coalitions which exist within the family, i.e. on different occasions there will be different sub-groups within the family. For example, on some occasions the males of the families may form a sub-group and decide to lobby the group to attend a football match, and on other occasions the young people in the family may want to visit the beach rather than go shopping. This reflects the importance of travel party decision making, and the importance of reviewing studies which have considered this aspect of tourism behaviour. For example, Thornton *et al.* (1997, p. 287), in a study of tourist parties in the UK, found that children influenced the behaviour of tourist parties 'either through their physical needs ... or through their ability to negotiate with parents'. Thus Holland's theory, which was originally designed to deal with individuals rather than with groups, needs to be adapted to group characterization. In addition, when estimating the codes of tourist attractions, rather than using experts or judges as done by Frew and Shaw (1997), there is a strong argument that the consumers themselves, i.e. the tourists, should be asked to characterize the attractions.

Conclusions

In recent years, two studies have confirmed the importance of developing tourist attractions which are of genuine interest to tourists. Martin and Mason (1993) suggest that visitors in the future will be increasingly selective about the attractions that they choose to visit. They suggest that the emphasis is likely to be more on visiting with a purpose, going to an attraction because it offers something of particular interest or relevance to the visitor, rather than just because the destination exists and there is time to be occupied. Similarly, a survey of agricultural tourists by Cox and Fox (1991) asked attraction operators why they thought visitors came to their attractions. The reason cited 84% of the time was that the attraction was of personal interest to the visitor. This reason was also given 51% of the time as the most important reason for visitors coming. These studies suggest that attractions must be of interest to visitors. However, they do not explain why these attractions are of interest to the tourists. This paper suggests that Holland's theory of personality types can be used to explain tourism choice behaviour and satisfaction in tourist settings, as it suggests that an attraction must be of personal interest to a person and reflect their personality type, before they are motivated to visit.

References

Argyle, M. (1996) *The Social Psychology of Leisure*. London: Penguin.

Astin, A.W. and Holland, J.L. (1961) The environmental assessment technique: a way to measure college environments. *Journal of Educational Psychology* 52, 308–316.

Beard, J.G. and Ragheb, M.G. (1983) Measuring leisure motivation. *Journal of Leisure Research* 15, 219–228.

Cairo, P.C. (1979) The validity of the Holland and basic interest scales of the Strong vocational interest blank: leisure activities versus occupational membership as criteria. *Journal of Vocational Behavior* 15, 68–77.

Campbell, R.A. (1973) *A study of the relationship between personality, work and leisure as it applies to men who work*. PhD thesis, State University of New York at Buffalo, New York. *Dissertation Abstracts International* 34 (09A), 5617.

Cattell, R.B. (1950) *Personality: A Systematic, Theoretical and Factual Study*. New York: McGraw-Hill.

Chesson, C.V. (1986) *Holland codes and congruency of life roles (Holland codes, leisure, work)*. PhD thesis, Texas Tech University, Lubbock, Texas.

Cox, L.J. and Fox, M. (1991) Agriculturally based leisure attractions. *Journal of Tourism Studies* 2, 8–27.

Fiske, D.W. and Maddi, S.R. (1961) *Functions of Varied Experience*. Homewood, Illinois: Dorsey Press.

Fodness, D. (1994) Measuring tourist motivation. *Annals of Tourism Research* 21, 555–581.

Frew, E.A. and Shaw, R.N. (1997) Personality, career choice and tourism behaviour: an exploratory study. In: R. Bushell (ed.) *Tourism Research: Building a Better Industry. Proceedings of the Australian Tourism and Hospitality Research Conference*. Canberra, ACT: Bureau of Tourism Research, pp. 275–287.

Graef, M.I. (1986) *A person–environment congruence approach to work–leisure relationships*. PhD thesis, Iowa State University, Ames, Iowa. *Dissertation Abstracts International* 47 (11B), 4687.

Hansom, J.C. and Campbell, D.P. (1985) *The Strong Manual*. Palo Alto, California: Consulting Psychologists Press.

Holland, J.L. (1958) A personality inventory employing occupational titles. *Journal of Applied Psychology* 42, 336–342.

Holland, J.L. (1973) *Making Vocational Choices*. Englewood Cliffs, New Jersey: Prentice-Hall.

Holland, J.L. (1977) *Self-Directed Search*. Palo Alto, California: Consulting Psychologists Press.

Holland, J.L. (1985a) *Making Vocational Choices: A Theory of Vocational Personalities and Work Environments*. Englewood Cliffs, New Jersey: Prentice-Hall.

Holland, J.L. (1985b) *The Self-Directed Search: A Guide to Educational and Vocational Planning*. Australian edn prepared by J.J. Lokan and M. Shears. Hawthorn, Victoria: Australian Council for Educational Research.

Holland, J.L. (1985c) *The Occupations Finder: For Use With the Self-Directed Search*. Australian edn prepared by M. Shears and J.J. Lokan. Hawthorn, Victoria: Australian Council for Educational Research.

Holland, J.L. (1985d) *Vocational Preference Inventory: Professional Manual*. Odessa, Florida: Psychological Assessment Resources.

Holland, J.L. (1985e) *Vocational Preference Inventory: Test Booklet*. Odessa, Florida: Psychological Assessment Resources.

Holland, J.L., Powell, A.B. and Fritzsche, B.A. (1994) *Self-Directed Search: Professional User's Guide*. Odessa, Florida: Psychological Assessment Resources.

Hoxter, A.L. and Lester, D. (1988) Tourist behavior and personality. *Personality and Individual Differences* 9, 177–178.

Hyland, A.M. and Muchinsky, P.M. (1991) Assessment of the structural validity of Holland's model with job analysis (PAQ) information. *Journal of Applied Psychology* 76, 75–80.

Iso-Ahola, S.E. (1980) *The Social Psychology of Leisure and Recreation*. Dubuque, Iowa: William C. Brown.

Kelso, G.I. (1986) An orientation to Holland's theory. In: J.J. Lokan and K.F. Taylor (eds) *Holland In Australia. A Vocational Choice Theory in Research and Practice*. Melbourne, Victoria: Australian Council for Educational Research, pp. xv–xxii.

Leiper, N. (1995) *Tourism Management*. Collingwood, Victoria: TAFE Publications.

Long, T.D. (1996) *An analysis of the Leisure Activities Finder based on congruence of personality and activity choice*. Master's thesis, Emporia State University, Emporia, Kansas.

Maddi, S.R. (1996) *Personality Theories: A Comparative Analysis*. Pacific Grove, California: Brooks/Cole.

Madrigal, R. (1995) Personal values, traveler personality type and leisure travel style. *Journal of Leisure Research* 27, 125–142.

Mannell, R.C. (1984) Personality in leisure theory: the self-as-entertainment construct. *Society and Leisure* 7, 229–237.

Martin, B. and Mason, S. (1993) The future of attractions: meeting the needs of the new consumers. *Tourism Management* February, 34–40.

McDonnell, I. (1994) *Leisure travel to Fiji and Indonesia from Australia 1982 to 1992: some factors underlying changes in market share.* Master's thesis, University of Technology, Sydney, New South Wales.

Meir, E.I., Melamed, S. and Abu-Freha, A. (1990) Vocational, avocational and skill utilization congruences and their relationship with well-being in two cultures. *Journal of Vocational Behavior* 36, 153–165.

Melamed, S. (1977) *Vocational and avocational choices and satisfaction: a test of Holland's theory.* PhD thesis, Department of Psychology, University of Sydney, New South Wales.

Melamed, S. (1986) Vocational and avocational choices and satisfaction. In: J.J. Lokan and K.F. Taylor (eds) *Holland In Australia: A Vocational Choice Theory in Research and Practice.* Melbourne, Victoria: Australian Council for Educational Research, pp. 78–89.

Melamed, S. and Meir, E.I. (1981) The relationship between interests – job incongruity and selection of avocational activity. *Journal of Vocational Behaviour* 18, 310–325.

Melamed, S., Meir, E.I. and Samson, A. (1995) The benefits of personality–leisure congruence: evidence and implications. *Journal of Leisure Research* 27, 25–40.

Miller, M.J. (1991) Accuracy of the Leisure Activities Finder: expanding Holland's typology. *Journal of Vocational Behavior* 39, 362–368.

Miller, M.J. and Tobacyk, J. (1987) Would a conventional/realistic type subscribe to National Geographic? Expanding Holland's typology. *Psychological Reports* 60, 561–562.

Nias, D.K.B. (1985) Personality and recreational behavior. In: B.D. Kirkcaldy (ed.) *Individual Differences in Movement.* Lancaster: MTP Press, pp. 279–292.

Nickerson, N.P. (1989) *Tourism and personality: a comparison of two models.* PhD thesis, Department of Recreation and Leisure, University of Utah, Salt Lake City, Utah.

Nickerson, N.P. and Ellis, G.D. (1991) Traveler types and activation theory: a comparison of two models. *Journal of Travel Research* 29, 26–31.

Norman, A. (1994) *Differentiating between recreation activity participants through use of dispositional profiles.* PhD thesis, Clemson University, Clemson, South Carolina.

Parker, B.L. (1990) *An investigation of the relationship between job satisfaction and vocational and avocational choice: a test of Holland's theory (vocational choice).* PhD thesis, University of Tulsa, Tulsa, Oklahoma. *Dissertation Abstracts International* 51 (12a), 4003.

Plog, S.C. (1972) Why destinations rise and fall in popularity. Paper presented to the Travel Research Association Southern California Chapter, Los Angeles, California, October 1972.

Plog, S.C. (1974) Why destination areas rise and fall in popularity. *Cornell Hotel and Restaurant Administration Quarterly* 14, 55–58.

Plog, S.C. (1990) A carpenter's tools: an answer to Stephen L.J. Smith's review of psychocentrism/allocentrism. *Journal of Travel Research* 29, 43–45.

Plog, S.C. (1991) *Leisure Travel: Making it a Growth Market ... Again!* New York: Wiley.

Pusz, R.C. (1993) *The relationship of work and leisure to Holland personality types.* PhD thesis, West Virginia University, Morgantown, West Virginia.

Randolph, P.D. (1992) *Construction and psychometric evaluation of the revised Leisure Preference Inventory: toward an understanding of leisure versus vocationally derived interests.* PhD thesis, Texas Tech University, Texas. *Dissertation Abstracts International* 52 (11B), 6070.

Ross, G.F. (1994) *The Psychology of Tourism*. Elsternwick, Victoria: Hospitality Press.

Schenk, C.N. (1996) *Sensation-seeking and occupational and leisure preferences*. PhD thesis, Florida State University, Tallahassee, Florida. *Dissertation Abstracts International* 58 (01B), 449.

Smith, S.J. (1991) The supply-side definition of tourism: reply to Leiper. *Annals of Tourism Research* 15, 179–190.

Staats, A.W. (1981) Paradigmatic behaviorism, unified theory, unified theory construction methods and the zeitgeist of separatism. *American Psychologist* 36, 239–256.

Taylor, K.F., Kelso, G.I., Cox, G.N., Alloway, W.J. and Matthews, J.P. (1979) Applying Holland's vocational categories to leisure activities. *Journal of Occupational Psychology* 52, 199–207.

Thornton, P.R., Shaw, G. and Williams, A.M. (1997) Tourist group holiday decision-making and behaviour: the influence of children. *Tourism Management* 18, 287–297.

Tourism Society (1979) *Handbook and Members' List*. London: The Tourism Society.

Tracey, T.J. and Rounds, J. (1993) Evaluating Holland's and Gati's vocational-interest models: a structural meta-analysis. *Psychological Bulletin* 113, 229–246.

Varca, P.E. and Shaffer, G.S. (1982) Holland's theory: stability of avocational interests. *Journal of Vocational Behavior* 21, 288–298.

Walsh, W.B. and Holland, J.L. (1992) A theory of personality types and work environments. In: W.B. Walsh, K.H. Craik and R.H. Price (eds) *Person–Environment Psychology: Models and Perspectives*. Hillsdale, New Jersey: Lawrence Erlbaum Associates, pp. 35–69.

Warren, G.D., Winer, J.L. and Dailey, K.C. (1981) Extending Holland's theory to the later years. *Journal of Vocational Behavior* 18, 104–114.

Chapter seven
An Analysis of Consumers' Risk Approach and Risk Behaviour in the Context of Gambling

Karin Weber and Wesley S. Roehl
Department of Tourism and Convention Administration, University of Nevada Las Vegas, Las Vegas, NV 89154-6023, USA

Introduction

By drawing on the notion that tourism involves the movement of people outside their area of normal residence, Roehl (1994) argued that casinos function as tourist attractions, as many people still have to and do travel to participate in casino gaming. Therefore casinos become part of the tourism system (Leiper, 1995). At the same time, gambling constitutes an increasingly popular leisure activity among local residents (e.g. Gagnon, 1994).

The casino gaming industry in the USA has experienced tremendous growth in the past decade. Until 1988 only Nevada and New Jersey permitted casino operations. By 1997, all but two states – Utah and Hawaii – had legalized gambling, and casinos can now be found in numerous states across the country.

Advocates of casinos often emphasize the potential of casino gaming acting as a catalyst for a region's economic development (Eadington, 1996). While not denying the economic value of casino gaming, opponents generally focus on potential social costs. The issue of problem gambling in particular has received considerable attention in recent years (e.g. Ladouceur *et al.*, 1994; Hraba and Lee, 1996; Volberg, 1996). One aspect of research on problem gambling is its potential link to under-age gambling (e.g. Lesieur and Klein, 1987; Devlin and Peppard, 1996; Govoni *et al.*, 1996). These studies have mainly focused on describing actual gambling behaviour. However, to the knowledge of the authors, only one study to date (Buchta, 1995) has assessed the relationship between gambling and risk-taking behaviour with a particular focus on under-age gambling. Buchta (1995), however, assessed this relationship only for under-age individuals, without contrasting it with that of other age groups.

The purpose of this study is two-fold. Firstly, it assesses the relationship between individuals' gambling behaviour, their risk approach motivation and their optimum stimulation level in general. Secondly, the gambling and risk-taking behaviour of under-age individuals is contrasted with that of individuals in other age groups. Finally, the influence of gender and nationality is examined.

Literature Review

While there are scattered items of useful knowledge and theory, systematic treatises on gambling are sadly lacking. Moreover, many of the treatments that do exist are speculative, impressionistic and moralistic, and many also lack adequate data (Devereux, 1968, p. 53).

Bromiley and Curley (1992), 25 years later, partly concurred with this statement by pointing to the fact that individual differences in risk-taking related to gambling in particular have not been adequately researched. This is in contrast to extensive efforts to research pathological gambling and the legal aspects of gambling (e.g. Eadington and Cornelius, 1991; Walker and Dickerson, 1996).

Gambling can be regarded as a form of risk-taking behaviour, as it satisfies the two criteria commonly associated with the notion of 'risk'. These are: (i) the nature of the outcome is probabilistic rather than certain; and (ii) there is uncertainty regarding the amount of potential loss (Slovik, 1964; Kogan and Wallach, 1964).

In discussing gambling it is important to make a distinction between games of chance and games of skill, since risk-taking strategies to these different types of games are said to vary (e.g. Sorrentino et al., 1992). Games of skill are, as the name implies, games which require certain skills to increase the chance of overcoming the house advantage and/or to win. Examples of games of skill include poker and horse-race betting. In the latter, for instance, skill is reflected in the methods of information collection and processing, interpretation, consideration of precedent, formulation of expectations, 'gut' feelings, and consultation of expert opinion (Bruce and Johnson, 1996, p. 69). Conversely, in games of chance no skills are required; the outcome of these games is chance-determined whereby the person gambling has no opportunity to apply his/her skills or to influence the outcome. Lotteries and standard slot machines represent examples of games of pure chance.

It is also important to distinguish between the study of gambling behaviour in artificial (laboratory) versus real settings. Anderson and Brown (1984), for instance, found significant differences in gambling behaviour and the relationship between sensation-seeking, arousal and gambling in real and artificial casino settings. Gambling in a real casino setting produced a higher level of excitement, and subjects placed higher bets than in an artificial environment.

Bauer (1960) introduced the concept of 'perceived risk' in the context of the consumer decision-making process. He proposed that a consumer perceives a decision as one involving risk if the consequence of the decision is uncertain. Cox (1964), expanding on this premise, suggested that perceived risk incorporates two distinct aspects – uncertainty about the outcome of the decision, and uncertainty concerning the consequences of the decision. Numerous authors have concurred with this general approach to defining risk (e.g. Kogan and Wallach, 1964; Slovik *et al.*, 1982; MacCrimmon and Wehrung, 1986).

While a consensus had been reached on the general definition of risk, the difficulty of operationalizing this concept remained. The latter can be partly attributed to the fact that, in many instances, risk had been operationalized as a single dimension, yet numerous studies subsequently suggested that risk is a multidimensional construct. These dimensions include the financial, functional, psychological, physical, social and time risks (Jacoby and Kaplan, 1972; Cheron and Ritchie, 1982; Brooker, 1983).

The existence of various types of risk underlies the argument of one school of thought on risk perception, namely that risk perceptions are specific to a situation (Kogan and Wallach, 1964; Weinstein and Martin, 1969). Depending on the situation, some risk dimensions become more important to the individual than others (Slovik, 1972). Situationalists would argue that environmental extremes can override most personality traits, with the character of certain situations becoming the primary influence on behaviour (Dietz and Humpf, 1984).

In contrast, personality trait theorists proposed that differences in risk behaviour are due to differences in individuals' traits which predispose them differently towards risk-taking (Coombs and Pruitt, 1960; Lichtenstein, 1965). With traits exhibiting temporal and cross-instance stability, this school of thought de-emphasized the effect of situational variables on risk perception. However, numerous studies found no evidence for this line of argument, with personality variables being unrelated or inconsistently related to individual differences in risk-taking behaviour (Kogan and Wallach, 1964; Slovik, 1964).

However, Knowles (1976), by making a distinction between motivational and stylistic/strategy aspects of risk-taking, found that people do behave consistently in their willingness to approach risk situations. The apparent lack of personal consistency referred to above was found only in regard to strategies in risk-taking. The risk-taking questionnaire (RTQ) was used to assess risk-approach motivation.

Knowles (1976, p. 307) further suggested that the optimum stimulation level (OSL) may be a personality dimension which is closely related to risk-taking motivation. The concept of OSL, introduced by Hebb (1955) and Leuba (1955), focuses on the interaction between an individual's psychological state and his/her reaction to environmental stimuli. It is suggested that each individual has a preferred or optimum stimulation level and is motivated to increase or decrease novelty and complexity if the environmental stimulation is below or above the optimum, respectively.

Berlyne (1960) proposed that the OSL is determined by an individual's personality, cultural factors, learning and the psychological state, and termed behaviour aimed at adjusting environmental stimulation 'exploratory behaviour'. Studies have assessed the relationship between OSL and demographic variables and personality traits (Raju, 1980), vacation preferences (Wahlers and Etzel, 1985), and leisure choice processes (Beard and Ragheb, 1983; Iso-Ahola, 1980).

The study by Wahlers and Etzel (1985) requires specific mention, as they found that 'it is possible for a person with a low OSL to be a stimulation seeker if the environment is providing a deficient level of stimulation' (p. 285). Conversely, a person whose lifestyle offers a high level of stimulation may avoid stimulation despite having a high OSL.

The sensation-seeking scale (SSS) of Zuckerman (1979) and the arousal-seeking tendency (AST) scale of Mehrabian and Russell (1974) represent the most frequently utilized OSL scales. Wahlers and Dunn (1987, p. 253) pointed out that these two scales are not equivalent measures of the OSL construct. However, the scales are similar in their assessment of risk-taking behaviour.

Several studies have assessed the relationship between sensation seeking and gambling behaviour. The results, however, are varied. Some studies support a direct relationship between sensation seeking and gambling (e.g. Kuley and Jacobs, 1988), whereas other studies found no evidence of a relationship (e.g. Anderson and Brown, 1984) or evidence of an inverse relationship (e.g. Dickerson et al., 1987). However, to the knowledge of the authors very little research has utilized the AST scale in the context of gambling behaviour – a scale which is regarded as superior to Zuckerman's sensation-seeking scale (Wahlers and Etzel, 1985).

This study utilizes the AST scale to establish individuals' OSL. It assesses the relationship between two personality traits, OSL and risk-approach motivation, and gambling behaviour. Following Knowles (1976), a distinction is made between risk approach and risk strategy. The frequency and type of play characterize risk approach, while the amount bet is indicative of the risk strategy adopted by the individual.

Methodology

A pre-tested, self-administered questionnaire was provided to samples of 136 and 56 undergraduate students at a university in the south-western USA, in the spring and fall, respectively, of 1997. The questionnaire completion took place in a controlled environment (classroom setting) which, together with the incentive of one credit point towards the completion of their course, contributed to the high response rate of 100% of students who had volunteered to participate in the study (192 students, or 80% of the students offered the extra credit).

The questionnaire inquired about respondents' gambling behaviour, reflected in the frequency of visiting gambling establishments in a specified time period and of playing various games of skill and of chance, the single largest bet placed, and the single largest amount lost. A modified version of Knowles's (1976) RTQ was utilized to measure subjects' risk-approach motivation. This version incorporated 10 instead of the original 20 items. Roehl (1988), in a study on risk in vacation travel, found the scale consisting of these 10 items to have an almost equally high internal consistency (Cronbach alpha coefficient of 0.83) as Knowles's original scale (a=0.85). The OSL was measured by Mehrabian and Russell's (1974)

AST scale rather than Zuckerman's SSS. A review of the literature suggested that the former scale is a favoured measurement of the OSL, for reasons outlined by Wahlers and Etzel (1985, p. 286). Finally, the age, gender and nationality of respondents were ascertained.

Data analysis

Tests of normality revealed that three variables – maximum amount bet, maximum amount lost and the frequency of gambling – displayed significant departures from normality (Kolmogorov–Smirnov test values of 0.323, 0.324 and 0.249, d.f.=191, $P<0.01$). Consequently, these variables were subjected to a log transformation which addressed the problem. (Note: since the log of 0 is undefined, a small value (0.2) was added to the zero values for these variables.)

The risk-approach measures (RTQ scale) and the OSL measures (AST scale) were subjected to a reliability analysis. This was deemed necessary to assess the properties of the measurement scales and the relationship of the items that make them up (Allen and Yen, 1979). Cronbach's coefficient alpha (Cronbach, 1951), the most frequently used reliability measure, provided a measure of the scales' internal consistency, based on the average inter-item correlations.

Chi-square analysis and one-way ANOVA were utilized to assess relationships among subjects with different risk-approach motivation/OSL and their gambling behaviour. Differences among subjects of different age groups were of particular interest.

Results and Discussion

The sample comprised 192 respondents. Since the data collection took place at different points in time, several tests were conducted to determine whether the samples differed significantly in regard to certain variables. However, both *t*-tests and chi-square analysis indicated that there were no significant differences between respondents from the two samples in terms of their gambling behaviour (frequency of gambling, maximum amount bet and maximum amount lost), selected demographics (age, gender, nationality), and risk-approach motivation and OSL scores.

Demographic profile of the sample

Most respondents were either in the 17–21-year (47.9%) or in the 22–29-year (41.1%) age group. Genders were about equally represented. In terms of respondents' nationality, US nationals had the strongest representation (69.3%), followed by Japanese nationals (12.5%) and Korean nationals (4.7%). Nationals from Asian countries totalled 47 respondents, accounting for 24.5% of the sample (Table 7.1).

Table 7.1 Demographic profile of the sample

Characteristics	Number of respondents (%)
Age	
17–21	92 (47.9)
22–29	79 (41.1)
30–54	20 (10.4)
Gender	
Male	86 (44.8)
Female	106 (55.2)
Nationality	
USA	133 (69.3)
Asia	47 (24.5)
Japan	24 (12.5)

n=192.

Gambling behaviour of the sample

As shown in Table 7.2, the majority of respondents bet and lost a relatively small amount of money. There was, however, also a considerable number of respondents who engaged in high-stake betting behaviour, with the maximum single bet amounting to $1100 and the maximum single loss of money in one gambling session totalling $2500. In terms of visiting gaming establishments, a considerable number of respondents (56) averaged between two and three visits per week for the specified time period (1 month).

Finally, the greatest number of respondents identified playing slots as the gambling activity engaged in on a frequent or occasional basis (119 respondents), followed by blackjack (65 respondents) and race/sports book (52).

Table 7.2 Gambling behaviour of the sample

Behaviour variable	No. of respondents (%)
Maximum amount bet ($)	
0	29 (15.1)
1–50	105 (54.7)
51–250	41 (21.4)
251–1100	16 (8.3)
Maximum Amount Lost ($)	
0	33 (17.2)
1–50	77 (40.1)
51–250	54 (28.1)
251–2500	28 (14.6)
Number of visits to gambling establishments*	
0	81 (42.2)
1–4	48 (25.0)
5–15	56 (29.2)
16–41	7 (3.6)
Frequency of playing various games†	
Blackjack	
Frequently	6 (3.1)
Occasionally	59 (30.7)
Rarely	127 (66.1)
Craps	
Frequently	3 (1.6)
Occasionally	19 (9.9)
Rarely	170 (88.5)
Slots	
Frequently	18 (9.4)
Occasionally	101 (52.6)
Rarely	73 (38.0)
Race and sports book	
Frequently	13 (6.8)
Occasionally	39 (20.3)
Rarely	140 (72.9)

$n=192$.
*Refers to number of visits in the 4 weeks preceding the questionnaire administration.
†Frequent gambling activity = more than four times a month; occasional gambling activity = twice a month to once every few months; rare gambling activity = once a year and less often.

Table 7.3 provides an overview of the gambling behaviour of under-age subjects. There is reason for some concern in view of the fact that 18.5% of under-
age subjects had lost amounts between $51 and $250. Almost 10% of subjects had
lost amounts between $251 and $2500 in a single gambling session. At the same
time there were a considerable number of under-age respondents (25 of 92
respondents) who engaged in frequent gambling, consistent with the high
amounts bet and lost. The most popular gambling activity among under-age
respondents was playing slots, with 47 subjects playing it on a frequent/occasional
basis, followed by blackjack (24 respondents). Craps was obviously not a popular
game for this age group. The popularity of slots machines among under-age
respondents can be partly attributed to their wide distribution, the ease of access,
the relative anonymity of people playing slots compared to table games, and the
consequent difficulties for casinos in preventing under-age gambling.

Focusing on the variable of interest – age – chi-square analysis revealed significant differences among the age groups in terms of overall frequency of gambling (χ^2=13.3, d.f.=6, P<0.05; Cramer's V=0.186). However, it was the two age
groups other than the under-age group that displayed a higher gambling frequency. The assessment of the maximum amount bet and the maximum amount
lost produced similar results, with chi-square tests pointing to significant differences ((χ^2=14.5, d.f.=6, P<0.05; Cramer's V=0.196 and (χ^2=23.3, d.f.=6,
P<0.01; Cramer's V=0.247, respectively) among age groups. Yet again, it was the
age groups other than the under-age group that engaged in significantly more
high-stake betting ($51–$1100) and that also incurred higher losses ($51–$2500).

Assessment of RTQ and OSL scales

Two scales were formed to assess respondents' risk-approach motivation (RTQ)
and their OSL. The RTQ scale, incorporating 10 items, returned a Cronbach alpha
coefficient of 0.8626. The AST scale, consisting of 40 items, had a Cronbach
alpha coefficient of 0.8861. Consequently, the items contained in the individual
scales can be regarded as internally consistent. (Detailed item-analysis statistics
are omitted due to space constraints.)

Relationship between respondents' risk-approach motivation, their gambling behaviour and demographics

Respondents were classified into low-, medium- and high-risk approach subjects,
depending on their RTQ score (31, 131 and 30 respondents, respectively). Chi-
square analysis indicated that high-risk approach subjects differed significantly in
their overall gambling frequency compared to low- and medium-risk approach
subjects (χ^2=12.7, d.f.=6; P<0.05; Cramer's V=0.182), displaying a higher gambling frequency. One-way ANOVA was carried out to determine whether subjects
in the low-, medium- and high-risk approach groups differed significantly in their
frequency of playing various games. Since for two variables the Levene test for
the equality of group variance was significant, appropriate transformations had to
be carried out. The one-way ANOVA results are presented in Table 7.4.

Table 7.3 Gambling behaviour of under-age subjects

Behaviour variable	No. of respondents (%)
Maximum amount bet ($)	
0	20 (22.0)
1–50	51 (56.0)
51–250	17 (18.7)
251–1100	3 (3.3)
Maximum amount lost ($)	
0	21 (22.8)
1–50	46 (50.0)
51–250	17 (18.5)
251–2500	8 (8.7)
Number of visits to gambling establishments*	
0	49 (53.3)
1–4	18 (19.6)
5–15	23 (25.0)
16–41	2 (2.2)
Frequency of playing various games†	
Blackjack	
Frequently	2 (2.2)
Occasionally	22 (23.9)
Rarely	68 (73.9)
Craps	
Frequently	1 (1.1)
Occasionally	5 (5.4)
Rarely	86 (93.5)
Slots	
Frequently	4 (4.3)
Occasionally	43 (46.7)
Rarely	45 (48.9)
Race and sports book	
Frequently	5 (5.4)
Occasionally	16 (17.4)
Rarely	17 (77.2)

n=92.
*Refers to number of visits in the four weeks preceding the questionnaire administration.
†Frequent gambling activity = more than four times a month; occasional gambling activity = twice a month to once every few months; rare gambling activity = once a year and less often.

Table 7.4 Respondents' risk motivation and their frequency of playing selected games

Games	F	P
Blackjack	4.936	0.008
Craps	6.539	0.002
Slots	2.209	0.113
Race/sports book	3.515	0.032

Post hoc Bonferroni tests indicated that subjects in the high-risk approach category displayed a higher frequency to engage in all games except slots (i.e. blackjack, craps and race/sports book) than subjects in the medium-risk approach category. Significant differences in gambling frequency were also found between low- and high-risk approach subjects in terms of playing blackjack and craps. No significant differences in gambling frequency were observed between these two groups for slots and race/sports book.

Earlier research indicates that 'heavy gamblers' generally prefer games that involve an appropriate mix of chance and skill (e.g. Vogelaar, 1986). Such a preference appears to be also prevalent among high-risk approach subjects in view of the above results. Consequently, a game of pure chance such as slots does not display a higher gambling frequency for high-risk approach subjects compared to low- and medium-risk approach subjects.

Turning from risk approach to risk strategy, it was found that there were no significant differences among low-, medium- and high-risk approach subjects in terms of the maximum amount bet (chi-square test: $\chi^2=8.4$, d.f.=6, P=0.210). These findings appear to lend support to Knowles's (1976) proposition that people differ in the way they approach risk and how they actually deal with it.

No statistically significant relationships were observed between respondents' risk approach and their gender, nationality and age (chi-square tests: $\chi^2=1.974$, d.f.=2, P=0.373; $\chi^2=3.433$, d.f.=4, P=0.488; $\chi^2=3.247$, d.f.=4, P=0.517, respectively). These results are somewhat surprising.

With regard to gender, several earlier studies found significant differences between male and females in their approach to risk situations (e.g. Kogan and Wallach, 1964). Zinkhan and Karande (1991) also found significant gender differences, with women being more conservative than men in their approach to risk situations. However, no such difference was evident in this study.

The lack of difference in risk approach among subjects of various ages was also unexpected, since a tendency among younger people (particularly the age group under investigation in this study) to possess a higher-risk approach motivation than older people is conceivable. The effect of age has been documented in the context of optimum stimulation level research. Zuckerman (1979) reported that sensation-seeking scores decrease with increasing age. This, however, does not appear to apply in the context of risk approach in this study.

Finally, with nationality being broadly grouped into USA and Asian nationalities, one could have expected differences in cultural background and consequent differences in risk approach to be evident. Yet again, that did not occur. However, it should be noted that nationality does not necessarily reflect respondents' cultural background, i.e. US nationals could have an Asian background, while Asian nationals could have grown up in the USA and therefore have been strongly influenced by US culture.

Relationship between respondents' optimum stimulation level, their gambling behaviour and demographics

According to their score on the AST scale, respondents were classified as either low, medium or high in terms of their optimum stimulation level. This resulted in groups of 28, 114 and 49 respondents, respectively. Chi-square analysis indicated that there was no association between respondents' OSL and the overall frequency of gambling (χ^2=6.05, d.f.=6, P=0.418). This is in contrast to Zuckerman's (1979) hypothesis that gamblers are higher than non-gamblers on measures of sensation seeking. It also contradicts Kuley and Jacobs' (1988) findings that the OSL is associated with high-frequency gambling. It is, however, consistent with the results of a study by Anderson and Brown (1984) who found no evidence of a relationship between the two variables.

The lack of evidence for a relationship between OSL and the overall frequency of gambling extends to the relationship between OSL and the frequency of playing individual games. One-way ANOVA, carried out to determine whether subjects with a low, medium and high OSL differed in their frequency of playing individual games, be they games of chance or games of skill, revealed no evidence to that effect. It is, therefore, suggested that factors other than the OSL influence the frequency both of gambling overall, and of engaging in particular games.

Further, an assessment was made on the relationship between respondents' OSL and the maximum amount bet. Again, there was no evidence of a significant relationship between these two variables (χ^2=4.749; d.f.=6, P=0.576).

Finally, the influence of the various demographics also yielded some interesting and partly unexpected results. The lack of association between OSL and age, in particular, was surprising (χ^2=0.781, d.f.=4, P=0.941). As mentioned earlier, Zuckerman (1979) reported that sensation-seeking scores decrease with increasing age. However, this did not appear to be the case in this study. The under-age group did not display significant differences in OSL compared to the other two age groups. The genders did not vary significantly in their OSL (χ^2=0.982, d.f.=2, P=0.612). There were, however, significant differences with regard to different nationalities (χ^2=13.7, d.f.=4, P<0.01). In particular, US nationals on average displayed a somewhat higher OSL than Asian nationals in this study.

Conclusions

The purpose of the study was to investigate the relationship between gambling and risk behaviour with a particular focus on under-age gambling behaviour. Results of the study supported the notion that people differ in their risk approach and their risk-strategy behaviour. There was a significant relationship between individuals' risk approach and gambling frequency, with high-risk approach subjects displaying a higher gambling frequency than both low- and medium-risk approach subjects. However, there were no significant differences among low-, medium- and high-risk approach subjects in terms of the maximum amount bet.

The analysis of the relationships between respondents' OSL, gambling behaviour and age yielded some interesting and surprising results. In contrast to several previous studies, this study found no significant relationship between the OSL and the frequency of gambling, both in terms of overall gambling frequency and frequency of playing individual games. This suggests that personality traits other than a person's OSL have an impact on gambling frequency. Neither were there significant differences found among ages in regard to the OSL, as measured by the AST scale, a scale judged superior to Zuckerman's SSS. This again contrasts with earlier research (Raju, 1980) which suggested a correlation between age and OSL, with the OSL being derived from the AST scale. Therefore, further research is required on whether the lack of a relationship between the two variables found in this study holds true in other studies utilizing the AST scale.

With regard to under-age gambling behaviour, the results of this study indicate that the majority of respondents in this age group gambled either not at all or on an infrequent basis. The amounts bet and the amounts lost by this age group were typically small. This is consistent with earlier findings of studies on college student gambling practices (e.g. Yuan et al., 1996). Therefore, in discussions on under-age gambling it is important to distinguish clearly between the public opinion and the actual state. The media often focus on individual cases of under-age problem gambling (e.g. Associated Press, 1998), thereby greatly influencing public opinion – perceptions of widespread under-age problem gambling are consequently not uncommon. Thus it is important to provide data that convey a more accurate picture of under-age gambling behaviour.

Nevertheless, there were also a considerable number of under-age respondents who reported relatively high gambling losses, consistent with high-frequency gambling. Several studies suggest a relationship between early gambling and an increased likelihood of gambling problems later in life (e.g. Dell et al., 1981, Lesieur and Klein, 1987). It may be these respondents who have started gambling at an earlier stage and may develop serious gambling problems later. In order to determine whether this is indeed the case, studies adopting a longitudinal rather than a cross-sectional research design would prove beneficial.

At the same time, it is important to promote an increase in awareness among under-age persons and their parents of issues related to problem gambling. In this context, not only educational institutions but also the casino gaming industry itself have an important role to play. The latter has to establish and enforce stricter measures to counter potential problem gambling among all age groups, particularly under-age persons.

References

Allen, M.J. and Yen, W.M. (1979) *An Introduction to Measurement Theory.* Belmont, California: Wadsworth.

Anderson, G. and Brown, R.I.F. (1984) Real and laboratory gambling, sensation seeking and arousal. *British Journal of Psychology* 75, 401–410.

Associated Press (1998) Spread of casinos may be increasing gambling among college students. *Las Vegas Review Journal* May 4, 3D.

Bauer, R.A. (1960) Consumer behavior as risk-taking. In: R.S. Hancock (ed.) *Dynamic Marketing for a Changing World.* Chicago: American Marketing Association, pp. 389–398.

Beard, J.G. and Ragheb, M.G. (1983) Measuring leisure motivation. *Journal of Leisure Research* 15, 219–228.

Berlyne, D.E. (1960) *Conflict, Arousal and Curiosity.* New York: McGraw Hill.

Bromiley, P. and Curley, S.P. (1992) Individual differences in risk taking. In: J.F. Yates (ed.) *Risk-taking Behaviour.* Chichester: Wiley, pp. 87–132.

Brooker, G. (1983) An assessment of an expanded measure of perceived risk. In: T.C. Kinnear (ed.) *Advances in Consumer Research*, No. 11. Provo, Utah: Association of Consumer Research, pp. 439–441.

Bruce, A.C. and Johnson, J.E.V. (1996) Decision-making under risk, effect of complexity on performance. *Psychological Reports* 79, 67–76.

Buchta, R.M. (1995) Gambling among adolescents. *Clinical Pediatrics* 34, 346–348.

Cheron, E.J. and Ritchie, J.R.B. (1982) Leisure activities and perceived risk. *Journal of Leisure Research* 14, 139–154.

Coombs, C.H. and Pruitt, D.G. (1960) Components of risk in decision-making, probability and variance preferences. *Journal of Experiential Psychology* 60, 265.

Cox, D.F. and Rich, S.U. (1964) Perceived risk and consumer decision making. *Journal of Marketing Research* 1, 32–39.

Cronbach, L.J. (1951) Coefficient alpha and the internal structure of tests. *Psychometrika* 16, 297–334.

Dell, L.J., Ruzicka, M.E. and Polisi, A.T. (1981) Personality and other factors associated with gambling addiction. *International Journal of Addiction* 16, 149–156.

Devereux, E.C. (1968) *Gambling. International Encyclopedia of the Social Sciences* Vol. 6. New York: Macmillan, pp. 53–62

Devlin, A.S. and Peppard, D.M. (1996) *Casino use by college students. *Psychological Reports* 78, 899–906.

Dickerson, M., Hinchy, J. and Fabre, J. (1987) Chasing, arousal and sensation seeking in off–course gamblers. *British Journal of Addiction* 82, 673–680.

Dietz, R. and Humpf, D.A. (1984) The gambling personality, an interactional approach. In: *Proceedings of the Sixth National Conference on Gambling and Risk Taking.* Reno, Nevada: Bureau of Business and Economic Research, UNR, pp. 146–157.

Eadington, W.R. (1996) The legalization of casinos, policy objectives, regulatory alternatives, and cost/benefit considerations. *Journal of Travel Research* Winter, 3–8.

Eadington, W.R. and Cornelius, J.A. (eds) (1991) *Gambling and Public Policy, International Perspectives.* Reno, Nevada: Institute for the Study of Gambling and Commercial Gaming.

Gagnon, L. (1994) The pitfalls of using human greed to fuel the economy. *Toronto Globe and Mail* July 23, D3.

Govoni, R., Rupcich, N. and Frisch, G.R. (1996) Gambling behavior of adolescent gamblers. *Journal of Gambling Studies* 12, 305–317.

Hebb, D.O. (1955) Drives and the CNS. *Psychological Review* 62, 243–254.

Hraba, J. and Lee, G. (1996) Gender, gambling and problem gambling. *Journal of Gambling Studies* 12, 83–101.

Iso-Ahola, S.E. (1980) *The Social Psychology of Leisure and Recreation.* Dubuque: Brown.

Jacoby, J. and Kaplan, L.B. (1972) The components of perceived risk. In: M. Venkatesan (ed.) *Proceedings of the 3rd Annual Conference of the Association for Consumer Research.* Chicago, Association for Consumer Research, pp. 382–393.

Knowles, E.S. (1976) Searching for motivations in risk-taking and gambling. In: W.R. Eadington (ed.) *Gambling and Society.* Springfield, Illinois: Charles & Thomas.

Kogan, N. and Wallach, M.A. (1964). *Risk Taking.* New York: Holt, Rinehart & Winston.

Kuley, N.B. and Jacobs, D.F. (1988) The relationship between dissociate-like experiences and sensation seeking among social and problem gamblers. *Journal of Gambling Behaviour* 4, 197–207.

Ladouceur, R., Boisvert, J.-M., Pepin, M. and Loranger, M. (1994) Social cost of pathological gambling. *Journal of Gambling Studies* 10, 399–409.

Leiper, N. (1995) *Tourism Management.* Melbourne: TAFE Publications.

Lesieur, H.R. and Klein, R. (1987) Pathological gambling among high school students. *Addictive Behaviour* 12, 129–135.

Leuba, C. (1955) Towards some integration of learning theories, the concept of optimal stimulation. *Psychological Reports* 1, 27–33.

Lichtenstein, S.C. (1965) Bases for preferences among three-outcome bets. *Journal of Experiential Psychology* 69, 162.

MacCrimmon, K.P. and Wehrung, D.A. (1986) *Taking Risks.* New York: Free Press.

Mehrabian, A. and Russell, J.A. (1974) *An Approach to Environmental Psychology.* Cambridge, Massachussetts: MIT Press.

Raju, P.S. (1980) Optimum stimulation level, its relationship to personality, demographics, and exploratory behavior. *Journal of Consumer Research* 7, 272–282.

Roehl, W.S. (1988) A typology of risk in vacation travel. PhD thesis, Texas A&M University.

Roehl, W.S. (1994) Casinos as tourist attractions, issues for the 1990s. *IAHA* August/September, 6–7, 37.

Slovik, P. (1964) Assessment of risk-taking behavior. *Psychological Bulletin* 61, 220–233.

Slovik, P. (1972) Convergent validation of risk taking specificity and the generality of risk taking behavior. *Journal of Personality and Social Psychology* 22, 128–134.

Slovik, P., Fischhoff, B. and Lichtenstein, S. (1982) Why study risk perception? *Risk Analysis* 2, 83–93.

Sorrentino, R.M., Hewitt, E.C. and Raso-Knott, P.A. (1992) Risk-taking in games of chance and skill, informational and affective influences on choice behavior. *Journal of Personality and Social Psychology* 62, 522–533.

Vogelaar, D.M. (1986) Skill versus chance, technical management. In: J. McMillen (ed.) *Gambling in the 80s*. Brisbane: National Association for Gambling Studies.

Volberg, R.A. (1996) Prevalence studies of gambling in the United States. *Journal of Gambling Studies* 12, 111–128.

Wahlers, R.G. and Dunn, M.G. (1987) Optimal stimulation level measurement and exploratory behavior: review and analysis. In: Belk, R.W., Zaltman, G. and Bagozzi, R. (eds) *Marketing Theory – 1987 Winter Educators' Conference*. American Marketing Association, Chicago, Illinois, pp. 249–254.

Wahlers, R.G. and Etzel, M.J. (1985) Vacation preference as a manifestation of optimum stimulation and lifestyle experience. *Journal of Leisure Research* 17, 283–295.

Walker, M.B. and Dickerson, M.G. (1996) The relevance of problem and pathological gambling, a critical analysis. *Journal of Gambling Studies* 12, 233–249.

Weinstein, E. and Martin, J. (1969) Generality of willingness to take risk. *Psychological Reports* 24, 499–501

Yuan, M., Yuan, S. and Jones, P. (1996) An examination of university student gambling practices. *Gaming Research and Review Journal* 3, 7–23.

Zinkhan, G.M. and Karande, K.W. (1991) Cultural and gender differences in risk-taking behavior among American and Spanish decision makers. *Journal of Social Psychology* 131, 741–742.

Zuckerman, M. (1979) *Sensation Seeking, Beyond the Optimal Level of Arousal*. Hillsdale, New Jersey: Erlbaum Associates.

Chapter eight
Tourism Constraints: the Neglected Dimension of Consumer Behaviour Research

Simon Hudson
Tourism Management Group, University of Calgary, 2500 University Drive N.W., Calgary, Alberta, Canada, T2N 1N4

David Gilbert
School of Management Studies, University of Surrey, Guildford GU2 5XH, UK

Introduction

It is important for marketing managers to understand how internal, psychological processes influence individuals to choose a certain holiday destination, or a particular type of tourism product. Behavioural concepts lie at the heart of marketing theory, and have been the subject of extensive literature in recent years. The understanding of marketing practitioners concerning how consumers make their product decisions influences all the subsequent decisions in the marketing process. In fact, effective marketing in competitive conditions is impossible without some understanding of buyers' motivations and decision processes. The company that really understands how consumers will respond to different product features, prices and advertising appeals has a great advantage over its competitors. As a result, researchers from industry and the academic world have studied in depth the relationship between marketing stimuli and consumer responses.

Many tourism texts have been written from a practitioner's point of view, discussing the structure and operation of particular sectors of the tourism industry, suggesting trends and their possible consequences. Examples are Burkart and Medlik (1974), Hodgson (1987), Lundberg (1989) and Holloway (1990). Several books combine the examination of management with marketing – Hawkins *et al.* (1980), Cooper *et al.* (1993), and Witt and Moutinho (1994) are examples – and there are texts dealing only with marketing that provide a general application to tourism. Books by Holloway and Plant (1988), Jefferson and Lickorish (1988), Horner and Swarbrooke (1996), and Middleton (1988) fall into this category. All these books include articles on consumer demand, as do journals such as *Tourism Management*, *Travel and Tourism Analyst* and *International Tourism Quarterly*.

However, there is little research on the tourism industry and its operation which is analytical in emphasis, and there is a general belief that the interrelationships between the industry, the consumer and the destination have been neglected, largely because modelling has not been sufficiently integrated.

In fact, even existing definitions of tourism are not adequate for marketers, as they have been derived for the economists. The simplistic view of tourist behaviour should be rejected and replaced with a new understanding of the tourist as a consumer who demonstrates particular actions of behaviour (Gilbert, 1991). These actions involve the needs, motivation, attitudes, values, personality and perceptions which all lead to specific preferences for tourism-related activities. To carry this argument further, the study of tourist consumer behaviour should not only seek to understand the choice process of tourists, but should endeavour to comprehend the range of constraints preventing non-tourists from becoming tourists.

An industry that would benefit from such research is the ski industry, where markets have matured worldwide, but communication is still directed primarily to the converted. If the sport is to be revitalized, then the audience cannot be restricted to skiers, and more effort is required to persuade non-skiers to take to the slopes. An understanding of their constraints is therefore vital to launching such a marketing initiative.

Problems with consumer behaviour models in tourism

The 'grand models' of consumer behaviour have been utilized or transformed by authors interested in the tourism choice process. Some of the models developed are quite basic (Wahab *et al.*, 1976; Mayo and Jarvis, 1981; Middleton, 1988), while others are more sophisticated (Schmoll, 1977; Mathieson and Wall, 1982). These last two are explained below.

Schmoll (1977) built a model based on the Howard–Sheth (1969) and Nicosia (1966) models of consumer behaviour. His model was based upon the following premises:

- the decision process and its eventual outcome are influenced by four sets of variables: customer goals, travel opportunities, communications effort, and intervening or independent variables;
- it is possible to identify these sets of variables and their individual components;
- the eventual decision is the result of a distinct process involving several successive stages or phases.

The model (see Fig. 8.1) is composed of four fields:

- field 1, external stimuli such as trade publications;
- field 2, travel needs and desires determined by personality, socioeconomic factors, attitudes and values;
- field 3, external variables such as confidence in the travel agent, destination image, previous experience, and cost and time constraints;
- field 4, destination- or service-related characteristics that have a bearing on the decision process and its outcome.

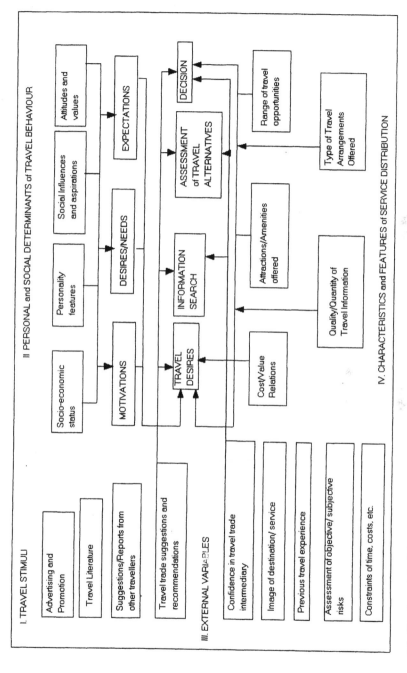

Figure 8.1 The travel decision process – a model (Schmoll, 1977).

Schmoll's model is descriptive – its purpose is to show the relevant variables and their interrelationships – but it cannot be quantified. Furthermore, the model is not a tool for prediction. It cannot serve as a basis for the forecasting of demand for a given destination or service. However, Schmoll's is the only model that pays respect to constraints, and their impact on the decision making process.

In the behavioural framework presented by Mathieson and Wall (1982), the decision-making process, as seen in Fig. 8.2, involves five principal phases:

- felt need or travel desire
- information collection and evaluation
- travel decisions
- travel preparations and travel experience
- travel satisfaction evaluation.

The components which are itemized in the framework, and their interrelationships, influence each of the five decision phases. In their book, mainly dedicated to the impacts of tourism, the authors consider the framework under four major headings, as detailed below.

- *The tourist profile.* This is viewed under the categories of the tourists' socio-economic and behavioural characteristics.
- *Travel awareness.* Potential tourists may be motivated to travel but, unless they are informed of what opportunities are available, they may be unaware of the means of meeting their requirements. A tourist image is conjured up from the information received, as interpreted through the personal and behavioural characteristics of the tourist.
- *Trip features.* These include such factors as distance, duration of stay, time constraints, trip cost, party size and perceived risk.
- *Resources and characteristics of destinations.* These include types of attraction, the availability and quality of services, environmental conditions, the attributes of the host population and their political organization.

Gilbert (1991) has criticized this model for omitting the important aspects of perception, memory, personality and information-processing, which is the basis of traditional models (although Mathieson and Wall could argue that these aspects are part of 'travel awareness' in their model). Also, this (like other models) seems to ignore 'type of holiday' in its trip features. With the increase in special interest and activity holidays, future models should take into account the plethora of holiday options available to the consumer. Despite its limitations, however, the framework was designed solely to indicate that the impacts of tourism are the consequence of tourist decisions, and it recognizes that the impacts of tourism are dynamic, changing with corresponding changes in destination features, trip characteristics, and the personal and behavioural attributes of tourists.

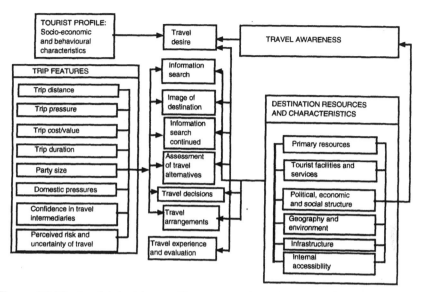

Figure 8.2 The tourist decision-making process (Mathieson and Wall, 1982).

The 'borrowing' of theories from those who have concentrated on more tangible products has hampered progress in developing realistic models. Tangible products can be assessed prior to purchase, but it is more difficult to develop and construct models of the decision process which relate to the purchase of tourism products. From a tourism marketing point of view, all of these recent models are not predictive for two reasons. Firstly, they are stereotypical and generalized, whereas in reality the decision process will vary significantly between different groups of tourists. Secondly, they have no time dimension, so they do not indicate to the practitioner when to intervene in the process in order to influence the decision. Additionally, just as in the marketing of consumer goods, people with a lack of motivation are ignored, typologies do not include the non-participant or non-user, and the models (with the exception of Schmoll's) do not take into account the constraints facing consumers in the decision-making process.

The non-user

Authors of works on consumer behaviour have occasionally referred to the non-user, usually during a discussion of user segmentation. For example, Evans *et al.* (1996) distinguished between brand-loyal users, brand switchers, new users and non-users. However, they paid scant attention to the latter group, suggesting that they are an unattractive target group for marketers. Likewise, Loudon and Della Bitta (1993), in a section on usage segmentation, advise that marketing efforts should generally be aimed at light to heavy users rather than at non-users. However, they do acknowledge that for many products, non-users may represent a significant marketing opportunity.

For tourism, while research on non-users is difficult, it is vital for marketers. Discovering why people are not purchasing the services provided by an organization is important, as most tourism organizations need to attract new customers if they are to thrive or even survive. Horner and Swarbrooke (1996) see the difficulty and high cost of finding out about non-users as a major marketing challenge for those in the tourism industry. Such research can help marketers identify different types of non-users, for whom different marketing messages need to be developed and transmitted. These groups may be ex-users who need to be tempted back, those who are aware of the product but need to be persuaded to buy it, and those who are not aware of the product's existence. Furthermore, an understanding of the constraints facing these groups can only help transform potential demand into purchase decisions.

One of the first researchers to investigate the non-user was Plog (1974). His psychographic classifications of tourists (allocentrics and psychocentrics) resulted from his examination of how to turn more non-flyers into flyers. At the request of 16 airline and travel companies, he interviewed a hard core of the population who refused to fly, even when disposable income was sufficient. He found that fear of flying, unfamiliarity with flight, and maintenance of old habits kept these people from flying. Plog became convinced that there was a strong emotional core to the problem which explained his personality-based exploratory research. Attempts have been made to segment the travel market based on their constraints to travel, but such efforts are limited, and they focus on travel in general rather than on specific tourism activities. Stemerding *et al.* (1996) suggested that travel segmentation models should take constraints behaviour explicitly into consideration; and Norman (1995) tried to identify homogeneous groups of individuals based on their perception of the influence of constraints to travel, as well as describing these market segments based on their motives for travel, level of involvement, past travel experience, travel intention, and a number of sociodemographic variables.

Leisure Constraints Research

In the past decade, a growing body of research has emerged regarding leisure constraints, and the diversity of this research necessitates some kind of classification. In this paper the authors have chosen to group investigations in terms of research into ceasing participation; constraints facing non-participants; and the constraints facing existing participants. Each category is discussed below, prior to the current theory of 'negotiation of leisure constraints'.

Research into ceasing participation

Ceasing participation is a measure of non-participation employed by one group of researchers. Jackson and Dunn (1988) proposed a model attempting to demonstrate how ceasing participation and other aspects of non-participation are interconnected. Former participants were shown as exhibiting deferred or potential demand, and the authors distinguished between these two categories and former participants who cease because of lack of interest. They introduced two new measures, 'dropout rate' and 'replacement rate', suggesting that these two concepts allow for a more accurate interpretation of changes in leisure behaviour than do raw data on ceasing participation. Their categories provide a useful framework for future research, and in a replication of their study McGuire *et al.* (1989) concluded that an understanding of ceasing leisure involvement can and should be effectively examined within a context of decision-making as a whole.

In another study involving the perception of constraints, Boothby *et al.* (1981) offer a more thorough interpretation of loss of interest. Their paper details the various reasons why people cease participation in sports activities. They felt that until that date too much emphasis had been placed on recruitment and the promotion of new interest, and that effort could also usefully be directed at minimizing 'wastage', i.e. reducing the numbers of people ceasing participation.

Chick and Roberts (1989) introduce the term 'antileisure', making the interesting argument that the structures of some games/sports, and the social contexts in which they are played, may contribute to the diminution of the qualities of perceived freedom and intrinsic motivation that are important to the leisure experience. This may in turn lead participants to discontinue. Robinson and Carron (1982) also looked at team sports and ceasing participation, and attempted to determine the motivational (personal) and situational (environmental) factors associated with participants' decisions either to maintain affiliation with a competitive sport team or to drop out.

Backman and Crompton (1990) make the distinction between active and passive discontinuers. Active discontinuers have discontinued using the activity and transmit negative information about it, whereas passive discontinuers do not. It would be interesting to further this research by determining the effect of negative word-of-mouth communication among potential and existing participants in tourism activities.

Constraints facing non-participants

Most of the literature dealing with the constraints of non-participants has focused on intervening constraints facing only those who have expressed an interest or desire to participate. Two types of intervening constraints have been identified in these studies, namely internal and external constraints (Jackson, 1988). The most common internal constraints include personal skills, abilities, knowledge, and health problems, whilst external ones typically include lack of time, financial cost, lack of facilities, and transportation problems. These constraints are labelled as 'reported constraints' or 'perceived constraints', since they are measured by asking respondents to report the presence or absence of each type of barrier to a preferred activity.

Some researchers have looked for correlations between constraints and social class. Haukeland (1990) examined the social situation of non-travellers in Norway, but he acknowledged that an unsatisfactory social situation is neither a necessary nor a sufficient condition explaining the phenomenon of non-travel. Similarly, Searle and Jackson (1985), after examining socioeconomic variations in the perception of barriers to participation, concluded that further research is required to enhance the understanding of people who perceive barriers to participation. Romsa and Hoffman (1980) found that individuals from the lower social strata and less active recreation groups give lack of interest as their main reason for non-involvement. The responses from the more active recreation segments of society indicate that price, time, and facilities are the main barriers to their pursuit of certain activities. They call for further investigation into factors responsible for the apparent lack of interest amongst non-participants. Recently, Davies and Prentice (1995) have suggested that the lack of interest expressed by non-participants may be a rationalization of constraints rather than a true lack of interest, concealing underlying motivations and constraints to behaviour.

The perspective of life cycle has proved to be a useful conceptual and analytical framework to investigate the experience of leisure constraints and support for strategies to alleviate them. Life-cycle issues have appeared in constraints research in one or other of two forms. Firstly, some researchers have investigated how constraints are experienced at given life stages, such as adolescence and later life (McGuire, 1984; Hultsman, 1993; Raymore *et al.*, 1994). Others have compared the constraints experienced by different age groups or people at different life stages (Witt and Goodale, 1981; Buchanan and Allen, 1985; Searle and Jackson, 1985; McGuire *et al.*, 1986). Together, these lines of research indicate that constraints are not experienced in the same way by people of different ages. Other authors have added gender as a mediating variable (Jackson and Henderson, 1995; Scott and Jackson, 1996). Raymore *et al.* (1994), Henderson *et al.* (1995), and Alexandris and Carrol (1997) have indicated that females are more constrained than males in their leisure behaviour.

Recent studies have supported the view that constraints do not work in isolation. Rather, constraints appear to be interrelated and thus can be evaluated in the context of underlying dimensions. Jackson (1993) identified six dimensions that represented commonalities found in previous studies. These he labelled as social isolation, accessibility, personal reasons, cost, time commitments, and facilities. Jackson suggests that the analysis of dimensionality of constraints is often more reliable than focusing on individual constraints, because the latter may be affected by the way that data are collected or by the wording used.

Constraints facing existing participants

Although most constraints research has focused on non-participants, some authors have expanded categories to include differences among participants exhibiting different levels of participation frequency and interest. Wright and Goodale (1991) recognize that participants can also be constrained, not from participating, but from participating as frequently as they desire. Shaw *et al.* (1991) tested the relationship between reported constraints and participation, and found little support for the hypothesis that reported constraints are associated with low levels of participation. On the contrary, many of the constraints were shown to have positive rather than negative relationships with participation.

Aas (1995), in a study on constraints to fishing, also found that participants reported stronger constraints than non-participants. In another study, Kay and Jackson (1991) also found contradictions between assumptions of how constraints affect participation and what people actually report. They suggested that these contradictions may be due to different levels of aspiration, or the presence of frustrated aspiration. Shaw *et al.* (1991) believe that a more plausible explanation could be that constraints may exist which researchers have not asked about, and/ or that constraints exist which people do not recognize as such.

Negotiation of Leisure Constraints

More recently, the concept of constraints negotiation has been introduced (Crawford and Godbey, 1987; Crawford *et al.*, 1991; Jackson *et al.*, 1993). Crawford *et al.* (1991) proposed that individuals who participate in a given leisure pursuit might have successfully negotiated a sequential or hierarchical series of constraints, whereas individuals who do not participate have experienced constraints that might have occurred at any one of several stages.

The Crawford *et al.* model, shown in Fig. 8.3, contains a clearly defined hierarchy of constraints, beginning with those that affect preferences and leading to those that affect participation. Each level of constraint must be overcome in order for an individual to face the subsequent level of constraint.

The first level of constraints is intrapersonal. Intrapersonal constraints involve individual psychological states and attributes which interact with leisure preferences rather than intervening between preferences and participation. Examples include stress, depression, religiosity, anxiety, perceived self-skill, and subject evaluations of the appropriateness of various leisure activities. Leisure preferences are formed following the negotiation or absence of intrapersonal constraints. The next stage of interpersonal constraints occurs as a result of interaction or the relationship between individuals' characteristics. For example, individuals may experience an interpersonal constraint if they are unable to find a partner or friends to participate with. Finally, once interpersonal constraints have been overcome, an individual may face structural constraints, the type of constraint that has received most attention in previous constraints research. Structural constraints are those 'intervening factors between leisure preference and participation' (Crawford and Godbey, 1987). Examples are economic barriers, availability of time, access and opportunity.

In explaining this hierarchy, Crawford *et al.* (1991) contended that there are psychological orientations that may prevent individuals from experiencing higher-level constraints. Therefore, individuals who are most affected by intrapersonal constraints would be less likely to want to participate in a given leisure activity and therefore would not reach higher-order constraints (interpersonal and structural constraints). If this hypothesis is valid then previous studies that have eliminated subjects from consideration because of 'lack of interest' have excluded individuals who were faced with intrapersonal constraints.

The negotiation model certainly changes the face of leisure constraints research. If negotiation rather than non-participation constitutes the dominant response to leisure constraints, then it is not surprising that some researchers have found no relationship between the reporting of some constraints and actual leisure participation (Kay and Jackson, 1991) and even a positive relationship in one study (Shaw *et al.*, 1991). Jackson *et al.* (1993) believe that such findings prove that people frequently respond to constraints actively, by negotiation, rather than passively, by non-participation.

It is clear from the literature review that constraints on leisure have received increasing attention from academics. However, the majority of previous literature on leisure constraints has examined structural constraints (those intervening factors between leisure preference and participation), whereas intrapersonal constraints have largely been ignored. Often, individuals with intrapersonal constraints have been labelled with a lack of interest and given no further consideration. Many authors have acknowledged that lack of interest may well mask more deep-seated constraints on participation (Jackson and Dunn, 1988; Boothby *et al.*, 1981), and others have called for further investigation into factors responsible for the apparent lack of interest amongst non-participants (Jackson *et al.*, 1993; Iso-Ahola *et al.*, 1994).

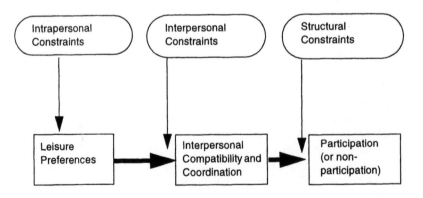

Figure 8.3 A hierarchical model of leisure constraints (Crawford *et al.*, 1991).

For much of this research, quantitative methods have dominated, and if qualitative methods are used, then they are typically reduced to help create and pose hypotheses which can then be tested and refined using statistical research methods and models. A conceptual, methodological and managerial challenge is to better understand constraints among low-interest or uninterested non-participants, because these groups are often a large part of the total population. For these groups, long lists of constraints have little meaning. Therefore, alternative methodological and theoretical approaches are needed.

As Jackson *et al.* (1993) have pointed out, the concept of negotiation lends further support to a conclusion reached by other constraints researchers, that the most apparent avenue for future research regarding leisure constraints involves the operationalization and simultaneous investigation of all three constraint levels – intrapersonal, interpersonal, and structural – if a complete picture of the nature and operation of leisure constraints is to be achieved. The latest theory of constraints negotiation takes into account intrapersonal constraints, and already researchers have adopted its principles in their studies on leisure constraints (Raymore *et al.*, 1993; Henderson *et al.*, 1995; Jackson and Rucks, 1995). However, the hierarchical model proposed by Crawford *et al.* (1991) requires further empirical verification.

Another area that appears to have been neglected is the constraints facing existing participants. Most researchers appear to be in agreement that participants as well as non-participants face constraints, and that they negotiate through these constraints. However, how the two groups differ in types of constraint requires further clarification. Blazey (1987) points out that the published research which examines differences between participants and non-participants in travel programmes is virtually non-existent.

Objectives

The objectives of this study are two-fold. Firstly, on purely theoretical grounds, the authors intend to operationalize the negotiation model proposed by Crawford *et al.* (1991) and to investigate the constraints to skiing. In addition, the authors intend to further this field of research by comparing the constraints of high-potential non-participants with the constraints of existing participants. Some recent studies have inferred that reported constraints do not always prevent participation (Kay and Jackson, 1991). It is therefore possible that loyal skiers have the same constraints as non-skiers, but still ski. This could have important implications for the industry.

The second objective is to gain a stronger understanding of high-potential non-skiers, with respect to what factors might heighten their interest and willingness to participate in skiing; what constraints have repressed their previous involvement; and what incentives and promotional messages might influence their future levels of skiing.

Methodology

A qualitative approach was used in order to operationalize the model in Fig. 8.3. Consumer behaviourists are increasingly embracing qualitative techniques and models in order to deal with relevant topics in meaningful and pragmatic ways (Walle, 1997). The authors felt that formal research methods could not pursue some of the deeper issues involved in understanding constraints to tourist behaviour. Both in-depth individual interviews and focus groups were used at this stage. Three focus groups with groups of non-skiers preceded the in-depth interviews, with each group made up of 10 members of the chosen sample. Conversations were taped and transcribed, and were captured on video for later interpretation.

Since the focus of the study was on high-potential non-skiers as well as existing skiers, the sample was taken from a membership listing of a health club chain in the south of England called Dragons. They attract mainly young, affluent, health-conscious men and women. ACORN profiles for each of the clubs were obtained by the authors, along with demographic details for the clubs, and these were compared to the demographics provided by Mintel (1996) for regular skiers and non-skiers, and also compared to the profile of a skier as suggested by Greer (1990) and *Precision Marketing* (Anon., 1993). A close correlation was found. Thirty in-depth interviews were undertaken and questions designed to allow skiers and non-skiers to talk about their leisure, and to provide insights into what constraints prevented their participation (or further participation) in the activity of skiing. The majority of interviews lasted between 40 and 55 minutes. Interviews were tape-recorded and transcribed for analysis.

The questions followed a semi-structured approach. A few main concepts were explored with all informants; however, wording of questions, ordering of questions, and questions regarding related concepts remained flexible. Broad areas of grounded theoretical interest, developed through prior data collection and analysis (focus groups and previous interviews), provided the basis for interview questions. For example, in the focus groups a pervasive theme that arose was that non-skiers felt different from skiers, who they believed were 'elitist', 'poseurs', 'materialistic' and 'ski bores'. This theme was addressed with all informants. A typical question which probed this theme was: What are your feelings about skiers themselves, and have these feelings prevented you from considering taking up the sport?

For the non-skier, the original interview guide included such questions as: What prevents you from doing all the things you'd really like to do?; What do you like to do for fun?; Have you ever considered going on a skiing holiday?; Do you have friends who ski?; What are your images of a skiing holiday?; Do you think you will ski in the future?; How could you be persuaded to take a skiing holiday? These questions were modified and enlarged as the data were collected. The latter part of the interview included more specific questions about how non-skiers were constrained from skiing, along with initial conclusions about how they could negotiate these constraints.

For existing skiers, the interview guide included such questions as: How were you first introduced to the sport?; Did your original perceptions of skiing match up with reality?; How many times have you been since?; Who do you normally go with?; What are your motivations when going on a skiing holiday?; Would you like to ski more often, and if so, what prevents you from doing so?; If these barriers were removed how often would you go? Interviewees were also asked if they had close friends or family who did not ski, and why this was the case.

Findings

Data analysis was done using the constant comparison technique (Glaser and Strauss, 1967) which is a systematic method for recording, coding, and analysing data. Constant comparison involved reading all the transcripts to develop a broad understanding of the content. The data were coded to reflect the major constraints, and categorized according to the hierarchy proposed by Crawford *et al.* (1991). This involved deciding whether the constraints were intrapersonal, interpersonal or structural. The focus groups were also analysed in this way, but in addition, the videos were scrutinized for significant body signals such as facial expressions during the discussions. The respondents' interpretations of the photographs given to them were also coded and categorized according to the constraints model. For example, one of the photographs (originally an advertisement for ski clothing), had a picture of two skiers on a chair lift, one smiling and enjoying herself, and the other looking very miserable and cold. Many of the respondents identified with the latter character, indicating that this was their image of the sport. These same people were likely to view the picture of a ski school as regimented and intimidating, as opposed to having fun with others.

Overall, the qualitative research provided interesting results. Non-skiers in particular revealed a surprising number of intrapersonal constraints, perhaps the 'hidden' constraints referred to earlier. They perceived skiing to be harder to learn than other sports, and suggested that they would feel self-conscious or embarrassed learning to ski. They also thought the activity would make them cold and wet, and that it would be dangerous, expensive, and too stressful. There was the feeling that skiing is an elitist sport, and that they were not 'chic and glamorous enough' to go. In fact, it was ascertained that non-skiers viewed themselves to be different from skiers. As in previous focus-group studies on non-skiers (Williams and Lattey, 1994), focus-group participants perceived that the literature promoting skiing portrayed the activity as being competitive, risk-taking and fashion-focused. Skiers, on the other hand, revealed in the interviews that they were mainly constrained by time, family or economic factors. Family constraints included the fact that the respondents' partners were often not interested in the sport.

A list of 30 constraints was developed directly from the results of the in-depth interviews and focus groups, and these have been abbreviated for the constraints model in Fig. 8.4.

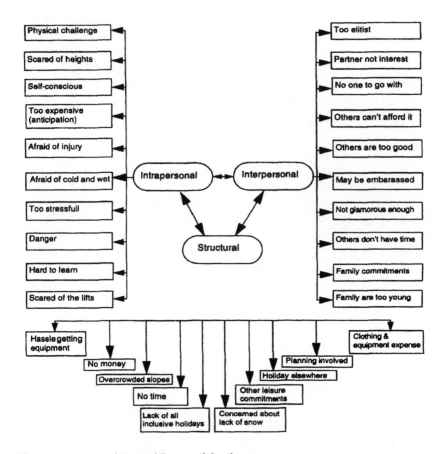

Figure 8.4 Constraints to skiing participation.

The results of this study provide guidance for the ski industry in strategy development. Perhaps the most important finding is that different constraints inhibit participants and non-participants, and therefore different strategies should be implemented for each group in order to increase participation. For the non-skier, changing preconceived attitudes requires education. Education has been cited as one of the most powerful influences on travel behaviour, and this includes information through advertising and use of the media. It may not be possible to overcome one's fear of heights, lack of desire for physical challenge, or being afraid of learning a new sport. However, it is clear that the decision to ski or not is income-sensitive, and creative marketers can influence travel behaviour by increasing the perceived income of the market or by reducing its influence through establishment of a sense of value and purchasing power in the minds of potential consumers.

For existing skiers, or those who have dropped out of the sport, rather than playing down the expense of the sport, promotion should state that it is an expensive activity, but remind skiers that the sport brings an emotional well-being worth the cost. Skiers are also concerned about the lack of snow, and over-crowded ski slopes, and destinations will have to adopt strategies to deal with these problems, by investing in snow-making equipment and applying capacity management techniques.

Conclusions

This paper has argued that the study of tourist consumer behaviour should not only seek to understand the choice processes of tourists, but should endeavour to comprehend the range of constraints preventing non-tourists from becoming tourists. In all of the models explaining consumer behaviour, people with a lack of motivation are ignored, typologies do not include the non-participant or non-user, and the models do not take into account the wide range of constraints facing consumers in the decision-making process. All of the models of consumer behaviour in tourism assume that purchase is the outcome, and there is no reference to the negotiation of constraints. This lack of research into the non-user and the associated constraints represents an important gap in consumer behaviour research. Non-users may represent a significant marketing opportunity, and with increased application of marketing research to understanding the motivations of different segments, greater success in converting non-users to users should occur in the future.

Although the majority of constraints research has concentrated on constraints to leisure participation in general, some studies have focused on particular tourist activities such as camping (Dunn, 1990), walking (Bialeschki and Henderson, 1988), and visiting museums (Davies and Prentice, 1995). However, such studies are scarce, and there is an opportunity for market development to be gained by broadening the customer profile and attracting more potential customers at present only latent in the customer profile of tourist organizations. Such research could focus on the accommodation sector, for example, and attempt to discover why certain people choose not to stay in hotels when they travel. Alternatively, understanding why people do not use particular methods of transport would be of interest to the transport sector.

On a broader scale, instead of continuing to try and understand why so many millions choose to go on package holidays each year, why not ask the people who do not go, why they choose not to? Similar questions could be asked of those who do not purchase niche tourism products such as safaris, golfing and sailing holidays, and educational tours. For many tourism products, such as skiing, demand has matured, and although growth via acquisition may satisfy the ever-demanding expectations of stakeholders in the short term, success for many tourist organizations in the long term could depend on converting non-users to users.

In this particular study, a qualitative approach was used in order to operationalize the negotiation model of leisure constraints. Distinct differences in constraints were found between participants and non-participants, especially for intrapersonal constraints. A logical extension of this study would be to test the model empirically on a larger sample, firstly, to establish the three types of constraint – intrapersonal, interpersonal and structural – as separate classes of constraint on skiing; and secondly, to test the existence of the proposed hierarchy on a specific tourism activity.

References

Aas, O. (1995) Constraints on Sportfishing and Effect of Management Actions to Increase Participation Rates in Fishing. *North American Journal of Fisheries Management* 15, 631–638.

Alexandris, K. and Carrol, B. (1997) Demographic differences in the perception of constraints on recreational sport participation: results from a study in Greece. *Leisure Studies* 16, 107–125.

Anon. (1993) Portrait of a skiing enthusiast. *Precision Marketing* 15 February, 8.

Backman, S.J. and Crompton, J.L. (1990) Differentiating between active and passive discontinuers of two leisure activities. *Journal of Leisure Research* 22, 197–212.

Bialeschki, M.D. and Henderson, K.A. (1988) Constraints to trail use. *Journal of Park and Recreation Administration* 6, 20–28.

Blazey, M.A. (1987) The difference between participants and non-participants in a senior travel programme. *Journal of Travel Research* 26, 7–12.

Boothby, J., Tungatt, M.F. and Townsend, A.R. (1981) Ceasing participation in sports activity: reported reasons and their implications. *Journal of Leisure Research* 13, 1–14.

Buchanan, T. and Allen, L. (1985) Barriers to recreation participation in later life cycle stages. *Therapeutic Recreation Journal* 19, 39–50.

Burkart, A.J. and Medlik, S. (1974) *Tourism: Past, Present, Future*. London: Heinemann.

Chick, G. and Roberts, J.M. (1989) Leisure and antileisure in game play. *Leisure Sciences* 11, 73–84.

Cooper, C., Fletcher, J., Gilbert, D. and Wanhill, S. (1993) *Tourism: Principles and Practice*. London: Pitman.

Crawford, D.W. and Godbey, G. (1987) Reconceptualising barriers to family leisure. *Leisure Sciences* 9, 119–127.

Crawford, D.W., Jackson, E.L. and Godbey, G. (1991) A hierarchical model of leisure constraints. *Leisure Sciences* 13, 309–320.

Davies, A. and Prentice, R. (1995) Conceptualising the latent visitor to heritage attractions. Tourism Management 16, 491–500.

Dunn, E. (1990) Temporary and permanent constraints on participation in camping. In: B.J.A. Smale (ed.) *Leisure Challenges: Bringing People, Resources and Policy into Play – Proceedings of the Sixth Canadian Congress on Leisure Research*. Toronto: Ontario Research Council on Leisure, pp. 360–363.

Evans, M.J., Moutinho, L. and Van Raaij, W.F. (1996) *Applied Consumer Behaviour*. Cornwall: Addison-Wesley.

Gilbert, D.C. (1991) An examination of the consumer behaviour process related to tourism. In: C. Cooper (ed.) *Progress in Tourism, Recreation and Hospitality Management*, Vol. 3. London: Belhaven Press, pp. 78–105.

Glaser, B.G. and Strauss, A.L. (1967) *The Discovery of Grounded Theory: Strategies for Qualitative Research*. Chicago: Aldine.

Greer, S. (1990) Snow business. *Leisure Management* 10, 34–35.

Haukeland, J.V. (1990) Non-travellers. The flip side of motivation. *Annals of Tourism Research* 17, 172–184.

Hawkins, D.E., Shafer, E.L. and Rovelstad, J.M. (eds) (1980) *Tourism Planning and Development Issues*. Washington: George Washington University.

Henderson, K.A., Bedini, L.A., Hecht, L. and Schuler, R. (1995) Women with physical disabilities and the negotiation of leisure constraints. *Leisure Studies* 14, 17–31.

Hodgson, A. (ed.) (1987) *The Travel and Tourism Industry*. Oxford: Pergamon.

Holloway, J.C. (1990) *The Business of Tourism*. Plymouth: MacDonald & Evans.

Holloway, J.C. and Plant, R.V. (1988) *Marketing for Tourism: A Practical Guide*. Harlow: Longman.

Horner, S. and Swarbrooke, J. (1996) *Marketing Tourism, Hospitality and Leisure in Europe*. Oxford: Thomson.

Howard, J.A. and Sheth, J.N. (1969) *The Theory of Buyer Behaviour*. New York: Wiley.

Hultsman, W.Z. (1993) Is constrained leisure an internally homogeneous concept? An extension. *Journal of Leisure Research* 25, 215–334.

Iso-Ahola, S.E., Jackson, E. and Dunn, E. (1994) Starting, ceasing and replacing leisure activities over the life-span. *Journal of Leisure Research* 26, 227–249.

Jackson, E.L. (1988) Leisure constraints: a survey of past research. *Leisure Sciences* 10, 203–215.

Jackson, E.L. (1993) Recognising patterns of leisure constraints: results from alternative analysis. *Journal of Leisure Research* 25, 129–149.

Jackson, E.L. and Dunn, E. (1988) Integrating ceasing participation with other aspects of leisure behaviour. *Journal of Leisure Research* 20, 31–45.

Jackson, E.L. and Henderson, K. (1995) Gender-based analysis of leisure constraints. *Leisure Sciences* 17, 31–51.

Jackson, E.L. and Rucks, V.C. (1995) Negotiation of leisure constraints by junior-high and high-school students: an exploratory study. *Journal of Leisure Research* 27, 85–105.

Jackson, E.L., Crawford, D.W. and Godbey, G. (1993) Negotiation of leisure constraints. *Leisure Sciences* 15, 1–11.

Jefferson, A. and Lickorish, L. (1988) *Marketing Tourism: A Practical Guide*. Harlow: Longman.

Kay, T. and Jackson, G. (1991) Leisure despite constraint: the impact of leisure constraints on leisure participation. *Journal of Leisure Research* 23, 301–313.

Loudon, D.L. and Della Bitta, A.J. (1993) *Consumer Behaviour. Concepts and Applications*. London: McGraw-Hill.

Lundberg, D.E. (1989) *The Tourism Business*, 6th edn. New York: Van Nostrand Reinhold.

Mathieson, A. and Wall, G. (1982) *Tourism: Economic, Physical and Social Impacts*. Harlow: Longman.

Mayo, E. and Jarvis, L. (1981) *The Psychology of Leisure Travel*. Boston: CBI Publishing.

McGuire, F.A. (1984) A factor analytic study of leisure constraints in advanced adulthood. *Leisure Sciences* 6, 313–326.

McGuire, F.A., Dottavio, D. and O'Leary, J.T. (1986) constraints to participation in outdoor recreation across the life span: a nationwide study of limitors and prohibitors. *Gerontologist* 26, 538–544.

McGuire, F.A., Yeh, C., O'Leary, J.T. and Dottavio, F.D. (1989) Integrating ceasing participation with other aspects of leisure behaviour: a replication and extension. *Journal of Leisure Research* 21, 316–326.

Middleton, V.T.C. (1988) *Marketing in Travel and Tourism.* London: Heinemann.

Mintel (1996) *Snowsports.* June. London: Mintel International Group, pp. 1–35.

Nicosia, F.M. (1966) *Consumer Decision Process: Marketing and Advertising Implications.* Englewood Cliffs: Prentice Hall.

Norman, W. (1995) Perceived constraints: a new approach to segmenting the vacation travel market. Paper presented at the NRPA Symposium on Leisure Research, San Antonio, Texas.

Plog, S.C. (1974) Why destination areas rise and fall in popularity. *Cornell Hotel and Restaurant Quarterly* 14, 55–58.

Raymore, L., Godbey, G., Crawford, D. and von Eye, A. (1993) Nature and process of leisure constraints: an empirical test. *Leisure Sciences* 15, 99–113.

Raymore, L.A., Godbey, G.C. and Crawford, D.W. (1994) Self-esteem, gender and socioeconomic status: their relation to perception of constraints on leisure among adolescents. *Journal of Leisure Research* 26, 99–118.

Robinson, T.T. and Carron, A.V. (1982) Personal and situational factors associated with dropping out versus maintaining participation in competitive sport. *Journal of Sport Psychology* 4, 364–378.

Romsa, G. and Hoffman, W. (1980) An application of nonparticipation data in recreation research: testing the opportunity theory. *Journal of Leisure Research* 12, 321–328.

Schmoll, G.A. (1977) *Tourism Promotion.* London: Tourism International Press.

Scott, D. and Jackson, E.L. (1996) Factors that limit and strategies that might encourage people's use of public parks. *Journal of Park and Recreation Administration* 14, 1–17.

Searle, M.S. and Jackson, E.L. (1985) Socioeconomic variations in perceived barriers to recreation participation among would–be participants. *Leisure Sciences* 7, 227–249.

Shaw, S.M., Bonen, A. and McCabe, J.F. (1991) Do more constraints mean less leisure? Examining the relationship between constraints and participation. *Journal of Leisure Research* 23, 286–300.

Stemerding, M.P., Oppewal, H., Beckers, T.A.M. and Timmermans, H.J.P. (1996) Leisure market segmentation: an integrated preferences/constraints-based approach. *Journal of Travel and Tourism Marketing* 5, 161–185.

Wahab, S., Crampon, L.J. and Rothfield, L.M. (1976) *Tourism Marketing.* London: Tourism International.

Walle, A.H. (1997) Quantitative versus qualitative research. *Annals of Tourism Research* 24, 524–536.

Williams, P.W. and Lattey, C. (1994) Skiing constraints for women. *Journal of Travel Research* 33, 21–25.

Witt, P.A. and Goodale, T.L. (1981) The relationship between barriers to leisure enjoyment and family stages. *Leisure Sciences* 4, 29–49.

Witt, S.F. and Moutinho, L. (eds) (1994) *Tourism Marketing Management Handbook*, 2nd edn. Hemel Hempstead: Prentice-Hall International.

Wright, B.A. and Goodale, T.L. (1991) Beyond non-participation: validation of interest and frequency of participation categories in constraints research. *Journal of Leisure Research* 23, 314–331.

Chapter nine
The Relationship Between Emotions, Mood and Motivation to Travel: Towards a Cross-Cultural Measurement of Flow

Jürgen Gnoth
Department of Marketing, University of Otago, PO Box 56, Dunedin, New Zealand

Andreas Zins
Institute for Tourism and Leisure Studies of the Vienna University of Economics and Business Administration, Augasse 2-6, 1090 Vienna, Austria

Ruediger Lengmueller
Department of Marketing, University of Otago, PO Box 56, Dunedin, New Zealand

Christo Boshoff
Department of Business Management, University of Port Elizabeth, PO Box 1600, Port Elizabeth 6000, South Africa

Introduction

Tourism motivation research (see e.g. Iso-Ahola, 1982; Fodness, 1994) has hitherto taken a strongly cognitive approach that matches mainstream achievement-motivation research (see Heckhausen, 1989 for a synopsis). However, the realization of the need for recreation and travel is an awareness of an affective state usually signalling physical and/or mental exhaustion, and/or social needs such as recognition or inclusion (Mundt and Lohmann, 1988). The need can also come about through a realization of curiosity for certain experiences. Both types of need are often linked with the habitualized opportunity to travel (Krippendorf, 1987), and usually follow the two basic movements of any organism. These can be classified according to either avoidance or approach behaviour. In tourism, the two behavioural directions are mostly described as escape from situations that bring such motivations about, or as a search for something new or an otherwise fulfilling experience that current situations do not afford (e.g. Iso-Ahola, 1982). Common to both of these directions is that they are triggered or accompanied by feelings.

To date, individual feelings have received little attention in tourism research (Floyd, 1997; Arnould and Price, 1993; Celsi *et al.*, 1993) and mostly have been treated as compounds. As such they have been discussed in the form of moods that underlie the need for recreation (Ragheb and Beard, 1982; Mundt and Lohmann, 1988), and are also contained in concepts surrounding 'flow' (Csikszentmihalyi, 1975) or in the theory of static versus dynamic orientation (Wicklund, 1986; Braun, 1989). Yet the relationship between these constructs and their relationship to individual emotions deserves ongoing attention, as this can form a platform for improving our understanding of motivations and consumption experiences.

Emotions

Frijda (1986) maintains that there is no generally held definition of emotions. This is due to the difficulty of observing all aspects of the instantiation or generation, expression and effect of emotions. There are feelings, terms (e.g. joy, anger) and verbal expressions (e.g. groaning) as well as metaphors for emotions (e.g. 'she is cold as ice'; Koevecses, 1995); all describing or expressing inherent motivational forces. The feeling of 'being stressed out', for example, thus motivates an inner-directed period of relaxation and often the removal of that person from the source of stress. How we spend the time to relax and how we choose to remove ourselves from work, whether mentally and/or physically such as through pursuing recreational activities or travel, differs from person to person. In general, emotions are a motivational force much older than cognitions and are part of a set of innate drives that serve the survival of organisms.

Tomkins (1962) suggests distinguishing between a basic drive system that signals needs through feelings of pain, for example, and an affective system that enforces these feelings in a way that they generate preferences and dislikes. Affect is an independent system from that of drives and can attach itself to a variety of stimuli. Whereas drives are unidimensional and basic, affect is complex and flexible. A person can learn to associate certain feelings with a variety of stimuli that have an effect which is either liked or disliked, that is, they have an affective consequence. The distinction between these two systems (drive and affect) helps explain differences in actions and reactions between individuals, groups of people and cultures, as the actual experience always implies situational parameters that differ from person to person, situations and (cultural) environments (Averill, 1982; Lazarus, 1991).

Scherer *et al.* (1986) conducted a cross-cultural study into the antecedents of emotions. While these authors expressed astonishment about the similarity of antecedents that caused certain emotions to occur and the similarities of expressions that followed, they also found differences between the eight (mostly European) nationalities they studied. These researchers focused on antecedents and a very small set of emotions – joy, sadness, anger and fear. Their reasons for these four were (i) because they appeared to be the most basic and universal; (ii) because others might be far more dependent on cultural interpretations, and (iii) for methodological reasons.

Despite Frijda (1986) and examples of widely differing expressions and understandings as to the nature of some emotions (e.g. Averill, 1982), there appears to be some consensus about which semantic categories are involved when discussing emotions. Thus we find basic and very similar sets of discrete emotions amongst common psychological emotion theories (Tomkins, 1962; Izard, 1977a; Plutchik, 1980; Scherer *et al.*, 1986). Plutchik (1980) proposes a set of eight basic emotions (joy, acceptance, fear, surprise, sadness, anger, disgust and expectancy). Their relationship to each other can be characterized according to levels of contiguity and opposition. Positioned in the shape of a circle, fear and anger are thus opposite to each other, whereas anger and disgust are more closely related and are located beside each other. While basic emotions can be regarded as distinct, Plutchik suggests that all other emotions are compounds or complex ones made up of at least two of the basic emotions. Accordingly, the contiguous emotions of anger and disgust form contempt, whereas the opposing basic emotions of fear and acceptance generate submission (Plutchik, 1980).

Izard (1977a) theorizes that there are prototypical emotions valid for all people across all cultures and 'part of the biological make-up of human beings' (1977b, p. 503). Accordingly, all humans are capable of experiencing at least ten basic emotions (interest, joy, anger, disgust, contempt, distress, anxiety, fear, shame and guilt). While there are variations in expressions and intensity across cultures, the set of emotions has proved useful in cross-cultural research.

The small number of basic emotions poses a problem for the needs of tourism management. In this context, the emotional terms mentioned so far hardly reflect the spectrum of experiences tourists feel before, during and after their voyages away from home. As a consequence, the limited number of terms, as well as their stark differentiation leave us with only a broad system. This system does not appear to match the levels of differentiation and sophistication tourists like to find themselves in, or situations that tourism facilitators like to provide.

Unlike approaches that try to distinguish discrete emotions, de Rivera (1977) maintains that 'an emotion exists, whenever a person is moved – whenever his relation to the world is transformed' (1977, p. 45). This stance differs from previous ones as it expressly includes relevant aspects of the environment. Accepting this socio-psychologically framed definition could help differentiate a person's relationship to the environment more subtly and would permit a much larger number of terms that express emotions. It would offer a basis from which we could differentiate complex emotions on the basis of the feeling person's relationship to the object of the emotion.

Analysing the transformation would thus result in two distinct sets of questions. Firstly, does an object induce the person to change (e.g. a dangerous situation induces fear), or does the person change due to his/her perception of an object (e.g. a person is sentimentally attracted to a scenery)? Secondly, does the emotion indicate a person's movement towards or away from the object (e.g. love versus fear; here the self moves) or, is the emotion indicating a movement of the object toward or away from the self (e.g. desire versus anger; here the object is moved)? Emotions can therefore be described as either self- or outer-directed, and contain information about a person's movement toward or away from an object. If any emotion persists, we often use the term mood to describe a more lingering emotional influence.

Moods

Feelings can be understood as physiological sensations and representations of emotions. Emotions signal a state of need preparing for certain tendencies to act (Izard, 1991), and/or they help create a state of tension that compels a person to act and remove that state (Lewin, 1942). Over time, when needs (as indicated by emotions) are not satisfied and tensions are not released, they accumulate (Behm, 1924; Mundt and Lohmann, 1988); a person may therefore feel easily tired, distracted or annoyed. When a person appears to behave accordingly over longer periods of time but is not usually known for it, we commonly say that the person's mood has changed. Travel is often seen as a suitable means of recreation and stimulation that alters such moods and helps reinstate a person to their desired self. A definitive relationship between emotions and moods has, however, not been established as yet. Indeed, moods have been treated as having no (Forgas, 1992, 1994) or unknown (Pieters and van Raaij, 1988) antecedent causes, while a recent literature review suggests that emotions can be seen as reactions whereas moods can be treated as both states and reactions (Luomala and Laaksonen, 1998). Although we offered a pre-scientific, popular notion of mood, it is difficult to determine whether individual emotions differ substantially from moods and whether moods can be described to any degree of sophistication. More detailed descriptions, however, would foster an understanding of needs and motivations as well as differentiating complex emotions that are hitherto still somewhat hazy and unspecified (for a compilation of the partly contradictory conceptualization and empirical results see Hibbert, 1998; Luomala and Laaksonen, 1998).

Moods have been described as complex affective states (Dunegan *et al.*, 1992) without a specific target (Groenland and Schoormans, 1994) that are pervasive in their effect (Morris and Reilly, 1987). Also, moods are less intense than emotions 'and tend not to disrupt ongoing activity' (Kraiger *et al.*, 1989, p. 13). They are transient (Zajonc and Marcus, 1984; Gardner, 1985; Smith *et al.*, 1993), yet compared to emotions they are 'relatively enduring... [and] have little cognitive content' (Forgas, 1994, p. 3). Consequently, mood measurements appear relatively unsophisticated with simple scales that are anchored by feeling good versus feeling bad, or feeling happy versus feeling sad. Other techniques use simple face drawings expressing differing emotions. Moods are known to influence perception and can be subject to mood-induction techniques (e.g. Petty *et al.*, 1993; Erber and Erber, 1994) that have found their way into consumer research (Gardner, 1985; Lutz, 1985).

Another cognitive school of thought that approaches the general subject area of moods derives from Lewin's (1942) ideas surrounding the concept of tension that is created in situations of a person feeling a need. Tension motivates a person to act. However, the interpretation of the environment and the type of action that ensues depends on the prevalent mood. Accordingly, the person is either statically or dynamically orientated.

Static versus Dynamic Orientation

From the research mentioned above, it can be assumed that the pervasiveness of a mood means, generally, that a person's attitude to any stimulus is affected by that mood. In other words, when a person feels exhausted and tired, lacking energy and concentration, instead of looking outwards, responding to and being interested in a variety of things, the person tends to look inward and is often considered indifferent or slow to respond (compare e.g. the empirical results of Cunningham, 1988). Wicklund (1986), following Lewin (1942), interprets such situations as ones that generate tensions within a person's mind, and these would be considered as statically orientated. Conversely, a person in harmony with the environment (or in a good mood) would express a dynamic orientation while being motivated to achieve.

The characteristics of a person with dynamic orientation are usually that he or she would be open to challenges and show an interest in problem-solving tasks, whereas a statically orientated person would shy away from such tasks, feeling unsure of their capabilities. Wicklund (1986) demonstrates how static orientation makes a person think about his or her lack of skills and often evaluates their capabilities as being lower than people with a dynamic orientation (see also Wicklund and Gollwitzer, 1981). In this sense, holidays could offer both types, either the challenges required to live out dynamic orientation or, in the case of static orientation, holidays could offer the environment that restores security and self-esteem.

As cognitivists, the above psychologists are interested in how the different orientations impact on cognitive achievement motivation and problem-solving behaviour, yet they reveal little or nothing about subjects' emotional states and the underlying characteristics of emotions that exist between a subject and the objects he/she is surrounded by. Most importantly, the orientations are said to occur only if a person is under the influence of such tensions. There is evidence that statically orientated persons tend to rebuild their tarnished self-esteem through activities that perform a symbolic function, replenishing that lack of self esteem (Wicklund and Gollwitzer, 1981). Holidays can easily allow such symbolic functions to come into play, for the tourist has time, money and choice. Yet we know little about the quality of the underlying feelings and emotions as antecedents to a tarnished self-esteem, and the resultant mood. These latter researchers assume that statically oriented persons tend to 'imbue' objects with a symbolic value that, through their acquisition (e.g. a ticket to a destination or a souvenir) or their mastery (learning a new skill; Braun, 1989), assist in 'completing the self' again

(Wicklund and Gollwitzer, 1981). It must be assumed that some objects are more successful than others in fulfilling this task. In this sense, orientations would have implications for decision and choice behaviour as well as for resource management when related to tourism.

For example, Friederichs (1985) details how search in choice and buying behaviour is always subject to emotional influences. Low levels of goal orientation accompanied by low interest levels (called stimulus situation) can have even trivial stimuli (called trigger stimuli) causing attention to occur. Contradicting the assumptions of rational and linear decision-making models (e.g. Engel *et al.*, 1968; Howard and Sheth, 1969), Friederichs maintains that both the triggering stimulus and the stimulus situation – which here include the prevalent mood – need to be considered. Their influence on individual aspects of behaviour as well as behaviour as a whole, encompasses both the evaluation of object attributes as well as levels of achievement aspirations (Weiner, 1976). Both interact with each other and with the prevailing mood. In other words, destination choice, for example, is not necessarily influenced by whether the tourist speaks the local language, but by his attitude toward the challenge it presents to find ways of communicating despite such an initial barrier. Neither should any other step in the decision-making process be necessarily presumed as rational.

Incidentally, Braun (1989) points to obvious similarities between the dynamic orientation and Csikszentmihalyi's (1975) theory of 'flow' in the context of skills and challenges. He notes that those who are dynamically orientated and those in flow are both in optimal harmony with their environment, their attention is directed towards their environment, and their skills are at a level that allows them to react in an adequate and competent manner.

The Characteristics of Flow

Csikszentmihalyi (1990, p. 17) regards humans' search for pleasure as a reflex response 'built into our genes for the preservation of the species, not for the purpose of our personal advantage'. Flow is the feeling of such pleasure during a situation of optimal experience. It comes about if the person is engaged in a voluntary activity, not concentrating on the self, and in harmony with their environment. Also, to gain the feeling of flow, the person is involved in and focused upon an activity that is pursued for its intrinsic value. Usually the activity involves a task that forms a challenge, yet the person's skills and these challenges are in balance. If the person encounters and/or creates such conditions he or she experiences flow. Consequently, a person who feels he/she is out of touch with his/her skills and fails to achieve would appear to feel the opposite, a kind of stasis.

We can assume that the goal of holiday facilitators is to assist tourists in achieving an 'optimal experience' as this is the process during which recreation takes place. The occasions that afford the experience of flow do not need to be exceptional. Csikszentmihalyi (1990) details how seemingly nonsensical and unproductive activities have been pursued for their intrinsic challenge throughout the history of mankind to create experiences of flow. Similarly, some tourists can find distraction and challenge in mundane activities such as shopping and thus experience flow. But what are the links between mood, orientation, motivation and flow? While these constructs appear to be related theoretically, are there any indications that they are related in the tourist's mind? And if so, what relationships can we distinguish, and how can we describe them in emotional terms?

The concepts of emotions, mood, static and dynamic orientation and flow discussed thus far all play an important part when trying to explain motivation for travel and tourism behaviour. Upset emotions, persistent negative moods, static orientation and the absence of feelings of flow, all create a sense of disorder, disharmony and tension that force the person to 'battle'. '... the battle is not really against the self, but against the entropy that brings disorder to consciousness. It is really a battle for the self; it is a struggle for control over attention' (Csikszentmihalyi, 1990, p. 41).

We can also assume that a negative state of mind (including feelings) turns the attention towards activities that, subjectively, help restore the self. But which emotions, if distinguishable, are connected to the accompanying mood? If they are distinguishable, strategies for product development and promotion could be developed to help tourists more effectively and in a targeted manner. Likewise, it appears, when a person is in flow and dynamically orientated, the mood is positive. But which emotions can be associated with the accompanying mood? Harking back to the notion of a set of emotions that appear to be common to all humans, is there a chance of determining more subtle emotions across cultures that would help explain the relationship between tourists and objects? When trying to find more subtle ways of describing moods and emotions as antecedents to motivation formation, how can culturally induced influences on perception and motivation formation (Gnoth, 1997) be distinguished?

With the above problem areas in mind, an empirical, cross-cultural study was conducted to explore the following questions:

- what is the relationship between a person's general mood and their feelings toward (e.g.) their skills and the challenges posed by the environment, prior to holidays?
- what is the general relationship between mood, emotions and motivations to travel and expectations?
- where do cross-cultural similarities end and culturally induced differences begin?

Methodology

The particular task of the present study was to investigate the relationship between emotions and moods prior to holidays, and how respondents' level of static versus dynamic orientation as a measurement of the state of flow affect motivations for holidays. Given that going on a holiday is often a necessary activity in order to recover from work and to do those recreational activities that work prevents due to lack of time, respondents needed to be interviewed in relation to their work. Following Csikszentmihalyi (1975), de Rivera (1977), Scherer *et al.* (1986) and Wicklund (1986), respondents needed to be questioned as to (i) their feelings about themselves in relationship to their work (skills and challenges); (ii) how they felt physically; (iii) how they perceived the atmosphere at their place of work as a measure of how that situation affected them, and (iv) how respondents felt in relation to their social environment (henceforth referred to as the four spheres).

In other words, respondents were asked to render an affective appraisal (Russell and Snodgrass, 1987) that involves attributing an affective quality to an object (skills, challenges and perceptions in relation to work). It would thus appear that the appraisal differs from an assessment of mood since it 'refers to a quality of the object appraised' (Russell and Snodgrass, 1987, p. 249; Cohen and Areni, 1990; Kacen, 1994). The present study therefore considers the relationship of affective appraisal to the person's general mood. Furthermore, the relationship of emotions towards work, mood and the motivation to travel will be scrutinized.

For the generation of items, three groups of students at three universities (South Africa $n=33$, Austria $n=28$ and New Zealand $n=95$) were presented with open-ended questions about their feelings regarding the four spheres mentioned above (see also Scherer *et al.*, 1986). Students were also asked what they expected from their holidays and what they intended to do. In addition, these students were given Schwartz's list of value items and their official translations (Schwartz, 1992; Boehnke, 1993) in order to verify different, culturally induced variations in value orientations. The analysis of the values showed a close match between Schwartz's findings regarding the three countries.

The content analysis of the written answers given by the students resulted in long lists of emotional statements regarding the four spheres from which we extracted descriptive adjectives. The latter were then developed into semantic differentials (Osgood *et al.*, 1957) whereby for each differential two adjectives became the anchors of seven-point scales. In addition, the development of the survey instrument included questions regarding demographics, prior types of holidays taken, and a list of motivations and expectations reflecting the particular flavour of the sample. Further items asked students how they felt before their holidays. The resulting questionnaire was then distributed to another sample of the student population at the three universities.

Results

In order to limit demographic variations across the samples of the selected countries, only campus students were invited to participate in this research project. Yet quotas – e.g. for gender, age or occupation – were not specified. As a consequence, the three convenience samples differ significantly in various respects. Students of the New Zealand (NZ, $n=111$) sample were much younger than those of the two other countries. The gender distribution was balanced in the NZ sample, and biased toward females in the South Africa (SA, *n*=100) sample and toward males in the Austria (AU, *n*=218) sample. However, there is no evidence that age and gender, for example, are sufficient indicators for explaining socialization processes and cultural differentiation.

Additional background data about the respondents signified that their living conditions were quite different. The habitat of NZ and AU students was far more characterized by the experience of a large city, whereas the SA students were more familiar with medium sized towns. The socio-economic situation was obviously not directly linked to the age of the respondents. The highest proportion of full-time students was found in the NZ sample, followed by the AU sample; only one-third of the SA respondents identified themselves as students. There was a strong relationship between income level and occupation, with the highest household income among the SA respondents. Of course, different frameworks for social security and income tax systems across the three countries may bias this comparison. Moreover, nothing can be said about the share of the household income that is disposable to the respondent, as no further details about the household structure have been investigated.

Some additional travel-related characteristics were monitored which may be essential when interpreting the stated holiday expectations. Almost every single descriptor (aspects of travel experiences, length of stay, type of destination, travel party) varied across the three countries. Respondents from Austria exhibited the least travel frequency over the past 3 years. However, independent and combined effects of income levels and country did not reveal significant influences on past travel activities. Austria, representing a tiny country geographically, urges travellers – especially young people – to gather their travel experiences from abroad. These circumstances are well reflected in the description of the past travel experience and the particular holiday travel in question. Yet the proportion of respondents qualifying the destination of this holiday as quite a new experience amounted to about 25% for each country. This might be seen as a common filter for harmonizing some of the general holiday expectations. Nevertheless, considering the length of stay (there is no information for the AU sample available) and the type of the travel party, substantial differences existed. Therefore, it can be concluded that the situation – as described by occupation and income levels – as well as the travel experience was extremely different for the three sub-samples.

Respondents were asked to think back to the time before leaving for their last holidays. As the respondents had different occasions to travel for leisure purposes, the elapsed times that were given were quite different from each other. The majority had to remember back from one up to several months. Interestingly, the distribution of the different periods did not vary significantly across the three countries. This helps to minimize the bias of memory effects, at least when comparing effects across countries.

Exploratory validation of the static–dynamic orientation as a measurement of flow

Following the conceptual discussion in the literature section above, the objective was to find consistent indicators which are able to (i) represent fields of challenges in the individual's life, and (ii) describe the status and shape of tension between those challenges and one's own skills and opportunities. The life domain of work was chosen as a major, common factor that influences people's view on life and is itself reflecting one area of personal resources where feelings of self-efficacy may materialize (Morris, 1989). Based on James (1890) and de Rivera (1977), three fields were differentiated that help determine the affective appraisal of work: (i) work with regard to the demanded tasks, the promotional opportunities, and the skills; (ii) atmosphere with regard to the job and the relation to colleagues/superiors; and (iii) social environment with regard to family and friends. Following Thayer's recognition of the role of biological factors in mood determination (Thayer, 1989), an additional domain addressing the physical condition of the individual was distinguished. The physical condition may be associated with each of the three fields, but may be influenced independently by other sources (life domains) as well.

Scales for these emotional domains have been constructed using the rich pool of pairs of semantic differentials generated by the first study (item generation) mentioned above. Factor analyses with principal axis extraction and varimax-rotation were applied for scale purification (Churchill, 1979). Items with loadings below 0.5 or with multiple loadings were eliminated. The particular goal at this stage was to generate the same factor structure for each country. In order to improve on the limited set of basic emotions, but with the reservation that these additional emotions should be cross-culturally valid, the purification reduced the number of variables dramatically. For example, in the case of 'Work' (see Table 9.1), the ten remaining items that make up the three factors were reduced from 29, while the remaining seven items on the 'Atmosphere' scale were reduced from 25. The divergent but nationally coherent factor solutions appearing during the purification stages, as well as a content analysis of the discarded items, support the assumption that many of the discarded items are subject to differences in cultural values and other, possibly situational influences. The emotional scales, their respective scale reliabilities, and factor patterns are documented in Tables 9.1 and 9.2.

Table 9.1 Pattern of the sub-scales constructing the second-order factor static–dynamic orientation compared across three different countries

Sub-scale items	New Zealand	South Africa	Austria
F1 Work: evaluation of self and work	0.85	0.89	0.89
Dissatisfied–satisfied	*0.77*	0.76	*0.86*
Disappointed–successful	*0.77*	*0.82*	0.71
Disillusioned–enchanted	0.69	0.66	*0.86*
Doubtful–self-confident	0.58	*0.76*	0.65
F2 Work: quality of physiological activity	0.82	0.71	0.76
Tense–relaxed	*0.82*	*0.74*	*0.68*
Pressured–calm	0.73	0.66	0.63
Exhausted–rested	*0.64*	*0.52*	*0.65*
F3 Work: potency and drive	0.73	0.72	0.70
Indifferent–eager	0.69	0.70	0.79
Disinterested–interested	0.68	0.50	0.56
Unambitious–ambitious	–	0.75	0.72
F4 Physiological: energy level	0.88	0.77	0.89
Tired–invigorated	0.74	*0.95*	*0.84*
Exhausted–refreshed	0.70	0.56	*0.83*
Empty–full of energy	*0.78*	*0.60*	0.80
Lethargic–energetic	0.79	–	0.72
Tense–relaxed	*0.70*	0.63	0.69
Uncomfortable–comfortable	0.67	–	0.63
Ill–healthy	0.54	–	0.62

Factors and items printed in italics are used to construct the second-order factor of static–dynamic orientation.

Table 9.2 Pattern of the emotional scales for work atmosphere and social interaction compared across three different countries

Emotional scale items	New Zealand	South Africa	Austria
S1 Social: evaluation and response	0.89	0.83	0.80
Hostile–friendly	*0.89*	*0.86*	*0.82*
Annoyed–pleased	*0.79*	0.86	*0.84*
Disinterested–interested	0.72	*0.50*	–
Withdrawn–sociable	0.66	–	–
Envious–generous	0.65	–	–
Unresponsive–responsive	–	–	0.60
Intolerant–tolerant	–	–	0.57
S2 Social: participation (activity)	0.85	0.76	–
Intolerant–tolerant	*0.76*	*0.65*	–
Grumpy–good-natured	*0.69*	–	–
Inattentive–attentive	0.62	–	–
Irritated–pleased	0.60	*0.77*	–
Jealous–faithful	–	0.62	–
S3 Social: potency	*0.76*	–	–
Doubtful–secure	*0.74*	–	–
Jealous–faithful	*0.65*	–	–
Guilty–innocent	0.64	–	–
A1 Atmosphere: evaluation and belonging	0.83	0.86	0.80
Annoyed–pleased	0.67	*0.77*	*0.71*
Grumpy–good-natured	*0.89*	*0.82*	*0.71*
Hostile–friendly	*0.73*	0.79	0.60
Aggressive–calm	0.59	0.74	0.66
Intolerant–tolerant	–	0.58	–
A2 Atmosphere: participation (activity)	0.71	–	0.74
Rejected–accepted	*0.85*	–	*0.64*
Unresponsive–responsive	*0.60*	–	*0.86*

Items printed in italics are used later for the structural equation models.

Overall, and except for the physiological dimension (Physiological: energy level) F4, the factor patterns for the remaining three parts of the data set measuring the affective appraisal (Work, Social, Atmosphere) reproduce the well-known semantic dimensions of evaluation, activity and potency (Osgood *et al.*, 1957). For this reason, these terms are included in the factor names. The 'Social' and 'Atmosphere' spheres (cf. Table 9.2) appear to follow the same pattern but are patchy when assuming the presence of similar factors across nationalities. This can have two causes. Firstly, the data lack sufficient validity; secondly, and this appears more likely, differences in normative and value structures do not permit the formation of similar factors.

The emotional scale Work: evaluation of self and work (F1) measures the affective result of the interaction with challenges at work whereby each significant differential expresses either an impact of the challenge on the person or the person's attitude towards work in the light of his/her skills.

The dimension Work: quality of physiological activity (F2) refers to the physical and mental state as well as reflecting on the impact of challenges on the feeling person. Lastly, Work: potency and drive (F3) indicates the level of emotional energy that a person has available to meet challenges. It refers to physical and mental openness and the level of attention the person affords.

Following Csikszentmihalyi's (1975) description of the phenomenon of flow (see literature review), it appears that we can state with some confidence that these dimensions measure students' current state of flow with respect to work in the sense that it represents a measurement of how far away these people are from experiencing flow. A person with a low score on all work dimensions will have to cover more ground to achieve flow than a person with high scores.

In the absence of an instrument that measures the process of flow, the related concept of static versus dynamic orientation can be utilized. While the work scales relating to skills and challenges involve those emotions that are of importance to the state of flow, they also reflect a person's position on the continuum between static versus dynamic orientation. Similar to flow, the underlying assumptions of these orientations were discussed and described as determining a person's level of openness and interest in new challenges and, in general, determining a person's level of confidence and mood. Prior to analysing the data with regard to the propositions that the descriptors of flow represent the status of static–dynamic orientation, further analyses regarding the stability of the dimensions found were conducted.

Regarding the dimensions relating to the social environment and atmosphere at work (Table 9.2), the emotional description of the work atmosphere found a rather limited convergence across the three countries. The factor Atmosphere: evaluation and belonging (A1) could be identified in each of the three samples, while the second factor, Atmosphere: participation (activity) (A2) could not be identified for the SA sample. When trying to detect a possible covariate, no significant variation could be identified between the type of occupation and atmosphere factors. However, given that South Africa is a less individualistic and more hegemonic society with more adherence to traditional values than New Zealand or Austria (Schwartz, 1992), it is possible that cultural influences are responsible for the somewhat different comprehension of the domain of work atmosphere. This, however, would have to be verified in a more extensive study.

Far more variations turned out to underlie the description of feelings about the non-work-related social environment. There are only two basic emotions that are responsible for the expression of a common factor (Social: evaluation and response, S1): hostile–friendly and annoyed–pleased. These variables can be considered as very similar to the basic emotions discussed above. The large proportion of conceptual variability of this factor, and even larger ones in the two following factors (Social: participation (activity), S2 and Social: potency, S3) points to the ever-increasing dependency on culturally specific values and norms.

Common patterns and reliabilities offer the Work (F1 to F3), the Physiological (F4) and the Atmosphere (A1) scales for the task of confirming the proposition that the life domain of work has a significant impact on overall mood. Mood was measured by the respondent's overall feeling before the holiday and anchored by 'extremely bad' and 'extremely good' on a seven-point Likert type scale.

In a first attempt, it was investigated whether the sub-scales F1, F2 and F4 have an invariant pattern across the three countries. Structural models using AMOS 3.6 (Arbuckle, 1997) were estimated using the ML method in order to compare a restricted model (holding the factor loadings constant over the three countries) with an unrestricted one. Comparing the fit statistics and applying the chi-squared difference test (χ^2=39.312, d.f.=16) we cannot assume that the factor pattern is similar for each of the three countries. In other words, while the dimensions across the countries are remarkably similar, the loadings of individual variables differ. As a consequence, the estimation of the second-order factor of static–dynamic orientation was done separately for each country.

In order to avoid over-identification, the sub-scales were estimated taking only two representative items (see italic items in Table 9.1). The theoretical construct of static–dynamic orientation is conceived to determine three emotional sub-scales covering the balance or unbalance between one's own skills and challenges. The three sub-scales are correlated with each other (correlations between 0.29 and 0.72). It can be postulated that a higher-order factor is responsible for this correlation (Bollen, 1989, p. 314), so a structural model may be designed with the first-order sub-scales having no direct effect on one another.

The factor pattern for each of the three countries is shown in Table 9.3. The static–dynamic orientation is strongly based on the Work: physiological (activity) scale. Overall, the disappointment and disillusionment (F1) associated with someone's work have a similar power compared to the physiologically based emotions. Thus both mental and physical exhaustion (or conversely, dynamism) contribute to the disposition of static–dynamic orientation. The factor loadings are very similar between New Zealand and South Africa. The Austrian data imply a stronger influence of the physiological sub-scale on the static orientation. Nevertheless, it was observed that the loading structure is somewhat dependent on the specified model. When additional latent factors were allowed to covary with the second-order factor of static orientation, factor loadings changed slightly in general. The factor pattern for the Austrian sample approached the loading structure of the other countries.

Relationship between mood, emotions and motivations to travel, and expectations

The external validation of the mood state reveals consistent correlations with the second-order factor of static–dynamic orientation which lie between 0.36 and 0.48 for the three different countries. The better people generally feel, the more in harmony they are with their environment. The same, yet somewhat weaker relationship was observed for the work atmosphere (significant correlations between 0.15 and 0.35) and for the social environment (significant correlations between 0.30 and 0.31).

It can be expected that strong emotions coming from one life domain irradiate and intermingle with feelings about other domains. From further analyses, it can be deduced that the feelings about the work atmosphere covary with the static–dynamic orientation. This means that a person who feels challenged by work obligation and feels at the same time apt to respond in a satisfying manner will bear in mind positive emotions about the work ambience and relationships to colleagues. These strong correlations cannot be observed with regard to the remaining social environment scales throughout the three countries. The lack of consistency again points towards the realm of existence that is strongly influenced by socio-cultural and situational factors.

As a final task, the links between the static–dynamic orientation and the holiday motivations and expectations were investigated. A hypothetico-deductively framed way to trace the veracity of the assumption that the affective evaluation of work dimensions is indeed a reflection of a static–dynamic orientation, is to use the students' expectations surrounding holiday experiences as evidence for the respective orientation.

For this kind of analysis, the variations of situative factors in addition to socio-demographic and cultural effects appeared to be most influential. For this reason, correlation analyses were done on an item-by-sub-scale basis in order to achieve a cogent discrimination. A common and concise factor structure for the entire list of 41 motivations and expectations used in this study across the three countries could not be obtained. However, some basic underlying factors, proposed and developed by e.g. Mo *et al.* (1993) and Ryan and Glendon (1998), could be identified across countries: destination-orientated, travel services, social contact; and social relationships, relaxation, intellectual, and competence–mastery. Other factors, such as attitudes towards group travel and contact with nature, could only be found in the NZ and AU samples. These dimensions are based on approximately half of the statement pool. The remaining holiday expectations and motivations could not be reduced to common dimensions.

Table 9.3 Factor pattern for the second-order factor of static–dynamic orientation compared across three different countries

Sub-scale	New Zealand	South Africa	Austria
F1 Work: evaluation of self and work	0.80	0.58	0.70
Factor loading	0.80	0.58	0.70
F2 Work: physiological (activity)	0.97	0.91	0.73
Factor loading	0.97	0.91	0.73
F4 Physiological: energy level	0.60	0.60	0.92
Factor loading	0.60	0.60	0.92

The correlations, though often weak, confirm the tendency that (i) those students who score low on the four scales tend to score particularly high on expectation and motivation scales which are stressing introversion, laziness, getting away from problems at home, etc. Overall, the negative correlations with the items mentioned express that the static orientation is closely related to escapism (comparable to the findings of Cunningham, 1988). In contrast, (ii) all those significant correlations that are positive relate to items that stress risk-seeking behaviour, curiosity, creativity, openness, and, in general, a search for new challenges. The dynamic orientation is therefore closely related to the motivation to search for new experiences.

When interpreting the motivational and expectational items closely, there also appears a tendency for the static orientation to target those needs on Maslow's hierarchy (1954) that are at the lower end, and the converse appears true for the dynamic orientation.

Discussion and Conclusions

The present study explored the relationships between mood prior to holidays and its underlying emotions with regard to the skills and challenges respondents face at work, their physical feelings, and their perceptions of the atmosphere at work and amongst their social peers and family. In his deliberations on the concept of flow, Csikszentmihalyi (1975) determined that the feeling of flow constitutes optimal experiences during which people recreate. It is also the ultimate goal for pleasure seeking. Its particular quality of experience comes about when a subject feels that his skills are in balance with the challenges posed. It was assumed here that 'work' constitutes a major life domain in which respondents develop a need for change driven by strong desires for (self-) fulfilment and instrumentalized by taking holidays and travelling around (for a discussion of desire and the contradicting economic model of need satisfaction see Belk *et al.*, 1998).

Furthermore, similarities between the concept of flow and those of static versus dynamic orientation (Wicklund and Gollwitzer, 1981; Wicklund, 1986) were found and discussed. These refer to the mental disposition of a person who, when under pressure to achieve, has an outer-directed and dynamic orientation that appreciates challenges and meets them with an appropriate level of skills. Conversely, a statically orientated person is one who is inwardly focused and doubtful of his or her skills to meet the challenges faced.

Based on de Rivera's (1977) socio-psychological approach to emotions and his definition that emotions are evident when a person is moved or transformed in relation to their environment, a list of semantic differentials was developed to help describe the emotions the respondents felt towards their work, its atmosphere and their social environment. Based on these descriptors, two dimensions overall (and a third, satisfying at least requirements for exploratory studies) could be extracted, that help qualify these particular emotions.

In general, the dimensions extracted reflect the factor structure that was found to exist in the measurement of meaning (Osgood *et al.*, 1957) and cover the semantic, psychological and physiological spheres that aptly describe Csikszentmihalyi's (1975) concept of flow. They can be regarded as a comparative measurement of flow in terms of indicating how far or close the respondent is from the achievement of flow.

Furthermore, it could be shown that distinct emotions could be related to a measure of general mood. Although some of the literature states that mood appears to have no (Forgas, 1992, 1994) or unknown antecedents (Pieters and van Raaij, 1988), the present study shows that there is now considerable evidence that mood can be traced back to distinct life domains and described by particular emotions.

In the absence of being able to measure flow as a process, the study also explored the meaning of static versus dynamic orientations in the context of emotions and expectations regarding travel. It could be demonstrated that the general tendency of a statically orientated person is introverted and that holiday expectations follow strongly the motivation to escape. Conversely, dynamically orientated respondents are open-minded, seek challenges and strongly follow motivations to search for new experiences. The poles of static versus dynamic orientation as represented by the emotional differentials that express respondents' feelings towards work, coincide with the context of flow.

Lastly, those measurements that have been extracted to describe feelings towards skills and challenges show strong reliability across all three nationalities. They are therefore worthy of further research as they manage to describe emotions in greater detail than general, basic emotions (see e.g. Izard, 1977a, b). Following de Rivera's (1977) approach to interpret the emotions in terms of transitivity and direction of movement, the dimensions and underlying variables permit a better understanding of resultant emotions. Further research would have to follow up on this and use, for example, actual advertisements that respond to one or the other orientation in order to verify current findings. Also, the contextual implications that derive from the items that make up the extracted dimensions are capable of giving the ads different semantic colourings, thus driving more refined segmentation and targeting.

Limitations

Although the findings are very encouraging because the samples showed significant differences in many aspects, the cross-cultural findings are preliminary and would need a much higher degree of external validation. The anchoring of different sample populations to reliable and valid cross-cultural dimensions would be necessary to refine the relationship between mood states, emotional reactions and the evolution of motivations and expectations.

In order to further clarify the causal relationships between mood and emotions, additional issues related to affect, such as intensity, duration, and amount of cognitive mediation, have to be addressed. Other – complementary – methodologies (e.g. longitudinal designs, observations, bio-technical measurement) should be applied in order to challenge the existing mood-related findings.

References

Arbuckle, J.L. (1997) *Amos Users' Guide*. Small Waters Corporation, Chicago, Illinois.

Arnould, E.J. and Price, L.L. (1993) River magic: extraordinary experience and the extended service encounter. *Journal of Consumer Research* 20, 24–45.

Averill, J.R. (1982) *Anger and Aggression – An Essay on Emotion*. New York: Springer.

Behm, K. (1924) Diskussionsbeitrag zur Klaerung des Begriffs 'Erholung'. Cited in: Stephanie, M. (ed.) (1981) Erholung and Erholungsfuersorge. Bericht ueber die Tagung der vereinigung Deutscher Kommunal-, Schul- und Fuersorgeaerzte vom 9. Bis 12. September 1924 im Kindererholundsheim Heuberf bei Stellen am kalten Markt. *Zeitschrift fuer Schulgesundheitsplege und soziale Hygiene* 37. Jahrgang, Ergaenzungsheft 12. Leipzig: Leopold Voss

Belk, R.W., Güliz, G. and Askegaard, S. (1998) Consumer desire. In: P. Andersson (ed.) *Track 6 Consumer Behaviour. 27th EMAC Conference*, Stockholm, 20–23 May 1998. Stockholm: Elanders Gotab, pp. 141–151.

Bollen, K.A. (1989) *Structural Equations with Latent Variables*. New York: Wiley.

Boehnke, K. (1993) Lehrerinnen und Lehrer als Wertemultiplikatoren im veraenderten Bildungssystem der neuen Bundeslaender: Probleme und Perspektiven. *Schulleitung Neue Laender* April, 57–77.

Braun, O.L. (1989) Vom Alltagsstress zur Urlaubszufriedenheit. Dissertation, University of Bielefeld.

Celsi, R., Randall, L.R. and Leigh, L.W. (1993) An exploration of high-risk leisure consumption through skydiving. *Journal of Consumer Research* 20, 1–23.

Csikszentmihalyi, M. (1975) *Beyond Boredom and Anxiety.* San Francisco: Jossey-Bass.

Csikszentmihalyi, M. (1990) *Flow: The Psychology of Optimal Experience.* New York: Harper & Row.

Churchill Jr, G.A. (1979) A paradigm for developing better measures of marketing constructs. *Journal of Marketing Research* 16, 64–73.

Cohen, J.B. and Areni, C.S. (1990) Affect and consumer behavior. In: T.S. Robertson and H.H. Kassarjian (eds) *Handbook of Consumer Behavior.* Englewood Cliffs, New Jersey: Prentice Hall, pp. 188–240.

Cunningham, M.R. (1988) What do you do when you are happy or blue? Mood, expectancies and behavioural interest. *Motivation and Emotion* 12, 309–331.

Dunegan, K.J., Duchon, J.D. and Barton, S.L. (1992) Affect, risk and decision criticality: replication and extension in a business setting. *Organisational Behavior and Human Decision Processes* 53, 335–351.

Engel, J.F., Kollat, D.T. and Blackwell, R.D. (1968) *Consumer Behaviour.* New York: Holt Rinehart & Winston.

Erber, R. and Erber, M.W. (1994) Beyond mood and social judgement: mood incongruent recall and mood regulation. *European Journal of Social Psychology* 59, 202–216.

Floyd, M.F. (1997) Pleasure, arousal, and dominance: exploring affective determinants of recreation satisfaction. *Leisure Sciences* 19, 83–96.

Fodness, D. (1994) Measuring tourist motivation. *Annals of Tourism Research* 21, 555–581.

Forgas, J.P. (1992) Affect in social judgments and decisions: a multiprocess model. *Advances in Experimental Social Psychology* 25, 227–275.

Forgas, J.P. (1994) The role of emotion in social judgments: an introductory review and an affect infusion model (AIM). *European Journal of Social Psychology* 24, 1–24.

Friederichs, W. (1985) *Der Einfluss von Gefuehlen auf Kaufentscheidungen, Europaeische Hochschulschriften: Reihe 5, Volks- und Betriebswirtschaft; Bd. 617.* Frankfurt/Main: Peter Lang.

Frijda, N.H. (1986) *The Emotions. Studies in Emotion and Social Interaction.* New York: Cambridge University Press.

Gardner, M.P. (1985) Mood states and consumer behaviour: a critical review. *Journal of Consumer Research* 12, 281–300.

Gnoth, J. (1997) Tourism motivation and expectation formation. *Annals of Tourism Research* 24, 283–304.

Groenland, E.A.G. and Schoormans, J.P.L. (1994) Comparing mood induction and affective conditioning as mechanism influencing product evaluation and product choice. *Psychology and Marketing* 11, 183–197.

Heckhausen, H. (1989) *Motivation und Handeln,* 2nd edn. Berlin: Springer.

Hibbert, S. (1998) In the mood – or not? Exploring the functional perspective of mood. In: P. Andersson (ed.) *Track 6 Consumer Behaviour, 27th EMAC Conference,* Stockholm, 20–23 May 1998. Stockholm: Elanders Gotab, pp. 585–605.

Howard, J.A. and Sheth, J.N. (1969) *The Theory of Buyer Behaviour.* New York: Wiley.

Iso-Ahola, S.E. (1982) Toward a social psychology theory of tourism motivation. *Annals of Tourism Research* 12, 256–262.

Izard, C.E. (1977a) *Human Emotions.* New York: Plenum Press.

Izard, C.E. (1977b) The emotions and emotion concepts in personality and culture research. In: R.B. Cattell and R.M. Breger (eds) *Handbook of Modern Personality Theory*. Washington, D.C.: Hemisphere.

Izard C.E. (1991) *The Psychology of Emotions*. New York: Plenum Press.

James, W. (1890) *The Principles of Psychology*. London: Macmillan.

Kacen, J.J. (1994) Moods and motivations: an investigation of negative moods, consumer behaviors, and the process of mood management. PhD thesis, University of Illinois at Urbana-Champaign, USA.

Koevecses, Z. (1995) Introduction: language and emotion concepts. In: J.A. Russell *et al.* (eds) *Everyday Conceptions of Emotion. An Introduction to the Psychology, Anthropology and Linguistics of Emotion*. Dordrecht: Kluwer Academic, pp. 3–16.

Kraiger, K., Billings, R.S. and Isen, A.M. (1989) The influence of positive affective states on task perception and satisfaction. *Organizational Behavior and Human Decision Processes* 56, 110–133.

Krippendorf, J. (1987) *The Holiday Makers*. London: Heinemann.

Lazarus, R.S. (1991) *Emotion and Adaptation*. New York: Oxford University Press.

Lewin, K. (1942) Field theory of learning. *Yearbook of National Social Studies of Education* 41, 215–242.

Luomala, H.T. and Laaksonen, M. (1998) Reviewing mood definitions and behavioral effects of negative mood: implications for consumer research. In: P. Andersson (ed.) *Track 6 Consumer Behaviour, 27th EMAC Conference*, Stockholm, 20–23 May 1998. Stockholm: Elanders Gotab, pp. 605–633.

Lutz, R.J. (1985) Affective and cognitive antecedents of attitude towards the ad: a conceptual framework. In: L.F. Alwitt and A.A. Mitchell (eds) *Psychological Processes and Advertising Effects: Theory, Research, and Application*. New Jersey: Lawrence Earlbaum.

Martin, B.A. (1997) Mood and framing effects in advertising. Dissertation, University of Otago, Dunedin, New Zealand.

Maslow, A.H. (1954) *Motivation and Personality*. New York: Harper.

Mo, C., Howard, D.R. and Havitz, M.E. (1993) Testing an international tourist role typology. *Annals of Tourism Research* 20, 319–335.

Morris W.N. (1989) *Mood – Frame of Mind*. New York: Springer.

Morris W.N. and Reilly N.P. (1987) Toward the self regulation of mood: theory and research. *Motivation and Emotion* 11, 215–249.

Mundt, J.W. and Lohmann, M. (1988) *Erholung und Urlaub: Zum Stand der Erholungsforschung im Hinblick auf Urlaubsreisen*. Starnberg: Studienkreis für Tourismus.

Osgood, C.E., Succi, G.J. and Tannenbaum, P.H. (1957) *The Measurement of Meaning*. Urbana, Illinois: University of Illinois Press.

Petty, R.E., Schumann, D., Richmann, S.A. and Strathman, J. (1993) Positive mood and persuasion: different roles for affect under high and low elaboration conditions. *Journal of Personality and Social Psychology* 64, 5–20.

Pieters, R.G.M. and van Raaij, W.F. (1988) Functions and management of affect: applications to economic behavior. *Journal of Economic Psychology* 9, 251–282.

Plutchik, R., (1980), *Emotion: A Psychoevolutionary Synthesis*. New York: Harper & Row.

Ragheb, M.G. and Beard, J.G. (1982) Measuring leisure attitudes. *Journal of Leisure Research* 14, 155–162.

de Rivera, J. (1977) *The Structural Theory of the Emotions.* Psychological Issues, Monograph 40. New York: International Universities Press.

Russell, J.A. and Snodgrass, J. (1987) Emotion and the environment. In: Altman, I. and Stockols, D. (eds) *Handbook of Environmental Psychology.* New York: Wiley, pp. 245–280.

Ryan, C. and Glendon, I. (1998) Application of leisure motivation scale to tourism. *Annals of Tourism Research* 25, 169–184.

Scherer, K.R., Wallbott, H.G. and Summerfield, A.B. (1986) *Experiencing Emotion: A Cross-Cultural Study.* Cambridge, UK: Cambridge University Press.

Schwartz, S.H. (1992) Universals in the content and structure of values: theoretical advances and empirical tests in 20 countries. *Advances in Experimental and Social Psychology* 25, 1–65.

Smith, R., Belk, R.W. and Sherman, E. (1993) Effects of store image and mood on consumer behavior: a theoretical and empirical analysis. *Advances in Consumer Research* 60, 631.

Thayer, R.E. (1989) *The Biopsychology of Mood and Arousal.* New York: Oxford University Press.

Tomkins, S.S. (1962) *Affect, Imagery and Consciousness. Vol. 1. The Positive Affects.* New York: Springer.

Weiner, W.B. (1976) Manifestations of mind: some conceptual and empirical issues. In: G.G. Globus, M. Grover and I. Savodnik (eds) *Consciousness and the Brain. A Scientific and Philosophical Inquiry.* New York: Plenum Press, pp. 5–31.

Wicklund, R.A. (1986) Orientation to the environment vs preoccupation with human potential. In: M. Sorrentino and E.T. Higgins (eds) *Handbook of Motivation and Cognition: Foundations of Social Behaviour.* NewYork: Guilford, pp. 64–95.

Wicklund, R.A. and Gollwitzer, P.M. (1981) Symbolic self-completion, attempted influence, and self-deprecation. *Basic and Applied Social Psychology* 2, 89–114.

Woodside, A.G. and Lysonski, S. (1989) A general model of traveler destination choice. *Journal of Travel Research* 27, 8–14.

Zajonc, R.B. and Markus, H. (1984) Affect and cognition: the hard interface. In: C.E. Izard, J. Kagan and R.B. Zajonc (eds) *Emotions, Cognition, and Behaviour.* Cambridge, UK: Cambridge University Press, pp. 73–103.

Chapter ten
A Hedonic Perspective on Independent Vacation Planning, Decision-Making and Behaviour

Kenneth F. Hyde
Manukau Institute of Technology, Private Bag 94006, Manukau City, Auckland, New Zealand

Introduction

Consumer psychology has traditionally focused on research into consumer purchase of packaged goods and durable products, while neglecting investigations of consumer purchase and consumption of the arts, popular culture, leisure and entertainment services (Holbrook and Hirschman, 1982). Wells (1993) criticized the field of consumer psychology for concentrating on investigations of early stage, low-level consumer decisions such as choice between brands of packaged goods. He implored consumer researchers to investigate more complex consumer decisions. This paper reports one such investigation.

This paper reports the results of research into one aspect of consumer behaviour in tourism, namely decision processes for choice of vacation itinerary by the independent traveller. Morrison *et al.*, 1993) define independent travellers as those 'who make their own transportation and accommodation arrangements, choosing not to buy prearranged packages or tours'. Independent travel is an important and growing sector of the tourism industry (World Tourism Organisation, 1993). Poon (1993) suggests that, because of changing demographics and lifestyles, a growing group of 'New Tourists' demand choice and flexibility in their vacations.

Until now, no piece of research has sought to model the independent vacation – from initial planning, through choice of itinerary items, to vacation behaviour. Compared with the general body of knowledge on consumer decision-making, the subject matter of this research is distinctive in four respects. Firstly the subject matter here concerns multiple decisions. Secondly, the subject matter relates to the purchase of intangible services, rather than tangible goods. Thirdly, tourism services are especially emotive products – we might expect decision processes for the choice of tourism and leisure services to be based on emotive mechanisms. And fourthly, the items being purchased here are all first-time purchases; they are not familiar brands; the consumer has no previous direct experience in purchasing any one of these services, on which to base their decision-making.

The discussion which follows introduces two perspectives on consumer psychology, and a number of models of consumer behaviour in tourism. It then summarizes research findings on the information search and travel planning of independent travellers, and discusses the role of affect in tourism.

Two alternative perspectives on consumer psychology

The field of consumer psychology is firmly rooted in the view of the 'consumer as problem-solver', a consumer seeking to maximize the outcomes of any purchase decision by carefully weighing the utility of each option available. Consumer decision-making is most often conceptualized as a problem-solving process of five steps: (i) recognition of a need, (ii) search for information, (iii) evaluation of alternatives, (iv) choice, and (v) post-purchase (Engel *et al.*, 1995). Modern consumer researchers borrow much from Newell and Simon's (1972) view of human beings as imperfect decision-makers. Consumers have limited information-processing capacity and are viewed as merely seeking sufficient information to make satisfactory purchase decisions (Bettman *et al.*, 1991). The process of consumer decision-making is viewed as dependent on the amount of cognitive effort the consumer is willing to expend (Bettman, 1979).

An alternative perspective on consumer psychology was provided by Holbrook and Hirschman (1982). These authors identified the seeking of emotional arousal as a major motivation for the consumption of certain product classes, including the arts, entertainment, sports, and leisure pursuits such as vacation tourism. The traditional view of the consumer as problem-solver seems inappropriate to describe those purchases which are based on satisfying emotional wants rather than utilitarian needs. The perspective of the 'consumer as hedonic person' suggests that in many instances consumers make purchases in order to create feelings, experiences and emotions rather than to solve problems (Mowen, 1988). Since the mid-1980s there has been increasing interest in the role of affect in consumer psychology.

Models of consumer behaviour in tourism

Research on consumer behaviour in tourism has by and large adopted a consumer as problem-solver perspective, and neglected the affective aspects of consumer behaviour in tourism. Over recent years, a number of models of consumer behaviour in tourism have been proposed. The models by van Raaij and Francken (1984), Moutinho (1987), Woodside and Lysonski (1989), and Um and Crompton (1991) have focused on a consumer's pre-vacation choice of tourism destination, while neglecting consumer behaviours which occur during the vacation.

Woodside and MacDonald's (1993) General systems framework of customer choice processes for tourism services is the only attempt to provide a framework which comprehensively covers consumer choice of all elements of the vacation itinerary. Many of the choices a consumer makes amongst tourism services are not planned before the start of the vacation. The Woodside and MacDonald model proposes that choices of tourism-related services are each interdependent to some degree. The services considered in the model are: destinations, accommodation, activities, attractions, travel modes and routes, dining, subdestinations (and scenic routes), self-gifts and durable purchases. Woodside and MacDonald call for research into the temporal sequence and the principal direction of influence amongst elements in this model. For example, does choice of subdestination influence choice of attractions and activities, or is it that choice of attractions and activities influences choice of subdestination?

Information search by independent travellers

Studies of tourists' information search and travel planning have often been studies of the independent traveller. Travellers *en route* to their destinations are known to make use of travel information centres and other people to learn about attractions and activities; such information can influence an independent traveller's length of stay and choice of attractions and activities in the destination area (Fesenmaier *et al.*, 1993).

Travellers taking routine trips to familiar destinations simply utilize past experience and advice of family and friends in their travel planning; travellers travelling longer distances, taking longer vacations, or visiting new and unfamiliar destinations are likely to seek a greater volume of information from a variety of sources (Gitelson and Crompton, 1983). In their study of travel information search and planning, Schul and Crompton (1983) identified an active search and a passive search group. Active searchers had longer planning horizons; their vacations displayed a preference for escape from the ordinary, and variety in things to see and do.

A number of writers have suggested that amount of information search and planning for the vacation might be related to levels of purchase involvement (Gitelson and Crompton, 1983; Fesenmaier and Johnson, 1989). Yet other researchers have suggested the role of involvement in decision processes for choice of tourism and leisure services might not be a simple, linear one. This is firstly because services are typically intangible and consumers can discover little about the attributes of a service prior to purchase; consumers may make a selection of a service after little pre-purchase information search (Murray, 1991). Secondly, purchase of leisure and tourism services might result in a high level of affective involvement rather than a high level of cognitive involvement; level of involvement might be unrelated to extensiveness of decision-making (Dimanche *et al.*, 1991; Otto and Ritchie, 1996).

Vacation planning by independent travellers

Most research on travel planning has taken a static view of the subject matter. In many instances the researcher's interest has simply been in the consumer's choice of a single vacation destination. In reality, all vacation decision-making involves multiple decisions, and many vacations involve travel to multiple destinations (Leu *et al.*, 1993). Amongst the multiple decisions involved in planning a vacation are: the date of the vacation, whether to take children, how long to stay, how much money to spend, destination point(s), choice of transportation, choice of accommodation, and choice of attractions and activities (Cosenza and Davis, 1981).

By definition, independent travellers have not pre-booked the details of their vacation itinerary, but have they pre-planned the details of their itinerary? Morrison *et al.* (1993) suggest independent travellers 'may use prearranged or fixed itineraries or they may have flexible itineraries', but precisely how flexible are the itineraries of independent travellers? In their study of visitors to Alachua County, Florida, Crotts and Reid (1993) found most visitors had decided upon recreational activities prior to departure. Those travellers who made their activity decisions after arrival in the county were typically long-haul and international visitors. In Tsang's (1993) survey of the information search and travel planning behaviour of international visitors to New Zealand, over 40% of respondents indicated they had no pre-planning of vacation activities. Only a minority of visitors had pre-planned their length of stay in each subdestination.

In a recent study, Jeng (1997) asked respondents to imagine a 2–4-day domestic vacation trip, and consider which itinerary elements they might plan before departure. Jeng identified a set of core subdecisions made before departure, including date of trip, primary destination, location of overnight stay, and travel route. He identified a set of secondary subdecisions, made before departure but considered to be flexible, including choice of attractions and activities, and secondary destinations. Thirdly, he identified a set of *en route* decisions, including where to dine, where to shop, and where to stop and rest. However, his results concern a short domestic trip to what is probably a familiar destination. We must question whether these results might apply to international independent travel.

From her study of international independent travellers, Parr (1989, p. 108) provides quite a different impression of vacation planning, stating 'some [travellers] had little idea of what they wanted to see and do ... Some people enjoyed the element of the unknown ... they felt they were on an adventure, full of surprises and spontaneity'.

Affect and independent travel

Research on consumer behaviour in tourism has seldom examined the hedonic aspects of tourist behaviour. This is surprising, given that a number of consumer researchers have identified tourism services as being especially hedonic purchases. Otto and Ritchie (1996, p. 168) recently gave expression to this point, stating

'Perhaps more than any other service industry, tourism holds the potential to elicit strong emotional and experiential reactions from consumers ... utilitarian and rational information processing schemes which focus on functional or purely attribute-based elements are incommensurate with leisure and tourism.' Hedonism was identified by these researchers as being of central importance in the consumption of tours and attractions.

Any examination of consumer purchase of tourism services should consider the affective aspects of such behaviour. Poon (1993) noted that the 'New Tourists' are more spontaneous, with a lower level of vacation planning, and a desire to do what comes on the spur of the moment. It is worth considering whether, as a source of hedonic pleasure, independent travellers might purposely avoid travel planning.

Objectives

The aim of this research was to build a model of the independent traveller's decision process for choosing elements of the vacation itinerary. This model would account for:

- extent of pre-trip information search
- extent of pre-trip travel planning
- timing of information search
- percentage of pre-trip travel plans which are actioned
- factors which influence amount of information search, amount of planning and percentage of travel plans actioned
- temporal sequence in which vacation subdecisions – choice of subdestinations, route, attractions and activities – are made
- role of involvement and affect in these decision processes.

Method

The research consisted of two phases, an inductive and a deductive phase. Research commenced with inductive model-building: data were collected from 12 sources, including interviews with tourism officials, documented observations and personal experiences of independent travel. Based upon themes identified in this inductive database and the existing research literature, a model of independent traveller decision-making processes was produced for testing. This model was expressed as a set of 18 testable propositions.

The use of visitors to New Zealand allowed a special opportunity to research independent travel behaviours. New Zealand is a destination where the key attractions are geographically dispersed, and travellers must decide upon an extended route to take them to their choice of attractions (Oppermann, 1992). All of the tourists studied were first-time visitors, not visiting friends and relatives; previous experience, or guidance from local friends and relatives, were not sources of information to assist travel planning or influence travel behaviours. A stratified purposeful sampling method was used (Patton, 1991). Three strata were judged critical to diversity in the study population, namely nationality of the traveller, travel party size, and mode of transportation.

To observe the process of tourist decision-making in action, a repeated-measures, before-and-after design was employed in the deductive phase, with data gathered on two separate occasions during each independent traveller's vacation. An initial interview was conducted with each of 20 travel parties (being single travellers or dyads) within 24 hours of arrival in New Zealand; a second interview was conducted with the same travel parties within 24 hours of their departure from New Zealand, at the end of their vacation. The interviews sought to probe and record content of cognitive sets at these points in time, rather than retrospectively. The initial interview investigated the extent and content of traveller research, awareness and planning relative to New Zealand subdestinations, attractions, activities and travel route. The second interview investigated actual vacation behaviour in terms of subdestinations visited, routes taken, and attractions and activities experienced.

Deductive testing of the model employed 'small t' case-study methodology (Wells, 1993). Case study produces in-depth information on a small number of individuals (Patton, 1991), and searches beyond simple snapshots of events, people or behaviours (Bonoma, 1985). Case study does not yield trustworthy estimates of population characteristics; rather, depth of understanding is based on a detailed knowledge of the each case, and its nuances in context (Stake, 1994). Rather than aggregating data across subjects, a detailed comparison was made between pre-vacation search and planning and actual vacation behaviours, on a case-by-case basis. Case study is especially useful for investigation of the sequence or process of a phenomenon (Eisenhardt, 1989).

According to Yin (1994), the least-developed procedures in case study research are deductive procedures for the testing of study propositions. One approach is the idea of 'pattern matching' described by Campbell (1975). The model one is tested is stated before data gathering commences. In addition, a counter-model is put forward for testing. Support is demonstrated for the model if the case data match the predicted pattern of outcomes of the model more closely than the predicted pattern of outcomes for the counter-model. If the results fail to show the entire pattern as predicted, the initial propositions need to be modified.

Each of four judges examined the 18 propositions of the model being tested against summaries and excerpts of transcript from each of the 20 cases. 4×18 judgements were brought to bear on each case, to see if the case supported the model as a whole.

Findings

Characteristics of travel parties

The 20 travel parties came from a diverse range of countries, occupations and age groups. Travellers came from continental Europe (*n*=7), North America (*n*=3), Australia (*n*=2), Scandinavia (*n*=2), Great Britain (*n*=2), East Asia (*n*=2), and the Middle East (*n*=2); this range represents well the diversity of international visitors to New Zealand. They travelled by a diverse range of transport modes – rental car, motorhome, purchase of a car, bus, train, flight and hitchhiking. Accommodation types used included four-star hotels, motels, youth hostels and a tent. The length of travellers' vacations varied from 10 to 88 days.

Extent of pre-trip information search

The travellers studied displayed considerable variation in amount of pre-trip information search; the amount of reading completed to research the vacation itinerary varied from nil to 40 hours for any one individual or travel party.

Extent of pre-trip travel planning

On average, travel parties had fewer than seven specifically planned elements for their vacation. Almost half of these specifically planned elements were subdestinations. Many fewer attractions or activities had been specifically planned. A minority of travel parties had a pre-planned travel route.

Travellers' vacations consisted of a mean of 33 elements. In other words, some 80% of vacation elements had been neither specifically nor generally planned. This finding provides some indication of just how flexible independent vacation itineraries might be.

The timing of information search

For the travellers studied, a majority of information search and planning occurred after arrival at the destination. Travellers made detailed plans for choice of attractions and activities only for the immediate 24-hour period. Only as travellers approached a subdestination did they seek detailed information on that subdestination and its attractions and activities.

The percentage of pre-trip travel plans which are actioned

No previous longitudinal studies were located describing the percentage of a consumer's travel plans which are put into action. The information presented here appears unique in this regard. Of the vacation elements these travellers had specifically planned, almost all – a mean of 72.9% – were actioned. This indicates that a knowledge of a consumer's specific travel plans might provide an accurate prediction of actual vacation behaviours.

The temporal sequence in which vacation subdecisions are made

Woodside and MacDonald's (1993) general systems framework of customer choice processes for tourism services identifies the key elements in a consumer's vacation itinerary, but leaves unanswered what the temporal sequence in choice of these elements might be. In this study of independent travellers to New Zealand, the decision sequence observed for choice of vacation elements was: subdestinations → travel route →attractions and activities.

Several findings point to subdestinations as being the central element in planning the vacation itinerary. Most specifically planned elements were subdestinations. High levels of information search were associated with precise planning of subdestinations, but bore no relationship to degree of planning of attractions and activities. Most planned subdestinations were actioned. Several findings point to the conclusion that alternative activities are substitutable. Individuals who had the highest number of planned activities were least likely to action these plans.

Factors influencing amount of information search and planning, and percentage of travel plans actioned – the role of involvement and affect

There were statistically significant relationships between level of purchase involvement and amount of information search ($r=0.4452$, $P=0.023$, $n=261$), degree of travel planning ($r=0.3310$, $P=0.099$, $n=26$), and percentage of vacation plans actioned ($r=0.4130$, $P=0.036$, $n=26$).

Of the constructs studied, amount of information search was identified as the factor most central to predicting other aspects of consumer behaviour in independent travel. Amount of information search was the strongest predictor of amount of travel planning, and percentage of travel plans which are actioned. A Low-Search group of travellers was identified, who were more likely to be backpackers (Fisher's exact test, $P=0.077$) in their twenties ($\chi^2=6.173$, d.f.$=2$, $P=0.046$), from English-speaking countries (Fisher's exact test, $P=0.088$), travelling alone (Fisher's exact test, $P=0.030$). These travellers generally displayed low purchase involvement and had few specific plans. What plans they had tended to feature a selection of activities, and yet these activities were readily substitutable. High-Search travellers tended to be couples, from non-English-speaking countries, aged in their thirties, and not backpacking. They generally displayed high purchase involvement, had many specific plans – especially a selection of 'must-see' subdestinations – and were highly likely to action these plans. Notwithstanding this, even the most planning of individuals experienced a vacation where the majority of elements are indeed unplanned.

Demographic characteristics of the traveller and level of involvement in the choice of vacation elements both predicted the travel variables of search, planning and action. But they did so independently.

A Model of Independent Traveller Decision-making for Choice of Vacation Itinerary

The aim of this study has been to build a model of the independent traveller decision process for choice of elements of the vacation itinerary. Such a model is presented in Fig. 10.1.

This model further develops three aspects of Woodside and MacDonald's (1993) general framework. Firstly, the model identifies which travel subdecisions take precedence in influence over the others. Secondly, the model indicates which processes occur before a consumer's arrival at their destination, and which occur after arrival. Thirdly, the model makes explicit which information sources are most influential at various stages of the vacation. Until now it has been unclear whether or not the vacation itinerary of the independent traveller is pre-planned. The model provides an indication of the type and extent of vacation planning undertaken by the independent traveller, and the extent to which such travel plans are actioned.

The independent vacation is like experiencing the 'fun of the fairground', a freewheeling experience of travelling from place to place, relatively unaware of what each subdestination has to offer. An integral feature of independent travel is the enjoyment the consumer experiences from not planning the details of the vacation but rather from experiencing the unknown and unexpected. Rather than following a fixed itinerary, the itinerary of an independent vacation evolves as the vacation proceeds.

Prior to departure on the vacation, the consumer undertakes research and planning of the vacation itinerary. Amount of information search and vacation planning varies greatly between individuals, dependent upon demographic characteristics of the traveller and level of involvement in choice of itinerary items. A set of planned subdestinations is formulated. This 'researched before' set of subdestinations is highly likely to be acted upon in the final vacation. The consumer's pre-vacation choices of attractions and activities are less likely to be acted upon.

The majority of vacation elements are chosen after arrival at the destination; a 'researched after' set of options is formulated. The sequence of vacation decision-making is firstly choice of subdestinations, then choice of travel route, then choice of attractions and activities. Consumers' choice of attractions and activities to experience at any one subdestination is generally delayed until within 24 hours of arrival at that subdestination.

In addition to researched before and researched after itinerary items, the consumer will take advantage of some serendipitous opportunities to experience a number of subdestinations, attractions and activities which they had neither actively researched nor planned.

Clearly, a continuum of alternative travel modes exists, from fully packaged and 'stay put' vacations, through varying degrees of independence, to fully independent travel. It appears that three characteristics distinguish fully independent travel: (i) the traveller experiences an evolving itinerary rather than a fixed itinerary; (ii) travellers are willing to take risks in their selection of vacation elements; and (iii) the traveller possesses a desire to experience the unplanned.

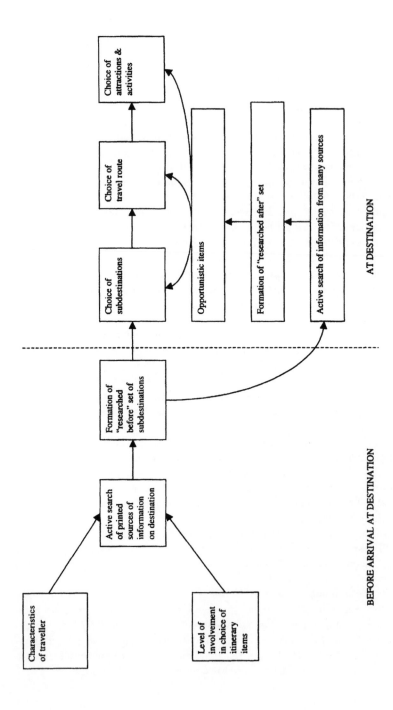

Figure 10.1 Model of independent travellers' decision processes for choice of vacation itinerary.

The conditions under which fully independent travel appear likely to arise are: (i) the vacation is a multi-destination vacation; (ii) forward bookings of accommodation and transportation have not been made; (iii) the traveller lacks familiarity with the destination; and (iv) levels of risk are perceived to be low or irrelevant.

Multi-destination tourism can occur at a number of levels of abstraction –a tour through several countries; a tour through a single international destination; or domestic tourism. It appears that such multi-destination tourism is likely to become fully independent travel when the above listed conditions exist.

Discussion

By its very nature, the vacation represents a different facet of consumer life. This is a facet of life where the usual constraints of responsibility, use of time and finances are somewhat relaxed. We might expect to observe quite different consumer behaviours during vacation time. The key feature of independent travel identified in this research has been the consumer's desire for flexibility of action, while avoiding planning and delaying decision-making.

The behaviours observed are analogous to a retail shopping trip. Before entering a supermarket or shopping mall, a consumer may have a written set of planned purchases. Yet by the end of their shopping trip, the actual shopping behaviours displayed involve a majority of unplanned purchases, and possibly a number of impulse purchases (Leeds, 1994). In the independent vacation, before arrival at a destination the consumer may have a researched before set of itinerary items. Yet by the end of the vacation, the actual behaviours displayed involve a majority of unplanned purchases, including researched after items and spontaneous purchases.

The model of independent travel presented here has similarities to Rook's (1987) description of impulse purchasing. In independent travel, the consumer at times displays risk-taking, sensation-seeking and a relative disregard for the consequences of their actions.

How do we explain this behaviour? Does the independent traveller display the actions of consumer as problem-solver, or the actions of consumer as hedonic person?

The consumer as problem-solver perspective offers some explanation of independent traveller behaviour. A consumer's behaviour regarding choice of vacation itinerary might reflect a desire to minimize cognitive effort, by delaying information search until absolutely necessary (see Bettman, 1979; Bettman *et al.*, 1991). Perhaps the consumer believes that a better decision can be made by delaying information search.

The factor of perceived risk may also explain the amount of vacation research and planning. Some consumers feel apprehensive about their future vacations – concerned about standards of accommodation, concerned for their own health and safety, concerned that transportation might not be available. Other consumers do not perceive this level of risk. But what must also be considered is that, for the majority of consumers, independent travel is about seeking risks; independent travellers are in many instances risk-takers (Mowen, 1995). The perspective of consumer as problem-solver does not allow for the possibility that consumers will seek risks rather than avoid them.

But the concepts of cognitive effort and perceived risk do not go far enough in explaining why the consumer wishes to delay decision-making, avoid vacation planning, and seek to experience the unknown. According to the consumer as hedonic person perspective, decision processes for choice of tourism and leisure services would not revolve around seeking to solve any problem; rather the consumer's goal would be to provoke feelings and emotions (Holbrook and Hirschman, 1982). This perspective provides a more parsimonious and convincing explanation of why the consumer avoids a fully planned vacation itinerary. The consumer avoids vacation planning because flexibility of action and experiencing the unknown are key amongst the hedonic experiences they are seeking when they choose independent travel.

The consumer psychology literature has yet to adequately explore the hedonic experience of tourism. The tourism and leisure literatures may provide more insights into the hedonic experience of independent travel. In the first instance, the tourism literature recognizes a human need for exploration, sometimes termed the 'Ulysses factor' (Anderson, 1970). In the leisure literature, Neulinger (1974) singles out freedom of choice as the defining character of leisure. Independent travel offers a rare opportunity for freedom of choice in where to go, what to see and do. Iso-Ahola (1979) recognizes intrinsic motivation as inherent in leisure; this includes experiences of challenge, mastery and adventure. Travel to a new destination places the consumer in an unfamiliar and challenging environment; independent travel might provide many consumers with experiences of mastery over the physical and social environments.

Gunter (1987) has identified six additional factors inherent in leisure experiences: escape from the everyday; timelessness; intense pleasure; spontaneity; fantasy and the exercise of creative imagination; and self-realization. Each of these factors may form part of the hedonic experience of independent travel. Vacations represent a facet of life different and apart from the everyday; a facet of life with perhaps fewer responsibilities, concerns and constraints. In independent travel, consumers may experience a loss of sense of urgency. Consumers undertake vacations because of the pleasures to be experienced. Some choices of tourism services are clearly impulse purchases; they involve a 'devil-may-care' approach to decision-making. Part of a consumer's vacation experience is the living out of fantasies held about places and activities. And for some consumers, independent travel may offer personal growth experiences, by exposing the consumer to new and unfamiliar situations where they may have to develop new skills and new confidence. In summary, then, independent travel provides an opportunity for the consumer to partake of a number of hedonic experiences.

Implications for the practice of tourism marketing

Fuelled by reports of growth in the numbers of independent travellers visiting New Zealand, large numbers of budding entrepreneurs have sought to establish small tourism businesses. But, what has been lacking is an understanding of these consumer and their needs. This research provides some basis for such an understanding, by describing the context in which tourism operators catering for the independent travel sector must operate.

By definition, the independent traveller is one who operates outside the normal conditions of commercial mass tourism. This research re-confirms that there is a sector of consumers who do not want to purchase travel packages. Instead, these consumers purchase just a destination, and leave the details of their itineraries flexible.

The research has identified two relatively distinct groups of independent travellers. The low-search backpacker group typically undertakes little pre-vacation information search and planning. The high-search, non-backpacker group typically undertakes much more pre-vacation search and planning. The effective placement of marketing communications would be quite different for each of these groups. Only the high-search group would appear to be receptive to marketing communications delivered offshore to intercept them during vacation planning. Effective placement of marketing communications could again be in travel guide books, but also internet home pages and 0800 numbers for request of information.

The research has suggested that both high-search and low-search independent travellers might delay most information search and decision-making for choice of attractions and activities until the final 24 hours upon approaching a subdestination. For operators of attractions and activities, the most efficient avenue for promotional expenditure is probably to concentrate their budget at the local level.

A final consideration is the role of modern electronic communications and the internet. Modern electronic communications are likely to lead to a shortening of travel sales and distribution channels, and to provide future travellers with the opportunity to source and book vacation details for themselves. The results of this study would suggest, however, that these new technologies might not lead to greater levels of planning of vacation elements by independent travellers.

References

Anderson, J.R.L. (1970) *The Ulysses Factor*. New York: Harcourt Brace Jovanovich.

Bettman, J.R. (1979) *Information Processing Theory of Consumer Choice*. Reading: Addison-Wesley.

Bettman, J.R., Johnson, E.J. and Payne, J.W. (1991) Consumer decision making. In:: T.S. Robertson and H.H. Kassarjian (eds) *Handbook of Consumer Behaviour*. Englewood Cliffs, New Jersey: Prentice-Hall.

Bonoma, T.V. (1985) Case research in marketing: opportunities, problems, and a process. *Journal of Marketing Research* 22, 199–208.

Campbell, D.T. (1975) "Degrees of freedom" and the case study. *Comparative Political Studies* 8, 178–193.

Cosenza, R.M and Davis, D.L. (1981) Family vacation decision making over the family life cycle: a decision and influence structure analysis. *Journal of Travel Research* Fall, 17–23.

Crotts, J.C and Reid, L.J. (1993) Segmenting the visitor market by the timing of their activity decisions. *Visions in Leisure and Business* 12, 4–7.

Dimanche, F., Havitz, M.E. and Howard, D.R. (1991) Testing the involvement profile (IP) scale in the context of selected recreational and touristic activities. *Journal of Leisure Research* 23, 51–66.

Eisenhardt, K.M. (1989) Building theories from case study research. *Academy of Management Review* 14, 532–550.

Engel, J.F., Blackwell, R.D. and Miniard, P.W. (1995) *Consumer Behaviour*, 8th edn. Fort Worth: Dryden.

Fesenmaier, D.R. and Johnson, B. (1989) Involvement-based segmentation: implications for travel marketing in Texas. *Tourism Management* December, 293–300.

Fesenmaier, D.R., Vogt, C.A. and Stewart, W.P. (1993) Investigating the influence of welcome centre information on travel behaviour. *Journal of Travel Research* 31, 47–52.

Gitelson, R.J. and Crompton, J.L. (1983) The planning horizons and sources of information used by pleasure vacationers. *Journal of Travel Research* Winter, 2–7.

Gunter, B.G. (1987) The leisure experience: selected properties. *Journal of Leisure Research* 19, 115–130.

Holbrook, M.B. and Hirschman, E.C. (1982) The experiential aspects of consumption: consumer fantasies, feelings, and fun. *Journal of Consumer Research* 9, 132–140.

Iso-Ahola, S.E. (1979) Basic dimensions of leisure. *Journal of Leisure Research* 15, 15–26.

Jeng, J. (1997) Facets of the complex trip decision making process. Paper presented at the Travel and Tourism Research Association's 28th Annual Conference, June 1997, Norfolk, Virginia.

Leeds, D. (1994) Accountability is in-store for marketers. *Brandweek* 35, 17.

Leu, C., Crompton, J.L. and Fesenmaier, D.R. (1993) Conceptualization of multi-destination pleasure trips. *Annals of Tourism Research* 20, 289–301.

Morrison, A.M., Hsieh, S. and O'Leary, J.T. (1993) Travel arrangement classifications for European international travellers. In: R.V. Gasser and K. Weiermair (eds) *Spoilt for Choice: Decision Making Processes and Preference Changes of Tourists. Proceedings of the Institute of Tourism and Service Economics International Conference*, November 1993, University of Innsbruck, pp. 221–235.

Moutinho, L. (1987) Consumer behaviour in tourism. *European Journal of Marketing* 21, 2–44.

Mowen, J.C. (1988) Beyond consumer decision making. *Journal of Consumer Marketing* 5, 15–25.

Mowen, J.C. (1995) *Consumer Behaviour*, 4th edn. Englewood Cliffs, New Jersey: Prentice-Hall.

Murray, K.B. (1991) A test of services marketing theory: consumer information acquisition activities. *Journal of Marketing* 55, 10–25.

Neulinger, J. (1974) *The Psychology of Leisure: Research Approaches to the Study of Leisure*. Springfield, Illinois: Charles C. Thomas.

Newell, A. and Simon, H.A. (1972) *Human Problem Solving.* Englewood Cliffs, New Jersey: Prentice-Hall.

Oppermann, M. (1992) Travel dispersal index. *Journal of Tourism Studies* 3, 44–49.

Otto, J.E. and Ritchie, J.R.B. (1996) The service experience in tourism. *Tourism Management* 17, 165–174.

Parr, D. (1989) Free independent travellers. MSc thesis, Lincoln College, University of Canterbury.

Patton, M.Q. (1991) *Qualitative Evaluation and Research Methods*, 2nd edn. Newbury Park: Sage.

Poon, A. (1993) *Tourism, Technology and Competitive Strategies.* Wallingford, UK: CAB International.

van Raaij, W.F. and Francken, D.A. (1984) Vacation decisions, activities, and satisfactions. *Annals of Tourism Research* 11, 101–112.

Rook, D.W. (1987) The buying impulse. *Journal of Consumer Research* 14, 189–199.

Schul, P. and Crompton, J.L. (1983) Search behaviour of international vacationers: travel-specific lifestyle and sociodemographic variables. *Journal of Travel Research* Fall, 24–30.

Stake, R.E. (1994) Case studies. In: N.K. Denzin and Y.S. Lincoln (eds) *Handbook of Qualitative Research.* Thousand Oaks: Sage.

Tsang, G.K.Y. (1993) Visitor information network study: visitors' information seeking behaviour for on-site travel-related sub-decision making and evaluation of service performance. MCom thesis, University of Otago, Dunedin.

Um, S. and Crompton, J.L. (1991) Development of pleasure travel attitude dimensions. *Annals of Tourism Research* 18, 500–504.

Wells, W.D. (1993) Discovery-oriented consumer research. *Journal of Consumer Research* 19, 489–504.

Woodside, A.G. and Lysonski, S. (1989) A general model of traveler destination choice. *Journal of Travel Research* 27, 8–14.

Woodside, A.G. and MacDonald, R. (1993) General system framework of customer choice processes of tourism services. In: R.V. Gasser and K. Weiermair (eds) *Spoilt for Choice: Decision Making Processes and Preference Changes of Tourists. Proceedings of the Institute of Tourism and Service Economics International Conference*, November 1993, University of Innsbruck, pp. 30–59.

World Tourism Organisation (1993) *Tourism to the Year 2000: Qualitative Aspects Affecting Global Growth.* Madrid: WTO.

Yin, R.K. (1994) *Case Study Research: Design and Methods*, 2nd edn. Thousand Oaks: Sage.

Chapter eleven
Tourist Motivation, Values and Perceptions

Irena Ateljevic
School of Business and Management, Victoria University of Wellington,
PO Box 600, Wellington, New Zealand

Introduction

'Out of the window, the vast land itself flitted by, so familiar from postcards but silent and untouchable from inside our glass case. I remember wanting to get off the train at every point and lie in the sweet summer fields. While it's nice to think that my image came from within, from the memory of authentic, animated real space, I know that it is also part of the repertoire of images of nature that tourist culture produces in great number and variety, and that in some ways are indistinguishable from nature itself' (Wilson, 1992, p. 19).

In conditioning consumer choice, perception is considered to be more important than reality. It has been argued that mental images of products form the basis of the selection process to interpret information and to guide consumer behaviour as people act upon what they believe to be true (Bruner, 1970; Spence and Engel, 1970; Papadopoulos 1993). Likewise, Meyer and Reynolds, explaining consumer behaviour, argue that perception is an important force of influence as: 'what we perceive is very often as much a product of what we want to perceive as of what is actually there' (1967, p. 3).

Similarly, the tourism literature argues that mental images of tourist destinations are essential in the tourist decision-making process, shaping the tourist flows of the world (Williams and Zelinsky, 1970; Britton, 1979; Stabler, 1988). Accordingly, an important element of effective destination positioning is the creation and management of a distinctive and appealing perception, or image of the destination (Calantone *et al.*, 1989). Similarly, a number of writers have highlighted the importance of favourable perception in influencing the consumer's destination choice (e.g. Goodrich, 1978; Gartner, 1989; Woodside and Lysonski, 1989). As Mayo and Jarvis (1981) argue, a traveller's evaluation of a destination's 'position' is based on perceived ability of the area to satisfy the travel needs of that individual.

However, the perceptions of a 'destination's ability' to satisfy tourist needs evolve with the socio-cultural context from which tourist motivations derive (Adler, 1989; Gnoth, 1997). This paper discusses how certain travel motivations are created by constantly evolving values and situational parameters within the cultural frame of everyday life in the generating countries. The dialectical relationship between the ordinary and extraordinary on which tourism is based (Urry, 1990) becomes important in relation to historically specific forces of different contexts. Put simply, when the ordinary changes, the motivations and perceptions for/of the extraordinary also have to change. This argument imposes critical implications for planners and marketers of tourist destinations who constantly need to (re)create and (re)invent the image of 'their' localities.

The findings discussed here are based on data collected in the author's survey of international visitors to New Zealand. Respondents' perceptions and key motivational forces for selection of New Zealand as a holiday destination have shown that emerging green values created the important socio-cultural frame for New Zealand's global appeal as a tourist destination. At some points, discussion is complemented by in-depth market research information of New Zealand's central government agency – the New Zealand Tourism Board (NZTB), as their research brings up similar arguments.

Methodology

The survey of international visitors was conducted in one of the most successful international resorts in New Zealand, Rotorua, during the summer of 1996. It is important to note that domestic and local visitors were omitted in this research: this was for practical reasons, as they would require a different approach to the investigation. The survey was part of the author's PhD project, and this text discusses only partial findings related to visitor images, motivations and their actual experiences once in the country. Administered using a semi-structured questionnaire, utilizing a combination of closed-format and open-ended questions, the survey aimed to obtain the whole spectrum of information related to tourist behaviour. Aiming for depth of interpretation, the methodology of open-ended questions has allowed acquiring tourists' perspectives expressed in their own words, without imposing the researcher's point of view (Squire, 1994). Dann *et al.* (1988) also make this point in a review of methodology in tourism studies, noting the potential for using interpretative qualitative approaches such as semi-structured and open-ended interviews. In particular, when researching the complexity of perceiving the image as a whole, Echtner and Ritchie (1991) suggest that unstructured methodologies of open-ended questions should be employed to gauge holistic impressions.

Through a face-to face interview procedure, the survey was conducted throughout the area of Rotorua District: at the information centre; at the sites of tourist attractions; and at accommodation establishments. Since the semi-structured schedule demanded at least 20 to 25 minutes, it was crucial that tourists had the time and willingness to participate. Accordingly, interviewers (myself and two other students) tried to meet tourists while they were resting after sightseeing, while they were waiting for their transport in the Travel Office, or while having their drink before or after dinner in their hotel.

Given the length of the interview and the language barrier, the majority of respondents were English-speaking tourists travelling independently, as they appeared to be more relaxed and not as hurried as the 'package' tourists on a fixed itinerary. Interviews with visitors from Japan and Central and Nordic Europe went smoothly, as the majority had at least competent knowledge of the English language. However, Korean and Taiwanese tourists emerged as the most difficult group to reach, being predominantly on guided tours with no time for the interview and/or with language barriers. In order to partially overcome this obstacle, contact was made with Korean and Taiwanese tour guides who live in New Zealand, speak English, and are employed by tour companies. They were willing to organise some time for interviews with travellers from their group, usually in the bus or at the hotel. They also acted as translators. However, given their 'culture of politeness', I was warned that visitors would not sincerely express their impressions, as 'they don't want to hurt their hosts' (Kwan Kim, Korean Tour Guide, pers. comm., 1996).

A total of 499 visitors were interviewed. The qualitative information was coded around sets of narrative themes to build analytical structures in the data. Full statements of individuals are quoted as they discover multiple layers of meaning attached to their impressions and experience. Within the social sciences, this is one way to situate a particular case study amidst wider patterns of culturally defined attitudes and values (Strauss, 1987). One of these values concerned links between New Zealand holidays and emerging green values in the context of increasing separation between nature and society.

Tourist perceptions, motivations and values

The perceptual process is a cognitive phenomenon that can be thought of as the process by which we make sense of the world. Since tourist consumers make decisions in conformity with their own view of reality, their behaviour follows from this view (Kassarjian and Robertson, 1968). An important beginning, then, toward understanding the tourist decision-making process is knowledge of perception. Berkman and Gilson (1986) have distinguished two groups of factors that influence perception, categorized as either stimulus or personal response factors. While stimuli are basically the characteristics of the stimulus being perceived (e.g. colour, shape or texture) and are hence outer-directed, personal factors are internal and are influenced by individual interests, needs and motives, expectations, personality and social position. In due course, when exploring the perception of travel, personal response factors have been far harder to measure scientifically than those relating to a stimulus (Mayo and Jarvis, 1981).

Along the same line, tourist motivation has been dominantly seen in the light of 'push' and 'pull' factors (Crompton, 1979; Dann, 1977; 1981). Push factors have been considered to be those socio-psychological motives that predispose individuals to travel. By contrast, pull factors are those that attract the potential traveller to specific destinations, once the decision to travel has been already made. In other words, the push factors have been always related to the inter/personal consumer 'world', and pull factors to the stimuli of destination. However, Crompton and McKay (1997) have recently argued that push–pull conceptualization should be refined by integrating with Iso-Ahola's (1982) escape-seeking dichotomy. From that perspective, it is possible to interpret the pull force in terms of intrinsic benefits: they divide both the seeking and escape forces into personal and interpersonal dimensions. Similarly, Gnoth (1997) argues that tourist perceptions and expectations are influenced by the interaction between two distinguished groups of motives and motivations. While motives relate to the emotional driving forces, motivations are related to cognitive situational parameters. Although both forces occur simultaneously, influencing the formation of perceptions and consequently expectations, the latter are produced by acquired values within peoples' everyday lives. In contrast to emotional urges and drives, such motivations are outer-directed, cognition-dominant, targeting particular objects (e.g. destinations, services, experiences) and are measurable. Gnoth goes further and suggests that contextual, socio-economic, cultural and situational influences:

'are operationalized as tourists' values expressing learned strategies to satisfy needs by either adapting the environment to suits one's needs, or to adapt oneself to given situations. In the case of holiday tourism, tourists can be assumed to choose an environment suitable to fit their motives and preferences. Those values and attitudes which come to bear on choices relating to destinations, activities, transport, and other tourism facilitators can be distinguished according to their amount of cognition vs. emotion they contain' (1997, p. 299).

Similarly, Parrinello (1993) claims that the motivation and anticipation of the tourist trip are interrelated phenomena and should be situated in the context of everyday life. She goes on to argue that post-industrial societies:

'are literally saturated with tourist culture, which originates from increasingly widespread and intensive channels of information, so that motivation and anticipation are now packed with meanings that would have been impossible to note 15 years ago' (1993, p. 241).

Broadening the simplistic approach of stimuli–response, Parrinello explains a holiday as a psychic journey that occurs in cycles, from planning and anticipation to recollection and re-elaboration. In this light, it becomes clear how the tourist consumer also becomes a 'producer', by negotiating and creating meanings from their individual perspectives and relaying them in their social worlds. Furthermore, by doing so they embody their perspective into the social and cultural structures within which producers negotiate and create new forms of tourist experience (Ateljevic, 1998). Consequently, tourist motivations and expectations are packed with the multiple layers of meaning induced by the socio-cultural context in which people live.

If tourism is a process that creates tourist experiences in the negotiation between the extraordinary and the mundane (Iso-Ahola, 1982; Mannell and Iso-Ahola, 1987), we can argue that historically specific forces of the 'everyday' context create tourist culture, influencing tourist motivations, perceptions and values. In like manner, Urry (1990) attests that the tourist gaze is directed towards places/ destinations that are in contrast to people's everyday environments, and is constructed through the anticipation. Various forms of non-tourist social practises, such as literature, film, TV, magazines, etc, feed the expectations. Urry (1987, 1988) explores this interplay through a study of seaside resorts in Britain, highlighting how socio-cultural and economic change, technological innovations and the internationalization of tourism have dramatically reduced the attractions of such resorts in the post-war period. However, in the 1990s, in the context of changing consumer tastes towards cultural experiences, those places are undergoing a resurgence as 'heritage' attractions (Foley, 1996). Likewise, Squire (1994) argues that one of the functions of tourism is that it enables people to indulge in dreams and idylls which are usually not part of their 'ordinary' life. Through her case study of visitors to the Lake District home of English children's writer Beatrix Potter, she found that this 'literary' tourist experience has been appropriated by tourists to fulfil a range of their social and cultural needs. In the nostalgia for a bygone age, many of her respondents valued the tourist experience as a medium to encounter a lost, hence idealized, rural past.

The perception process and destination images

Images represent a means of portraying perceived information in the individual's working memory (MacInnis and Price, 1987). Images can be likened to a mental picture constructed to represent personal beliefs, ideas and impressions. Imagery processing tends to deal with a multi-attribute or holistic view of an object (Dichter, 1985), as compared to discursive or single attribute-based processing (MacInnis and Price, 1987). Gestalt theory suggests that we perceive objects as an organized whole (Mayo and Jarvis, 1981).

To create the overall image of an object (destination), perceptual organization is based on the principles of selective attention, comprehension (categorization) and integration by selective retention (Mayo and Jarvis, 1981; Assael, 1987). In the phase of selective attention or 'perceptual defence', travel expectations are particularly important as: 'to an extent, a person perceives what he [sic] expects to see ... because [such expectations] determine what he [sic] pays attention to' (Mayo and Jarvis, 1981, p. 30).

The stage of comprehension is intrinsically linked to this process as people tend to conceive a consistent and uniform account by categorizing places, people, behaviour, events and objects into stereotypes, according to preconceived categories of meaning (Downs and Stea, 1977; Assael, 1987). Psychologists explain this by the mechanism called perceptual distortion, which helps people to cope in the way they seek information with a vast amount of data that agrees with their beliefs, but to ignore data that does not (Spence and Engel, 1970). Preconceived codes of established meanings and 'preferred readings' are usually constructed and transmitted by dominant cultural institutions (e.g. the media), and these views and ideologies subtly 'become "naturalized" as part of everyday common sense' (Dyer, 1982; Jackson, 1989, p. 3).

Destination images within the individual's mind are constructed by a wide range of information sources and 'are the sum of ideas and beliefs about a destination' (Oppermann and McKinley, 1996, p. 281). Gunn (1988) and Gartner (1989) suggest that images are formed on a number of conceptual levels. He explains the image formation process as evolving through three stages: organic, induced, and complex. While organic images are based primarily upon general sources of information, such as the general media, education, and word of mouth, the induced are related to tourist-directed information such as brochures or travel agents. Finally, impressions gained by visiting the destination produce the complex image. Accumulation of expectations and images in the phase of anticipation and planning for a trip is further negotiated when tourists step into the actual spaces of consumption. However, once on the actual trip, dreaming and playing continue, as people try to harmonize their feelings and their beliefs (Burch, 1965; Goodrich, 1978; Mayo and Jarvis, 1981).

The Meaning of Nature: the Tourist Gaze and Imagination of New Zealand

In cultures with highly developed technologies, where nature and society have become increasingly separated, the 'everyday' environment is becoming increasingly unhealthy and crowded, and members of society more alienated. Given this backdrop, Wilson argues that nature has become: 'the one place we can both indulge our dreams of mastery over the earth and seek some kind of contact with the origins of life – an experience we don't usually allow urban settings to provide' (1992, p. 25). In this context, tourism becomes an overarching structure through which it is possible to experience a romanticized appreciation of nature (Lash and Urry, 1994; Milne *et al.*, 1998). The opportunity of temporary escape from urbanization to gaze upon things lost to an industrialized world form the major cultural context for how New Zealand is apprehended in the tourist gaze and the imagination.

The overall perceptions of the international visitors interviewed confirm this argument. Themes of New Zealand being 'clean, green, fresh and peaceful', the 'farm life', 'scenery and diversified landscape', 'open space/freedom', 'low population' and 'friendliness' were the most common responses. As one young female student (in her twenties) from Holland said of New Zealand: 'The most beautiful country in the world for dreaming, relaxing and enjoying the nature'. A male professional (in his thirties) from Germany anticipated New Zealand: 'Just lovely – a place of serenity – yet still with the city rush'. The fear of development and 'progress' destroying nature constantly emerged – a middle-aged female professional from Germany imagined New Zealand as 'the last natural country in the world'.

Imagining these associations as a contrast to their everyday life and environments were frequently invoked, as one German professional (in his forties) explained: 'I imagined New Zealand as a very sunny country with few people and not that much stress like we have in Germany'. Similarly, one middle-aged administrative worker from Taiwan remarked: 'I knew it would be almost entirely in contrast to us – with fertile lands, plentiful water and life'. In this light, it becomes clear that there are geographical and socio-cultural variations in the construction of what constitutes the elements of attraction in the tourist gaze. More than 50% of tourists from Japan, Korea and Taiwan, who increasingly live in highly populated urban areas, commented open space, freedom, and room to move as an immediate association of New Zealand in their minds. In contrast, Australians in the sample who live on a relatively scarcely populated continent did not mention open space at all. Similarly, while 39% of British tourists imagined New Zealand to be like Britain (very often they said 'like England 20 years ago'), Asian tourists did not express that association at all (see Table 11.1).

These perceptions were almost equally reflected in the key motivations to visit New Zealand. Themes of 'unpolluted nature', 'freshness', 'diversified landscape', 'freedom/space', 'outdoor activities/adventure', 'peaceful/natural/relaxed holiday', 'natural paradise', 'beautiful country' were stated as leading factors in most cases. Full statements express clearly how tourists immerse themselves in a dream world and idylls of tourism consumption. A difference from their own country's sights (routine) and a romanticized appreciation of nature was the dominant theme, as a Korean clerical worker explained his motive to travel to New Zealand: 'to experience freedom, lots of space and greenness, which is so opposite to Korea'. Similarly, a female home-maker from Taiwan commented simply: 'for relaxation, to escape Taiwanese busy life and crowds'. A female administrative worker from Canada needed: 'a break from every day schedules'. A young female clerical worker from Australia simply wanted 'time-out and I needed somewhere slow and relaxing to go'.

Table 11.1 Images of New Zealand held by Australian, British, Japanese, Korean and Taiwanese tourists before their visit

Image of New Zealand	Australia	Japan	Korea	Taiwan	UK
	% (n=62)	% (n=36)	% (n=41)	% (n=32)	% (n=84)
Clean, green, fresh	55	75	85	78	31
Diversified landscape	21	8	5	0	21
Farm life, agricultural	19	42	37	40	21
Beautiful scenery	16	8	7	37	25
Friendly, safe	11	19	15	40	12
Like Britain	5	0	0	0	39
Low population	3	33	44	6	12
Maori culture	2	3	2	31	7
Peaceful, slow pace of life	2	6	5	0	10
Open space, freedom, room to move	0	64	54	59	7
Other	27	28	29	18	37

Source: International Visitors' Survey, Rotorua fieldwork, 1996.

Another layer of meaning consistently emerged whereby a generalized fear was expressed of environmental destruction and deepened social alienation caused by urbanization and industrialization. To a male professional (in his early forties) from Korea: 'New Zealand is what I consider to be a free country. We wanted to taste a relaxed lifestyle'. For a young female professional from Germany and her partner: 'it was our dream to experience nature, which we do not have in Germany'. A male agriculture worker from Holland (in his late thirties) wanted 'to see one of the last natural countries in the world before it's gone'. A middle-aged, female clerical worker from Germany asserted 'It's a place that's quite relaxed, we did not want to have a holiday in a place that is crowded and fast'.

Similarly, NZTB research interprets that one of the primary motivations for the Korean, Taiwanese, Singaporean and Thai groups to come to New Zealand is to 'be close to nature', and New Zealand is considered unique in that sense since it offers untouched beauty and space (New Zealand Tourist Board, 1995). Coming mainly from urban settings of crowds and traffic chaos, New Zealand's serenity 'delights' Asian visitors. One related the experience of driving through a flock of sheep: 'There are so many sheep, you cannot imagine it. They are not only in the fields but also on the roads – you have to see it to imagine it' (New Zealand Tourist Board, 1995).

Although the main motive for travel might be to experience a contrasting way of life from their own, fears of unfamiliarity and a lack of comfort came to the surface, as a male professional from USA (in his mid-thirties) expressed it: 'I wanted to travel in a place that was foreign but enough like home to get by'. Honeymooners from Australia wanted : 'to have a romantic honeymoon while still being in a familiar, Anglo-Saxon environment'. A young female professional from Australia selected New Zealand for her holiday destination because 'it's close to home – and similar – but still has its own personality'. A female home-maker (in her fifties) from Britain 'always felt New Zealand is part of England, so why not see it'.

NZTB research reveals similar sentiments, as one American visitor made this point directly:

'I enjoy travelling to new places – exotic in my mind but not really risky. I didn't expect such beautiful scenery, you go round every corner and see beautiful beaches and exotic forests and tree ferns. New Zealand is great because you can see all the fantastic scenery and still stay in nice hotels, you don't have to tramp for days to get to it. I had a great time flying to Milford Sound, I had not flown in something that small before – it was unique flying so close to the snow, a different point of view and very beautiful' (New Zealand Tourist Board, 1997, p. 32).

For visitors from the UK in particular, New Zealand offers cultural familiarity and at the same time the nostalgic experience of travelling from their increasingly alienated society back in time, perhaps even to the United Kingdom of the 1960s – as one British visitor interpreted:

'New Zealand is not just a holiday experience. New Zealanders are the same sort of people. Most people here speak English and they drive on the right side of the road. Its attractive to people from the UK – it's an uncrowded place. There's also a perception that the people "get up and go". When New Zealand turns its hand to something, then they do it well' (New Zealand Tourist Board, 1997, p. 30).

Another British visitor confirms:

'The people are proud. It doesn't compare to the UK. We've heard the National Anthem more here than in the UK. They like to tell you about their country. It's green and fertile land. The vegetation is impressive. There's a healthy lifestyle, good quality – it's a lovely country' (New Zealand Tourist Board, 1997, p. 30).

The safety of the country and assurance of reliable travel conditions appeared important, which can be interpreted as an awareness of the increasing uncertainty of international travel. A honeymoon couple from Taiwan selected New Zealand: 'to have a romantic honeymoon and New Zealand is a safe country to make own, relaxing, slow pace itinerary'. A middle-aged professional from Austria said: 'we travel a lot for hiking, trekking and cycling – we thought New Zealand would be a good place to come as you don't need to travel too far from urbanized area to get to a national park. It's also very safe for something like that'. A female professional from Japan (in her thirties) who travelled with her partner emphasized: 'it's safe and friendly to travel independently, to enjoy open space and beautiful scenery and to experience farm stay, life'.

Word-of-mouth promotion, underpinning New Zealand's increasing popularity and fashion as a 'newly discovered tourist destination', emerged as an influencing force. As a female clerical worker from the Netherlands put it: 'it was highly praised by my friends. They loved it here and I had to see it for myself'. One American journalist was sent to experience personally a 'motorbike adventure trip' by his magazine in order to do a story about it. He stated: 'New Zealand has currently an image in the States as an exotic, adventurous place, comparatively new'. A male professional from Japan explained it simply: 'everyone in Japan comes to New Zealand, and I wanted too'. A young female professional from the USA had 'heard a lot about it. It's a newly discovered place'. A male professional from Germany elucidated: 'all people talk about it and everybody who visited is fascinated'. A young student from Israel noted that New Zealand has become 'more and more popular in Israel. I heard a lot of stories about New Zealand. It contradicts Israel in terms of culture, relaxed life and views'. The images of landscape as portrayed by various media appealed, as a male professional from Germany (in his forties) explained: 'when I have seen documentaries on various parts, even Rotorua, I just had to see it'. A retired professional from USA interpreted: 'what we saw it just looked so beautiful and as our friends described it. We just had to see it'. Nearly 20% of respondents explicitly stated that one of the influencing reasons to travel to New Zealand was the current popularity of New Zealand at home, as 'so many people talk about it'.

As already argued, preconceptions and images that tourists assimilate and store (both in the past and present) during preparations for the trip are often (re)created beyond tourist image production by broader factors external to a tourism industry (e.g. TV, film, literature, magazines). Table 11.2 shows that 'the imagination' of New Zealand has been (re)constructed from a wide range of media and informational sources, within and beyond the dominion of tourism production forces. The high score of 75% assigned to friends and relatives clearly shows the importance of individual/social (re)production processes. This can be particularly linked to family/friends links in New Zealand as 30% of interviewed respondents came to visit friends and relatives, which was in most cases a convenient opportunity 'to have a holiday and to see a beautiful country' (see Table 11.3).

Table 11.2 Sources of information about New Zealand accessed by international visitors in their home country

Source of information	Ranking of importance (%) (*n*=499)				
	Very important		→		Not important
Friends/relatives/work colleagues	75	50	16	4	4
Guide/travel book	66	20	25	9	10
Travel agents	59	14	18	16	8
Travel brochure	45	10	20	8	6
Television documentaries	16	3	5	3	1
Television advertising	14	2	4	5	1
Film/cinema/video	14	2	4	4	2
Newspaper/magazine advertising	12	1	4	3	2
Newspaper/magazine articles or features	10	1	3	4	1
Visited NZ before	8	6	1	0	<1
NZ Tourist Office	5	1	3	1	1
Airline/airport	1	1	<1	<1	0
Other	4	4	<1	<1	0

Percentages are not equal to 100 because respondents were giving multiple responses.
Source: International Visitors' Survey, Rotorua fieldwork, 1996.

Table 11.3 Reason(s) for visiting New Zealand by international visitors

Reasons for visiting	Percentage (*n*=499)
Holiday	77
Visiting friends and relatives	30
Honeymoon	6
Education (English language)	4

Source: International Visitors' Survey, Rotorua fieldwork, 1996.

Tourist Participation on the Site

Aggregation of expectations and images in the phase of anticipation is further 'played out' when tourists step into the actual spaces of consumption. As Galbraith asserts: 'the tourist is physically transported to the site of attraction where he or she proceeds to see, hear, smell, touch or move through the experience. The individual is at the heart of this venture ... with his or her fulfilment of desire being the whole point to the exercise' (1992, p. 42). Squire, in her assessment of how people were interpreting the literary place through a case study of visitors Beatrix Potter's home, states that 'In adopting the Beatrix Potter setting for diverse purposes, visitors were consciously indulging in escapist fantasies, filtering out those elements that did not conform to the dictates of popular mythology' (1994, p. 117).

In a similar manner, to my question about how the country was experienced after arrival, respondents confirmed the continuous play on anticipated dreams and fantasies. A male managerial worker from Denmark (in his forties) remarked: 'New Zealand filled our dreams. It is simply beautiful'. Social values attached to the countryside and the rural, evoked in motivations and perceptions, consistently (re)emerged in the actual experience of New Zealand. Yet that would be hardly possible if there were not actual green spaces in New Zealand, as a female sales worker from Australia explained: 'I expected beautiful nature but I am impressed how beautiful it really is'. A female service worker from England complained about the weather but was still 'glad how really green it is, hilly and diversified'. Similarly, a female home-maker from Taiwan explained that her experience of New Zealand was 'better than imagined, so many beautiful trees, parks, you can sit freely everywhere'. A male administrative/managerial worker from Korea described his experience as 'Fantastic! Experience is much more realistic than image'. A female administrative/managerial worker from England (in her twenties) found New Zealand 'even more beautiful than imagined, absolutely amazing place'. A male administrative/managerial worker from Japan commented: 'New Zealand is so green. It's great. There are no road blocks or long traffic lines. It's so lovely. I wish I could take New Zealand back to Japan with me'. A female professional from France in her thirties asserted: 'it's so beautiful, you can only see for yourself New Zealand's true beauty'. Similarly, a female sales worker from Niue noticed: 'it's so pretty, unlike what I imagined. I had to see it for myself. You can't picture in your mind what New Zealand is'. A journalist from the USA noted details of the actual geography of New Zealand: 'amazing how the country differs from corner to corner, from farm over the mountain to water. I'm fascinated by trees, by little things making the difference from my home country, there are so many unusual things'. In all, almost 90% expressed their positive impressions about New Zealand's natural landscape in a variety of wordings such as great, fascinating, incredible, amazing, beautiful, breathtaking, fabulous, unreal, extraordinary, impressive, awesome, majestic.

However, in some cases the 'reality' of the physical landscape was not the only actuality captured. One respondent (male professional Irish) who was a 'professional' traveller, working for up to a year in each country noted: 'it's quite expensive; I have been lucky in the employment area but I've noticed there are a lot who are unemployed; but overall a very nice, friendly relaxed country'. Similarly, a female student from Spain noticed 'some poverty, but not as much as at home. What I like are very nice people and lovely nature'. A repeat visitor from England also found 'prices more expensive than last time and people are not so reliable as they used to be'. Among unexpected realities were: 'wet weather and high prices', as a male professional from Holland emphasized his disappointment. Similarly, for a female sales worker from Ireland: 'if it weren't always raining, it would be fantastic'. A male professional from the USA found New Zealand 'richer to experience than in the book, but disappointed by the weather'.

The significance of people's psychological immersion consistently arose, as a female artist from Canada expressed her experience of New Zealand: 'It's much more than what the eye sees, you have to look deeper to see New Zealand's real beauty'. A male professional from the USA (in his forties) remarked: 'it's absolutely fascinating, the landscape is amazing, there are so many different aspects of environment. Trees are a special story'. In that sense, a male service worker from Germany here on a second visit came: 'for more experience as there is so much to explore'. An emotional engagement of tourists was clearly evidenced, as one female professional from Germany (in her thirties) commented: 'people and the atmosphere is relaxed; just so much to see and experience beyond eye-view'. A retired man from the USA found it 'fabulous, just amazing, around every bend there's some hidden spectacular sight. It's just amazing'.

The need to turn the above intangibility of experience into tangible forms of memorable experience was expressed. A male professional from Germany explained: 'I've found myself stopping to take photos along the way all the time. It's so graceful, it's an awesome country, so friendly and relaxed'. Similarly, a female student from Australia found it: 'very scenic, little areas tucked away, that I've got great shots of'. A female sales worker from the USA took a lot of 'shots of nature', although slightly disappointed that she had not seen 'very many Kiwi birds around, I did not realize they were quite rare. You can take photos and I did, lovely pictures of the rivers, little waterfalls just coming out of nowhere on the sides of the hills.'

Overcoming the alienation of everyday life in one's own society was mentioned. A male professional from Germany observed: 'in Germany when you come alone into the pub, you stay alone, but here it's different'. In the same way, a male administrative/managerial worker from the USA found it 'truer and more genuine than where I come from'. In all, some 24% of respondents stated the 'friendliness and hospitality' of New Zealanders as an important part of their impressions.

NZTB research brings up similar arguments, quoting one German tourist:

'We came because of landscape. The light is different – there is not much pollution in the air. It's an untouched landscape. In Europe or the USA it would be built out. We saw the gannets, seals, and penguins here. You can get close to them – almost touch them. We cannot do that in Germany. We took a flight to White Island. The pilot could tell us everything – history, geology. We walked on the volcano. It is the ultimate experience' (NZTB, 1997, p. 31).

Contrast to life in contemporary, urban culture and nostalgia for spontaneity and the rural past are seized upon by tourists, enabling people 'to stop and think' away from the pressure, as one visitor from Netherlands remarked:

'You realise more about the things underneath the ground. Look at that mud – what is underneath there. Wonder and think. Talked about the eruptions – it is more likely that it happens here. We went to a local pub in the Coromandel and had a great night. Sat and drank with a lot of local people – Maori people. It was just great. Feel at home' (NZTB, 1997, p. 30).

Linked to this sense of 'warmth and freedom' is a feeling of safety, particularly for independent travel; as a service worker from Canada noted: 'a tourist like myself can get around easily, New Zealand is great, it's country where you can do anything you please, in your own time'. In the same way, a female service worker from Canada stated: 'definitely friendly people, really amazing country, easy to get around, people are laid back, really good for travellers'. Likewise, a male professional from Switzerland 'fell in love with this country; the climate is great, the hiking is just magnificent and it's so safe here'.

To summarize, several persistent themes emanate from the quotations of the tourists interviewed. Firstly, although visitors with different value systems and interests necessarily obtain distinct meanings from the experience, certain interpretations emerge almost universally. Despite their different positions conditioned by age, occupation, or country of residence, a value system that assigns virtue to rural and natural land as opposed to negative ratings of urban settings prevails cross-culturally. Secondly, their motivations to travel to New Zealand show other layers of meaning which express people's generalized fears of environmental destruction in the context of increasing urbanization. However, in the search for difference, the socio-cultural variations of people's everyday lives excite the diversity of the tourist gaze. Thirdly, consumption on site within New Zealand's natural landscape is in an important dialectic with the emotional engagements and signification given by tourists themselves. This was expressed in a variety of different wordings of their experience of natural landscape – 'fascinating, amazing, awesome, marvellous, fabulous, beautiful, attractive, remarkable, breathtaking'. Tourists universally visit New Zealand 'to gaze and do', to 'explore, relax, tramp, enjoy, have fun and adventures, feel, listen and see beyond the eye-view'.

Conclusions

A few key issues emerge from this New Zealand case study. Firstly, the methodological angle of open-coded queries employed in this research has shown how more interpretative, qualitative techniques allow us to gauge the multiple layers of meanings attached to tourist perceptions and impressions. Secondly, this approach reveals how tourism as a medium allows people to live out certain fantasies, imagining, idealizing and appropriating the experience which can satisfy a range of culturally constructed attitudes and values. The propensity to access a wide range of information sources about New Zealand illustrates how the tourist gaze/experience is socially constructed, anticipated and imag(in)ed within the everyday context, thereby influencing motivational and perceptual processes. For example, the images of 'New Zealand's incredible beauty', as described by visitors' friends and families who have already visited the country, created a perception of 'the country which cannot be missed to be seen' (as it might disappear in the progress of urbanization). In this sense, image of destination becomes the goal of motivation and perception (Parrinello, 1993). Thirdly, it can be argued that situational influences of progressive urbanization and alienation underpin the creation of green values and environmental consciousness, which then in turn influence tourist motivations, and the evaluation of destinations.

Finally, people's generalized fear of environmental destruction suggests that tourists mainly come from a global urban culture, which leads towards generalized tourist behaviour at an international level. On the other hand, however, in the search for difference, the socio-cultural variations of people's everyday lives inspire the diversity of the tourist gaze, maintaining the pattern of the motivational process and its own specific socio-cultural identity. In the light of this discussion, therefore, it is important for marketers to conceive this global–local dialectic as a simultaneously generalized trend towards global values and motivations of travel with, at the same time, locally specific situational influences of people's everyday lives. The tourism experience, as a negotiation between the extraordinary and the mundane, provides a focus for marketers to identify more thoroughly how people's suppressed personal, social and cultural needs can be satisfied through tourism consumption.

References

Adler, J. (1989) Travel as performed art. *American Journal of Sociology* 94, 1366–1391.

Assael, H. (1987) *Consumer Behaviour and Marketing Action*, 3rd edn. Boston: PWS-Kent Publishing Company.

Ateljevic, I. (1998) Circuits of tourism: (re)producing the place of Rotorua, New Zealand. PhD thesis, University of Auckland, New Zealand.

Berkman, H.W. and Gilson, C. (1986) *Consumer Behaviour: Concepts and Strategies*, 3rd edn. Boston: Kent Publishing Company.

Bruner, J.S. (1970) Social psychology and perception. In: D.T. Kollat, R.D. Blackwell and J.F. Engel (eds) *Research in Consumer Behaviour*. New York: Holt, Rinehart & Winston.

Britton, R.A. (1979) The image of the Third World in tourism marketing. *Annals of Tourism Research* 6, 318–329.

Burch, W.R. (1965) The play world of camping: research into the social meaning of outdoor recreation. *American Journal of Sociology* 70, 604–612.

Calantone, R.J., di Benetto, C.A., Hakam, A. and Bojanic, D.C. (1989) Multiple multinational tourism positioning using correspondence analysis. *Journal of Travel Research* 28, 25–32.

Crompton, J.L. (1979) Motivations for pleasure vacation. *Annals of Tourism Research* 6, 408–424.

Crompton, J.L. and McKay, L.S. (1997) Motives of visitors attending festival events. *Annals of Tourism Research* 24, 425–439.

Dann, G.M.S. (1977) Anomie, ego-enhancement and tourism. *Annals of Tourism Research* 4, 184–194.

Dann, G.M.S. (1981) Tourism motivation: an appraisal. *Annals of Tourism Research* 8, 187–219.

Dann, G., Nash, D. and Pearce, P. (1988) Methodology in tourism research. *Annals of Tourism Research* 15, 1–28.

Dichter, E. (1985) What's an image? *Journal of Consumer Marketing* 2, 75–81.

Downs, R.M. and Stea, D. (1977) *Maps in Minds: Reflections on Cognitive Mapping*. New York: Harper & Row.

Dyer, G. (1982) *Advertising as Communication*. London: Methuen.

Echtner, C.M. and Richie, J.R.B. (1991) The meaning and measurement of destination image. *Journal of Tourism Studies* 2, 2–12.

Foley, M. (1996) Heritage tourism in the United Kingdom. In: J. Richards (ed.) *Culture Tourism in Europe*. Wallingford, UK: CAB International.

Gartner, W.C. (1989) Tourism image: attribute measurement of state tourism products using multidimensional scaling techniques. *Journal of Travel Research* Fall, 16–20.

Gnoth, J. (1997) Tourism motivation and expectation formation. *Annals of Tourism Research* 24, 283–300.

Goodrich, J.N. (1978) The relationship between preferences for and perceptions of vacation destinations: application of a choice model. *Journal of Travel Research* 16, 8–13.

Gunn, C. (1988) *Vacationscapes: Designing Tourist Regions*. New York: Van Nostrand Reinhold.

Iso-Ahola, S.E. (1982) Towards a social psychology theory of tourism motivation: a rejoinder. *Annals of Tourism Research* 9, 256–262.

Jackson, P. (1989) *Maps of Meaning. An Introduction to Cultural Geography*. London: Unwin Hyman.

Kassarjian, H.H. and Robertson, T.S. (eds) (1968) *Perspectives in Consumer Behavior*. USA: Scott, Foresman & Co.

Lash, S. and Urry, J. (1994) *Economies of Signs and Space*. London: Sage.

MacInnis, D.J. and Price, L.L. (1987) The role of imagery in information processing: review and extensions. *Journal of Consumer Research* 13, 473–491.

Mannell, R.C. and Iso-Ahola, S.E. (1987) Psychological nature of leisure and tourism experience. *Annals of Tourism Research* 14, 314–331.

Mayo, E. and Jarvis, L.P. (1981) *The Psychology of Leisure Travel*. Boston: CBI Publishing.

Meyer, J.H. and Reynolds, W.H. (1967) *Consumer Behaviour and Marketing Management*. Houghton-Mifflin.

Milne, S., Grekin, J. and Woodley, S. (1998) Tourism and the construction of place in Canada's Eastern Arctic. In: G. Ringer and C.L. Cartier (eds) *Destinations: Cultural Landscapes of Tourism*. London: Routledge.

New Zealand Tourism Board (1995) *Product Development Opportunities for Asian Markets*. Wellington: NZTB.

New Zealand Tourism Board (1997) *Product Development Opportunities for European and North American Markets*. Wellington: NZTB.

Oppermann, M. and McKinley, S. (1996) Sex and image: marketing of tourism destination. In: *Pacific Rim Tourism 2000: Issues, Interrelations, Inhibitors. Conference Proceedings*. Rotorua, New Zealand: Centre for Tourism Studies, Waiariki Polytechnic.

Papadopoulos, N. (1993) What product and country images are and are not. In: N. Papadapoulos and L.A. Heslpo (eds) *Product–Country Images: Impact and Role in International Marketing*. New York: International Business Press.

Parrinello, G.L. (1993) Motivation and anticipation in post-industrial tourism. *Annals of Tourism Research*, 20, 233–249.

Squire, S.J. (1994) The cultural values of literary tourism. *Annals of Tourism Research* 21, 103–120.

Spence, H.E. and Engel, J.F. (1970) The impact of brand preference on the perception of brand names: a laboratory analysis. In: D.T. Kollat, R.D. Blackwell and J.F. Engel (eds) *Research in Consumer Behaviour*. New York: Holt, Rinehart & Winston.

Stabler, M.J. (1988) The image of destination regions: theoretical and empirical aspects. In: B. Goodall and G. Ashworth (eds) *Marketing in the Tourism Industry*. Beckenham, UK: Croom Helm.

Strauss, A.L. (1987) *Qualitative Analysis for Social Scientists*. Cambridge, UK: Cambridge University Press.

Urry, J. (1987) Some social and spatial aspects of services. *Environment and Planning D: Society and Space* 5, 5–26.

Urry, J. (1988) Cultural change and contemporary holiday making. *Theory, Culture and Society* 5, 35–55.

Urry, J. (1990) *The Tourist Gaze: Leisure and Travel in Contemporary Societies*. London: Sage.

Williams, J.E. and Zelinsky, W. (1970) On some patterns of international tourist flows. *Economic Geography* October, 549–567.

Wilson, A. (1992) *The Culture of Nature: North American Landscape from Disney to the Exxon Valdez*. Cambridge, UK: Blackwell.

Woodside, A.G. and Lysonski, S. (1989) A general model of traveller destination choice. *Journal of Travel Research* 17, 8–14.

Chapter twelve
The Problem of Motivation in Understanding the Demand for Leisure Day Visits

Scott McCabe
Derbyshire Business School, University of Derby, Kedleston Road, Derby DE22 1GB, UK

Introduction

Motivation is the 'thorn in the side' of leisure and tourism research. Some attempts have been made to propose theories of motivation for leisure travel, but the operational methods used to study motivation are extremely complex, even unwieldy, and lack predictive power. The continuing dominance of the behaviourist notions of 'needs' as motivations, or the cognitivist notions of 'attitudes', have tended to stifle debate on the subject, since both focus inherently on 'drives' as the basic notion behind motivation. In this paper we review the literature on motivation theory and the empirical evidence. We commend the very useful progress made and the contribution to the debate made by psychology in the conceptualization of drives as internal needs, but we conclude that epistemological concerns render the study of motivation as needs derived from analyses of 'reasons' inherently inconclusive, and therefore an inevitably equivocal area for further inquiry. This is not to dismiss the role of drives, or needs, in leisure and tourism behaviours, rather that inquiry may be more fruitfully directed through alternative conceptualizations. In this paper, we propose that modern leisure and leisure travel are social constructions and therefore that reasons for doing leisure and leisure travel are within the remit of the social science disciplines, the rationale being that social science is interested in the actions and interactions of individuals as members of a social system. However, even within sociology, motivations research has tended to be driven by the need to reinforce psychological notions of drives, through the design and interpretation of quantitative surveys using the attitude construct within positivist methodology. We argue to re-orient the debate towards the context of social reality, and within this context to locate the unit of research as the individual social actors, inseparable from their social setting. Through the use of an ethnomethodological study of the experiences of day visitors to the Peak National Park in the central UK, we hope to explain how complex, multi-dimensional, and often apparently contradictory reasons may give us clues to 'meanings' that may explain social action in leisure and leisure travel. Examples are presented through an analysis of conversational data and the justifications for actions uncovered through a search for the 'because' and 'in order to' motives explained by Schutz (1972 [1938]).

The motivations for leisure and leisure travel

De Charms and Muir (1978) classify the origins of motivational theories in Freud, Hull and Lewin as, respectively, psychodynamic theory, stimulus–response theory, and cognitive psychology. Parrinello (1993) states that in reality these three classifications can be broadly split into two groups: the homoeostatic theories (including behaviour theories), and cognitive theories. Parrinello (1993) further argues that although behaviouristic models were initially influential, after the work of Berlyne (1960, 1978) and Deci (1975) gradual acceptance of cognitive processes in motivation was achieved, based on the exploratory, self-deterministic and competence-seeking behaviours particular to humans. Motivation theory as an idea underpinning action was operationalized as a set of needs by Murray (1938), and gained currency after the work of Maslow (1943). Without going into all the details of the 'hierarchy of needs', we should state here that the theory entailed a logical progression in a five-stage hierarchy, from basic human needs of food and shelter though a series of stages that concluded with the pinnacle of 'self-actualization', where the individual attains a kind of self-fulfilment, realizing his or her potential. Ryan (1997) notes that until Maslow, psychology had been concerned with the study of abnormal behaviours, and that Maslow's contribution was that to understand psychological health, normative behaviour should be analysed. Witt and Wright (1992), in a thorough review of Maslow's work, claim that the hierarchy was developed in the context of the clinic, and further that Maslow himself had concerns about the applicability of the theory to work motivation, let alone tourist motivation. However, the theory's popularity is probably due to its simplicity for non-psychologists, and it is today almost ubiquitous in consumer studies, marketing, and leisure and tourism texts (Cooper *et al.*, 1993). But the theory lacks empirical support in the field of leisure and tourism – the only published work found that used it as a framework for the analysis of tourism motivation is that by Pearce and Caltabiano (1983), who inferred travel motives from tourists' experiences.

Possibly the earliest contribution specific to the motivation for travel, in particular leisure travel, was the work of Plog (1977). Based on in-depth interviews about destination preferences in the USA, Plog developed a typology of travellers along a continuum in which all citizens could be included. Plog's theory was indeed useful as a general classification, but in operational terms, travel is more complex than the model allows. Travellers have different motivations for different trips, and the model could not account for the changing nature of tourist destination preferences (Cooper *et al.*, 1993). Although the theory developed by Plog was not grounded in the notions of homoeostatic theories, the analysis was heavily interpretive. In terms of social psychology, the major contribution to the theory of motivation for leisure and tourism must be the work of Iso-Ahola (1980), which built on the notion of intrinsic motivation proposed by Deci (1975), linked to a level of optimal arousal, i.e. levels of boredom or over-stimulation. The ensuing academic discussion that followed with Dann (1977, 1981) made a lasting impression on the study of tourism motivation, and serves as a useful context for the major issues in the debate in psychology and social psychology. Dann preferred to view the 'push' and 'pull' factors of tourist motivation as to do with 'anomie' and 'ego-enhancement' (Dann, 1977, 1981), as opposed to Iso-Ahola's analysis of the individual 'escaping' and 'seeking' based on environment and stimulation levels (Iso-Ahola, 1980, 1982; see also Mannel and Iso-Ahola, 1987). Mansfield (1992) has argued against this apparent link between the escape from a mundane or urban environment associated with everyday life, coupled with a seeking that is based on either destination attributes or a compensation mechanism, on the basis of a lack of supporting evidence. Dun Ross and Iso-Ahola (1991, p. 284) explored the links between motivation and satisfaction, and found that seeking and escaping dimensions were important motives and satisfaction factors, with seeking factors being more significant. However, Moore *et al.* (1995, p. 72) state that the argument may be academic, since the psychological literature views the external event, especially stimuli associated with goal objectives, as incentive motivation.

Pearce (1993) developed the concept of a 'career travel ladder' that built on the notion that stage in the life cycle held value in determining the motivation for leisure travel, which was similar to the notions of family life cycle developed by Rapoport and Rapoport (1975). Pearce (1993) argued that at different stages of the life cycle, individuals were motivated by different factors that would influence their travel choices and decisions, and extended this analysis to claim that motivations can change within the one holiday experience. Gray (1979) proposed a simplified motivational theory based on two main determinants, wanderlust and sunlust. Krippendorf (1987) identified eight sets of reasons why people travel: recuperation and regeneration; compensation and social integration; escape; communication; freedom and self-determination; self-realization; happiness; and to broaden the mind. These motives are all connected by a going-away-from motive (as opposed to a seeking motive), and the motives are personal and self-directed. Crompton (1979) similarly identified nine motives for vacation travel, seven of which he claimed were social–psychological, the remaining two being cultural motives (which were found to be relevant to particular destination attributes). Crompton found that the motives were: escape from a perceived mundane environment; exploration and evaluation of self; relaxation; prestige; regression; enhancement of kinship relations; and facilitation of social interaction. The latter two cultural motives were novelty, and education. Crompton based his findings on his own empirical research, consisting of 39 unstructured interviews, and through his analysis pinpointed one of the fundamental and recurring problems of tourist motivation: that although individuals put effort into the destination selection process, the benefits and satisfactions derived were not related to, or derived from, a destination's attributes (Crompton, 1979, p. 415). Despite agreeing that motivational research findings are often unreliable, Ryan (1997) accepts the view that although experiences may be expressed in many different forms, the underlying motivations may be few in number (Ryan, 1997, p. 28). Ryan takes the leisure motivation scale developed by Beard and Ragheb (1983) as representing the continuing themes that emerge from an analysis of the research findings in tourism motivation, and classifies them into the four categories of motivational need adapted from Maslow: intellectual need; social need; competence-mastery; and stimulus avoidance. Fodness (1994), in an exhaustive empirical study, sought to formalize the conceptual relationships between motivations and the attitudes of tourists in Florida, using functional theory. On the premise that individuals' reasons for holding certain attitudes are based on the notion that the attitudes serve psychological needs, Fodness sought to extend this framework to tourism through assigning reasons to four dimensions of functional theory:

> 'The reasons people give for their leisure travel behavior represent the psychological functions (the needs) the vacation serves (satisfies) for the individual. This approach has intuitive appeal. It directly addresses the question of why tourists behave as they do' (Fodness, 1994, p. 445).

However detailed and extensive the construction of the research method developed by Fodness, the issue remains that the reasons given by the respondents bear little relation to the functional theory concepts utilized. Witt and Wright (1992, p. 45) propose an econometric, rational, utility approach to the study of motivation, and they apply the expectancy theory, where expectation of a given outcome, or consequence of a decision, will be determined by the value or attractiveness of that outcome to the individual. They point out that the major limitation of this approach is the complexity of the methods required to test it, and that it would be difficult to use the model to predict behaviour.

Many researchers prefer to avoid the problems of motivation by shifting the point of analysis away from internal states driving the process toward less problematic grounds. Notably, sociologists and social anthropologists have concerned themselves with the documentation, classification and typification of tourism experiences in a long tradition of qualitative and theoretical research, in the pursuit of linking typologies of tourists or typologies of experience to understanding behaviour (e.g. Boorstin, 1964; MacCannell, 1976; Cohen, 1972, 1974, 1979, 1988; Smith, 1977; Gottleib, 1982). Other researchers of consumer studies prefer to consider the actual decision-making characteristics of trips in terms of perceptions, attitudes, purpose of trip and benefits sought, so that segmentation of travellers into groups can be achieved (Middleton, 1994). Middleton argues that lists of motives are only one of a range of techniques that can be used to segment tourists. Certainly in terms of the marketing and consumer behaviour fields, research has been directed more towards understanding the decision-making processes of tourists within a framework that views tourism as a consumption process (see e.g. Howard and Sheth, 1969; Moutihno, 1987 for models of decision-making; Van Raaj and Francken, 1984; Um and Crompton, 1990; Crompton and Ankomah, 1993; Lue *et al.*, 1993; Dimanche and Havitz, 1994; Gitelson and Kerstetter, 1994; Sirakaya *et al.*, 1996 for examples of tourist choice research). No matter how relevant and interesting a discussion of these other areas might be to the debate, due to considerations of space this paper must confine discussion to the specific topic of motivation as a construct. We conclude this discussion with the assertion that the motivation construct that is credited with generating the whole leisure and tourism process is far from fully conceptualized, that it is still perceived as the grand prize, the big fish of tourism research that was never near being caught in empirical research findings. Let us detail some of the evidence for this assertion.

The theoretical and empirical problem of motivation

What is worrying from a reading of the tourism motivation literature is an apparent lack of concern about the epistemological basis of motivation as a construct in either the theory of needs, as it has been appropriated by many subsidiary disciplines, or the functional utility and expectancy theories, and the validity of the methods used to measure and test the construct. This is in part due to the multidisciplinary nature of leisure and tourism studies, the atheoretical character of much tourism research which is symptomatic of tourism studies (Tribe, 1997), and the complex nature of the touristic and leisure phenomena (Smith, 1995).

The theoretical problem of motivation is a question of epistemology. It is a question about what we can reasonably expect to 'know' about individuals' drives by asking them about their motivations and needs. Are these drives available to us as part of our consciousness? Or do we simply repeat the needs that have been suggested to us as needs through our immediate social peers, the wider contexts of our particular social realities in this place at this time, and the influence of the media?

Parrinello (1993, pp. 234–235) hints that recent psychological theories suggest that motivation involves much more complex processes which may not be understood solely in psychological terms, that social and environmental psychology may have important contributions to make, and further, that tourist motivation today is possibly so complex (in that the actual choice is a consequence of much wider experiences) that traditional notions of motivation are perhaps not relevant. Moore *et al.* (1995, p. 74), in their analysis of the relationships between leisure and tourism, cite the work of Leiper (1990a), who found that the range of needs and motivations identified from tourism studies closely paralleled those for other forms of leisure. The point being that motivation for tourism, as defined as a list of needs particular to, and responsible for, the tourism act, appears to be applicable at least to other forms of leisure, and perhaps even other forms of activity such as sex or religious ritual, and which may not exclude work, especially where motives to do with the notion of 'flow' (where the individual attains a high level of involvement in an activity) (Csikszentmihalyi, 1975) are considered. More recent efforts have sought to clarify the attitude construct and its relation to motivation and expectation as the central measurement device used in both psychological and sociological studies of tourism motivation (Gnoth, 1997). Gnoth argues against a uni-dimensional notion of motivation, and distinguishes between motive and motivation, whereby the former is derived from need formation and drives, and the latter indicates object-specific preferences (Gnoth, 1997, p. 291). This conception holds common-sense value and bears similarities to notions developed out of early empirical findings by this author (McCabe, 1997). Gnoth goes further than earlier attempts to problematize motivation as a construct in tourism (e.g. Parrinello, 1993), which were more interested in describing the construct.

As early as 1982, Pearce bemoaned a lack of coherent theory of tourist motivation which builds on previous studies. The lack of a consistent and coherent theory is only part of the problem, however. Efforts in theory development for tourist motivation are further hampered by the methodological traditions of the disciplines. We have noted that a wide selection of authors refer to the inability of empirical research to predict actual behaviour (Pearce, 1982, 1993; Parrinello, 1993; and notably, Mansfield, 1992; Ryan, 1997). The criticisms of the empirical body of knowledge have been addressed briefly in the preceding discussion of the literature – lack of space excludes a full description – but it is certain that the two problems are mutually exclusive. Howard and Sheth (1969), in their description of the theory of consumer behaviour, pointed out the operational problems associated with combining highly abstract concepts (including motivation) with relatively objective intervening variables within the same framework. The problems are rooted within questions about what are legitimate areas of study concerning human behaviour or action, as well as the legitimacy of the way academics assign abstract concepts to their observations of, and questions to, tourists. Can we conduct empirical research into the question of motivation? This theoretical question can be translated into another. Is it possible to construct abstract concepts about internal drives from a positivist analysis of survey data concerning the reasons why individuals indulge in leisure travel? Both questions are to do with academic beliefs that underpin the structures of empirical inquiry, yet both appear to be given little consideration in the literature. However, this paper is not concerned with a defence, or criticism, of other positions, but a presentation of a new approach that may overcome some of these problems.

Another view of motivation for leisure and leisure travel

It is appropriate to state here that it is not the premise of this paper that motivation is a legitimate subject of inquiry in this context. Motivation is an abstract concept that is beyond the realm of empirical inquiry in this case. We must make this assertion since consistency in the research process through ontological beliefs, epistemological positions and research methods is necessary to heighten confidence in the analysis of research findings (Glaser and Strauss, 1967; Strauss, 1987; Strauss and Corbin, 1990). However, it is the intention of this paper to present a brief outline of the beliefs, assumptions and methodologies underpinning the empirical evidence that could shed light on the problems associated with findings of motivation research.

The main beliefs that underpinning the empirical research presented here are that day visits (and here we could also include all forms of leisure and leisure travel) are a part of normal everyday life in the UK. This is not to say that day visits to the Peak National Park are undertaken by all members of society, but rather that day visits to the National Park are one type of a whole range of leisure trips available to members of society. In this sense, then, it is possible to locate day visits within the theoretical territory of the everyday world of social reality described by Berger and Luckmann (1966). Grounded in the tradition of social phenomenology (Schutz, 1972 [1938]), the study of everyday life concerns the mundane processes and actions of cognitive actors as they are oriented towards and ordered by the social world. To those who argue that leisure, and tourism especially, represent actions oriented towards an 'escape' from the mundane world of everyday life, we counter that it is still possible to conceive these actions and meanings as part of the paramount reality of everyday life, either as discreet spheres of reality within paramount reality (Berger and Luckmann, 1966), or as they may be the result of 'escape attempts' (Cohen and Taylor, 1976). Cohen and Taylor (1992), in the second edition of their book, define this attempt, in terms of holiday taking, as an ironic, staged, '(in-)authentic' event (after MacCannell, 1976) where the individual creates a fantasy image, yet knows that it is a false one. We do not necessarily accept this analysis. The basic premise here, however, is simply that of Schutz, who;

> '...insisted that the social world is, in the first instance, experientially interpreted by its members as meaningful and intelligible in terms of social categories and constructs' (Heritage, 1984, p. 45).

As such, day visits to the Peak National Park are not bestowed with meanings of authenticity seeking, but rather conceived as meaningful social action as part of everyday life performed in leisure time. Through the axiomatic notion that the social world is not a place of external happenings, but is understood as infused with subjective meaning and intention, where all social events are oriented to those who participate in them or attend in any way (Heritage, 1984, pp. 47–48), day visitor experiences can become the legitimate focus of study. This is not to say that understanding social reality in terms of mundane, everyday actions is achieved through empathetic observations. It is not possible to gain access to the exact experiences of the social actor, but rather, understanding is achieved through the application of common-sense constructs to events, experiences and actions for the time being, or until demonstrated otherwise (Heritage, 1984, p. 49). Although this signals a problem of intersubjectivity, Heritage argues that Schutz overcomes this problem by proposing that actors assume their experiences are similar to those of others and, possibly more importantly, act as if they were the same, for all practical purposes (Heritage, 1984, p. 54). It is through these assumptions that a social stock of knowledge, or recipe knowledge, is established and maintained, and typified through language (Berger and Luckmann, 1966). Data can then be collected and analysed using the techniques and devices of ethnomethology, to uncover the ways in which social actors, through their actions, engage in reproducing intelligible representations of their actions as choices accountable to other knowledgeable subjects (Garfinkel, 1967 cited by Heritage, 1984). This use of 'experience structures' as a method of understanding social actions views motivation for normative, appropriate conduct as part of actors' awareness of their accountability for different courses of action. Using conversational data (Psathas, 1995) it is proposed that actors account for their behaviour in terms of normative role presentations of self, directed towards other social actors (Goffman, 1959). These accounts appear in the texts as reasons which can be analysed as, and can be conceived from, the Schutzian notion of the 'because of' motive and the 'in order to' motive (Schutz, 1972 [1938]). In the conversational narratives, the actors construct accounts for their behaviour in terms of reasons that relate to previous lived experiences (because of) and intentional objects (in order to) that allows an analysis of reasons to be located within the theory of social action.

Although this paper cannot present a full discussion of the tenets of the epistemological assumptions of this position (or an analysis of the findings of the research, as in essence the work is ongoing), it is hoped that this brief introduction can be supplemented by an explanation of some of the issues that led to the development of this position and these techniques, and to present some examples of the research findings and some tentative analysis. It is first necessary to explain some of the issues that led to the development of this approach, to contextualize the analysis that follows.

Day Visitor Behaviour in the Peak National Park

The Peak National Park is located in central England and is surrounded by large cities including Greater Manchester, Sheffield, Birmingham, Derby, Nottingham, Rotherham, and the coalfield towns of north-east Derbyshire and South Yorkshire. Indeed, a third of the population of the UK live within one-and-a-half hours' drive from the park borders. The park receives somewhere between 22 and 26 million visits each year and is the second most visited National Park in the world after Mount Fuji (*Peakland Post*, 1997). The Peak District was the site of mass trespasses in the late 1930s as part of a movement to create National Parks in Britain, and was the first National Park to be created in the UK in 1951. There can be no doubt about the importance of the place to people from central and northern England as an area of beauty and as a place for recreation. In terms of the research, though, the impacts of tourism, given this volume of usage and the planning structure of the National Park authority, were well known and understood, but upon initial observations there appeared to be striking anomalies in the intentions and actual behaviours of visitors to the park. The park authority's own research showed that people wanted to get away from their usual environments, the hustle and bustle of the towns and cities, and to experience some quiet enjoyment of the countryside in the wilderness setting of the park (from a selection of Peak Park Annual Reports 1989–1993). Yet the sheer volume of usage in some places (it must be stressed that visitors are concentrated in particular 'honeypot' areas) makes this desire incongruous with common understandings of what getting away and quiet enjoyment actually mean. This alerted the author to the possible problems of motivational research findings and the vicarious nature of reasons as a topic of empirical inquiry. But first there was the problem that day visits are not well conceptualized in the literature in terms of either leisure, recreation or tourism (Clarke and McCabe, 1997). Rather than becoming embroiled in a conceptual debate concerning the experience of day visiting as leisure or tourism, the assumption was made that day visits to the Peak Park are, in part, a product of this particular socio-spatial configuration, as well as the macro-social organization of leisure, but also determined by social actors within that framework. This was a common-sense assumption on the basis that not all people want to, or do, visit the Peak National Park from the surrounding area, but it nevertheless appeared germane. Then the theoretical framework of consumer behaviour provided the focus for the empirical study, which also was a common-sense decision based on the comprehensive inclusiveness of the theory, covering all aspects of the consumer action process (Howard and Sheth, 1969). Howard and Sheth (1969) had already warned of the problematic nature of the theory in its bringing together of objective and subjective, abstract components. In terms of consumer processes as they had been applied to tourism (Moutinho, 1987), a strong concentration on the main stay, or overnight tourism, was evident, and indeed there appeared to be no studies centring on the leisure day visit consumer process.

The emergent design of the study

The study had to be qualitative in nature in order to be consistent with the tenets of the study of everyday action and interaction. Crompton (1979) had already identified some problems to do with the qualitative study of motivations. A pilot study was undertaken using open-ended, semi-structured interviews with 16 day visitors in May–June 1996, which alerted the researcher to further problems of motivation (McCabe, 1997). The questions in the pilot study hoped to explore the dimensions of day visitor decision-making, and to test the framing of questions themselves. In many cases, respondents answered questions asking them to describe their reasons for visiting the park that day, as intentional objects. Responses included such phrases as

> 'To get out of town, to be out in the fresh air, enjoy the scenery, and we like coming to Chatsworth because it's got the amenities as well as that. The toilets, the shop, and obviously we can buy sweets and that for the kids.'

The notion of getting out of town, getting away from the home environment, getting out in the fresh air, and the fact that the weather was good for the first time in the year (the interviews were conducted in the spring holidays) were all responses given to this type of question. Yet when the interviewer asked other questions, which were intended to be concerned with the decision-making process, other reasons for making the trips were cited by respondents. Questions such as 'what made you come here today?' and 'how did you decide to come to the Peak Park today?' were particularly useful in providing answers that were reasons. In the case of the respondent quoted above, his response to the question 'what made you come here today?' provided the following response:

> 'We had to choose something that we could do ... our visitors wanted to walk, but they have got two young children so we couldn't do anything strenuous, we have done this walk before once, we have been here before, so we knew fairly well the routes and how difficult it was, and so that made it the ideal choice ... so we have been up in the back of the Stand Wood and we have been up there looking at the lakes, and we have now come to the house and then we have got to walk back to the car, so we have got a variety of things to hopefully keep the children interested.'

There were some striking features of these two responses. The respondent had already made it known that in the party visiting that day were some friends of the family as well as his own family. But here we get a sense that the choice of a leisure day trip, as well as the choice of activity level and type, were out of the immediate control of the individual being interviewed. Moreover, the reasons given in the second response bear little correlation to the intentional reasons proposed by the respondent in the first answer, apart from the amenities available in the specific place. This in itself indicates that some account is made in the decision of the wishes, or wants, of the children in the group, and so the reason for the visit may not be solely for individual, personal benefits accrued to the respondent, but for many, complex considerations of friends and family wants or duties. Further, we may speculate upon the ways the respondent, rather than re-stating his initial intentional reasons, moves to produce more pragmatic reasons constructed as an account of behaviour. All we can say on this subject is that the respondent can be heard to be giving an account of his actions as normal social behaviour. We can hear that he shifts the subject of the account from his own intentions to the concerns and reasons of his friends as an example of this work, as he constructs his actions with reference to others in his social sphere.

In essence, the analysis of these pilot interviews revealed that the more one asks questions of respondents about their behaviours, the more elaborate and diverse accounts one will receive. It is this notion that led to a general questioning of the findings of motivational research in the literature and then the methodological assumptions underpinning those findings. Analysis of the more pragmatic accounts of reasons in itself would not help to understand the reasons behind day visitor actions, and a more sophisticated analysis would be required to attempt to understand what respondents were doing when they give intentional reasons for actions.

The second stage of the research project focused on *post hoc* conversations with day visitors. The sample was drawn from a convenience sample of friends and friends-of-friends, as well as from a leafleting campaign conducted by the author over a 6-month period in 1997. Respondents were asked to talk about their experiences of their day visits to the Peak National Park. The conversations contained only one pre-set question, 'Tell me in as much detail as you can about your last visit to the Peak Park?', and the interviews were conducted in an informal manner. Respondents were allowed to talk on a totally free range of subjects. The talk was tape-recorded, and five conversations were fully transcribed.

The texts were then analysed for the discursive structures that they contained in the constructions of experiences, and in terms of the accounting practices of the members in their accounts of behaviour using the 'in order to' and 'because of' indicators. An example follows, taken from a conversational interview with a couple describing their beginnings in their involvement in mountain biking in the Peak District (I = interviewer; E = Emma; S = Sam).

- I: So you say you were living in Kent last year, or a year ago?
- E: Two years ago.
- I: Did you do the same type of thing down there?
- E: Yes, but it...
- S: The countryside is just not the same, so we did go cycling but it was mostly on little side roads and B roads, there's ... one of the main reasons for me moving up here was because of the peak district being so close.
- E: There wasn't so much open and free countryside if you like, as there is, I mean the south-east is like overcrowded so...
- S: Some of it is very pretty, but you can't get away from it all.

We can hear in this small fragment of text that there appears to be a disorderliness in the way that the talk is constructed. The respondents appear to be collaborating in the production of the talk, but similarly they both appear to find it difficult to explain the intentions of the talk as a projected answer. However, using the 'in order to' and 'because of' motives, this section can be reconstructed as follows.

- I: So you say you were living in Kent last year, or a year ago?
- E: Two years ago.
- I: Did you do the same type of thing down there?
- E: Yes, but it...
- S: The countryside is just not the same, so we did go cycling but
- (a.1) **because** it was mostly on little side roads and B roads, there's ... one of the main reasons for me moving up here was
- (b.1) **in order to**
- (because of the) Peak District being so close.
- (a.2) **because**
- E: There wasn't so much open and free countryside if you like, as there is,
- (a.3) **because**
- I mean the south-east is like overcrowded so ...
- S: Some of it is very pretty,
- (b.2) in order to
- (but you can't) get away from it all.

As we can see from the reconstruction above, there are clearly two topics of conversation going on in the piece. Firstly, there is the explanation of differences between the two places (topic a), and secondly there are the reasons given for Emma's and Sam's move away from the south-east (topic b). These topics can be re-ordered to show a logical sequence.

Topic a:
- S: The countryside is just not the same, so we did go cycling but
- (a.1) **because**
- it was mostly on little side roads and B roads
- (a.2) (and) **because**
- There wasn't so much open and free countryside if you like,
- (a.3) **because**
- I mean the south-east is like overcrowded so...

Topic b:
- S: One of the main reasons for me moving up here was
- (b.1) **in order to**
- (because of the) Peak District being so close.
- (b.2) **in order to**
- (but you can't) get away from it all.

The two topics are mutually inclusive in that they must be heard in the context of each other. Further, there is a confusing aspect to the use of the 'because of' and 'in order to' statements in topic b that must be clarified. Sam uses the 'because of' statement as he is providing a justification for a past event, his move up from

Kent. However, he is justifying the move in terms of a sequential construction of the intended project of that move, in order to be close to the Peak District, so that (or in order to) get away from it all, which is not possible in the south-east for the reasons Sam and Emma describe in topic a. In a sense, the analytical work recreates the text in this instance in order to gain access to the orderliness of the conversation. It is important to stress that not all the interviews contain this disorderliness, and in fact most of the conversations were taken with individual members, yet the same method of analysis reveals that respondents resort to the same accounting 'work' in talking about their day visitor experiences. Indeed the most notable finding from a reading of the texts was that the respondents constructed their experiences, in large part, as lists of 'doings' and accounts for behaviour. It is these accounts of behaviour that form the bulk of the analytical work of the project, not only in an effort at unravelling the myriad reasons that respondents give in accounts of behaviour, but also to link these reasons to constructions and representations of self. It is beyond the task of this paper, however, to account for motivation as a construct, or propose some new theory behind leisure and leisure travel motives in a new method of analysis. The aim is merely to present for discussion the possible value of an alternative approach to the problem of motivation that follows a logical, rigorous procedure, and has a strong philosophical/theoretical heritage, which can be used to provide another dimension in the effort to understand consumer processes in leisure and tourism.

Conclusions

In this paper, we have reviewed the literature concerning the dominant constructs that underpin research into the reasons, or motivations, for leisure and tourism behaviour. This literature we found to contain problems from both theoretical and operational perspectives. Theory development is piecemeal and lacks a solid foundation, and research has varying degrees of predictive ability. Some methods linked to traditional methodological foundations have developed instruments that are unworkable. Other researchers have chosen to explain behaviour without recourse to motivation as the basic construct. We proposed that by taking the perspective of social constructionism, motivation problems can be avoided, and also that through the application of the analytical technique proposed by Shutz, and the perspective of ethnomethodology, 'reasons', as a device used to account for behaviour, can form the basis of an inquiry that may be used to help explain and understand consumer behaviour processes.

References

Beard, J.G. and Ragheb, M.G. (1983) Measuring leisure motivation. *Journal of Leisure Research* 15, 219–228.
Berger, P.L. and Luckmann, T. (1966) *The Social Construction of Reality*. New York: Doubleday.

Boorstin, D. (1964) *The Image: A Guide to Pseudo Events in American Society.* New York: Harper.

Clarke, A. and McCabe, S. (1997) What's in a name: conceptualising tourism, leisure and recreation. Paper presented to the EIRASS workshop *The Battle for the Tourist,* Eindhoven, Netherlands, 1997.

Cohen, E. (1974) Who is a tourist? A conceptual review. *Sociological Review* 22, 27–53.

Cohen, E. (1979) A phenomenology of tourist experiences. *Sociology* 13, 179–201.

Cohen, E. (1988) Traditions in the qualitative sociology of tourism. *Annals of Tourism Research* 15, 29–46.

Cohen. S. and Taylor, L. (1992) *Escape Attempts,* 2nd edn. London: Routledge.

Cooper, C., Fletcher, J., Gilbert, D. and Wanhill, S. (1993) *Tourism Principles and Practice.* Essex: Longman.

Crompton, J.L. (1979) Motivations for pleasure vacations. *Annals of Tourism Research* 6, 408–424.

Crompton, J.L. and Ankomah, P.K. (1993) Choice set propositions in destination decisions. *Annals of Tourism Research* 20, No. 3.

Csikszentmihalyi, M. (1975) *Beyond Boredom and Anxiety. The Experience of Play in Work and Games.* San Francisco: Jossey-Bass.

Dann, G. (1977) Anomie, ego-enhancement and tourism. *Annals of Tourism Research* 4, 184–194.

Dann, G. (1981) Tourist motivation. An appraisal. *Annals of Tourism Research* 8, 187–219.

De Charms, R. and Muir, M.S. (1978) Motivation: a social approach. *Annual Review of Psychology* 29, 91–113.

Deci, E.L. (1975) *Intrinsic Motivation.* New York: Plenum.

Dimanche, F. and Havitz, M. E. (1994) Consumer behavior and tourism: review and extension of four study areas. *Journal of Travel and Tourism Marketing* 3, 37–57.

Dun Ross, E.L. and Iso-Ahola, S. (1991) Sightseeing tourists' motivation and satisfaction. *Annals of Tourism Research* 18, 226–236.

Fodness, D. (1994) Measuring tourist motivation. *Annals of Tourism Research* 21, No. 3.

Gitelson, R. and Kerstetter, D. (1994) The influence of friends and relatives in travel decision making. *Journal of Travel and Tourism Marketing* 3, 59–68.

Glaser, B.G. and Strauss, A. *The Discovery of Grounded Theory: Strategies for Qualitative Research.* New York: Aldine Publishing Co.

Goffman, E. (1959) *The Presentation of Self in Everyday Life.* London: Penguin.

Gottlieb, A. (1982) Americans' vacations. *Annals of Tourism Research* 9, 165–187.

Gray, H.P. (1979) *International Travel: International Trade.* Lexington, Massachusetts: Heath Lexington.

Heritage, J. (1984) *Garfinkel and Ethnomethodology.* Cambridge: Polity Press.

Howard, J.A. and Sheth, J.N. (1969) *The Theory of Buyer Behavior.* New York: Wiley.

Iso-Ahola, S.E. (1980) *The Social Psychology of Leisure and Recreation.* Dubuque: W.M.C. Brown.

Iso-Ahola, S.E. (1982) Toward a social psychological theory of tourism motivation: a rejoinder. *Annals of Tourism Research* 9, 256–262.

Krippendorf, J. (1987) *The Holiday Makers.* London: Heinemann.

Lue, C.-C., Crompton, J.L. and Fesenmaier, D.R. (1993) Conceptualization of multi-destination pleasure trips. *Annals of Tourism Research* 20, No. 2.

MacCannell, D. (1976) *The Tourist: A New Theory of the Leisure Class.* London: Macmillan.

Mannel, R.C. and Iso-Ahola, S. (1987) Psychological Nature of Leisure and Tourism Experience. *Annals of Tourism Research* 14, 314–331.

Mansfield, Y. (1992) From motivation to actual travel. *Annals of Tourism Research* 19, 399–419.

McCabe, A.S. (1997) Towards a conceptual framework of day visitor behaviour. Paper presented at the EIRASS workshop *The Battle for the Tourist*, Eindhoven, Netherlands, 1997.

Middleton, V.T.C. (1994) *Marketing in Travel and Tourism*. Oxford: Heinemann.

Mill, R.C. and Morrison, A.M. (1985) *The Tourism System: An Introductory Text*. Englewood Cliffs, New Jersey: Prentice-Hall.

Moore, K., Cushman, G. and Simmons, D. (1995) Behavioral conceptualization of tourism and leisure. *Annals of Tourism Research* 22, 67–85.

Moutinho, L. (1987) Consumer behavior in tourism. *European Journal of Marketing* 21, 5–44.

Parrinello, G.L. (1993) Motivation and anticipation in post-industrial tourism. *Annals of Tourism Research* 20, 232–248.

Pearce, P.L. (1982) *The Social Psychology of Tourist Behaviour*. Oxford: Pergamon.

Pearce, P.L. (1993) Fundamentals of Tourist Motivation. In: D.G. Pearce and R. Butler (eds) *Tourism Research: Critiques and Challenges*. London: Routledge.

Pearce, P.L. and Caltabiano, M.L. (1983) Inferring travel motivations from travelers' experiences. *Journal of Travel Research* 12, 16–20.

Plog, S. (1977) Why destinations rise and fall in popularity. In: E.M. Kelly (ed.) *Domestic and International Tourism*. Wellesley, Massachusetts: Institute of Certified Travel Agents, pp. 26–28.

Psathas, G. (1995) *Conversation Analysis: The Study of Talk in Interaction*. Thousand Oaks, California: Sage.

Rapoport, R. and Rapoport, R.N. (1975) *Leisure and the Family Life Cycle*. London: Routledge & Kegan Paul.

Ryan, C. (ed.) (1997) *The Tourist Experience. A New Introduction*. London: Cassell.

Schutz, A. (1972) *The Phenomenology of the Social World*. London: Heinemann.

Sirakaya, E., McLellan, R.W. and Uysal, M. (1996) Modeling vacation destination decisions: a behavioral approach. *Journal of Travel and Tourism Marketing* 5, 57–75.

Smith, S.L.J. (1995) *Tourism Analysis: A Handbook*, 2nd edn. Harlow, Essex: Longman.

Smith, V.L. (1977) *Hosts and Guests: The Anthropology of Tourism*. Philadelphia: University of Pennsylvania Press.

Strauss, A. (1987) *Qualitative Analysis for Social Scientists*. Cambridge, UK: Cambridge University Press.

Strauss, A. and Corbin, J. (1990) *Basics of Qualitative Research: Grounded Theory Procedures and Techniques*. Newbury Park, California: Sage.

Tribe, J. (1997) The indiscipline of tourism. *Annals of Tourism Research* 24, 638–657.

Um, S. and Crompton, J.L. (1990) Attitude determinants in tourism destination choice. *Annals of Tourism Research* 17, 432–448.

Van Raaj, W.F. and Francken, D.A. (1984) Vacation decisions, activities and satisfactions. *Annals of Tourism Research* 11, 101–112.

Witt, C.A. and Wright, P.L. (1992) Tourist motivation: life after Maslow. In: P. Johnson and B. Thomas (eds) *Choice and Demand in Tourism*. London: Mansell.

Chapter thirteen
Personal Aspects of Consumers' Decision-Making Processes Revisited Through a Grounded Theory of Belgian Vacationers

Alain Decrop
Department of Business Administration, University of Namur, Rempart de la Vierge 8, 5000 Namur, Belgium

Introduction

In this chapter, we explore such important factors as socio-demographics, personality, product experience, and push factors, which characterize the individual vacationer. These constructs have recently been discussed, especially in positivist terms, in consumer behaviour literature as well as in travel, hospitality and leisure journals: demographics and life cycle (Gitelson and Kersteller, 1990; Fodness, 1992; Oppermann, 1994); product experience and involvement (Reid and Crompton, 1993; Havitz and Howard, 1994); personality and lifestyles (Plog, 1974, 1994; Mayo and Jarvis, 1981; Mazanec, 1994); and motivation (Crompton, 1979; Fodness, 1994; Gnoth, 1997). In this study, these personal aspects are revisited from an interpretivist perspective to gain a better insight into their nature and the way they influence vacation decisions (destination choice in particular) and decision-making processes. The focus is on understanding and interpretation rather than on generalization and prediction. Based on a grounded theory approach, a set of propositions is developed which stimulates further empirical research. This paper is part of a global dissertation project on vacationers' decision-making processes (Decrop, 1999b).

Methodology

In-depth semi-structured interviews were used to collect the data. Informants could freely and spontaneously talk about three central themes: (i) general vacation and travel behaviour; (ii) definitions and motives; and (iii) current vacation plans and evoked vacation destinations. The open-ended format of the interviews is important for several reasons. Firstly, as the interview evolves to a kind of conversation, the informant becomes less and less aware of the interview process. This opens the way to his/her automatic (unbiased) thinking. Secondly, in-depth interviewing means both listening to people and sharing social experiences (Rubin and Rubin, 1995). This brings much additional information (how and in which context things are said) to the straight content of the interview, and often makes interpretation easier and more reliable. Finally, by adapting the content and flow of the interview to each informant, we do not force them into preconceived answer patterns: there is more room for discovering particular situations and atypical behaviours. This is extremely important for theory generation.

The analysis and interpretation process is based on Glaser and Strauss's grounded theory approach (1967), which is 'a qualitative research method that uses a systematic set of procedures to develop an inductively derived grounded theory about a phenomenon' (Strauss and Corbin, 1990, p. 24). Categories, patterns and propositions emerge from the interview transcripts (through a coding process) rather than being imposed beforehand. The grounded theory approach is further characterized by the following basic principles:

- concurrent data collection and analysis
- theoretical sensitivity: thinking descriptively, analytically, interpretively and critically at the same time
- categories and theory evolve as new material is gathered and analysed
- coding procedures (open, axial and selective coding) lead the way to the final formulation of an explanatory framework that fits emerging theory
- permanent questioning and comparing data, categories and concepts.

In the past few years, several authors have used a grounded theory approach to study problems in tourism behaviour (Teare, 1994; Riley, 1995; Hernandez *et al.*, 1996; Decrop, 1999a, b). Connell and Lowe (1997) have recently reviewed the application of inductive methods in tourism and hospitality management research.

Informants were recruited according to theoretical sampling (Strauss and Corbin, 1990), i.e. looking for information-rich cases in order to maximize theory development. The search for enough variation and informational saturation guided the selection of 25 Belgian decision-making units (DMUs). The four basic types of vacation DMUs are represented: singles (representing vacationers who decide on their own); couples (encompassing the man–woman relationship, be it married or unmarried); families with children; and groups of friends. A real-situation, longitudinal research design was chosen:

- Subjects were recruited only if they intended to go on vacation in the summer of 1996. This was to avoid problems linked to the intention–behaviour discrepancy (Belk, 1985) when hypothetical instead of actual decision questions are asked.
- A few studies (van Raaij and Francken, 1984; Moutinho, 1987) have shown that vacation choices involve a long decision-making process which takes

place over many months. Therefore the same informants were interviewed up to four times over the year: two or three times before the summer vacation (February, April and June) and once after (November).

A few definitions

Before describing and interpreting the research findings, the core concepts of the study must be defined. The following definitions emerge from the data rather than being imposed beforehand.

Two key constructs deserve particular attention, i.e. vacation (used as the American synonym for 'holiday') and travel. Language is the first reason for this: French is poorer than English regarding the travel vocabulary. In French, there is only one translation for travel, tour, trip and journey, i.e. 'voyage'. Secondly, vacation and travel may encompass very different realities from one individual to another. To avoid interpretation biases, each interviewee was asked what vacation, travel and going on vacation mean for him/her. For a large part of the sample, vacation and travel are assimilated: vacation involves travelling (at least ideally) because travel strengthens the vacation feeling. A summer vacation without going away cannot really be called a vacation, and travelling is as such a synonym for vacation. However, the travel–vacation association is stronger than the vacation–travel association. By this we mean that:

- Except for people who travel for business, travelling is always connected with vacation. Travelling and going on vacation are often synonyms, and the vacation begins with the journey itself: 'For me, the journey is already part of the vacation: once I step into my car and I leave, it is part of the vacation'. However, for some people travelling means more than going on vacation: it involves a more active vacation type where one moves from one place to another with the major goal of discovering and visiting the destination. In this sense, travel is assimilated with a tour, while going on vacation is associated with staying in the same spot.
- Vacation does not always include leaving home and, even less, travelling. For many informants, vacation is first of all a state of mind: vacation is a break from work and worries, living at one's own pace, and doing activities other than the daily routine. As a consequence, one can feel on vacation at home or when doing particular activities such as reading or gardening. In the same way, vacation is not a question of duration, or of distance.

Put simply, vacation is a broader concept than travel, which itself is often associated with going on vacation. Vacation is more like a lifestyle, an abstract construct. In contrast, travel is more concrete and goal-oriented. To avoid ambiguity, when speaking of travel and vacation below, we always mean leaving home for leisure purposes for more than 3 days.

Travel and vacation being defined, we now look at the decision items that may be involved in vacation and travel choices. Next to vacation destinations (which is the primary focus of our research), other vacation subdecisions were discussed with informants. Coding results in a typology of 16 travel decision items, which are defined in Table 13.1. A star indicates that the particular sub-decision is part of Woodside and McDonald's (1994) general system framework of customer choice decisions for tourism services.

Table 13.1 A typology of vacation decision items

Vacation	Definition
Accommodation*	Includes lodging but also the general infrastructure (pool, tennis, disco...) of the place of stay
Accompaniment	People with whom one spends the vacation (can be different than a DMU: e.g. a single decision-maker can decide to accompany a conducted tour)
Activities*	What people do during their vacation time: sports, cultural visits, reading, entertainment...
Attractions*	Types of attractions tourists like to visit: museum, cities, monuments, national parks, events...
Budget and expenses	Amount of money that is spent on vacation and the way money is spent
Destination*	Place(s) where the vacation will be spent (most of the time a country, but this can also be a region or a particular spot)
Duration	Duration and timing of the vacation
Formula	Global type of vacation: staying in one spot or touring, sea or mountains, city or countryside...
Meals*	Eating patterns (what and where does one eat for breakfast, lunch, dinner?)
Organization	Planning and booking of the vacation: by one's self or by an intermediary (travel agent, tour operator, association...)
Period	Period of the year (season, month, particular dates) when one goes on vacation
Purchases*	Anything that is purchased and (or) taken back home from the vacation (souvenirs, self-gifts, postcards, photos...)
Route*	Route that is followed to reach the vacation destination (one or more overnight stops, country roads or highways...)
Tour*	Destination area visited, and route followed for that purpose
Transportation*	Transportation modes used to reach the vacation destination and to make excursions while there
Vacation style	Vacation lifestyle. Two typical cases: - comfort level of the vacation (backpacker vs comfortable vacationer) - integration in local life (incognito vs arrogant tourist)

Old-Fashioned but Still Useful: Socio-Demographics

Socio-demographic variables are widely used to discriminate between groups of consumers, e.g. vacationers. This privileged position, while often criticized, is justified by our data. Important differences in decisions and decision-making styles result from such classical criteria as age, family situation, socio-economic status and occupation. Before considering each of these aspects, it should be kept in mind that age and family situation are inextricable factors, which are usually regrouped in the 'family's life cycle' (Wells and Gubar, 1966). Based on the data, life cycle seems still to be one of the best ways to segment vacationers. We suggest the typology given in Table 13.2, which additionally illustrates the composition of our sample.

The influence of age can be interpreted in terms of anticipation and maturity. As vacationers become conscious of the weight of years, they are willing to anticipate health and mental constraints due to age. This results in a higher travel involvement for younger people ('it is better to travel when one is fit and well', 'staying at home will be for my old days'); more active vacation types; and more distant or less touristy destinations ('one shouldn't consider Indonesia after the age of 70'). In many instances, it is 'now or never', that is: travel now, rest later. In contrast, older vacationers are characterized by growing maturity. Involvement weakens ('As I grow older, I think I attach more and more importance to the quality of my everyday life than to 15 days, which would be more enjoyable'), cultural discovery and knowledge acquisition are the major motives, and destination preferences are given more easily (one realizes that some dreams will never be fulfilled so that priorities are given). Next to destinations, age influences other vacation subdecisions such as activities, vacation style, accompaniment, formulae, organization mode and travel purchases. A final emerging observation about age is price discrimination: one single is completely reconsidering his travel behaviour just because he cannot benefit from discounts for youth travel by train any more.

The family situation is another major factor in vacation choices and decision-making processes. Having children involves many constraints that can be divided into structural and interpersonal constraints.

Structural constraints. Babies and younger children require more care and attention so that parents often decide not to go on vacation. Even if they don't like it, they choose closer and more secure destinations (including always returning to the same place), they prepare the trip in more depth and for longer before departure (decisions are taken earlier), and they select accommodation where children will be at ease (swimming pool and beaches). Staying in the same spot is also preferred to a tour. The influence of family situation is often explained by risk aversion: parents of young children are not willing to improvise and to live as adventurous vacationers. Another practical constraint related to family is money. Larger families cannot afford to take a vacation each year or are forced to choose cheaper vacation formulae and accommodation (camping, apartment, family cottage). They tend to seize any opportunity to go on free vacations (invitation by family members or friends).

Table 13.2 A typology of vacationers based on the family life cycle (FLC)

Position in FLC	Definition
Younger single	From 20 to 40 years old, bachelor (2 DMUs) or divorced (but without children)
Younger couple	From 20 to 40 years old, married or unmarried (1 DMU) but without children
Younger family	Head of household under 45 with young children (less than 12 years) (unmarried: 1 DMU, newly made family: 2 DMUs)
Mid-life family	Head of household over 40 with (young and) older children (at least one over 12 years), could be married (5 DMUs), unmarried (1 DMU); sometimes children have left the household while others still participate in vacation decisions (2 DMUs)
Single-parent family	Head of the household is divorced or widowed with children (1 DMU)
Older couple	Over 50 years old, with no child accompanying because they have left the household (2 DMUs) or they don't want to go on vacation with their parents any more (2 DMUs)
Older single	Over 50 years old, bachelor (1 DMU), widow and no children present (2 DMUs) or divorced
Group of friends	Most often involves younger people (under 40); can be a group of younger singles (2 DMUs), a group of younger couples (1 DMU) or a mixed group (singles, couples and sometimes also a younger family) – this type of DMU is less stable over time and often involves mixed DMUs, i.e. people who don't only go on vacation with friends

Interpersonal constraints. As children enter adolescence, they build their own definitions of a vacation with their own motives and expectations, which may obviously differ from those of their parents. In a few families, there are no conflicting values or they are held back because of strong parental authority. In other families, teenagers dare to express their own values, which results in two possible situations:

- parents take children's requests into consideration and adapt their vacation regarding destinations, formulae and, most of all, activities
- children refuse to accompany their parents any more – this can lead to a durable modification of the DMU.

Switching from being single to a couple, the birth of a baby, or the death of the usual travel partner are other events which cause deep changes to the family structure and thereby to the DMU. One's everyday and consumer life are affected as well as vacation behaviour and decision-making processes.

The family situation also influences vacation motives and involvement. As children grow older, parents become either more strongly or less involved in going on vacation. Involvement can become stronger because destinations, formulae and activities may become more in accordance with parents' expectations. In contrast, involvement can weaken because children are not enthusiastic any more about going on vacation with their parents or because they have left the DMU. However, children leaving the household can also relax the financial constraints, so that involvement grows again. The death of a family member can also either strengthen ('I cannot spend my leisure time at home any more') or weaken ('since I am alone, I have become stay-at-home') travel involvement. In the same way, vacation definitions and motives change: with young children, vacations are seen as a period of rest, relaxation and play. There is no need to go far away to spend a nice vacation, staying at home is even considered. In contrast, parents with older children are primarily motivated by sharing social experiences (they complain: 'we don't see our children during the year') and acquiring knowledge. When children have left, there is more room for culture, learning and discoveries.

Next to age and family, occupation is a determinant of vacationers' decision-making processes. The influence of occupation is related to both the working/non-working dichotomy, and to the nature of the job.

While the desire to have a break and to get away from daily routine is constant (see below), there is an occupational differentiation of vacation definitions and motives. For working people, vacation primarily means not going to work. Motives are linked to rest, leaving the stress and the (boring) tasks of daily work, spending more time with the family. In contrast, for non-working people, vacation definitely means leaving home, travelling and choosing accommodation where the household tasks will be minimized (so hotels instead of camp-sites). They are motivated by a more active vacation type, including discovering new things and meeting other people. The working/non-working dichotomy is strongly linked to gender. When there is only one source of income in the household, this nearly always comes from the man (husband). This is a reflection of Belgian society, which is still characterized by a strong patriarchy: the man is the *pater familias* who provides for the household's needs while the woman cares for the children and the household tasks. As a consequence, non-working women have a dramatically different perspective on vacations from their working partners. Note that this gender-occupational differentiation of vacation definitions remains after retirement. In contrast to women, men consider (or anticipate) the period following retirement as 'continuous vacation', confirming the yin–yang of the concept: vacation exists just because work exists. Modification of occupational status, like the passage from student life to occupational life, or retirement, has a durable effect on time (the vacation period, often dictated by occupational requirements, becomes a real choice when one retires) and on income.

For working people, the nature of the job also affects vacation involvement and motives. For instance, going away is the only means for professional people to escape their work environment, since they have their office at home. They have different vacation drives (i.e. they regain the energy necessary for their busy occupational life by resting and relaxing) than teachers (i.e. they discover, acquire knowledge or even confront the information they give to their students with reality). Moreover, the nature of occupation has a considerable influence on discretionary time, i.e. the time that is spent on leisure purposes, including travelling and going on vacation, but also planning and preparing the trip. So, many people cannot really choose their vacation period: it has to fall into the school vacation (in Belgium, July and August) or into a fixed period of vacation for the industry (judicial vacation). For others, it depends on the employer's planning or good will (with the consequence that the period cannot be fixed long beforehand). Duration is also constrained by the job: while teachers or soldiers do not suffer very much from it, other active people cannot usually afford more than 2 weeks' summer vacation. Finally, some jobs allow more free time for thinking of and planning vacations (civil servants), or suggest greater and earlier attention to the content of the trip (teachers, travel agents). This is not to say that these people take their decisions earlier. For others (self-employed workers), the vacation preparation consists in anticipating and delegating tasks in such a way that the business still runs during the break.

Finally, the nature of occupation influences destination choice, as illustrated by the examples of a professor of ancient history wishing to visit Turkey, or a soldier who requires special authorization to visit non-NATO countries. Sometimes, this effect is mediated by the vacation period (a teacher can only travel in July and August, which means that he/she will never visit the south of Chile or Argentina, where it is winter time); duration (distant countries often require more time to visit); and cost (travelling during the high season means higher prices so that destinations such as China or Egypt are not available to people who are forced to take their vacation during that period).

Economic status, which itself strongly depends upon age, family and occupation, has a direct influence on the vacation and travel experience. DMUs with lower incomes (students, unemployed, or large families with only one salary) tend to have a limited vacation experience. Financial constraints lie at the origin of many vacation lapses in the individual's life cycle. This influence is interpreted by two mental states: trade-offs, and frustrations.

There may be trade-offs in the allocation of discretionary income, as illustrated by the following quote:

'[During that period], we asked ourselves: "we have this amount of money, what do we do with it? Do we go on vacation or ... do we do some more work?" And therefore, for a while, we have chosen to do up our house because we stay longer there than on vacation.'

Note that trade-off choices don't result just from the objective economic situation, but are also influenced by more subjective factors such as risk aversion, relationship with money (see below), and vacation involvement. This is illustrated by a woman who can afford both to buy new lounge chairs and to go on vacation, but who is urged into the trade-off just because she doesn't want to put her future in danger. Further, trade-offs don't always lead to a complete renunciation of vacation; because of financial constraints, some DMUs decide to shorten their vacation, to choose cheaper accommodation, to travel by their own means (this is especially a problem for families where everyone has to pay for his/her own plane, train or bus seat) or, most obviously, to spend less during the vacation period. So, five interviewees insist that money is not an absolute limitation: 'it is possible to have a very interesting vacation for very affordable prices'. Other people are less compromising: 'one goes well, or one doesn't go at all'.

Financial trade-offs can also involve family members, as suggested by these two contrasting examples:

- parents who sacrifice the family vacation for their children's own vacation plans
- in a mixed DMU, parents who refuse to spend too much on a trip with friends in order not to cut down on the family vacation.

Frustrations are experienced when travel involvement is high and income is low. This feeling can prepare the way for a feedback effect: once the financial constraint is lifted, the involvement is still higher, there is a desire to make up for lost time.

Economic status has a strong influence on destination choice. DMUs with a lower income are forced to choose closer or touristy destinations, offering cheap accommodation types and a reasonable cost of living. Capital cities such as Paris and Vienna are excluded, while domestic destinations such as the Belgian coastline and the Ardennes, as well as border countries, are more popular.

Each Person is Unique: Personality and Lifestyle

Personality is a complex psychological phenomenon. It could be defined as the reflection (because it is the visible part of one's character as it impresses others) of a person's enduring and unique characteristics that urge him/her to respond in persistent ways to recurring environmental stimuli (Decrop, 1999a). Related to personality, lifestyle refers to unique patterns of thinking and behaving that characterize differences among consumers. These are reflections of self concept and help to understand vacationers' patterns of time, spending and feeling. For example, life habits such as being vegetarian or an early riser influence the content of vacation subdecisions. Personality and lifestyle are such intertwined concepts that we don't want to deal with them separately (Mayo and Jarvis, 1981; Plog, 1994). Note that findings are based on both the content and discourse analysis of our data. They are a reflection of both the interviewee typifying his/her own behaviour (emic perspective) and the researcher interpreting the interviewee's behaviour (etic perspective).

The individual's enduring characteristics are often approached as traits. In this study, more than 40 different character traits were identified. The more frequent are: resourceful, optimistic, nostalgic, passive, altruist, stubborn, organized, improviser, emotional, impulsive, inquisitive, crowd-averse, and prospective. These traits can be regrouped in broader personality types. A first distinction is between emotional and rational vacationers. Emotional people may be characterized by impulsiveness, instability, adventurousness and improvisation. Another possible distinction is active versus passive vacationers. Active vacationers are characterized by a high activity propensity, they cannot keep still ('staying home makes me inert and more tired', 'I leave home for the smallest reason'), while passive vacationers are rather 'stay-at-home' ('I need stability', 'I can enjoy my leisure time at home'). Risk aversion (see below) lies at the origin of a third continuum: adventurous versus careful vacationers.

Personality types have a major influence on the nature of vacation destinations, activities, style, organization, souvenirs and formulae. For example, the stay-at-home will prefer vacationing in the same spot, while the cannot-keep-still will prefer touring. Careful vacationers will avoid such 'dangerous' destinations as Egypt (political violence) or Madagascar (sanitary conditions). Personality types also have an effect on other individual variables, such as involvement and motives, and on aspects of decision-making processes including planning, information search, choice criteria, heuristics, decision timing, and brand loyalty. For example, adventurous travellers don't book anything beforehand and are searching for ever-new vacation destinations and experiences.

Risk aversion is another major personality aspect, although it is less enduring and more situational. Following Bauer (1960), risk is the anticipation that a particular action will result in a failure or a loss or, more simply, uncertainty about the product. In our sample, the level of risk aversion varies strongly from one DMU to the other (and sometimes within one DMU, from one person to the other). It is influenced by the type of DMU (risk perception is stronger for singles because they travel alone) and by age (older people tend to be more risk averse). Risk perception also depends on the vacation decision item. While activities, attractions, period, meals and purchases are not considered as risky, this is not the case for the vacation budget, transportation, organization, accompaniment and formulae. Vacationers are even more sensitive to risk with regard to their destination choices. Risk can originate from sanitary conditions (a pregnant woman doesn't want to go to Madagascar); tourist infrastructure (a single traveller would not be willing to travel alone in Africa); political violence (a family prefers to wait a few years before going to Egypt); gangsterism and delinquency (a mother seeks to avoid some particular beaches in France to protect her children from drugs). Risk aversion doesn't always lead to the rejection of a particular destination, but to compromising other vacation subdecisions if that destination is chosen. For example, a single woman who usually goes on vacation on her own will prefer to book an organized trip if she is to visit Egypt.

Risk aversion also affects vacation preparation. This is not to say that risk aversion involves more preparation, but rather that preparation (especially bookings) occurs beforehand instead of on the spot. Brand loyalty is another logical consequence of risk aversion. Two examples of this: a single vacationer who always books her trips in the same travel agency, and a family who always go on vacation to the same spot. Finally, risk aversion intervenes in trade-off choices (see above).

Informants' activities and interests (hobbies) emerged spontaneously from the discussion while no particular question was asked for this. The most popular activities are music (in an active sense, e.g. singing in a choir), sports and youth associations (scouts). The latter two involve groups and children. Other popular activities are reading and walking. Photography, do-it-yourself, fishing, boating, painting, dance, hiking, student-exchange organization and tourist guiding are other hobbies. There is also a wide range of interests in the sample: from history (the most popular) and geography to animals, nature, tales and legends, and to more specific passions such as railway stations and chiming of bells.

Activities and interests influence destination choice, as well as vacation activities and attractions. They often lie at the core of additional vacation plans, which are particular to some members of the DMU. This affects the number of vacations, vacation timing (one has to combine the different projects), and accompaniment (children cannot always join the family vacation because they have their own summer activities such as camps or training courses). Involvement, motives and information search are also affected.

A last interesting lifestyle aspect is the relationship with money. It influences vacation decisions and decision-making in two instances: the general expense behaviour of the individual and the particular position of vacation in the household's budget.

The relationship with money in everyday life. A distinction can be made between avaricious and prodigal people. Avaricious people don't like to spend much, either by constraint ('we live a frugal life all through the year'), or by risk aversion ('we don't know what the future of our children will be'). The latter save a lot based on the motto 'little streams make big rivers'. Prodigal people are Epicurean in the sense that 'it is better to live well today'. They buy something as soon as they long for it. A consequence of this is their lack of savings. Most DMUs in our sample are not that extreme, but could be considered as thrifty: they don't want to throw their money down the drain and are not ready for financial excess. This reflects a basic characteristic of the Belgian population, which is financially careful and saves a large part (about 20%) of its income. Next to reasonableness, money considerations reveal other character traits including altruism (parents who will deprive themselves but who are not willing to deprive their children, including for their holiday) and resourcefulness (bargaining or comparing prices to save money).

The position of travel and vacation in the household's budget. Most of the time, this position is related to trade-off problems and risk aversion (see above). In addition to travel, people have to consider major expense entries such as house (maintenance, reparations or housing), health, leisure, clothes, furnishing, car and books. Again, many DMUs declare that they are careful: they do not want to use up savings or to upset the family budget by going on vacation. As a consequence, they are not ready to sacrifice anything for a vacation; in contrast, vacations are often sacrificed for other items such as house maintenance and new furnishings. Those people go on holiday only when they can afford it or if they have an opportunity to go for free (invitation by family or friends, winning a contest). This means that they go on vacation less often or they choose closer destinations. The data also reveal an asymmetrical income elasticity:

> 'If there is not enough money, the first item to be sacrificed is vacation. However, if there is money, this is not to say that I will go on vacation immediately.'

On the other hand, there are DMUs who spend a lot (sometimes everything they have) on vacation and travel. Some have no problem with doing this because they can afford it. Others have to make sacrifices (no more smoking, no more 'caprices') that can be 'protected' by savings. These sacrifices sometimes occur after the vacation experience. Between these two extremes, other vacationers adapt their vacation budget to their income.

People can have a specific vacation entry in the household's budget (in this case, they often save for it), or no vacation budget as such. A fixed budget can lead to vacation trade-offs: travelling more often but for shorter periods or on smaller budgets. For other people, what is relevant is spending money well. This is defined as a good quality/price ratio of the vacation, or more original, climate/price, destination/price or time/price. One last thing to note is that the relationship with money can also differ on vacation from that during the year (money comes more easily from your pocket).

The Importance of Vacation Experience

Prior product experience is a key personal factor influencing both the nature of vacation subdecisions and aspects of decision-making processes. An emerging distinction is between the number of trips and vacations in the past, and the experience (in variety and intensity) of each vacation subdecision and, in particular, vacation destinations. The two dimensions do not always go hand in hand, although there is often a correlation. There are households who often go on vacation but always to the same place. The distinction is rather between brand loyalists and variety seekers. Brand loyalists (families with children) have an intensive vacation experience for particular decision items: they often go to the same destination, always around the same time period, in the same type of accommodation and for the same type of activities. Variety seekers have an extensive vacation experience, which is primarily related to destinations. Three dimensions of this variety seeking behaviour are identified:

- collection behaviour or the absolute will to visit another country, just because it is a different political entity: 'I must admit that I did already travel a lot: I already visited Norway, Sweden, Denmark, Germany, Austria, Italy completely, France completely. Therefore I have to go to Spain, Portugal, and England to see something I don't know'
- the desire to visit another country which is similar to some destinations visited before
- the desire to visit another region or to choose another place to stay in the same country.

The time dimension of vacation experience also emerges. Vacation or travel lapses resulting from socio-demographic factors have already been described. Moreover, an individual's experience in the current DMU can dramatically depart from his/her experience in previous DMUs ('she almost never traveled before she knew me'). As a consequence, members of the same DMU can have very different vacation and travel backgrounds. This can result in conflicting values or, in contrast, in the will of one member to make the other travel partner(s) benefit from his/her experience ('I want to show you the place').

Experience is often a good indicator of vacation involvement. However, it is not the only indicator: there are people who are travel fanatics but who have hardly travelled before because of structural or interpersonal constraints. Another point is that experience strengthens involvement and causes an upwards shift of the expectation level, in quantity or (and) in quality: 'I have already travelled a lot and seen many things but I would like to see still more and be dazzled'. Experience also leads to a shift in definitions and motives. People who have never travelled before don't realize what they are missing. After going on vacation abroad for the first time, a young girl admits: 'I have now given a real meaning to the word vacation'. For each of the vacation subdecisions, previous experience influences future choice through the post-experience evaluation process and the mediation of situational variables. Finally, the level of destination experience, resulting in destination knowledge, seems to affect judgements. A better destination knowledge makes perception judgements (informants were asked to describe their future vacation destination in a few words) easier but, in contrast, makes preference judgements (informants were asked to give the three destination aspects that attracted them the most) more difficult.

The push factors

The question of what drives consumers to behave as they do is of paramount importance for understanding vacation decisions and decision-making processes. When asked why she considered a particular vacation formula, one person answered:

> '... There is also the social contact: meeting people. But is this the result of
> the type of vacation I take or, additionally, of the person I am?'

In her question, that person unwittingly introduces the differentiation between 'push' and 'pull' factors (Dann, 1977). The first are considered as socio-psychological forces (motivators) that predispose the individual to go on vacation. The latter represent the product attributes that attract (as a result of the evaluation process) the individual towards a particular vacation decision.

Two levels of push factors are emerging from the data. Firstly, there is one basic push factor for all DMUs: the need to break from routine, to get away (a change of scenery). This need to get away is further refined into a temporal and spatial escape:

- The temporal escape pertains to getting away from everyday life (work, household tasks): leaving the pace and stress linked to occupational or household activities is the primary motivation. There is a kind of transition from everyday life time to vacation time. Those people can feel on vacation at home (at least, if they are not disturbed by daily tasks) and want to avoid an excessive disorientation due to travelling to far-away countries.
- The basic spatial escape is to get away from home: there is a need to leave home to really feel on vacation. It is argued that even if the vacation period is there, one tends to continue the daily routine or, even worse, to work more than during the year. The break is not sharp enough. This is particularly true for non-working women and professional people (see above). A more object-

specific escape is to get away from Belgium, as travelling in Belgium doesn't really give a vacation feeling. Escape is linked to the simple (psychological) fact of crossing a border; to experience (which causes weariness); the duration of the stay (shorter if in Belgium); the change in climate; and not only to geographical distance.

- People can also be motivated by an escape in both time and space. Some want to relive experiences and revive memories by going to certain places. Others desire a change after painful events (like the death of the partner), to escape dark memories by just leaving home for another environment, or by avoiding particular destinations associated with those memories. A final remark is that the change of place can alter time perception: 'Time is not the same when one stays at home as when one leaves. Time is elastic, definitely.'

Next to this basic push factor, there are a lot of more specific, goal-directed motives that vary (in importance and combination) from one individual (or DMU) to the other. Six categories emerge from the coding process:

- Discovering new things and visiting the destination in order to acquire knowledge. The goal is often well defined: to see how other people (the locals) live, to discover other cultures, or to visit sites which are historically or currently important. There is a desire to come back with something learned from the vacation. This motive is often contrasted with the relaxation motive, which is associated with beach and tanning, and is not considered as a profitable vacation.
- Resting and relaxing in order to take breath and eliminate stress. This is being out of one's element in the broad sense of breaking with routine and habit. The lust for sun is often associated with this motive. Vacation has a utilitarian function: people look for long term benefits such as a better mood, working better, or recovering health. Vacation is like a therapy: it creates necessary conditions for forgetting daily problems or for solving them through recovered clear-mindedness.
- Looking for people in order to share social experiences (be it with the locals, with other tourists or with travel partners). This motive is particularly strong for single DMUs, which leads to the following proposition: being a single decision-maker doesn't mean a trip alone.
- Doing exciting activities and having fun in order to take a big bite out of life and forget everything just for a few days. Excitement and fun are related to particular leisure (most often sport) activities, social togetherness or romantic experiences. Vacation has a clear hedonic function: people look for direct benefits during their consumption experiences.
- Looking for personal values (prestige, richness, knowledge...) in the vacation experience in order to impress others ('I was there!') or to go back to roots ('My family has lived in Africa for a long time'). Vacation is an opportunity to develop self-image and ego-enhancement.

- Going to 'true' places in order to experience an authentic environment that has not been corrupted by tourists. Both tourist traps and 'staged authenticity' (MacCannell, 1973) must be avoided:

'I accept to go to India but I will go on my own to discover the true face of the country and not the artificial face. We have other friends who travelled to Thailand ... They went to the south of Thailand to see the giraf women and they say that it is artificial; they advise us not to go and see that because they are people who only live from tourism, it is awful! If you want to take a picture of a child, you have to pay ... There is nothing natural any more.'

Table 13.3 Propositions for a renewed perspective on vacationers' decision-making processes

1	There is a gender-occupational differentiation of vacation definitions and motives
2	The influence of age on vacation decisions and aspects of decision-making processes can be interpreted in terms of anticipation (related to health) and maturity
3	The person's position in his/her life cycle is a major determinant of the nature of vacation decisions and of the decision-making style. Transition moments (from single to couple, the birth of a baby, children leaving the family DMU, the death of a partner) can be identified
4	Age, family, occupation and personality are the primary roots from which all personal influences originate. Vacation experience and push factors are secondary personal variables. Time and money are 'only' intervening conditions
5	The influence of personal factors on vacation decisions is often explained by trade-offs involving how discretionary time and money are spent between different items (including vacation items), or different members of the DMU. Mental states such as frustration and conflict can result from those trade-offs
6	Emotionality vs rationality, activity propensity, and risk aversion are major personality types influencing vacation choices and decision modes
7	The distinction between brand loyalists (intensive experience) and variety seekers (extensive experience) is better used to distinguish vacation experience levels
8	There are two levels of vacation push factors: a generic need to break from everyday life, and a typology of six more specific motives

Meeting and living the life of the locals, going off the beaten track, and bringing preconceived ideas or information into reality are other authenticity motives.

Conclusions

In this paper, personal constructs related to the vacationer's socio-demographics, personality and lifestyles, experience, and push factors are reconsidered through an interpretivist perspective. Emerging findings shed new light on the nature of these individual aspects and the way they influence vacation decisions and decision-making aspects. In Table 13.3 the major findings are synthesized and formulated as propositions. These stimulate further empirical research and the elaboration of broader decision-making frameworks that will take cognitive and affective processes as well as contextual and dynamical influences into account (see Decrop, 1999b).

References

Bauer, R.A. (1960) Consumer behavior as risk taking. In: R.S. Hancock (ed.) *Dynamic Marketing for a Changing World, Proceedings of the 43rd Conference*. Chicago, Illinois: American Marketing Association, pp. 389–400.

Belk, R.W. (1985) Issues in the intention–behavior discrepancy. In: J.N. Sheth (ed.) *Research in Consumer Behavior*, Vol. 1. Greenwich, Colorado: Jai Press, pp. 1–34.

Connell, J. and Lowe, A. (1997) Generating grounded theory from qualitative data: the application of inductive methods in tourism and hospitality management research. *Progress in Tourism and Hospitality Research* 3, 165–173.

Crompton, J.L. (1979) Motivations for pleasure travel. *Annals of Tourism Research* 6, 408–424.

Dann, G.M. (1977) Anomie, ego-enhancement and tourism. *Annals of Tourism Research* 4, 184–194.

Decrop, A. (1999a) Tourists' decision-making and behavior processes. In: A. Pizam and Y. Mansfeld (eds) *Consumer Behavior in Tourism and Hospitality*. New York: Haworth Press (in press).

Decrop, A. (1999b) Consumers' decision making processes revisited through a grounded theory of Belgian vacationers. PhD thesis, University of Namur.

Fodness, D. (1992) The impact of family life cycle on the vacation decision-making process. *Journal of Travel Research* 31, 8–13.

Fodness, D. (1994) Measuring tourist motivation. *Annals of Tourism Research* 21, 555–581.

Gitelson, R. and Kersteller, D. (1990) The relationship between socio-demographic variables, benefits sought, and subsequent vacation behavior: a case study. *Journal of Travel Research* 28, 24–29.

Glaser, B. and Strauss, A. (1967) *The Discovery of Grounded Theory*. Chicago: Aldine.

Gnoth, J. (1997) Tourism motivation and expectation formation. *Annals of Tourism Research* 24, 283–304.

Havitz, M.E. and Howard, D.R. (1994) How enduring is enduring involvement in the context of tourist motivation? In: R.V. Gasser and K. Weiermair (eds) *Spoilt for Choice. Decision Making Processes and Preference Changes of Tourists: Intertemporal and Intercountry Perspectives*. Thaur: Kulturverlag, pp. 120–124.

Hernandez, S.A., Cohen, J. and Garcia, H.L. (1996) Residents' attitudes towards an instant enclave resort. *Annals of Tourism Research* 23, 755–779.

MacCannell, D. (1973) Staged authenticity: arrangements of social space in tourist settings. *American Sociological Review* 79, 589–603.

Mayo, E.J. and Jarvis, L.P. (1981) *The Psychology of Leisure Travel*. Boston: CBI.

Mazanec, J.A. (1994) Segmenting travel markets. In: R. Teare, J.A. Mazanec, S. Crawford-Welch and S. Calver (eds) *Marketing in Hospitality and Tourism: A Consumer Focus*. London: Cassell, pp. 99–166.

Moutinho, L. (1987) Consumer behaviour in tourism. *European Journal of Marketing* 21, 2–44.

Oppermann, M. (1994) Travel life cycles: a multitemporal perspective of changing travel patterns. In: R.V. Gasser and K. Weiermair (eds) *Spoilt for Choice. Decision Making Processes and Preference Changes of Tourists: Intertemporal and Intercountry Perspectives*. Thaur: Kulturverlag, pp. 81–97.

Plog, S.C. (1974) Why destination areas rise and fall in popularity. *Cornell Hotel and Restaurant Administration Quarterly* 14, 55–58.

Plog, S.C. (1994) Developing and using psychographics in tourism research. In: J.R. Brent Ritchie and C.R. Goeldner (eds) *Travel, Tourism, and Hospitality Research*. New York: Wiley, pp. 209–218.

Reid, I.S. and Crompton, J.L. (1993) A taxonomy of leisure purchase decision paradigms based on level of involvement. *Journal of Leisure Research* 25, 182–202.

Riley, R. (1995) Prestige worthy leisure travel behavior. *Annals of Tourism Research* 22, 630–649.

Rubin, H.J. and Rubin, I.S. (1995) *Qualitative Interviewing: The Art of Hearing Data*. Thousand Oaks: Sage.

Strauss, A. and Corbin, J. (1990) *Basics of Qualitative Research: Grounded Theory Procedures and Techniques*. Newbury Park: Sage.

Teare, R. (1994) Consumer decision making. In: R. Teare, J.A. Mazanec, S. Crawford-Welch and S. Calver (eds) *Marketing in Hospitality and Tourism: A Consumer Focus*. London: Cassell, pp. 1–96.

van Raaij, W.F. and Francken, D.A. (1984) Vacation decisions, activities and satisfactions. *Annals of Tourism Research* 11, 101–112.

Wells, W.D. and Gubar, G. (1966) The life cycle concept. *Journal of Marketing Research* 2, 355–363.

Woodside, A.G. and MacDonald, R. (1994) General system framework of customer choice processes of tourism services. In: R.V. Gasser and K. Weiermair (eds) *Spoilt for Choice. Decision Making Processes and Preference Changes of Tourists: Intertemporal and Intercountry Perspectives*. Thaur: Kulturverlag, pp. 30–59.

Chapter fourteen
The Myers–Briggs Type Indicator and Leisure Attribute Preference

Robyn L. McGuiggan
School of Marketing, University of Technology Sydney, PO Box 222, Lindfield, NSW 2070, Australia

Introduction

Since the mid-1960s, there have been hundreds of studies dealing with the relationship between personality and various aspects of leisure. Vealey (1989) identified 463 articles on sport and personality from a limited selection of journals published between the years 1974 and 1987. The literature is extremely fragmented, with studies published in journals from a diverse array of disciplines ranging from leisure, recreation, sport, travel and tourism, to psychology and counselling, medicine, marketing, organizational management and education. The studies fall into one of three categories. The first group attempt to establish a link between personality profile and participation in certain leisure activities, for example camping or bush walking. In the second group of studies, a segmenting approach is taken and the researcher/s attempt to develop leisure profiles of those with particular personality characteristics. The third type of study endeavours to establish the personality variables associated with success in a particular activity such as chess, golf or football. The studies have predominantly focused on participation in sport and to a lesser extent on recreational activities. In spite of the volume of research, results have been disappointing. These findings have encouraged the belief that personality is of minor (if any) importance in the determination of leisure choice. This is despite reviewers such as Eysenck *et al.* (1982), Kirkcaldy (1985), Nias (1985), Vealey (1989), Kirkcaldy and Furnham (1991), Furnham (1990, 1992) and Davis and Mogk (1994) pointing out conceptual problems and design limitations in many of these studies. These reviewers argue that personality should not be dismissed as a possible determinant of leisure choice, but rather that more research is required in this area, avoiding the weaknesses inherent in previous studies.

Leisure Choice

Most previous research assumes that personality has a direct influence on leisure activity choice. However, research to date has provided little support for this assertion. There are two issues that need to be addressed here. Firstly, is leisure activity (for example tennis, watching television) the correct unit of measure? And secondly, can personality be expected to influence choice directly or does it exert its effect indirectly?

Leisure activity

The question arises as to whether leisure activity is a simple and unambiguous natural unit of analysis. A number of problems can be identified with this unit of analysis. Firstly, it is not possible to produce an exhaustive list of activities that can be classified as leisure, since all activities have the potential to be leisure and all activities have the potential to be non-leisure (for example competition golf for the professional golfer). Secondly, Kelly (1983, p. 159) draws attention to the fact that activity labels do not take account of the diverse types of activity and interaction which may occur in a single activity setting. For example, if a person indicates they have been 'swimming' what does this tell us about their actual activities – have they swum laps, played with the children, socialized with friends, or read a book by the pool? Moreover as Neulinger points out (1974, p. 35), if a list is produced, a decision as to what constitutes a unit of activity has to be made. Number of hours may be an appropriate measure for involvement in reading or watching television, but may not be a good measure for bungy jumping or skydiving. Even if the unit of analysis is established, self-reported participation in leisure activities may be biased, respondents tending to overestimate leisure activity participation (Chase and Cheek, 1979; Hultsman et al., 1989). Furthermore, using leisure activities as the unit of analysis limits the generalizability of the research. Leisure activities change over time. For example, bungy jumping, grass skiing and inline skating were unheard of in the 1970s, as were electronic games.

From the above discussion it would appear that far from leisure activity being a 'simple and unambiguous natural unit of analysis', it seems to be fraught with insurmountable problems. A number of researchers have dealt with this problem by using groups of leisure activities as the unit of analysis, for example social activities, outdoor activities, sports and hobbies. However, a review of the literature does not indicate any agreement as to the way activities should be grouped. A further argument against using activity groupings is provided by Kelly (1978b) who points out that dealing with classifications of activities will invariably obscure significant differences among particular activities. Duncan's (1978) work, showing that Q and R factor analyses of leisure activities provide very different pictures of leisure groupings, suggests that it is not the activity itself that is important to the individual but the underlying attributes of the activity as perceived by the individual. This suggests that predicting 'generic behavior', or attribute preferences, should be less difficult than predicting specific forms of behaviour.

It would appear then that the solution is not to profile a person's actual participation in leisure activities, but rather the attributes or meaning of those activities. The same conclusion has been reached by a number of authors such as Coleman (1976), Kelly (1978a, b), Kabanoff (1980), Crandall and Slivken (1980), Iso-Ahola (1980) and Bergier (1981). In support of this approach, Kabanoff (1981, p. 383) argues that task attributes have consistently been used to predict job satisfaction, and therefore he sees no reason why they should not also predict leisure satisfaction. A further argument for focusing on leisure attributes and meanings is provided by Balderjahn's (1988) causal model of ecologically conscious consumer behaviour, in which he suggests that greater correlation should be found between personality and leisure attributes than between personality and participation in specific activities. Foxall's (1984, pp. 115–116) contention that to measure accurately the association between two variables, both must be conceptualized and measured at the same level of generality/specificity, adds even further support for using attributes rather than activities. Personality tests apply to global views of behaviour and not to the specific. Attributes are not activity-specific; they can be used to describe any leisure activity.

Leisure choice

The second issue that needs to be addressed is that of choice. It is proposed that rather than personality influencing leisure choice directly, personality exerts its influence indirectly through establishing leisure preferences. Choices are made, but within the constraints that order our lives. Many researchers in the leisure area have identified constraints on our actual choice. These may be external to the individual, such as culturally determined roles, laws and regulations, availability/accessibility of appropriate facilities; or internal, such as physical ability, health, and competing obligations such as family or work. Whether constraints are internal or external, perceived or real, surveys such as the General Recreation Surveys administered by the Alberta government in 1988 and 1992, in which approximately 50% of respondents reported the desire to start a new recreational or leisure activity but were unable to because of various constraints (Jackson and Witt, 1994), indicate that actual choice is likely to be difficult to predict. In the words of Kelly (1978b, p. 328), 'leisure is found to be a complex and varied combination of activities, relationships, and meanings which are neither determined by social and environmental factors nor separate from them. In fact, leisure decisions contain so many factors that they are very difficult to predict at all' (Kelly, 1982, p. 172). Therefore, although we may prefer to engage in a particular activity, intervening variables may lead to a totally different activity being chosen or a compromise being made. Some support for expecting personality to influence leisure choice indirectly through preference is provided by Webster and Wakshalg's (1983) model of television programme choice. Although they present no empirical data to support their theory, they propose that 'specific program preference is a cause of program choice' (p. 432) and that psychological variables, e.g. needs, influence actual choice through establishing preferences. It is therefore proposed that personality influences leisure choice indirectly, as depicted in Fig. 14.1.

The aim of this study is to focus on the first part of the model, to determine whether a relationship can be established between personality and leisure attribute preference.

Measuring Personality

One of the major criticisms levelled at past research is the choice of personality instrument. Literally hundreds of personality questionnaires are available commercially. However, many of the previous studies on personality and leisure choice have been criticized by authors such as Wilde (1977), Iso-Ahola (1980) and Furnham (1990, 1992) for the inappropriate selection and use of personality instrument. The instruments themselves have been criticized as being based on weak theory, invalid or inappropriate (Furnham, 1990). Many researchers do not use well established instruments, but choose obscure and unsatisfactorily validated scales (Iso-Ahola, 1980) for the measurement of their chosen personality constructs. Often these are poorly defined and operationalized. Others, wishing to shorten their total questionnaire, use a shortened version of a personality questionnaire. They may use the questions that have the highest loading on a personality factor as a measure of that personality attribute (e.g. Ergün and Stopher, 1982), or they may not even state how the shortened version was derived (e.g. Douse and McManus, 1993). Some researchers have even re-worded the questions in the personality questionnaire to reflect a leisure context (e.g. Taylor *et al.*, 1979), or have added items to measure additional personality constructs they thought might be useful (e.g. Kirkcaldy, 1990). A significant number focus on abnormal personality profiles and deficiencies rather than personality strengths (Furnham, 1992).

Although the above criticisms point to the necessity of choosing a theoretically based instrument that has been adequately tested in terms of reliability and validity, there must also be a theoretically sound justification for expecting a relationship between the personality trait/s to be measured and the leisure activity. In Iso-Ahola's (1980) words:

> 'In no study have researchers offered any theoretical reasons why certain activities have been selected for their investigation. ... Like the selection of leisure activities, the choice of traits to be correlated with activities has, without exception, been made for no apparent theoretical reasons' (p. 207).

The personality constructs chosen, even though appropriately conceived and measured, may simply not be related to the leisure behaviour being measured. One personality indicator that addresses these criteria is the Myers–Briggs type indicator (MBTI).

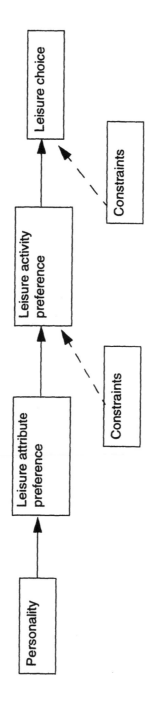

Figure 14.1 Proposed relationship between personality and leisure choice.

The Myers–Briggs type indicator

Katherine Briggs and Isabel Briggs Myers developed the MBTI to operationalize Carl Jung's (1971 [1921]) theory of psychological types. It is extensively used in counselling (both career and personal), teacher training (learning styles) and organizational contexts such as team building, conflict resolution and staff development. With translation into 33 languages (Pearman and Fleenor, 1996) and claims that over 3,000,000 people per year take the MBTI (Spoto, 1995), the MBTI is one of the most widely used personality indicators for non-psychiatric populations in the world.

The MBTI describes a person's personality on four dichotomous dimensions, indicating a person's preference for source of psychological energy (extroversion versus introversion), perception (sensing versus intuition), making judgements (thinking versus feeling), and orientation to the outer world (judging versus perceiving). The four preferences combine to generate 16 personality types. The MBTI questionnaire is a forced-choice, self-report inventory, virtually self-administering and designed for use with normal subjects. The questions consist of behavioural preferences and a number of preferred self-descriptive adjectives. Each individual question is designed to elicit a preference for one of the four dimensions. The responses for each question are weighted and a total score for each of the eight preferences recorded. The scores are then converted to a preference score for each of the four scales that reflect the relative preference for one pole over the other (taking omissions into account). These four preferences indicate a person's MBTI type.

Countless papers have been written reviewing the reliability and validity of the MBTI. Generally these support the view that the four MBTI scales have construct validity and measure important dimensions of personality which approximate those in Jung's typology (Steele and Kelly, 1976; Coan, 1978; Levy and Padilla, 1982; Geer et al., 1984; Tzeng et al., 1984; Sipps et al., 1985; Thompson and Borrello, 1986; Wiggins, 1989; Murray, 1990). Both test–re-test reliability (coefficients range between 0.60 and 0.91) and internal consistency (coefficients range between 0.77 and 0.90) have been established for the instrument (Pearman and Fleenor, 1996) and are generally accepted as satisfactory (Carlson, 1989).

Thus the MBTI questionnaire would appear to address a number of the criticisms levelled at previous studies. It has a strong theoretical framework, being based on Carl Jung's theory, and there exists extensive validity data supporting the underlying constructs. It has also shown good reliability in many and varied situations. Moreover the MBTI does not have negative connotations associated with being a particular type. All personality types are seen as positive. The MBTI questionnaire asks about everyday, commonplace events, and so is suitable for all types of respondents. The MBTI is designed as a self-administered questionnaire and thus is appropriate for inclusion as part of a broader, self-completion survey.

In addition, a number of arguments can be advanced for expecting a relationship to exist between MBTI type and leisure choice. Firstly, Jung's and Myers' theories imply that a relationship should exist. Both are type theories, which advocate that people of similar personality can be expected to react in a similar way to many situations in life. A number of authors, such as Kroeger and Thuesen (1988), Hirsh and Kummerow (1989), Provost (1990), Provost and Anchors (1991), to name just a few, have hypothesized on the relationship between MBTI type and leisure choice. In fact many MBTI advocates suggest that this relationship may be stronger than that between personality and work. Secondly, extensive data are available on the relationship between MBTI type and occupational preference or choice. If choice of both work and leisure are influenced by a common third variable such as personality, as suggested by authors such as Kraus (1978), Iso-Ahola (1980) and Kabanoff and O'Brien (1980), the data already collected on the MBTI showing a strong relationship between MBTI type and career choice would suggest that a relationship between type and leisure choice should also exist. Thirdly, the sensing–intuitive and thinking–feeling functions measured by the MBTI refer to the way people gather information and arrive at decisions. This parallels consumer behaviour theory in terms of information search and decision-making. In fact the MBTI has been used in organizations to estimate decision styles of executives (Henderson and Nutt, 1980; Moore, 1987). So one can extend the argument by asking a simple question. Why wouldn't the same be true for decisions on product or leisure choice?

However, as pointed out by Pearman and Fleenor (1996), although numerous books and papers have been published on psychological type, these are mostly based on the authors' observations rather than on empirical data. Thus this study aims to determine whether the leisure attribute preferences predicted by MBTI theory can be substantiated empirically.

Method

Development of the questionnaire

Numerous books and articles on the MBTI were scanned to determine any predictions that had been made regarding the relationship between type and leisure preferences. Other MBTI type characteristics that might be applicable to leisure attribute preference were also noted. For example, it could be expected that people who like to plan their work would also prefer to plan their leisure activities. Four distinct leisure areas were covered: reading, general leisure, sport, and vacations. One hundred and twenty questions were developed under 25 broad headings suggested by the literature (see Table 14.1). For a full list of the MBTI scales and types suggested by the literature, by question, see McGuiggan (1996). A summary of the expected MBTI scales is presented together with the results. Because the MBTI questions are presented as forced-choice answers, the leisure questions were developed to replicate this format. The intention was to make questionnaire completion easier for the respondent and also to aid in analysis. Furthermore, completion time would be minimized. For a full description of the development of the actual questions, see McGuiggan (1996).

The questions were pre-tested using a convenience sample of undergraduate business students enrolled in first-year marketing at the University of Technology, Sydney (UTS), Australia. One hundred and three questionnaires were completed. The questions were analysed for skewness (non-discriminating questions), and high inter-question correlation. After skewed questions were deleted and highly correlating questions either deleted or re-worded, 101 questions remained.

The final questionnaire thus contained the 94 scoring questions from the MBTI Form G (the instructions having been modified to facilitate self-completion) and the 101 questions asking about the respondent's vacation and leisure attribute preferences.

Table 14.1 Broad headings used to develop leisure questions

Heading	Sub-headings
Planning	Vacation planning
	Leisure planning
	Acceptability of changes to plans
	Carry through with plans
	Complete planned projects
	Follow rules
People	Number of people vacation with
	Number of people spend leisure with
Depth of involvement in activities	
Length of vacation	
Reading	General questions
	Preferred type of reading
Variety	Variety of vacations
	Variety of activities on vacation
	Level of comfort on vacation
	Variety of sports
	Variety of leisure activities
	Risk involved in sports
Sports	Watching or engaging in sports
	Pace of activities engaged in
	Team or contact sports
	Competition
Household tasks	
Traditional or modern activities	
Other aspects of leisure	

Participants

A purposive sample was sought with the aim of achieving a large sample made up of a relatively even distribution of the 16 MBTI types. Personal dropping off and collection of the questionnaire was the preferred method of data collection, because of the length of the questionnaire and also the concern that the forced-choice format might increase the number of questionnaires returned with missing data. To achieve enough respondents of each type, data were collected in two phases.

Phase I

As part of their course requirement, undergraduate students completing the subject Marketing Research at UTS were required to collect data for this study. Students were divided into groups of between four and six for this project. Each student was required to have six questionnaires completed by appropriate respondents. Groups were asked to balance their respondents in terms of gender and age (18–25 years; 26–55 years; over 55 years). Furthermore, students were instructed that university students and staff were not acceptable respondents. This directive was given to try to maximize the variation in respondent personality type. Each student was given six questionnaires, six envelopes in which the respondents could seal the completed questionnaires to ensure anonymity, a check sheet for the later verification of questionnaire completion, and an introductory letter to read to and leave with the respondents. The students returned 880 completed questionnaires. Two respondents were randomly chosen from each student's check sheet and contacted to ascertain whether they had completed the questionnaire. Each questionnaire was also checked for completeness and having been properly answered. Following these checks, 98 of the questionnaires were discarded, leaving 782 completed questionnaires. After establishing the MBTI type of the respondents, it was found that 12 of the MBTI types contained fewer than 30 respondents with four of the types having less than 20 respondents. Therefore further respondents were sought to boost the numbers in these 12 groups.

Phase II

A list of possible participants of 'known' MBTI type in each of the 12 groups sought was provided by the Director of the Institute for Type Development, Sydney, on the understanding that the list would be destroyed upon completion of data collection and that respondent questionnaires would be anonymous. Each of these people was mailed a package which included a copy of the questionnaire, a reply-paid envelope and a covering letter on Institute for Type Development letterhead, signed by the Director, requesting their help with the project. After 3 weeks a follow-up letter was sent out to improve the response rate. Approximately 50% of the questionnaires were returned and, after checking the questionnaires, a further 126 cases were added to the data bank, giving a total sample size of 908 cases.

Men comprised 49% of the sample, and the mean age was 35–39 years (range 18–65+ years). Seventy two percent were born in Australia and 70% were working (58% full-time and 12% part-time) with an average household income of $75,000 per year. The MBTI type distribution of the sample is presented in Table 14.2.

Results

SPSS, a statistical package for the social sciences, was used to analyse the data. Before correlations could be calculated, 17 of the leisure questions that allowed respondents to choose between three or more options required re-coding. Five were re-coded into dichotomous variables by combining categories, and the other 12 were re-coded 1, 1.5 and 2 since the choices provided an ordinal scale. Preference and continuous scores were created for the MBTI scales as described in the MBTI Manual (Myers and McCaulley, 1992, p. 9).

Table 14.2 MBTI type distribution of the sample

Type	No. in sample	Percentage of total
ISTJ	133	14.6
ISFJ	60	6.6
INFJ	33	3.6
INTJ	41	4.5
ISTP	65	7.2
ISFP	31	3.4
INFP	54	5.9
INTP	49	5.4
ESTP	64	7.0
ESFP	83	9.1
ENTP	65	7.2
ESTJ	96	10.6
ESFJ	43	4.7
ENFJ	27	3.0
ENTJ	29	3.2

To assess whether the MBTI predictions could be verified from the data, a correlation matrix was created between the 101 leisure questions and the four MBTI continuous scales and 16 types. Due to the nature of the data, point biserial correlations were completed between 89 of the leisure questions and the MBTI continuous scales, and phi correlations between these questions and the 16 MBTI types. The other 12 leisure questions being on a three-point continuum necessitated the use of Pearson's product moment correlations and point biserial correlations, respectively. In all correlations, pairwise deletion of missing cases was specified. The correlation analysis revealed that 94% of the leisure questions were significantly associated with at least one of the four MBTI scales at the 0.01 level. Although the large number of significant results provides some support for a relationship existing between the MBTI scales and leisure preference, two issues remain. Firstly, only 15 of the correlations had correlation coefficients above 0.3, and 69 above 0.2. Although these values are consistent with those published in the MBTI manual (Myers and McCaulley, 1992), and high coefficients cannot be expected due to the categorical natural of the data and the imbalance in the marginal distributions, how useful are the relationships seen in the correlation matrix? Secondly, how important and useful is knowing how each MBTI type is likely to respond to any particular question of the 101 asked in this study? Data reduction would provide a solution to both of these concerns.

A principal components factor analysis with varimax rotation and pairwise deletion of missing data was attempted (dummy variables having been created for the 12 questions with three categories). Thirty-five factors with eigenvalues greater than 1, accounting for 56.2% of the variation in the data, were obtained. On the other hand, the scree plot suggested only six distinct factors accounting for 23.5% of the variation. However the factors were not clearly interpretable in either case. The problem with this factor analysis seemed to be the large number of questions that were being factored together. A possible solution would be to redo the factor analysis on smaller groups of questions. The dilemma centres on the basis for choosing the questions to put into each factor analysis. Going back to the MBTI theory used to generate the questions suggests that the initial 25 groups, resulting from the MBTI literature and used in the development of the questions, be used as the basis for choosing the questions for the factor analyses. Three of these groups – reading, preferred type of reading and other aspects of leisure – were dropped from the analysis, since the correlation analysis indicated that the questions within each of these groups were not closely related. A drawback to the use of factor analysis on the 22 remaining groups is the small number of questions in some of them. For example, 'the number of people you vacation with', and whether 'you complete planned projects', contain only two questions each, making it impossible to use factor analysis. A solution to this problem would be to combine groups. However, this would create the same dilemma as before – which groups to combine? Instead of using trial and error to determine the groups to combine, it was decided to leave the groups as they were and create a simple scale by adding the question scores together. This would then provide 22 new variables. The questions were re-scored such that a score of 1 meant the respondent answered negatively on the scale, and a 2 meant a positive association with the scale. Once the 22 scores were created, a factor analysis of the scales was undertaken to determine whether some should be combined. The analysis gave six factors with eigenvalues exceeding 1, explaining 51.7% of the variance in the data, while the scree plot indicated three factors accounting for only 34.9% of the variance. Neither solution was easily interpreted. However, going back to the predictions made from MBTI theory, it was felt that a number of the scales might logically be expected to fit together. Therefore a factor analysis was carried out on the groups of scales indicated in Table 14.3. The analysis of the planning questions showed that these six scales could be reduced to two: a planning factor consisting of 'vacation planning', 'leisure planning' and 'acceptability of changes to vacation plans'; plus a follow-through factor comprising 'carry through with plans', 'complete planned projects' and 'follow rules'. Similarly, the variety scales reduced to two: a variety factor which incorporated 'variety of vacations', 'variety of activities on vacation', 'variety of leisure activities', and 'variety of sports'; plus a risk factor which combined 'level of comfort on vacation' and 'risk involved in sports'. The sports scales also reduced to two factors: pace of activities comprising 'competitive sport' and 'pace of sporting activities'; and team sports which combined 'watch or engage in sport' and 'team or contact sports'. Finally the two people scales factored into one. Scores were created for each of the seven new combined scales.

Table 14.3 Leisure scales factored together

Planning	Vacation planning
	Acceptability of changes to vacation plans
	Carry through with plans
	Leisure planning
	Follow rules
	Complete planned projects
Variety	Variety of vacations
	Variety of activities on vacation
	Level of comfort on vacation
	Variety of leisure activities
	Variety of sports
	Risk involved in sports
People	Number of people vacation with
	Number of people spend leisure with
Sport	Watch or engage in sport
	Pace of sporting activities
	Team or contact sports
	Competitive sport

Since a Pearson's product moment correlation showed significant correlations between a number of the leisure scales, a factor analysis was completed on the 11 scales to check that the optimal number of scales had been achieved. Only one of the five factors was clearly interpretable: a planning factor consisting of both 'planning' and 'follow-through with plans'. Two distinct factors having emerged when the six original planning scales were factored, it was decided that planning should remain as two separate scales. It appeared that nothing could be gained by further data reduction. Thus 11 leisure scales were created. The reliability of the scales was not at issue, since creation of leisure attribute scales was not the aim of the research. However, because the questions assigned to each of the original 25 scales were determined subjectively, reliability analysis was used to determine whether all the questions included in a scale were appropriate. Where a question reduced the Cronbach alpha, it was removed from the scale. The questions removed were then tested with other possible scales to determine whether they more appropriately belonged to those. Questions not improving the Cronbach alpha of any scale were dropped from the analysis. Seventy-nine questions were included in the final 11 scales: Planning, 14; Follow-through, 6; Variety, 18; Risk, 3; People, 6; Pace of activities, 5; Team sports, 5; Length of vacation, 2; Household tasks, 4; Involvement, 8; and Modernity, 8. For full details and the actual questions in each of the scales, refer to McGuiggan (1996). New scores were created for each of the 11 cleaned scales. These were then correlated with the MBTI four continuous scales. The results are presented in Table 14.4. From this table, it can be seen that 10 of the 11 leisure scales are significant, with at least one of the MBTI scales at the 0.001 level. Since 'length of vacation' showed no significant relationship with any of the MBTI scales (or types), it was excluded from further analysis. Furthermore, the significant correlation coefficients obtained using the leisure scales were of a more impressive magnitude than those achieved using the individual questions. Significant correlations with more than one of the MBTI scales were found for nine of the ten remaining leisure scales, some of which were not predicted from the literature. Relying on the size of the correlation coefficients to determine which of the MBTI scales has the greatest predictive power for a particular leisure scale could be misleading, since the impact of one variable on another may depend totally or partly on its relationship to other variables. Therefore using only a coefficient of association to determine explanatory importance would seem fraught with danger (Reynolds, 1984, p. 71). To overcome this problem, stepwise multiple regression analysis was used to determine which of the MBTI scales were, in fact, accounting for the variation in the leisure scales. The results are presented in Table 14.5: it is evident that the power of the MBTI to explain the variability in the leisure scales differs greatly from a low of 6.1% for the Involvement scale to a high of 46.4% for the Planning scale. Split-half samples were used to verify that the results were not due to chance and all assumptions underlying regression analysis were checked. A summary of the predictions and actual results are presented in Table 14.6.

Table 14.4 Pearson's product moment correlations of the eleven leisure scales with the MBTI continuous scores

Leisure scale	ContEI	ContSN	ContTF	ContJP
Planning	0.16***	−0.32***	−0.14***	−0.68***
Follow-through	−0.01	−0.23***	−0.12***	−0.31***
Variety	−0.42***	0.28***	−0.00	0.30***
Risk	−0.26***	0.30***	−0.06	0.35***
People	−0.44***	0.09**	0.06	0.30***
Pace of activities	−0.25***	0.07*	−0.13***	0.22***
Team sport	−0.45***	0.08*	−0.04	0.24***
Length vacation	0.05	0.02	−0.01	0.01
Household tasks	0.17***	−0.22***	0.02	−0.33***
Involvement	−0.02	0.06	−0.23***	−0.03
Modernity	−0.25***	−0.01	−0.06	0.26***

*$P<0.05$, **$P<0.01$, ***$P<0.001$.

Table 14.5 Stepwise multiple regression analysis with leisure scales as the dependent variable and the MBTI continuous scales as the independent variables

Leisure scale	MBTI scales entered	B	R^2	Adjusted in order of entry
Planning	JP	−0.06	−0.68	0.46
Follow-through	JP	−0.13	−0.28	0.11
	SN	−0.01	−0.11	
	EI	−0.004	−0.08	
Variety	EI	−0.05	−0.37	0.26
	SN	0.03	0.21	
	JP	0.02	0.15	
	TF	−0.01	−0.10	
Risk	JP	0.01	0.26	0.21
	EI	−0.01	−0.19	
	SN	0.01	0.21	
	TF	−0.01	−0.17	
People	EI	−0.02	−0.39	0.23
	JP	0.01	0.21	
Pace of activities	EI	−0.01	−0.21	0.12
	JP	0.01	0.21	
	TF	−0.01	−0.18	
Team sport	EI	−0.23	−0.41	0.23
	JP	0.01	0.18	
	TF	−0.01	−0.10	
Household tasks	JP	−0.01	−0.28	0.14
	SN	−0.01	−0.13	
	TF	0.01	0.11	
	EI	0.005	0.10	
Involvement	TF	−0.02	−0.25	0.06
	SN	0.01	0.12	
Modernity	JP	0.02	0.29	0.13
	EI	−0.02	−0.21	
	SN	−0.01	−0.12	
	TF	−0.01	−0.11	

All significant at $P<0.001$. All SE $B<0.001$

Table 14.6 Results of the stepwise multiple regression analysis compared with predictions from the MBTI literature

Leisure scale	Preferences predicted	Actual results
Planning	J, S	J
Follow-through	J, S	J, S, E
Variety	E, N, P	E, N, P, T
Risk	E, N, P, F	E, N, P, T
People	E, F	E, P
Pace of activities	E, T, P	E, T, P
Team sport	E	E, T, P
Household tasks	J, S, I	J, S, I, F
Involvement	S, T	N, T
Modernity	E, P, N	E, P, S, T

As predicted by the MBTI literature, the Planning scale is closely tied to the judging–perceptive scale (46.4% of the variance accounted for), with people having a preference for judging wanting to plan, and those with a preference for perception wanting to be spontaneous and flexible. Only 11.1% of the variability in the Follow-through scale is accounted for by the three MBTI scales judging–perceptive, sensing–intuitive and extroversion–introversion. Association was predicted with the judging–perceptive and sensing–intuitive scales – a person with a preference for judging being more likely to follow through with plans than a person with a preference for perception. A preference for intuition predisposed one towards newness and change, and a preference for sensing implied focus, detail and step-by-step execution of tasks. The last scale to be entered into the regression equation was the extroversion–introversion scale, adding only 0.56% to the explanatory power of the equation. This scale was not significantly correlated with the Follow-through scale and no association had been predicted. However, it appears from the regression analysis that extroverts are more likely than introverts to follow through with their plans.

All four MBTI scales were entered into the regression equation for the Variety scale, even though Table 14.4 shows that the thinking–feeling scale was not significantly correlated with this scale. As predicted in the literature, a preference for extroversion, intuition or perception leads to a preference for variety. These three scales account for 25.76% of the variability in the Variety scale, while the preference for thinking–feeling (which was not predicted) adds only another 0.8% to the total explanatory power of the equation. Those with a preference for thinking appear to be more inclined to seek variety. Although the thinking–feeling scale was not found to be significantly correlated with the Risk scale, the regression analysis does seem to indicate that all four scales would influence a person's perception of risk. As suggested by the MBTI literature, those having a preference for extroversion, intuition, or perception are much more likely to partake in activities involving risk than those with a preference for introversion, sensing, or judging. On the other hand, the results indicate that a preference for thinking also predisposes towards risk (adding 2.7% to the explanatory power of the equation), when in fact the literature had suggested the opposite. Together, the four MBTI scales explain 21.08% of the variation in risk-taking behaviour.

The MBTI literature indicated that extroverts should score more highly on the People scale than introverts. This was indeed the case, as can be seen from Table 14.6. However, it was not foreseen that a preference for perception would also lead to a higher score. Nevertheless, inclusion of the judging–perceptive scale in the regression equation improved explanatory power by 4.3% to 23.36%.

Table 14.5 indicates that the MBTI scales extroversion–introversion, judging–perceptive and thinking–feeling explain only 12% of the variability in the Pace of activities scale. It was easy to predict the inclusion of the extroversion–introversion and the thinking–feeling scales from the MBTI literature, and to a lesser extent the judging–perceptive scale. It appears that a preference for extroversion, thinking or perception predisposes one to a preference for faster paced competitive activities. These same three MBTI scales were much better at explaining involvement in team sports (22.77%) than the pace of the activities undertaken (12%). From the literature, only a preference for extroversion had been predicted to predispose a person towards involvement in team sports, whereas a preference for thinking and perception also appear to be involved.

The MBTI predicts that people with a preference for judging, sensing or introversion would be more likely to do household tasks than those with a preference for extroversion, intuition or perception. This is borne out by the results of the regression analysis, which also indicates a preference for feeling to be associated with doing household tasks. However, the explanatory power of the equation is relatively weak (13.46%) compared to a number of the other scales.

The variance in the Involvement scale is least explained (6.1%) by the MBTI scales. From the literature, it was expected that a preference for sensing or thinking was likely to be associated with deeper involvement in activities rather than intuition or feeling. The correlation matrix (Table 14.4) and the regression analysis (Table 14.5) show that the opposite is in fact true for the sensing–intuitive scale. In other words, a preference for intuition or thinking rather than sensing or feeling predisposes towards deeper involvement in activities. A preference for modern versus traditional was predicted by the literature to be associated with the preferences of extroversion, intuition and perception. All four MBTI scales entered into the regression analysis and accounted for 12.98% of the variance in the scale. Extroversion and perception were indeed associated with a preference for modern cultural activities. However, a preference for sensing rather than intuition and also thinking were positively associated with the Modernity scale.

In summary, although not all of the above results were predicted from the MBTI literature, a large number were. This in itself is quite impressive considering the fact that in the main, the literature is based not on empirical data but on observation and the various authors' personal experiences with people of different preferences.

Discussion

The results of this study provide strong support for continued investigation of the relationship of personality and leisure preferences using the MBTI. Eighty per cent of the predictions made at the MBTI scale level could be substantiated by empirical data. As the following discussion indicates, this may in fact be an underestimation, since reasonable explanations can be found for almost all of the results obtained using the MBTI descriptions of the eight preferences.

Even though the MBTI had predicted an association between the sensing–intuitive scale and the Planning scale and the two were found to be highly correlated, the sensing–intuitive scale did not enter the Planning regression analysis. This appears to be due to the overriding nature of the judging–perceptive scale in predicting the desire to plan. In other words, a preference for judging implies a strong need to plan regardless of other preferences. However, it does appear that a person with a preference for perception is more likely to plan if they have a preference for sensing rather than intuition (see Table 14.4).

The finding that the People scale was not correlated with the thinking–feeling scale was probably due to the differences in the two underlying constructs. A preference for feeling, as described by the MBTI, relates to decision-making rather than the desire to be with people, while the leisure questions comprising the People scale were more oriented toward social involvement with people. This would more closely reflect the MBTI extrovert–introvert scale and this was reflected in the results.

In the regression analyses, the three results that ran contrary to prediction had not shown a significant correlation with the respective MBTI scale. Yet inclusion in the regression equation did add between 1.17 and 2.7% to the explanatory power of the equations. A possible explanation for the association between thinking and a reported preference for activities involving risk could be risk perception. People with a preference for thinking may be more likely to perceive risk in activities than others. Alternatively it is possible that they seek out risky activities for the challenge they present. Deeper involvement in activities being associated with intuition rather than sensing could be due to interest in the complexity of the situation and the opportunity provided to explore creative solutions. A preference for sensing predisposes towards seeing what is, a preference for reality, which could explain the association with modern cultural events.

Of the seven results where no prediction had been made, but the MBTI scale had entered the regression equation, only two (both involving the judging–perceptive scale) showed a significant correlation with the respective leisure scales (People and Team sport scales). No clear explanation for these results can be found in the MBTI literature, but perhaps people with a preference for perception being more open to change may provide a partial explanation for the relationships found. Of the remaining five results, four involved the thinking–feeling scale. Doing household tasks was associated with a preference for feeling, which could be explained by a desire for harmony in the household and a predilection for the consideration of others. A preference for thinking was associated with seeking variety, involvement in team sports and a preference for modern cultural events. Although an explanation is not obvious from the MBTI literature, it is possible that the desire of people with a thinking preference for logical choice, competition, truth and reality may partially account for the results. The other result that was not predicted was a preference for extroversion being associated with a desire to follow through with tasks. An extrovert's desire for continual activity could go some way to explaining this finding.

It is difficult to compare the results of this study with previous studies carried out in the leisure area using the MBTI, for two reasons. Firstly, previous studies used very specific samples and measured very specific leisure activity, e.g. long-distance running and sub-3-hour marathoners (Gontang *et al.*, 1977); gambling problems among members of Gamblers anonymous (Malkin and Syme, 1986); collecting in baseball-card collectors (Dodgen and Rapp, 1992). Secondly, correlation coefficients were rarely reported, even when results were significant. In most cases results were not significant and discussion focused around reporting trends in the data. The one outstanding result from these studies was that found by Morehouse *et al.* (1990). They found that when respondents were asked if they received stimulation more from thoughts or from activities and behaviours, those with a preference for extroversion reported stimulation to come from activity and behaviours ($r=0.39$). Even though the results are not directly comparable, this result does appear to be consistent with the findings of this study, where extroverts were found to prefer a variety of activities ($r=0.42$).

The ability of the MBTI scales to explain leisure attribute preference varied between 6.1% for the Involvement scale to 46.35% for the Planning scale. For five of the leisure scales, Planning, Variety, Risk, People, and Team sport, more than 20% of the variance could be explained by the MBTI scales. In all cases, bar that of the Involvement scale, the MBTI scales could explain at least 10% of the variance. Compared to previous research on personality in both the consumer behaviour and leisure studies areas, this is a good result. Neulinger (1974) reports correlations of 0.3 or higher to be rare in personality research; Kamphorst (1987) describes typical correlations in social psychology to be around 0.25; and Kabanoff

(1981) says 0.2 and 0.3 are virtually modal values in personality research. There-fore the correlations found in this study could be described as varying from aver-age to extremely good, depending on the leisure attribute.

Conclusions

The significant correlation coefficients reported in the MBTI manual range between 0.07 and 0.47, with the vast majority in the range 0.11 to 0.29 (Myers and McCaulley, 1992). The results of this study compare extremely favourably with these, providing support for the research proposition that personality, as measured by the MBTI, is associated with leisure attribute preference. Therefore it does appear that MBTI theory can be used to predict leisure preference. In fact, com-paring the size of the correlation coefficients in this study with those reported in the MBTI manual, the MBTI may be a better predictor of leisure attribute prefer-ence, than a predictor in other areas of life, such as occupation, with which it has traditionally been associated. This should not be surprising, since freedom of choice can more easily be exercised in the leisure domain of life than the work or maintenance areas. Thus the results of this study provide further evidence of the validity of the MBTI theory, at least at the scale level.

This study has indeed shown that it is, as yet, too early to dismiss personality as a major contributor in determining leisure activity preferences. In particular, attributes of leisure such as planning, variety, risk, pace of activities, competition and modernity seem to be influenced by personality. The study has shown the importance of using leisure attributes based on theory rather than specific leisure activities. However, many leisure activities can be described in terms of the attributes used in this study, and therefore the results may provide only a partial explanation for preference of specific activities. The study has also shown the importance of a sound theoretical basis in the choice of personality indicator, and specifically the applicability of the MBTI to leisure attribute choice.

The results of this study also indicate that not all attributes of leisure are equally likely to be influenced by personality. A possible explanation for the var-iability in the proficiency of the MBTI to explain the leisure attributes could be the differing reliabilities of the various leisure scales. An improvement in the internal reliability of the leisure scales may enhance the explanatory power of the MBTI. Of course, other explanations for the variation in explanatory power are possible. For example, the leisure attribute may not in fact be related to personal-ity, but rather to demographics, situational variables, or other factors. Alterna-tively, the respondent may not see the attribute as leisure, and therefore lower correlations might be expected. Further research should involve the development of better leisure scales and the inclusion of other variables.

References

Balderjahn, I. (1988) Personality variables and environmental attitudes as predictors of ecologically responsible consumption patterns. *Journal of Business Research* 17, 51–56.

Bergier, M.J. (1981) A conceptual model of leisure-time choice behavior. *Journal of Leisure Research* 13, 139–157.

Carlson, J.G. (1989) Testing the test affirmative: in support of researching the Myers–Briggs Type Indicator. *Journal of Counseling and Development* 67, 484–486.

Chase, D.R. and Cheek Jr, N.H. (1979) Activity preferences and participation: conclusions from a factor analytic study. *Journal of Leisure Research* 11, 92–101.

Coleman, D.V. (1976) Biographical, personality, and situational determinants of leisure time expenditure: with specific attention to competitive activities (athletics) and to more cooperative activities (music). *Dissertation Abstracts International* 37 (1-B July), 520-B.

Crandall, R. and Slivken, K. (1980) Leisure attitudes and their measurement. In: S.E. Iso-Ahola (ed.) Social psychology perspective on leisure and recreation, 1st edn. Springfield, Illinois: Charles C. Thomas, pp. 261–284.

Davis, C. and Mogk, J.P. (1994) Some personality correlates of interest and excellence in sport. *International Journal of Sport Psychology* 25, 131–143.

Dodgen, L. and Rapp, A. (1992) An analysis of personality differences between baseball card collectors and investors based on the Myers–Briggs Personality Inventory. *Journal of Social Behavior and Personality* 7, 355–361.

Douse, N.A. and McManus, I.C. (1993) The personality of fantasy game players. *British Journal of Psychology* 84, 505–509.

Duncan, D.J. (1978) Leisure types: factor analyses of leisure profiles. *Journal of Leisure Research* 10, 113–125.

Eysenck, H.J., Nias, D.K.B. and Cox, D.N. (1982) Sport and personality. *Advances in Behavior Research and Theory* 4, 1–56.

Foxall, G. (1984) The meaning of marketing and leisure: issues for research and development. *European Journal of Marketing* 18, 23–32.

Furnham, A. (1990) Personality and demographic determinants of leisure and sports preference and performance. *Journal of Sport Psychology* 21, 218–236.

Furnham, A. (1992) *Personality at Work: the Role of Individual Differences in the Workplace*. London: Routledge.

Geer, C., Ridley, S.E. and Roberts, A. (1984) Jungian personality as a predictor of attendance at the black college day march. *Psychological Reports* 54, 887–890.

Gontang, A., Clitsome, T. and Kostrubala, T. (1977) A psychological study of 50 sub-3-hour marathoners. *Annals of New York Academy of Sciences* 301, 1020–1028.

Henderson, J.C. and Nutt, P.C. (1980) The influence of decision style on decision-making behavior. *Management Science* 26, 371–386.

Hirsh, S. and Kummerow, J. (1989) *Life Types*. New York: Warner Books.

Hultsman, W.Z., Hultsman, J.T. and Black, D.R. (1989) Response peaks as a component of measurement error: assessment implications for self-report data in leisure research. *Journal of Leisure Research* 21, 310–315.

Iso-Ahola, S.E. (1980) *The Social Psychology of Leisure and Recreation*. Dubuque, Iowa: William C. Brown.

Jackson, E.L. and Witt, P.A. (1994) Change and stability in leisure constraints: a comparison of two surveys conducted four years apart. *Journal of Leisure Research* 26, 322–336.

Jung, C.G. (1971) Psychological types. In: H. Read, M. Fordham and G. Adler (eds) *The Collected Works of Carl Jung* (Vol. 6) A revision by R.F.C. Hull of the translation by H.G. Baynes. London: Routledge.

Kabanoff, B. (1980) A task attributes description of leisure: its relation to personality. *Australian Psychologist* 15, 268–269.

Kabanoff, B. (1981) Validation of a task attributes description of leisure. *Australian Journal of Psychology* 33, 383–391.

Kabanoff, B. and O'Brien, G.E. (1980) Work and leisure: a task attribute analysis. *Journal of Applied Psychology* 65, 596–609.

Kamphorst, T.J. (1987) The underlying dimensions of leisure activities: the example of watching television. *Society and Leisure* 10, 195–208.

Kelly, J.R. (1978a) A revised paradigm of leisure choice. *Leisure Sciences* 1, 345–363.

Kelly, J.R. (1978b) Situational and social factors in leisure decisions. *Pacific Sociological Review* 21, 313–330.

Kelly, J.R. (1982) *Leisure*. Englewood Cliffs, New Jersey: Prentice Hall.

Kelly, J.R. (1983) *Leisure Identities and Interactions*. London: George Allen & Unwin.

Kirkcaldy, B.D. (1985) The value of traits in sport. In: B.D. Kirkcaldy (ed.) *Individual Differences in Movement*. Lancaster, UK: MPT Press, pp. 257–277.

Kirkcaldy, B. (1990) Gender and personality determinants of recreational interests. *Studia Psychologica* 32, 115–121.

Kirkcaldy, B. and Furnham, A. (1991) Extraversion, neuroticism, psychoticism and recreational choice. *Personality and Individual Differences* 12, 737–745.

Kraus R. (1978) *Recreation and Leisure in Modern Society*, 2nd edn. California: Goodyear.

Kroeger, O. and Thuesen, J.M. (1988) *Type Talk: The 16 Personality Types that Determine how we Live, Love, And Work.* New York: Bantam Doubleday Dell.

Levy, N. and Padilla, A. (1982) A Spanish translation of the Myers–Briggs Type Indicator Form G. *Psychological Reports* 51, 109–110.

Malkin, D. and Syme, G.J. (1986) Personality and problem gambling. *International Journal of Addiction* 21, 267–272.

McGuiggan, R.L. (1996) The relationship between personality, as measured by the Myers–Briggs Type Indicator, and leisure preferences. PhD thesis, Macquarie University, Australia.

Moore, T. (1987) Personality tests are back. *Fortune* 115, 76–81.

Morehouse, R.E., Farley, F. and Youngquist, J.V. (1990) Type T personality and the Jungian classification system. *Journal of Personality Assessment* 54, 231–235.

Murray, J.B. (1990) Review of research on the Myers–Briggs Type Indicator. *Perceptual and Motor skills* 70, 1187–1202.

Myers, I. and McCaulley, M.H. (1992) *Manual: A Guide to the Development and Use of the Myers–Briggs Type Indicator.* Palo Alto, California: Consulting Psychologists Press.

Neulinger, J. (1974) *The Psychology of Leisure: Research Approaches to the Study of Leisure.* Springfield, Illinois: Charles C. Thomas.

Nias, D.K.B. (1985) Personality and recreational behaviour. In: B.D. Kirkcaldy (ed.) *Individual Differences in Movement.* Lancaster, UK: MTP Press, pp. 279–292.

Pearman, R.R. and Fleenor, J. (1996) Differences in observed and self-reported qualities of psychological types. *Journal of Psychological Types* 39, 3–17.

Provost, J.A. (1990) *Work, Play, and Type.* Palo Alto, California: Consulting Psychologists Press.

Provost, J.A. and Anchors, S. (1991) *Applications of the Myers–Briggs Type Indicator in Higher Education.* Palo Alto, California: Consulting Psychologists Press.

Reynolds, H.T. (1984) *Analysis of Nominal Data,* 2nd edn. Quantitative Applications in the Social Sciences Series No. 07-001. Newbury Park, California: Sage.

Sipps, G.J., Alexander, R.A. and Friedt, L. (1985) Item analysis of the Myers–Briggs Type Indicator. *Educational and Psychological Measurement* 45, 789–796.

Spoto, A. (1995) What would Jung say about the MBTI? and does it really matter? *Australian Journal of Psychological Type* 4, 3–12.

Steele, R.S. and Kelly, T.J. (1976) Eysenck personality questionnaire and Jungian Myers–Briggs Type Indicator of extraversion–introversion. *Journal of Consulting and Clinical Psychology* 44, 690–691.

Taylor, K.F., Kelso, G.I., Cox, G.N., Alloway, W.J. and Matthews, J.P. (1979) Applying Holland's vocational categories to leisure activities. *Journal of Occupational Psychology* 52, 199–207.

Thompson, B. and Borrello, G.M. (1986) Construct validity of the Myers–Briggs Type Indicator. *Educational and Psychological Measurement* 46, 745–752.

Tzeng, O.C.S., Outcault, D., Boyer, S.L., Ware, R. and Landis, D. (1984) Item validity of the Myers–Briggs Type Indicator. *Journal of Personality Assessment* 48, 255–256.

Vealey, R.S. (1989) Sport personology: a paradigmatic and methodological analysis. *Journal of Sport and Exercise Psychology* 11, 216–235.

Webster, J.G. and Wakshalg, J.J. (1983) A theory of television program choice. *Communication Research* 10, 430–446.

Wiggins, J.S. (1989) Review of Myers–Briggs Type Indicator. In: J.C. Conoley and J.J. Kramer (eds) *Tenth Mental Measurements Yearbook.* Lincoln, USA: University of Nebraska Press, pp. 537–538.

Wilde, G.J.S. (1977) Trait description and measurement by personality questionnaires. In: R.B. Cattell and R.M. Dreger (eds) *Handbook of Modern Personality Theory.* Washington, D.C.: Hemisphere, pp. 69–103.

Chapter fifteen
Deciphering Day-Trip Destination Choice Using a Tourist Expectation/Satisfaction Construct

Peter Schofield
Department of Business Studies, University of Salford, The Crescent, Salford M5 4WT, UK

Introduction

It is generally accepted that traditional market-segmentation bases are becoming less reliable determinants of consumer behaviour. This results, in part, from the closure of income gaps between skilled and unskilled manual jobs, increased spending on activities where a greater expression of individual beliefs and values occurs, and a breakdown in the homogeneity of values within any given social class (Ryan, 1991). Under these conditions, attitudes, values and perceived benefits are likely to be more reliable determinants of consumer behaviour. Tourism managers therefore require information about the response of visitors to both the 'secondary' and 'primary' stimuli (Phelps, 1986) of a tourist destination, their likes and dislikes regarding various attractions and amenities, and what constitutes a satisfactory or unsatisfactory experience (Haywood and Muller, 1988).

Consumer satisfaction is one of the most important issues in consumer behaviour, and during the past 15 years, the expectation–disconfirmation paradigm has been dominating research in this area. Within this paradigm, consumer satisfaction is hypothesized to be a function of expectations and disconfirmation, with expectations used as the standard of comparison (Yi, 1990). In other words, if the performance is above expectations (positive disconfirmation) the consumer will be satisfied; if the performance is below expectations (negative disconfirmation) the consumer will be dissatisfied. Moreover, research by Oliver (1980), Churchill and Suprenant (1982) and Tse and Wilton (1988), among others, showed that expectation, through its influence on perceived performance, had a direct impact on consumer satisfaction.

Pizam *et al.* (1978) argued that tourism goods and services could be treated as a subset of goods and services in general, and that satisfaction could, therefore, be defined as the result of the interaction between a tourist's experience at a destination area and his/her prior expectations. Chon (1990) also conceptualized tourist satisfaction in this way. This 'evaluative congruity' model of tourist satisfaction is apparently valid and useful as a general framework, but it does not identify the separate components and dimensions of tourist expectation and satisfaction. Given the multi-faceted nature of products generally, but tourism products in particular, it is important to identify and measure tourist satisfaction with each component in order to gain an insight into the consumer's evaluation process (Swan and Coombs, 1976; Echtner and Ritchie, 1993). The purpose of this paper was, therefore, to identify and assess the relative importance of the determinant attributes of consumers' expectations about, and satisfaction with, day-trip destinations, by developing an appropriate construct. The objective was then to examine the relationship between the variables, using principal components analysis, and identify any meaningful dimensions.

The development of the expectation/satisfaction construct formed part of a wider-ranging study which included an evaluation of consumer attitudes towards, and satisfaction with, Castlefield Urban Heritage Park in Manchester and its position in three-dimensional perceptual space relative to competitors' tourism products. Attitude, in this context, was defined as a psychological tendency that is expressed by evaluating a particular entity on a cognitive, an effective or a behavioural basis (Eagly and Chaiken, 1993). To this end, an expectancy-value multi-brand, multi-attribute model (after Scott *et al.*, 1978) was used to structure the analysis; this model represents an extension of Fishbein and Ajzen's (1975) model of reasoned action. The original expectancy-value model (Fishbein, 1967) describes a predicted relationship between the attractiveness of some object or action, A_j, and two variables: B_{ij}, 'belief' about whether a particular object or action (j) possesses a given quality (i); and V_i, 'value' placed on the desirability of quality i to predict the attitude or opinion a person holds about a particular choice. Thus an individual's attitude toward or opinion about an object is a composite of his/her evaluation of that object in terms of attaining certain goals, weighted by the relative importance or saliency of the goals. The model has received considerable empirical support (Wilson *et al.*, 1975; Glassman and Fitzhenry, 1976; Bowman and Fishbein, 1978; Ryan and Bonfield, 1980; McCarty, 1981; Kantola *et al.*, 1982; Warshaw *et al.*, 1986; Sheppard *et al.*, 1988). Moreover, notwithstanding several conceptual challenges with respect to the multi-dimensionality of expectancy-value components, crossover effects, and the effect of prior behaviour (Miniard and Cohen, 1981; Bagozzi, 1981, 1982; Shimp and Kavas, 1984; Oliver and Bearden, 1985), there have been a wide range of applications, not least within the leisure and tourism literature (Scott *et al.*, 1978; Young and Kent, 1985; Cable *et al.*, 1987; Tourism Canada, 1988; Saleh and Ryan, 1992).

The fieldwork for the overall project involved a timed sequence of four successive surveys using the same sample of respondents. Repeated access to this sample was required because of the cumulative nature of both the questionnaire designs and the information required. Freely elicited data from the first questionnaire were incorporated into the expectation/satisfaction construct and a day-trip destination preference grid in the second questionnaire. The subjects were asked to rate each attribute in the construct in terms of its importance for a day trip. They were then asked to rate Castlefield Urban Heritage Park in Manchester (after visiting the destination) on each attribute in terms of how much or how little of each item the destination had. A third survey was used to assess the stability of subjects' mental categorization of day-trip destinations over time, and the validity of the 'evoked set' concept (Howard and Sheth, 1969) within this context (in terms of actual visitation or otherwise during the year after they were elicited during the first survey). Finally, the factor-analysed responses to the ratings obtained from the second questionnaire formed the basis of MDS similarity/dissimilarity scales in the fourth questionnaire. Sample stability was, therefore, critical for this process. The selection of the sample was also influenced by such practical considerations as the length and complexity of the questionnaires and the amount of detailed information required from the respondents. In order to satisfy these specific requirements, the sample consisted of undergraduates studying at Salford University (*n*=320).

A Comparative Analysis of Attitude-Scale Construction Techniques

One of the main problems with assessing consumers' expectations of, and satisfaction with, tourism products stems from the fact that these products are 'complex human experiences' (Gunn, 1988). As such, the attributes identified by managers may not be the most important ones from the consumers' perspective. Moreover, attributes which have been found to be significant in one particular market, such as a summer package holiday, may not be important in another, in this case the day-trip market.

Given that the study of consumer behaviour deals with multiple causes and compound variables, and that the choice of measurement technique is, therefore, of special importance, there have been relatively few studies reported in the consumer literature that have empirically compared attitude-scale construction techniques or strategies for determining the importance of attributes (Ryan and Etzel, 1976; Wiley *et al.*, 1977; Myers and Alpert, 1977; Neslin, 1981; Jaccard *et al.*, 1986). There are significant differences between the available techniques in terms of complexity, ease of use, and time- and budget-related criteria, and according to Lego and Shaw (1992), tourism research, in practice, is often subject to significant time and budgetary pressures. Therefore, if there is a relatively high degree of convergence between the results obtained from different methods which have been employed in a particular study, the selection of a technique for use in subsequent studies of a similar nature may be dictated primarily by practical concerns. For example, such convergence would probably favour the selection of a direct-rating approach and the use of predetermined attribute profiles based on previous studies in the literature, rather than the development of constructs based on freely elicited attributes or focus group subjects' personal constructs. Alternatively, where attribute assessment methods are relatively uncorrelated, the implication is either that one or more of the methods is suspect, or that they are measuring different constructs. Not surprisingly, Ryan (1995) suggests that tourism researchers must be prepared to adopt more than one perspective in order to gain a broader understanding of the concept.

The aim of this part of the study was, therefore, to compare empirically, and to assess the convergent validity among, a number of alternative methods of attitude-scale construction in terms of the specific attributes they produced. Firstly, as a basis for the comparison, the researcher conducted a review of the pertinent literature, which predominantly focused on vacations, to identify the attributes that were found to be relevant in that context. A summary of these attributes together with their research sources is provided in Table 15.1. These *a priori* attributes were considered by the researcher to be generally applicable, although their specific relevance to the day-trip market was unknown at that stage. In the second approach, a repertory grid test was used to obtain relevant attributes. Finally, attributes were obtained from subjects using the technique of free elicitation. The attributes from all three sources formed the basis of a composite expectation/satisfaction construct comprised 74 attributes. This was presented, within a questionnaire, to subjects who were asked to rate each attribute on a seven-point Likert scale in terms of its importance for a day trip. The ratings were then subjected to principal components analysis in order to reduce the data to more manageable proportions and identify the underlying dimensions.

Table 15.1 *A priori* attributes (from previous research)

Attribute	Source
Good value for money	1, 10, 13, 15, 19
Ease of access/accessibility	1, 10, 13
Availability of facilities for sport	1, 2, 10, 11, 16, 17
Availability of entertainment	1, 2, 4, 11, 16, 17
Variety of activities available	10, 15, 18
Architecture/buildings	19
Availability/cleanliness of toilets	19
Atmosphere	19
Facilities for the disabled	19
Quality attractions	4, 15
Familiarity with the destination	15

Table 15.1 (Continued) *A priori* attributes (from previous research)

Attribute	Source
An exciting place to visit	10, 13
Friendly and hospitable people (Welcoming)	1, 2, 8, 9, 10, 11, 13, 14, 15
Organized events	5, 8
Historical and cultural interest (museums, monuments, historical buildings, etc.)	1, 2, 4, 5, 8, 10, 11, 12, 15, 16, 17
Markets	5
Opportunities for walking or strolling	14
Historical attractions	5, 8, 15
Distinctive local features	8
Interesting sights	1, 7
Very commercialized	4, 15, 16, 17
An all-year-round destination	15
Evening/night-time recreation	8, 14
Better in warm than in cold weather	18
A change from the usual destinations	1
Not overcrowded or congested	13, 14, 15, 19
Expensive day out	14, 15, 16, 17, 18
Opportunity for rest and relaxation	2, 11, 15, 16, 17, 18
Quality shopping facilities	2, 4, 5, 11, 15, 19
Quality of/good eating facilities	2, 11, 16, 17, 19
Good public houses	5
Unspoilt environments	16, 17
Setting and scenic beauty	14, 15, 16, 17
A clean environment	13, 14, 15, 19
Opportunity for sightseeing	2, 11
Beautiful landscape	13, 15
A safe place to visit	3, 10, 12, 14
Good car-parking facilities	16

Table 15.1 (Continued) *A priori* attributes (from previous research)

Attribute	Source
Good tourist signposting	5, 16
Adequacy of healthcare in case of emergency	14
Interpretation of the history/heritage (signs, displays, trails, information, etc.)	19
Visual attractiveness of the presentation of the district's heritage	19
Waterside locations	19
Tourist information quality	4, 15, 19
Quality of the promotional literature	4
Green areas	5
Unpleasantness of weather during the visit	14, 19
Open spaces	5
A boring place	6, 12
Many interesting things to do	6, 15
Making a visit because friends or family members want to go there	18
Others have recommended this destination as a place to visit	18
Suitable for a visit with friends/family	18
A visit to this destination will enhance my feeling of well being	18
The visit is likely to improve togetherness with my family and friends	18

1. Haahti (1986); 2. Goodrich (1977); 3. Chon (1991); 4. Scott *et al.* (1978); 5. Perry *et al.* (1976); 6. Pearce (1982); 7. Var *et al.* (1977); 8. La Page and Cormier (1977); 9. Shih (1986); 10. Gartner (1986); 11. Bojanic (1991); 12. Reilly (1990); 13. Haywood and Muller (1988); 14. Calantone and Johar (1984); 15. Pizam *et al.* (1978); 16. Sternquist-Witter (1985); 17. Um and Crompton (1990); 18. Glasson (1994); 19. Driscoll *et al.* (1994).

The repertory grid test

The repertory grid is based on Kelly's (1955) personal construct theory in which individuals arrange features of their perceived environment by discrimination on the basis of its attributes and construct a set of 'personal constructs' which are used in deciding on future behaviour (Bannister and Muir, 1968). Therefore, in constructing the measurement instrument, the emphasis was on the subjects' idiosyncratic judgement and interpretation of relevant stimuli. This is clearly preferable to the researcher making assumptions about which attributes are relevant to day-trip decision-making and how best to express them.

The repertory grid test was conducted with a subset (n=30) of the sample (15 females and 15 males). Harrison and Sarre (1975) found that comparatively small sample sizes, often with as few as 20 respondents, produce valid constructs because the number of constructs being used by members of any given group tends to be repeated. The objective was to establish the constructs that respondents use to describe similarities and differences between day-trip tourism products, and thereby indirectly determine the attributes which were relevant from the subjects' perspective. These constructs are assumed to involve 'dimensionality', that is, the notion of a continuum along which products might vary. The repertory grid test subjects were not included in the sample that was used for the surveys.

The typical procedure for eliciting respondents' personal constructs was followed. The theoretical orientation of Kelly's (1955) repertory grid demands that the range of stimuli that is presented to the subject must be meaningful and representative of the entire semantic domain for the elements to be judged (Bannister, 1962). The repertory grid test subjects' 'evoked set' destinations (Howard and Sheth, 1969) were therefore used as the 'stimuli of interest'. These elements were employed for two reasons. Firstly, it is likely that the repertory grid test subjects had more knowledge of, and interest in, these places than would have been the case with an alternative set of destinations, for example, subjects' 'awareness set' destinations (Howard and Sheth, 1969). Therefore, it was felt that subjects would be more able to make accurate and meaningful distinctions between the destinations in the triads. Secondly, the use of respondents' evoked set destinations produced a manageable number of triads (n=559) before equal numbers were selected from each category. Initial pilot tests with other subjects using a larger group of destinations taken from subjects' awareness sets produced an unmanageable number of triads.

The repertory grid test subjects' evoked sets included 31 different destinations; many places were popular choices and were listed frequently. The 31 destinations were subjected to a pre-test in which the respondents were asked to delete those with which they were not familiar. As a result of this process, 15 destinations were eliminated from the test. The remaining 16 were sorted by subjects into groups on the basis of similarity, so that the perceived intra-group similarity between destinations was greater than the inter-group similarity.

The total number of possible combinations was then determined for within-category triads (where all elements were selected from one group); mixed-category triads (where two elements were selected from one group); and cross-category triads (where one element was selected from each group). The three categories were established with the aim of producing both fine distinctions between the elements (i.e. constructs with a narrow range of convenience, within-category triads) and broad distinctions with a wide range of convenience (mixed-category and cross-category triads). All 55 triad combinations from the within-category group were used, and 55 were selected randomly from both the mixed-category ($n=378$) and cross-category ($n=126$) groups, so that the maximum number of triads could be used whilst the balance between the triad categories was maintained.

The triads were then presented to the subjects, who were asked to produce constructs for each one by distinguishing between the elements in response to the following question (after Frain, 1986): 'In what important way are any two of these alike and in that way different from the third?' The constructs were recorded until the respondents failed to elicit any further distinctions between the destinations and all subjects had exhausted their repertory of constructs. All constructs from each respondent were pooled and subjected to an initial content analysis, in which numerous duplicated constructs were removed. The large number of repeated constructs supported the findings of Harrison and Sarre (1975) noted above. The following numbers of distinct constructs were elicited by respondents from each triad category:

- Within-category triads ($n=63$)
    Group 1: $n=7$
    Group 2: $n=21$
    Group 3: $n=35$
- Mixed-category triads ($n=130$)
- Cross-category triads ($n=99$)

The 292 constructs were then sorted into similar content categories, and constructs that were unsuitable for use in this context were rejected. The exercise produced 50 usable attributes which reflected both a broad and a narrow range of convenience. Thirty-four of these attributes were common with the predetermined, *a priori* construct derived from published research.

Free elicitation of attributes

Free elicitation is a relatively simple, inexpensive, but powerful technique that can be used in a range of different survey modes, and the data are relatively easy to analyse (Reilly, 1990). Like the repertory grid test, this technique was used in the present context to enable respondents to describe the stimulus in their own terms rather than responding to either the researcher's predetermined dimensions or those derived from relevant published research.

According to Krippendorf (1980), words are the smallest and most reliable recording unit. The elicitation measure was therefore derived from the open-ended question 'what 10 words would you use to describe the things you are looking for when you go out for a day trip? (they may be 'things' or 'feelings')'. All of the words elicited by the respondents were content analysed. By using this procedure, the problems associated with sampling from a more detailed text such as recorded interviews or lengthy statements from a more open-ended questionnaire format were avoided.

In order to establish the construct validity of the measure, a comparative analysis was undertaken of the attributes produced from the free-elicitation technique, the repertory grid test, and the literature review. The relationship between the attributes or constructs derived from the three techniques is shown in the Venn diagram in Fig. 15.1. A total of 74 attributes was produced from the three techniques. The free-elicitation methodology produced 60 attributes (81.08% of the total). This compares with 50 (67.57%) from the repertory grid analysis and 55 (74.32%) from the literature search. A list of all attributes and details of their derivative sources is given in Table 15.2. There is a high level of convergence between the results obtained from the three techniques, particularly between the *a priori* and free-elicitation methods. Clearly, many of the attributes which were found to be relevant in the research on vacations are also relevant in the context of day trips.

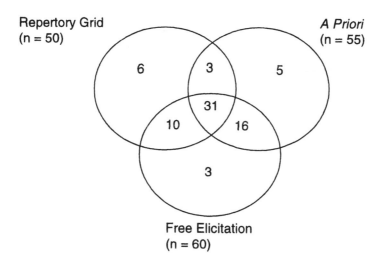

Figure 15.1 A comparison of the free-elicitation-, repertory grid- and literature search (*a priori*)-derived attributes. *n*=74 combined attributes.

Table 15.2 The day trip expectation/satisfaction construct by source of
individual attribute

Attribute	Derivation
Good value for money	RG, PC, FE
Convenient location	RG, PC, FE
Availability of facilities for sport	RG, PC, FE
Availability of entertainment	PC, FE
Variety of activities	RG, PC, FE
Attractive buildings	PC, FE
Quality attractions	RG, PC, FE
Familiarity with the destination	PC, FE
An exciting place to visit	PC, FE
Friendly and hospitable people (welcoming)	PC, FE
Organized events	PC, FE
Special interest, e.g. museums	RG, PC, FE
Markets	RG, PC, FE
Opportunities for walking/strolling	RG, PC, FE
Historical attractions	RG, PC, FE
Distinctive local features	RG, PC
Not over-commercialized	RG, PC
An all-year-round destination	RG, PC, FE
Dry-weather facilities	RG, PC, FE
Wet-weather facilities	RG, PC, FE
Nightlife	RG, PC, FE
A change from the usual destinations	RG, PC, FE
Not overcrowded/congested	RG, PC, FE
An inexpensive place to visit	RG, PC, FE
Opportunity for rest and relaxation	RG, PC, FE
Quality shopping facilities	RG, PC, FE
Good eating and drinking facilities	RG, PC, FE

Table 15.2 (Continued) The day trip expectation/satisfaction construct by source of individual attribute

Attribute	Derivation
Good public houses	RG, PC, FE
Scenic beauty	RG, PC, FE
Uncongested roads	RG, PC, FE
A clean environment	PC, FE
Opportunity for sightseeing	PC, FE
A safe place to visit	PC, FE
Good car-parking facilities	RG, PC, FE
Good tourist signposting	PC, FE
Adequacy of healthcare in case of emergency	PC
Heritage displays, trails and information	RG, PC
Waterside location	RG, PC, FE
Quality of tourist information	PC, FE
Quality of the promotional literature	PC
Green areas	RG, PC, FE
Good weather during the visit	PC, FE
Open spaces	RG, PC, FE
Many interesting things to do	RG, PC, FE
Good public transport links	RG, PC, FE
A good atmosphere	PC, FE
Convenient layout/size	RG, PC, FE
Toilet facilities	PC, FE
Clean toilets	PC, FE
Facilities for the disabled	PC, FE
A place where friends and/or family could go	RG, PC, FE
Friends/family have recommended the place	PC
A place where friends and/or family would want to go	RG, PC, FE

Table 15.2 (Continued) The day trip expectation/satisfaction construct by source of individual attribute

Attribute	Derivation
A visit to the place is likely to enhance my feeling of well-being	PC
A visit is likely to improve togetherness with my family and friends	PC
Good picnic sites	RG, FE
A variety of eating facilities	RG, FE
Good cafes	RG, FE
Educational value	RG, FE
A fun place to visit	RG, FE
Something for everyone	RG, FE
Appeal to younger people	RG
Appeal to older people	RG
Fairground rides	RG, FE
Boat trips	RG
A busy place	RG, FE
A place to go in fair weather	RG
A place to go in wet weather	RG, FE
A place to go in any weather	RG
A lot going on there	RG, FE
Beautiful gardens	RG
Opportunity for active participation	FE
Opportunity to meet people	FE
A good reputation	FE

n=74.
RG = Repertory grid-derived attributes.
PC = Predetermined (literature search)-derived construct.
FE = Free-elicitation-derived attributes.

Notwithstanding this convergence, each technique also made an exclusive contribution to the construction of the expectation/satisfaction scale. Three attributes (4.05% of the total) were exclusively derived from the free-elicitation method, compared with six (8.11% of the total) from the repertory grid test and five (6.76%) from previous research. Clearly, there are certain attributes (elicited from both the free-elicitation and repertory grid techniques) which were not found to be significant in previous research; equally, the literature search identified attributes which were not obtained by using the other techniques. Moreover, several of these exclusive attributes were found to be particularly important when they were rated by subject in terms of their importance for day trips. For example, 'a good reputation' (derived from free-elicitation technique) was subsequently rated, by subject, as the sixth most important of the 74 attributes in the construct. This also demonstrates the advantage of using more than one scale-construction method.

The Composite Expectation/Satisfaction Construct

The results from the analysis of the subjects' ratings, on a seven-point scale, for each attribute in the 74-item composite construct, are summarized in Table 15.3. The 10 highest-ranked attributes are 'clean toilets' (mean: 6.26), 'toilet facilities' (6.14), 'good atmosphere' (6.07), 'having something for everyone' (6.06), 'a fun place to visit' (6.04), 'a good reputation' (6.03), 'good value for money' (5.97), 'many interesting things to do' (5.96), 'a clean environment' (5.93) and 'a safe place to visit' (5.92). It is interesting that the two highest-ranked attributes relate to common functional facilities (the secondary features of destinations) rather than distinctive or unique attractions (the primary elements of place). Given that the attributes: 'having something for everyone', 'a fun place to visit', 'good value for money' and 'many interesting things to do' were the most frequently listed by respondents in the free-elicitation exercise, it is surprising that they did not achieve a higher rank. However, the importance attributed to 'clean toilets' probably reflects their use as an indicator of the overall quality of the amenities provided by a tourist destination.

The sixth-ranked 'a good reputation' reinforces the importance that subjects attached to word-of-mouth communication; this may help to minimize the risk of disappointment from an unsatisfactory visit experience. Moreover, the importance attached to 'a clean environment' and 'a safe place to visit' indicates that the subjects do not take these qualities for granted. It should also be noted that the majority of these high-ranking attributes represent the 'expressive performance' of the product (Swan and Coombs, 1976) or the 'psychological end of the functional–psychological continuum' (Echtner and Ritchie, 1993, p. 3). At the other end of the scale, the subjects consider 'familiarity with the destination' (3.32) to be the least important attribute. This was not expected, given the high proportion of previous visits to the destinations in respondents' awareness sets and evoked sets found elsewhere in the study. This variable may therefore be important at a subconscious level, where reassurance and comfort are gained by revisiting a destination.

Table 15.3 Subjects' rank-ordered ratings of the attributes in the expectation/satisfaction construct in terms of their 'importance' for a day trip

Name	Mean	S.D.	Label (importance of...)
ICLEANTO	6.25524	1.12448	Clean toilets
ITOILETS	6.13636	1.23072	Toilet facilities
IATMOSPH	6.06643	1.00129	A good atmosphere
IEVERYON	6.05944	1.07277	Something for everyone
IFUNPLAC	6.03846	1.07046	Being a fun place to visit
IGOODREP	6.03497	0.96546	A good reputation
IVALUE	5.96853	1.11877	Good value for money
IMANYINT	5.96154	1.07046	Many interesting things to do
ICLEANEN	5.92657	1.10097	A clean environment
ISAFEVIS	5.92308	1.11498	Being a safe place to visit
IEATDRIK	5.87413	1.04204	Good eating/drinking facilities
IFRENDLY	5.86014	1.13076	Being a friendly place
IFAMCUD	5.85315	1.08552	Being a place for the family
IEXCITIN	5.84266	1.18458	Being an exciting place
ITOURSIN	5.83566	1.07161	Good tourist signposting
INITELIF	5.83566	1.36276	Nightlife
IDISABLE	5.80070	1.43103	Facilities for disabled
IVARIETY	5.77622	1.10767	A variety of activities
IQALATTR	5.77273	1.01951	Quality attractions
IALOTON	5.76923	1.21217	A lot going on there
IPUBTRAN	5.73077	1.25694	Good public transport
IENTERTN	5.72727	1.17089	Entertainment
IANYWETH	5.70280	1.09182	Being an any-weather place
IVARIEAT	5.58392	1.19573	A variety of eating facilities
IEMERGFA	5.58042	1.30270	Healthcare in emergencies
IFAMWANT	5.55944	1.18542	Being a place family wants
ICARPARK	5.54545	1.54114	Good car park facilities

Table 15.3 (Continued) Subjects' rank-ordered ratings of the attributes in the expectation/satisfaction construct in terms of their 'importance' for a day trip

Name	Mean	S.D.	Label (importance of...)
IACHANGE	5.54196	1.20961	A change from the usual
IGOODCAF	5.50699	1.29165	Good cafes
INOTOVER	5.48252	1.35519	Not being overcrowded
IGUDPUBS	5.47552	1.51174	Good public houses
IDRYFACS	5.45804	1.36497	Dry weather facilities
IWEATHER	5.45804	1.43514	Weather conditions during visit
IINEXPEN	5.44755	1.36461	Being an inexpensive place
IQALSHOP	5.41608	1.28074	Quality shopping facilities
IROADUNC	5.34266	1.35131	Uncongested roads
ILAYOUT	5.31818	1.33515	A convenient layout
IMEETFOK	5.29720	1.32947	Opportunities to meet folk
IFAMREC	5.26923	1.29814	Recommendation by family
IQALINFO	5.23427	1.31296	Quality of tourist information
IWETFACS	5.19580	1.65119	Wet-weather facilities
IAPEALYU	5.16434	1.47883	Appealing to young people
IOPRELAX	5.06294	1.47121	Opportunities for relaxation
ILOCATON	5.03846	1.39997	A convenient location
IALLYEAR	5.03497	1.58020	Being an all-year attraction
IGREEN	5.03147	1.45905	Green areas
IOPSIGHT	4.98951	1.36236	Opportunities for sightseeing
IIMPWELB	4.97203	1.32424	Visit enhancing well-being
IFERWETH	4.97203	1.40397	Being a fair-weather place
ISCENIC	4.91608	1.64369	Scenic beauty
IOPENSPA	4.82168	1.43381	Open spaces
IQALPROM	4.78671	1.29776	Quality of promotional material
IIMPTOG	4.72727	1.50639	Visit enhancing togetherness
IORGEVEN	4.52797	1.50003	Organized events

Table 15.3 (Continued) Subjects' rank-ordered ratings of the attributes in the expectation/satisfaction construct in terms of their 'importance' for a day trip

Name	Mean	S.D.	Label (importance of...)
IRIDES	4.52797	1.69134	Fairground rides
IAPEALOL	4.47902	1.63017	Appealing to older people
IEDUCATE	4.45804	1.62545	Educational value
IWETWETH	4.40909	1.76629	Being a wet-weather place
IPARTIC	4.40210	1.60127	Opportunities for participation
IPICSITE	4.33566	1.45310	Good picnic sites
IGARDENS	4.27273	1.70317	Beautiful gardens
IHERITAG	4.22378	1.53289	Heritage trails/information
IBUSY	4.19580	1.59718	Being a busy place
ISPECINT	4.19231	1.42709	Special interests, e.g. museums
IWATERSY	4.18182	1.34887	A waterside location
IBOATRIP	4.17133	1.45892	Boat trips
INOTOCOM	4.10490	1.56816	Not being overcommercial
IBUILDIN	4.10490	1.58153	Attractive buildings
IWALKING	4.03846	1.51782	Opportunities for walking
ILOCFEAT	3.90909	1.59345	Distinctive local features
ISPORTFA	3.88462	1.81146	Facilities for sport
IMARKETS	3.79720	1.49178	Markets
IHISTORY	3.76573	1.60406	Historical attractions
IFAMILAR	3.32168	1.50135	Familiarity with a destination

n=320.

It is interesting to note that the free-elicitation method produced all 10 of the highest-ranked attributes. By comparison, seven of the ten were derived from previous research (the top three and the seventh, eighth, ninth and tenth ranked attributes) and the repertory grid test produced only four of the attributes (the fourth, fifth, seventh and eighth ranked attributes). The pattern was similar when the 20 highest-ranked attributes were examined. This demonstrates the effectiveness of the free-elicitation technique, and the risk involved in using only a predetermined construct based on a review of the literature and consisting of attributes which were found to be relevant to other tourism markets. The results may also reflect the relatively indirect nature of the approach taken in the repertory grid test in comparison with the free-elicitation method, notwithstanding the use of subjects' evoked set destinations as the stimuli of interest.

The Principal Components Analysis

In order to reduce the data to more manageable proportions and to examine the relationship between the variables, the respondents' ratings were subjected to principal components analysis.

The reliability of the instrument was assessed using Cronbach's alpha coefficient to measure the internal consistency or degree of covariance that exists between the items in the scale. A coefficient of 0.8917 was produced with a standardized item alpha of 0.8970, indicating that the items on the scale have fairly comparable variances (Norusis, 1994). The split-half alpha coefficients were 0.8187 (part one) and 0.7938 (part two) with a Spearman Brown coefficient of 0.8824. Cronbach's alpha coefficient can produce quite high results if the number of items on the scale is large, even where the average inter-item correlation between the variables is quite small. Therefore, since the variables must be related to each other for the factor model to be appropriate, the correlations between the items were subjected to further tests.

Bartlett's test for sphericity produced a statistic of 9860.6638. This is large, and the associated significance level was small, so the hypothesis that the correlation matrix was an identity was rejected. The correlation matrix showed that there was a high correlation between each variable and at least one other variable in the set. The Kaiser–Meyer–Olkin (KMO) measure of sampling adequacy produced an index of 0.72173. Kaiser (1974) characterizes measures in the 0.70s as 'middling'. This indicates that the sum of the squared partial correlation coefficients between all pairs of variables was small when compared to the sum of the squared correlation coefficients. This also indicated that the model was an appropriate one to use.

The final statistics (Table 15.4) show that 23 principal components with eigenvalues of greater than 1 explained 70.40% of the variance in the data, and that a high proportion of the variance is explained by the common components according to the communality data. Only the IWEATHER variable ('the importance of weather conditions during a visit') and the IGOODREP variable ('the importance of a good reputation') produced figures of less than 0.60 (0.554 and 0.598, respectively). The combination of a relatively large number of components needed to represent the data and the absence of singularly important unique variables, together with the good fit between the model and the data (only 12.00% of the residuals had absolute values greater than 0.05), indicate that the relationship between the variables is complex.

Table 15.4 Final statistics from the principal components analysis of the expectation/satisfaction construct ratings

Variable	Communality	Factor	Eigenvalue	Percentage of variation	Cumulative percentage
IACHANGE	0.69686	1	9.48012	12.8	12.8
IALLYEAR	0.70409	2	5.40578	7.3	20.1
IALOTON	0.70964	3	4.26920	5.8	25.9
IANYWETH	0.77533	4	2.98975	4.0	29.9
IAPEALOL	0.72308	5	2.70510	3.7	33.6
IAPEALYU	0.69257	6	2.45947	3.3	36.9
IATMOSPH	0.72734	7	2.04044	2.8	39.7
IBOATRIP	0.68520	8	2.01270	2.7	42.4
IBUILDIN	0.65432	9	1.90100	2.6	45.0
IBUSY	0.65351	10	1.72574	2.3	47.3
ICARPARK	0.64519	11	1.67395	2.3	49.5
ICLEANEN	0.75030	12	1.59972	2.2	51.7
ICLEANTO	0.84801	13	1.56347	2.1	53.8
IDISABLE	0.67598	14	1.53266	2.1	55.9
IDRYFACS	0.63309	15	1.42579	1.9	57.8
IEATDRIK	0.73366	16	1.37723	1.9	59.7
IEDUCATE	0.72915	17	1.26184	1.7	61.4
IEMERGFA	0.76727	18	1.25140	1.7	63.1
IENTERTN	0.76262	19	1.18058	1.6	64.7
IEVERYON	0.69608	20	1.13227	1.5	66.2
IEXCITIN	0.66149	21	1.07290	1.4	67.7
IFAMCUD	0.63323	22	1.03936	1.4	69.1
IFAMILAR	0.70669	23	1.02618	1.4	70.4
IFAMREC	0.71853				
IFAMWANT	0.77544				
IFERWETH	0.68708				
IFRENDLY	0.65933				

Table 15.4 (Continued) Final statistics from the principal components analysis of the expectation/satisfaction construct ratings

Variable	Communality	Factor	Eigenvalue	Percentage of variation	Cumulative percentage
IFUNPLAC	0.68636				
IGARDENS	0.70909				
IGOODCAF	0.76445				
IGOODREP	0.59768				
IGREEN	0.66906				
IGUDPUBS	0.71368				
IHERITAG	0.73357				
IHISTORY	0.68762				
IIMPTOG	0.73569				
IIMPWELB	0.68569				
IINEXPEN	0.65078				
ILAYOUT	0.71537				
ILOCATON	0.60127				
ILOCFEAT	0.72951				
IMANYINT	0.71142				
IMARKETS	0.65752				
IMEETFOK	0.69674				
INITELIF	0.76516				
INOTOCOM	0.65020				
INOTOVER	0.70719				
IOPENSPA	0.73299				
IOPRELAX	0.78528				
IOPSIGHT	0.69831				
IORGEVEN	0.65310				
IPARTIC	0.69851				
IPICSITE	0.71355				
IPUBTRAN	0.63928				

Table 15.4 (Continued) Final statistics from the principal components analysis of the expectation/satisfaction construct ratings

Variable	Communality	Factor	Eigenvalue	Percentage of variation	Cumulative percentage
IQALATTR	0.64626				
IQALINFO	0.75635				
IQALPROM	0.70209				
IQALSHOP	0.68203				
IRIDES	0.71570				
IROADUNC	0.74145				
ISAFEVIS	0.68606				
ISCENIC	0.70823				
ISPECINT	0.70923				
ISPORTFA	0.73178				
ITOILETS	0.81476				
ITOURSIN	0.69603				
IVALUE	0.65804				
IVARIEAT	0.79479				
IVARIETY	0.69920				
IWALKING	0.70473				
IWATERSY	0.72077				
IWEATHER	0.55401				
IWETFACS	0.73866				
IWETWETH	0.77235				

Only the first nine principal components could be labelled with any confidence. Component 1 is a 'general factor' (Child, 1970) because it includes significant loadings from a large number of the variables in the analysis. It correlates quite highly with 'many interesting things to do' (0.57), 'convenient layout' (0.53), 'educational value' (0.53), 'a good atmosphere' (0.53), 'a good reputation' (0.52), 'something for everyone' (0.50), 'quality of tourist information' (0.49), 'clean toilets' (0.49), 'toilet facilities' (0.48), and 17 other variables at a level of 0.40 or above.

Inasmuch as this component is accounting for the single most important contribution to total variance, such a pattern of correlation is to be expected. Component 1 was, therefore, named 'comprehensive leisure opportunities and amenities'. The remaining principal components which were labelled are 'group factors' (Child, 1970) because a number of variables with significant loadings appear in the same component.

Component 2 has an environmental orientation whereby 'historical attractions' (0.68), 'distinctive locational features' (0.61), 'opportunities for walking' (0.56), 'scenic beauty' (0.55), 'not being over commercialized' (0.51), 'opportunities for sightseeing' (0.50), 'attractive buildings' (0.48) and 'heritage trails and information' (0.47) correlate closely. This component was labelled 'scenic interest and environmental quality'.

Component 3 correlates most highly with 'quality shopping facilities' (0.55), 'nightlife' (0.54), 'eating and drinking facilities' (0.52), 'dry-weather facilities' (0.49), 'a change from the usual' (0.46), 'entertainment' (0.44), 'being an exciting place to visit' (0.42) and 'good public houses' (0.41). As a result, it was named 'shopping and nightlife'.

Component 4 is an example of a 'bipolar factor' because it incorporates contrasting groups of variables. In geometric terms, some of the test vectors have been resolved in one direction, others in opposite quadrants, thereby giving rise to both positive and negative values. It is positively correlated with 'sports facilities' (0.37), 'boat trips' (0.34), 'a convenient location' (0.34) and 'being a busy place' (0.31). However, it has higher negative correlations with 'clean toilets' (−0.53), 'toilet facilities' (−0.51), 'a variety of eating facilities' (−0.49) and 'good cafes' (−0.45). Component 4 was, therefore, labelled 'outdoor activity'.

Component 5 consists, for the most part, of items relating to 'being a busy place' (0.42), 'recommendation by friends and family' (0.41), 'fairground rides' (0.41), 'a lot going on there' (0.36). It is also negatively correlated with 'educational value' (−0.35). Consequently, 'fun and amusement' seemed to describe this component.

The variables with the highest positive scores on Component 6 are 'good picnic sites' (0.39), 'quality shopping facilities' (0.33) and 'enhancing togetherness' (0.31). The component is also negatively correlated with 'a fun place to visit' (−0.37) and 'many interesting things to do' (−0.31). This implies that 'opportunities for relaxed and undemanding leisure' are important.

Component 7 appears to be related to 'healthcare in emergencies' (0.50), 'an all-year-round attraction' (0.33), and 'organized events' (0.30), with a loading on 'heritage trails and information' of 0.28. This suggests 'security, comfort and familiarity'.

Component 8 is comprises items relating to 'social interaction and conviviality': 'opportunities for participation' (0.39) and 'a variety of eating facilities' (0.31). It also loads on 'good cafes' (0.29) and 'opportunities to meet people' (0.28), and is negatively correlated with 'being a place family could go to' (−0.38).

Component 9 is positively correlated most highly with 'value for money' (0.37), 'being an any-weather place' (0.35), 'good public houses' (0.34), 'appealing to older people' (0.32) and 'wet-weather facilities' (0.32). It was, therefore, labelled 'good-value wet-weather facilities'.

The first nine principal components accounted for 63.92% of the variance explained by the first 23 principal components, and 45.00% of the total variance. All of the remaining principal components were characterized by low positive and negative correlations with a large number of variables, thereby precluding any further identification and labelling. The principal components analysis has, nevertheless, highlighted a number of important elements which are influential in the day-trip decision process.

Conclusions

Many of the attributes which were found to be relevant in previous research on vacations were also found to be important in the context of day trips. The comparative analysis of the scale-construction techniques has, nevertheless, demonstrated the benefits of using more than one methodological approach both for confirming the validity of each technique and to demonstrate their exclusive contributions. It also highlighted the effectiveness of the free-elicitation method.

A wide range of attributes were considered by respondents to be relevant to day-trip destination choice. Moreover, the principal components analysis demonstrated the complexity of the relationship between the variables and identified a number of key components in the day-trip destination choice process. The relative importance of both the primary and secondary features of day-trip destinations, and the psychological aspects of the experience, are of particular interest given that both the primary features and the tangible attributes of these destinations are typically prominent features of the official promotional literature.

Overall, the analysis has highlighted a number of issues which should be examined further in terms of their relevance to a broader cross-section of the day-trip market. Further research is needed, both to refine the instruments which are used to construct the day-trip tourist expectation/satisfaction construct, and to further our understanding of the day-trip destination choice process. This is a considerable challenge, given the wide range of individual motivations, the increasing variety of options available for day trips, and the influence of situational constraints, all of which are likely to affect the stability of determinant attributes and their relative importance over time.

References

Bagozzi, R.P. (1981) Attitudes, intentions, and behaviour: a test of some key hypotheses. *Journal of Personality and Social Psychology* 41, 607–627.

Bagozzi, R.P. (1982) A field investigation of causal relations among cognitions, affect intentions and behaviour. *Journal of Marketing Research* 19, 562–584.

Bannister, D. (1962) Personal construct theory: a summary and experimental paradigm. *Acta Psychologica* 20, 105–120.

Bannister, D. and Muir, J.M.M. (1968) *The Evaluation of Personal Constructs*. London: Academic Press.

Bojanic, D.C. (1991) The use of advertising in managing destination images. *Tourism Management* December, 352–355.

Bowman, C.H. and Fishbein, M. (1978) Understanding public reactions to energy proposals: an application of the Fishbein model. *Journal of Applied Social Psychology* 8, 319–340.

Cable, T, Knudson, D.M., Udd, E. and Stewart, D.J. (1987) Attitude changes as a result of exposure to interpretive messages. *Journal of Park and Recreation Administration* 5, 47–60.

Calantone, R.J. and Johar, J.S. (1984) Seasonal segmentation of the tourist market using a benefit segmentation framework. *Journal of Travel Research* 23, 14–24.

Child, D. (1970) *The Essentials of Factor Analysis*. London: Holt, Rinehart & Winston.

Chon, K.S. (1990) The role of the destination image in tourism: a review and discussion. *Tourist Review* 45, 12–9.

Chon, K.S. (1991) Tourist destination image modification process: marketing implications. *Tourism Management* March, 68–72.

Churchill, G.A. and Suprenant, C. (1982) An investigation into the determinants of customer satisfaction. *Journal of Marketing Research* 19, 491–504.

Driscoll, A., Lawson, R. and Niven, B. (1994) Measuring tourists' destination perceptions. *Annals of Tourism Research* 21, 499–511.

Eagly, A.H. and Chaiken, S. (1993) *The Psychology of Attitudes*. Fort Worth: Harcourt Brace Jovanovich.

Echtner, C.M. and Ritchie, J.R.B. (1993) The measurement of destination images: an empirical assessment. *Journal of Travel Research* 3, 3–12.

Fishbein, M. (1967) A consideration of beliefs, and their role in attitude measurement. In: Fishbein, M.A. (ed.) *Readings in Attitude Theory and Measurement*. New York: Wiley, pp. 257–266.

Fishbein, M. and Ajzen, I. (1975) *Belief, Attitude, Intention, Behaviour: An Introduction to Theory and Research*. Reading, Massachusetts: Addison-Wesley.

Frain, J. (1986) *Principles and Practice of Marketing*. London, Pitman.

Gartner, W.C. (1986) Temporal influences on image change. *Annals of Tourism Research* 13, 635–644.

Glassman, M. and Fitzhenry, N. (1976) Fishbein's subjective norm: theoretical considerations and empirical evidence. In: B.B. Anderson (ed.) *Advances in Consumer Research, 3*. Ann Arbor, Michigan: Association for Consumer Research, pp. 477–484.

Glasson, J. (1994) Oxford: a heritage city under pressure. *Tourism Management* 15, 137–144.

Goodrich, J.N. (1977) Differences in perceived similarity of tourism regions: a spatial analysis. *Journal of Travel Research* 16, 10–13.

Gunn, C. (1988) *Tourism Planning*, 2nd edn. New York: Taylor & Francis.

Haahti, A.J. (1986) Finland's competitive positioning as a destination. *Annals of Tourism Research* 13, 11–26.

Harrison, J. and Sarre, P. (1975) Personal construct theory in the measurement of environmental images. *Environment and Behaviour* 7, 3–58.

Haywood, K.M. and Muller, T. (1988) The urban tourist experience: measuring satisfaction. *Hospitality Research and Education Journal* 12, 453–459.

Howard, J.A. and Sheth, J.N. (1969) *The Theory of Buyer Behaviour*. New York: Wiley.

Jaccard, J., Brinberg, P. and Ackerman, L.J. (1986) Assessing attitude importance: a comparison of six methods. *Journal of Consumer Research* 12, 463–468.

Kantola, S.J., Syme, G.J. and Campbell, N.A. (1982) The role of individual differences and external variables in a test of the sufficiency of Fishbein's model to explain behavioural intentions to conserve water. *Journal of Applied Social Psychology* 12, 70–83.

Kaiser, H.F. (1974) An index of factorial simplicity. *Psychometrica* 39, 31–36.

Kelly, G.A. (1955) *The Psychology of Personal Constructs*. New York: Norton.

Krippendorf, K. (1980) *Content Analysis: An Introduction to its Methodology*. London: Sage.

La Page, W.F. and Cormier, P.L. (1977) Images of camping – barriers to participation. *Journal of Travel Research* 15, 21–25.

Lego, R. and Shaw, R.N. (1992) Convergent validity in tourism research: an empirical analysis. *Tourism Management* 13, 387–393.

McCarty, D. (1981) Changing contraceptive usage intentions: a test of the Fishbein model of intention. *Journal of Applied Social Psychology* 11, 192–211.

Miniard, P.W. and Cohen, J.B. (1981) An examination of the Fishbein–Ajzen behavioural intention models – concepts and measures. *Journal of Experimental Social Psychology* 17, 309–339.

Myers, J.H. and Alpert, M.I. (1977) Semantic confusion in attitude research: salience versus importance. In: W.D. Perreault (ed.) *Advances in Consumer Research, 4*. Atlanta, Georgia: Association for Consumer Research, pp. 106–110.

Neslin, S.A. (1981) Linking product features to perceptions: self-stated versus statistically revealed importance weights. *Journal of Marketing Research* 18, 80–86.

Norusis, M.J. (1994) *SPSS Professional Statistics 6.1*. Chicago: SPSS Inc.

Oliver, R.L. (1980) A cognitive model of the antecedents and consequences of satisfaction decisions. *Journal of Marketing Research* 17, 460–469.

Oliver, R.L. and Bearden, W.O. (1985) Crossover effects in the theory of reasoned action: a moderating influence attempt. *Journal of Consumer Research* 12, 324–340.

Pearce, P.L. (1982) *The Social Psychology of Tourist Behaviour*. Oxford: Pergamon.

Perry, M., Izraeli, D. and Perry, A. (1976) Image change as a result of advertising. *Journal of Advertising Research* 16, 45–50.

Phelps, A. (1986) Holiday destination image – the problem of assessment: an example developed in Menorca. *Tourism Management* 7, 168–180.

Pizam, A., Neuman, Y. and Reichel, A. (1978) Dimensions of tourist satisfaction with a destination area. *Annals of Tourism Research* 5, 314–322.

Reilly, M.D. (1990) Free elicitation of descriptive adjectives for tourism image assessment. *Journal of Travel Research* 28, 21–26.

Ryan, C. (1991) *Recreational Tourism: A Social Science Perspective*. London: Routledge.

Ryan, C. (1995) *Researching Tourist Satisfaction: Issues, Concepts, Problems*. London: Routledge.

Ryan, M. and Bonfield, E.H. (1980) Fishbein's intention model: a test of external and pragmatic validity. *Journal of Marketing* 44, 82–95.

Ryan, M. and Etzel, M.J. (1976) The nature of salient outcomes and referents in the extended model. In: B.B. Anderson (ed.) *Advances in Consumer Research, 3*. Ann Arbor, Michigan: Association for Consumer Research, pp. 485–490.

Saleh, F. and Ryan, C. (1992) Client perception of hotels – a multi–attribute approach. *Tourism Management* 13, 163–168.

Scott, D.R., Schewe, C.D. and Frederick, D.G. (1978) A multibrand/multiattribute model of tourist state choice. *Journal of Travel Research* 17, 23–29.

Sheppard, B.H., Hartwick, J. and Warshaw, P.R. (1988) The theory of reasoned action: a meta-analysis of past research with recommendations for modifications and future research. *Journal of Consumer Research* 15, 325–343.

Shih, D. (1986) VALS as a tool of tourism market research: the Pennsylvania experience. *Journal of Travel Research* 24, 2–10.

Shimp, T.A. and Kavas, A. (1984) The theory of reasoned action applied to coupon usage. *Journal of Consumer Research* 11, 795–809.

Sternquist-Witter, B. (1985) Attitudes about a resort area: a comparison of tourists and local retailers. *Journal of Travel Research* 24, 14–19.

Swan, J.E. and Coombs, L.J. (1976) Product performance and consumer satisfaction: a new concept. *Journal of Marketing* 40, 25–33.

Tse, D.K. and Wilton, P.C. (1988) Models of consumer satisfaction formation: an extension. *Journal of Marketing Research* 25, 204–212.

Tourism Canada (1988) *Pleasure Travel Markets to North America – Switzerland, Hong Kong, Singapore – Highlights Report, March.* Ottawa, Ontario: Market Facts of Canada, Tourism Canada.

Um, S. and Crompton, J.L. (1990) Attitude determinants in pleasure travel destination choice. *Annals of Tourism Research* 17, 432–448.

Var, T., Beck, R.A.D. and Loftus, P. (1977) Determination of touristic attractiveness of the touristic areas in British Columbia. *Journal of Travel Research* 15, 23–29.

Warshaw, R., Calantone, R. and Joyce, M. (1986) A field application of the Fishbein and Ajzen intention model. *Journal of Social Psychology* 126, 135–136.

Wiley, J.B., MacLachlan, D.L. and Moinpur, R. (1977) Comparison of stated and inferred parameter values in additive models. An illustration of a paradigm. In: W.D. Perrault (ed.) *Advances in Consumer Research, 4.* Atlanta, Georgia: Association for Consumer Research, pp. 106–110.

Wilson, D.T., Mathews, H.L. and Harvey, J.W. (1975) An empirical test of the Fishbein intention model. *Journal of Consumer Research* 1, 39–48.

Yi, Y. (1990) A critical review of consumer satisfaction. In: Zeithaml, V.A. (ed.) *Review of Marketing.* American Marketing Association.

Young, R.A. and Kent, A. (1985) Using the theory of reasoned action to improve the understanding of recreation behaviour. *Journal of Leisure Research* 17, 90–106.

Chapter sixteen
The Application of the Guttman Scaling Procedure in the Measurement of Consumer Behaviour: A Marketing Myopia

Yüksel Ekinci and Michael Riley
School of Management Studies, University of Surrey, Guildford GU2 5XH, UK

Introduction

The reliability and validity of measurement, as well as consistency between theory development and empirical testing, have been of particular concern to marketing researchers for a long time (Churchill, 1979; Parameswaran *et al.*, 1979; Oh and Parks, 1997). In practice, this concern mainly involves the validity and reliability of the measurement instrument. Consequently, scales used should not only provide a true measurement but also measure a certain construct which purports to be acceptably unidimensional. This is an essential element of construct validity (Hattie, 1985; Gerbing and Anderson, 1988).

However, assessing the unidimensionality for a measurement scale has caused a circular debate due to a persistent misapplication of analytical techniques. Factor analysis, item to total correlation, coefficient alpha or a different form of correlation analysis are some of the techniques which attempted to establish scale unidimensionality even in today's marketing and hospitality literature (Knutson *et al.*, 1990, Cronin and Taylor, 1992; 1994; Winstead, 1997). These studies appear to omit Gerbing and Anderson's (1988) early revision which addressed these issues in constructing a unidimensional scale. For example, the fact that exploratory factor analysis was used as an ultimate method rather than as a preliminary method in constructing unidimensional scale can be found in the literature. Similarly, coefficient alpha, or variety of inter-correctional analyses (item to total correlation) are used to measure unidimensionality rather than as a measure of scale reliability, internal consistency or homogeneity (Green *et al.*, 1977, Hattie, 1985)

Although it provided some insight regarding the proper use of these analytical techniques, and offered some alternative methods for constructing a scale, the Guttman scaling (Guttman, 1944) was originally developed to set for unidimensionality in a scale. This original purpose received a little attention from the marketing and hospitality researchers (Brown *et al.*, 1965; Landis, 1965; McFall,

1969; Wierenga *et al.*, 1994). Because of this, the possible applications of Gutt-man methodology have been largely ignored as a way of improving the quality of consumer behaviour research. However, in other areas of advanced psychometric theory, the properties of Guttman have proved fruitful (Hambleton *et al.*, 1991).

The purpose of this paper is twofold. Firstly, it aims to introduce the Guttman methodology, and then to demonstrate how it can be used in assessing scale uni-dimensionality. Secondly, other possible applications in consumer behaviour measurement will be discussed.

Unidimensionality and the Guttman Scale

Unidimensionality is evidence for the existence of a single trait or single construct which is underlying a set of measures (Hattie, 1985). It also implies that the items in a test or scale are ordered along a single continuum according to a set of criteria they manifest, such as item difficulty or item agreement.

Guttman scale, sometimes known as scalogram analysis, is a kind of scaling where items and respondents can be scaled at the same time, unlike the Likert and Thurstone scaling techniques where either subjects-only or items-only are scaled. The two main properties of Guttman scaling are being ordinal and being cumulative, and these properties provide a unidimensional status for Guttman scaling (Gutt-man, 1944; Oppenheim, 1966; McIver and Carmines, 1981). For example, salt, rock and diamond can be ordered according to their cumulative degree of hardness. Furthermore, the structure of cumulativeness can be checked according to a pre-determined single criterion – hardness in this example. On a purely unidimenisonal scale, if a person accepts that salt is hard, he/she must accept that rock is harder.

The Methodology of Guttman Scaling

The construction of the Guttman scale involves either dichotomous (1 = yes, 0 = no) or trichotomous (0 = disagree, 1 = neutral, 2 = agree) rating scale (Edwards, 1957). The scale can be constructed in two ways: using a ready-made ordinal scale, or constructing an ordinal scale. In the first case, a number of statements are organized in a hierarchical order on the basis of the items' content. For instance, salt, rock and diamond may be ordered according to their degree of hardness. Then the cumulative structure of these items is checked through the subjects' response patterns. By the same token, if a respondent says that salt is hard, he/she should also agree the hardness of the diamond (cumulative principle). If this struc-ture is not supported, the rule of cumulation is violated. The unidimensionality of children swinging development-behaviour scale, the adolescents' substance-use scale, and Moslow's motivation scale were examined through this procedure (Fox and Tipps, 1995; Andrews *et al.*, 1991; Porat, 1977, respectively).

In the second method, the frequency scores of items are used in constructing a hierarchical structure between the items. A single stimulus which is assumed to have two poles is useful in order to place the items in a hierarchical order (McIver and Carmines, 1981). If the measured construct is an attitude, the hierarchical order would be the degree of agreement along the continuum of statements rang-ing from favourable to unfavourable, or it can be a continuum from agree to dis-agree. Alternatively, if the content is quality, it can be the degree of excellence on the agree–disagree continuum. The perception and attitude assessment studies are good exemplars of this category (Koslowsky *et al.*, 1976; Lever and Samooha, 1981). The Cornell technique and the scalogram board technique are also based on this principle (Guttman, 1947; Suchman, 1950, respectively).

As it is hard to observe a perfect (ideal) Guttman scale in real life, the meas-ured construct is subjected to an error assessment procedure according to a perfect Guttman scale matrix. It is also notable that the cumulative order of perfect scale matrix varies on the basis of scale items and the form of rating scale, such as whether it is dichotomous or trichotomous. Figure 16.1 shows a hypothetical observed matrix which is formed in a hierarchical order with four items according to the items' positive frequency score, which means that a favourable response is indicated as 1 and unfavourable as 0 (dichotomous). Figure 16.2 illustrates a per-fect Guttman scale matrix with four items.

Item 1	Item 2	Item 3	Item 4	Total Score
1	1	1	1	4
1	1	1	0	3
1	0	1	1	3
1	1	0	0	2
1	1	0	0	2
freq	freq	freq	freq	
5	4	3	2	

Figure 16.1 The observed pattern matrix.

Item 1	Item 2	Item 3	Item 4	Total Score
1	1	1	1	4
1	1	1	0	3
1	1	0	0	2
1	0	0	0	1
0	0	0	0	0

Figure 16.2 The perfect scale matrix.

With reference to Fig. 16.1, if a measured construct is an attitude, item 4 is the least-agreed item compared to the other items in the scale, whereas item 1 is the most-agreed item. If the scale is cumulative, a respondent who endorses item 4 positively should also endorse the other items positively. Similarly, a person who has a total score of 2 along the four items should have endorsed only the first and the second items positively, and the third and fourth items negatively. The next stage in the scale analysis involves computing the scalability which is expressed by coefficient of reproducibility (CR). The process basically involves assessing the scale error. The Goodenough–Edwards error-assessment technique is adopted here in preference to alternatives such as Guttman's 'principles of error minimization' or 'H technique' (Guttman, 1950; Stouffer *et al.*, 1952; Edwards, 1957).

The error-assessment technique concerns comparing the performance of observed scales with an ideal cumulative scale. Through this comparison the number of errors, that is the number of times the cumulative scale of the item diverges from the ideal template, can be calculated. Guttman (1950) set the standard of 10% error as the maximum, and therefore an item needs a CR of 90%. By a successive process of elimination, the output is a set of items (or a scale) that reach the 90% level. To achieve this, the process re-eliminates in turn the item with the highest error, then recalculates the cumulative order and compares it again with the ideal scale. To illustrate the error-assessment process, an example from Fig. 16.1 is useful. Looking again at this figure, the third respondent assigns a total score of 3 on the four-item scale with the following observed pattern (1,0,1,1 = 3). That response pattern gives two errors when it is compared to the ideal scale pattern in Fig. 16.2 (1,1,1,0 = 3), since the response pattern deviates on items 2 and 4 (compare the italic number on the observed pattern with the bold number in the ideal pattern). No other subjects produced error, as their observed response pattern matches the ideal pattern. The error assessment is carried out for every single respondent participating in the survey, and the numbers of errors are added up to find the total scale error. Furthermore, the scale CR is computed by using the following formula (Guttman, 1950):

$$CR = 1 - \text{total error} / \text{total responses}$$
$$CR = 1 - \text{total error} / (\text{items} \times \text{respondents})$$

where total error is divided by the number of total responses (total responses is computed by multiplying the number of scale items by the number of subjects participating in the study). According to this statistic, the CR should be 0.90, if the examined construct is unidimensional (Guttman, 1950).

Once the proposed scale provides unidimensionality between the items, it is then required to test the consistency of this relationship with a further test. The perfect pattern involves a weak monotonic relationship between the scale items. A number of alternative statistical tests were offered to examine the significance of this relationship (McIver and Carmines, 1981). Yule's Q correlation is a good choice for a dichotomous and a trichotomous rating scale (Koslowsky *et al.*, 1976).

Application of Guttman Methodology to the SERVQUAL Dimensions

The lack of consistency between the theory and its empirical assessment has been well documented in service quality literature, in particular in SERVQUAL scale development studies (Cronin and Taylor, 1992; Buttle, 1996; Oh and Parks, 1997). These studies emphasize validity and reliability issues in measurement of consumer behaviour.

At the outset of their study, SERVQUAL researchers implied that service quality consists of ten overlapping dimensions from the consumer-perception point of view: Accessibility, Communication, Competence, Courtesy, Credibility, Reliability, Responsiveness, Security, Tangibles and Understanding/knowing the customer (Parasuraman *et al.*, 1985). The SERVQUAL research group took a further decision to develop a shorter instrument with relatively discriminate dimensions. As a result of the exploratory factor analysis, these ten overlapping dimensions were merged into five distinct factors: Assurance, Empathy, Tangibles, Reliability, Responsiveness (Parasuraman *et al.*, 1988). Basically, the first two dimensions were formed by the combining initial items of seven dimensions (communication, credibility, security, competence, courtesy, understanding/ knowing customers). However, in the scale purification study conducted by exploratory factor analysis, the dimensions again displayed an overlapping pattern where tangibles split into two parts, responsiveness and assurance merged in a single factor, and reliability and empathy remained distinct (Parasuraman *et al.*, 1991).

As a result of various criticisms of the SERVQUAL scale, the researchers attempted to develop an alternative measurement method which mainly concerned modification of the rating scale, but is based on the same five dimensions. However, the observed factor structure in exploratory and confirmatory analysis was again problematic, confirming the three-dimensional model rather than five-dimensional (Parasuraman *et al.*, 1994). As Parasuraman *et al.* (1988) imply that the SERVQUAL dimensions are generic, the original scale and the content-specific scale based on these five dimensions have been tested in different service settings in order to confirm their findings. However, the result was patchy and the existence of these dimensions was thought by some to be dubious (Buttle, 1996).

The case study aims to investigate the SERVQUAL scale dimensional structure, in particular whether or not the certain items measure five distinct dimensions. Evidence of the existence of dimensions would be observation of a unidimensional structure between the five sub-scale items that measure the purported dimensions. In other words, the study is using Guttman scaling from a hypothesis-testing perspective rather than a scale-development perspective (Edwards, 1957, p. 172)

The instrument

The questionnaire instrument was the 22-item SERVQUAL scale (Appendix 1). In order to provide face validity, the scale items were slightly modified in the light of expert opinion. Firstly, the overall instrument tense was changed from present simple to past, to make the items more comprehensible and suitable for performance-only measurement. Secondly, the following three SERVQUAL items' wordings have been changed to simplify their meanings:

- the 'reliability' item of SERVQUAL: 'XYZ insists on error-free-record' was changed to 'The hotel paperwork was accurate';
- the 'tangible' item of SERVQUAL: 'XYZ's physical facilities are visually appealing' was changed to 'The hotel's facilities were visually appealing';
- the 'responsiveness' item of SERVQUAL: 'Employees of XYZ tell you exactly when services will be performed' was changed to 'Employees of the hotel told you exactly when services were available'.

The seven-point Likert scale format, as suggested by Parasuraman *et al.* (1988, 1991), was used. The methodology was similar to previous SERVQUAL generation and assessment studies; however, performance-only measurement was used as suggested by recent studies in this area (Cronin and Taylor, 1992; Smith, 1995). A question about the overall quality of service was inserted to assess the scale external validity (concurrent validity).

The sample

The field survey was conducted in 1996 in two Turkish seaside resorts. The survey was completed with the assistance of two local travel agencies. The questionnaires were filled in as the holiday-makers were leaving the resort to return to the airport.

A total of 115 questionnaires were collected but three were excluded due to missing information. The sample size was sufficient according to Guttman (1950). The sample contained 49% female, 50% male. The age distribution was as follows: 16–24, 11%; 25–34, 25%; 35–44, 18%; 45–54, 23%; 55–64, 19%; 64 and over, 4%. Ninety six per cent of the subjects had visited the hotel for the first time, and all the respondents were British.

Analysis of the data

The data displayed a skewed distribution to the negative end of the scale. Peterson and Wilson (1992) define this type of distribution as a characteristic of satisfaction surveys. By the same token, the data are biased towards the negative end when the customers satisfied with the services and therefore the mean-based measurement might be misleading due to the inflated ratings. Therefore the data were dichotomized according to items' median scores rather than mean scores.

With reference to this conversion, those items which are below the median are accepted as the least-agreed items (0) and those items above and on the median score are accepted as the most-agreed items (1). For an example of the type of conversion, see Koslowsky *et al.* (1976).

Following this procedure, the cumulative order of SERVQUAL's dimensions was examined. The construction of hierarchical order and the error-assessment process are illustrated for four tangible items in Table 16.1.

Overall analysis of items' frequency of positive response suggests that question 6 is the most agreed item which represents the premium quality, whereas question 19 is the least agreed item that represents poor quality. If a respondent gives a positive rating (1) to question 19, it means that he/she is satisfied with this hotel feature, and must rate all the other items positively. Alternatively, if a respondent rates item 19 negatively (0), but question 3 positively, he/she is again expected to rate the other items positively in order to confirm the cumulative structure. If this pattern is not observed then an error occurs in the scale. The error is assessed simply by comparing the respondent's observed pattern against the perfect scale pattern.

From the first-stage error-assessment process, no satisfactory CR value has been provided for the Tangible items (the CR value is less than 0.90). Therefore an item which possesses the highest number of error was deleted from the scale. The same analysis was followed for the remaining items in response to Guttman's suggestion (1950). At the end of the third iteration, a satisfactory result (CR=0.93) was obtained for the two items Q16 and Q19. This finding suggests provisional evidence for the existence of a Tangible dimension. The unidimensionality of the five SERVQUAL scales (Reliability, Assurance, Tangibles, Empathy, Responsiveness) were investigated by employing the same process. The overall findings are shown in Table 16.2.

Table 16.1 Tangibles dimension: the cumulative ordering structure of items, number of error and the coefficient of reproducibility (CR)

Iteration process	Error for per statement (*n*=112)				Total error	CR
	Q6	Q16	Q3	Q19		
Stage 1	23*	18	21	22	84	0.81
Stage 2		13	17*	16	46	0.86
Stage 3		7		7	14	0.93
Positive response	72	65	59	49		

*To be excluded for the next stage.

Table 16.2 Final result of Guttman scale analysis

Iteration process	Reliability		Assurance		Tangibles		Empathy		Responsiveness	
	Items	CR	Items	CR	Items	CR	Items	CR	Items	CR
Stage 1: Analysis with all the items (Dimension I)										
Iteration 1	15, 20, 13, 18, 21	0.81	12, 9, 1, 2	0.87	6, 16, 3, 19	0.81	8, 5, 22, 7, 11	0.81	14, 17, 10, 4	0.84
Iteration 2	15, 20, 13, 18	0.81	12, 1, 2	0.91	16, 3, 19	0.86	8, 5, 22, 7	0.84	14, 17, 10	0.84
Iteration 3	15, 20, 13	0.84			16, 19	0.93	8, 5, 22	0.86	14, 10	0.97
Iteration 4	15, 20	0.88					5, 22	0.90		
STAGE 2: Analysis with the redundant items (Dimension II)										
Iteration 1	13, 18, 21	0.86			6, 3	0.86	8, 7, 11	0.85	17, 4	0.89
Iteration 2	18, 21	0.89					8, 7	0.93		

From the analysis of stage one, four of the dimensions, Assurance (12, 1, 2; CR=91), Tangibles (16, 19; CR=93), Empathy (5, 22; CR=90), and Responsiveness (14, 10; CR=97) provided a minimum degree of CR values. This gave provisional support for the unidimensionality of these constructs. In the second stage, the existence of an additional dimension was also searched with those items that were redundant in the first stage. Having used same analysis, a second empathy dimension was found (8, 7; CR=93).

It was also notable from Table 16.2 that some of the dimensions' CR values (0.89) were very close to the minimum acceptable CR score (Reliability and Responsiveness). Consequently, it was worth employing two additional scalability methods, minimal marginal reproducibility (MMR) and coefficient of scalability (CS), for these dimensions. The MMR and CS values of Reliability I (15, 20; MMR=0.60, CS=0.70), Reliability II (18, 21; MMR=0.57, CS=0.74) and Responsiveness II (7, 4; MMR=0.56, CS=0.75) were sufficient to confirm their existence at this stage (McIver and Carmines, 1981).

In order to test the weak monotonic relationship between the items, a follow up test called Yule's Q was performed between the validated dimensions. The intention of this test was to check whether this relationship was significant. To do this, a cut-off value is required in order to make a judgement as to whether the relationship is consistent. Koslowsky *et al.* (1976) recommend 0.70% for a consistent relationship between the items. On the other hand, the maximum value can be 1, if this relationship is perfectly consistent. The results are presented in Table 16.3.

From Yule's Q correlation, the relationship between the assurance items and the first Empathy dimension items was spurious, and therefore items 2, 5 and 22 should be excluded from the scale, whereas the consistency of relationship between the other items was encouraging. This study also suggests that the Reliability and Responsiveness scales are multidimensional rather than unidimensional, supported by two items. (The MMR scores of four dimensions, Assurance, Tangibles, Empathy, and Responsiveness I, are less than 0.64, and CS scores are greater than 0.70.)

Although this methodology is useful in terms of searching for the existence of dimensions and validating the scale unidimensionality, the unidimensional scale should also be reliable and valid. This condition was necessary in terms of providing an accurate measurement. Therefore, the modified SERVQUAL scale was subjected to internal consistency analysis. Coefficient alpha was considered to be the first measure to assess the scale reliability (Churchill, 1979). Table 16.4 shows the reliability of sub-scales and the item-to-total correlation by using the original Likert scale.

From the computed coefficient alpha values, four of the dimension reliability scores, Assurance, Empathy, Responsiveness II, and Reliability I, are low for a mature scale (Churchill, 1979). This means that these scales contain more than 30% measurement error. Three of the sub-scales, Tangibles, Responsiveness I, and Reliability II, displayed sufficient reliability. All the items contributed to the measured construct, so that the item-to-total correlation was moderately high.

Table 16.3 Yule's Q correlation between the validated items

Assurance

	12	1	2
12	1		
1	0.83	1	
2	0.43	0.63	1

Tangibles

	16	19
16	1	
19	0.82	1

Empathy

	5	22
5	1	
22	0.66	1

	8	7
8	1	
7	0.75	1

Responsiveness

	14	10
14	1	
10	0.84	1

	17	4
17	1	
4	0.74	1

Reliability

	15	20
15	1	
20	0.71	1

	18	21
18	1	
21	0.79	1

Table 16.4 The modified SERVQUAL scale: seven-point Likert scale

Item number	Dimension	Cronbach's alpha	Item to total correlation
	Assurance	0.69	
1	Employees of the hotel were consistently courteous with you		0.55
12	The behaviour of employees of the hotel instilled confidence in customers		0.55
	Tangibles	0.77	
16	The hotel's facilities were visually appealing		0.63
19	The materials associated with the service (such as menu, furniture) were visually		0.63
	Empathy	0.69	
7	Employees of the hotel understood your specific needs		0.53
8	The hotel had operating hours convenient to all its customers		0.53
	Responsiveness I	0.87	
10	Employees of the hotel were always willing to help you		0.78
14	Employees of the hotel gave you prompt service		0.78
	Responsiveness II	0.60	
17	Employees of the hotel told you exactly when services were available		0.45
4	Employees of the hotel were never too busy to respond to your request		0.45
	Reliability I	0.58	
15	The hotel's paperwork was accurate		0.43
20	The hotel provided its services at the time it promised to do so		0.43
	Reliability II	0.74	
18	The hotel performed services right the first time		0.59
21	When the hotel promised to do something by a certain time, it did it		0.59

From a broader perspective, the validity of a scale is concerned with whether it is a useful instrument in measuring a particular concept, in this example, service quality. The validity assessment also contains different types of criteria in the literature (Kaplan and Sacuzzo, 1989). Tull and Hawkins (1993) define concurrent validity in the following statement:

'It is the extent to which one measure of variables can be used to estimate an individual's current score on a different measure of the same or, a closely related variable' (Tull and Hawkins, 1993, pp. 318).

The concurrent validity of the modified SERVQUAL scale was tested by regressing the present 14 items over to the single item 'overall quality' scale. The correlation coefficients were high (0.76) between these two scales ($P<0.000$). This finding demonstrates that the scale has a concurrent validity.

Discussion and Conclusions

The application of the Guttman methodology in the SERVQUAL scale demonstrates that some of the scales are multidimensional rather than unidimensional. With reference to these findings, the three additional sub-dimensions were identified. These findings implicitly confirm Carmen's (1990) findings, in which the service quality dimensions were broke down into the further sub-dimensions in different service environments. These findings may be related to the SERVQUAL scale's original combination procedure where it was attempted to merge the initial ten dimensions into five dimensions. As some additional dimensions were observed in this study, the combination process may not have been done properly in the SERVQUAL development studies. This result suggests that the five-dimensional structure may be flawed.

The iteration process which is aims to search for the unidimensionality of the scale suggests that some of the SERVQUAL statements need to be deleted, since they do not define any associated construct.

The reliability and validity of the modified SERVQUAL scale needed to be confirmed, as even the observed sub-scales were unidimensional. Although the reliability of four sub-scales was low, the other dimensions provided satisfactory findings. Further analysis suggested that the modified scale is a valid instrument in terms of predicting respondents' 'overall quality judgement'. However, there are some limitations in this case study, in terms of generalizing the results. Firstly, the dimensions are confirmed by only two items, which may cause a reliability and validity problem in the measurement. Therefore the scale should contain a minimum of three items, which means that more items are needed. Increasing the number of statements will also improve the scale reliability (Green *et al.*, 1977). Secondly, despite providing a sufficient sample size, the study should be repeated with a larger sample size. Thirdly, the scale can be tested with a dichotomous rating scale.

Guttman scaling is a useful methodology for assessing scale unidimensionality, which is an important element of construct validity. Furthermore, this methodology offers some other contributions and implications for consumer behaviour in terms of theory testing and measurement. The error-assessment process is a useful item-analysis technique which can be used in scale analysis. The structure of the multidimensional models can be tested with this methodology. Through this examination, the existence of the dimensions can be validated and the relevant construct probed in detail. This examination provides not only more accurate information about the underlying trait, but also better implications for practitioners. This means that the marketing strategy can be formulated more precisely, based on a clear idea of how consumers evaluate. Then marketing activities can be planned and used more efficiently.

The above discussion has been central in using Guttman scaling to test the hypothesis that certain dimensions exist. However, if the process reiterates, the Guttman methodology can be used to construct a unidimensional scale.

References

Andrews, J.A., Hopes, H., Ary, D., Lichtenstein, E. and Tildesley, E. (1991) The construction, validation and use of a Guttman scale of adolescent substance use: an investigation of family relationships. *Journal of Drug Issues* 21, 557–572.

Brown, D.A., Buck, S.F. and Pyatt, F.G. (1965) Improving the Sales Forecast for Consumer Durables. *Journal of Marketing Research* 2, 229–234.

Buttle, F. (1996) SERVQUAL: review, critique, research agenda. *European Journal of Marketing* 30, 8–32.

Carmen, J.M. (1990) Consumer perceptions of service quality: an assessment of the SERVQUAL dimensions. *Journal of Retailing* 66, 33–35.

Churchill Jr, G.A. (1979) A paradigm for developing better measures of marketing constructs. *Journal of Marketing Research* 16, 64–73.

Cronin Jr, J.J. and Taylor, S.A. (1992) Measuring service quality: a re-examination and extension. *Journal of Marketing* 56, 55–68.

Cronin Jr, J.J. and Taylor, S.A. (1994) SERVPERF versus SERVQUAL: reconciling performance-based and perceptions-minus-expectations measurement of service quality. *Journal of Marketing* 58, 125–131.

Edwards A.L. (1957) *Techniques of Attitude Scale Construction.* New York: Appleton-Centry Crofts.

Fox, J.E. and Tipps, R.S. (1995) Young children – development of swinging behaviours. *Early Childhood Research Quarterly* 10, 491–504.

Gerbing, D.W. and Anderson, J.C. (1988) An updated paradigm for scale development incorporating unidimensionality and its assessment. *Journal of Marketing Research* 15, 186–192.

Guttman, L. (1944) A technique for scale analysis. *Educational and Psychological Measurement* 4, 179–190.

Guttman, L. (1947) The Cornell technique for scale and intensity analysis. *Educational and Psychological Measurement* 7, 247–280.

Guttman, L. (1950) The basis for scalogram analysis. In: S.A. Stouffer, L. Guttman, E.A. Suchman, P.F. Lazarsfeld, S.A. Star and J.A. Claussen (eds) *Measurement and Prediction*, Vol. 4. Princeton, New Jersey: Princeton University Press, pp. 60–90.

Green, S.B., Lissitz and Mulaik, S.A. (1977) Limitations of coefficient alpha as an index of test unidemensionality. *Educational and Psychological Measurement* 37, 827–838.

Hattie, J. (1985) Methodology review: assessing unidimensionality of tests and terms. *Applied Psychological Measurement* 9, 139–164.

Hambleton, R.K., Swaminathan, H. and Rogers, H.J. (1991) *Fundamentals of Item Response Theory*. London: Sage.

Kaplan, M.R. and Sacuzzo, P.D. (1989) *Psychological Testing Principles – Applications and Issues*. California: Brooks/Cole, pp. 119–136.

Knutson, B., Stevens, P., Patton, M., Wullaert, C. and Yokoyama, F. (1990) The service expectation index: a comparison of confirmatory analysis and factor analysis as methods of index testing and refinement. *Hospitality Education and Research Journal* 14, 277–284.

Koslowsky, M., Pratt, G.L. and Wintrob, R.M. (1976) The application of Guttman scale analysis to physicians' attitudes regarding abortion. *Journal of Applied Psychology* 61, 301–304.

Landis, J.B. (1965) Exposure probabilities as measure of media audiences. *Journal of Advertising Research* 5, 24–29.

Lever, H. and Smooha, S. (1981) A part–whole strategy for the study of opinions. *Public Opinion Quarterly* 45, 560–570.

McIver, J.P. and Carmines, E.G. (1981) *Unidimensional Scaling: Quantitative Applications in the Social Sciences*. London: Sage.

McFall, J. (1969) Priority patterns and consumer behaviour. *Journal of Marketing* 33, 50–55.

Oh, H. and Parks, S. (1997) Customer satisfaction and service quality: a critical review of the literature and research implications for the hospitality industry. *Hospitality Research Journal* 20, 35–64.

Oppenheim, A.N. (1966) *Questionnaire Design and Attitude Measurement*. London: Heinemann.

Paramaswaran, R., Greenberg, B.A., Bellenger, D.N. and Robertson, D.H. (1979) Measuring reliability: a comparison of alternative techniques. *Journal of Marketing Research* 16, 18–25.

Parasuraman, A., Zeithaml,V.A. and Berry, L.L. (1985) A conceptual model of service quality and its implications for future research. *Journal of Marketing* 49, 41–50.

Parasuraman, A., Zeithaml, V.A. and Berry, L.L. (1988) SERVQUAL: a multiple-item scale for measuring consumer perception of service quality. *Journal of Retailing* 64, 13–40.

Parasuraman, A., Berry, L.L. and Zeithaml, V. (1991) Refinement and reassessment of the SERVQUAL scale. *Journal of Retailing* 67, 421–450.

Parasuraman, A., Zeithaml, V.A. and Berry, L. (1994) Alternative Scales for Measuring Service Quality: A comparative assessment based on psychometric and diagnostic criteria. *Journal of Retailing* 70, 193–199.

Peterson, R.A. and Wilson, W.R. (1992) Measuring customer satisfaction – fact and artefact. *Journal of The Academy of Marketing Science* 20, 61–71.

Porat, A.B. (1977) Guttman scale test for Moslow need hierarchy. *Journal of Psychology* 97, 85–92.

Smith, A.M. (1995) The consumer's evaluation of service quality: an examination of the SERVQUAL methodology. PhD thesis, Manchester School of Management, UMIST, UK.

Suchman, E.A. (1950) The scalogram board technique for scale analysis. In: S.A. Stouffer, L. Guttman, E.A. Suchman, P.F. Lazarsfeld, S.A. Star and J.A. Claussen (eds) *Measurement and Prediction*, Vol. 4. Princeton, New Jersey: Princeton University Press, pp. 91–121.

Stouffer, S.A., Borgatta, E.F., Hays, D.G. and Henry, A.F. (1952) A technique for improving cumulative scales. *Public Opinion Quarterly* 16, 273–291.

Tull, D.S. and Hawkins, D.I. (1993) *Marketing Research Measurement and Method*. New York: Macmillan.

Wierenga, B., Oude Ophuis, P.A.M., Huizingh, E.K.R. and Van Campen, P.A.F.M. (1994) Hierarchical scaling of marketing decision support systems. *Decision Support Systems* 12, 219–232.

Winstead, K.F. (1997) The service experience in two cultures: a behavioural perspective. *Journal of Retailing* 73, 337–360.

Appendix 1

The SERVQUAL Scale (1991)

Tangibles

1. XYZ has modern-looking equipment
2. XYZ's employees are neat appearing
3. XYZ's physical facilities are visually appealing
4. Materials associated with the service (such as pamphlets or statements) are visually appealing at XYZ Reliability
5. When you have a problem, XYZ shows a sincere interest in solving it
6. XYZ insist on error-free records
7. XYZ performs the service right the first time
8. XYZ provides its services at the time it promises to do so
9. When XYZ promises to do something by a certain time, it does so Assurance
10. Employees of XYZ are consistently courteous with you
11. Employees of XYZ have knowledge to answer your questions
12. You feel safe in your transaction with XYZ
13. The behaviour of employees of XYZ instils confidence in customers Responsiveness
14. Employees of XYZ are never too busy to respond to your request
15. Employees of XYZ are always willing to help you
16. Employees of XYZ give you prompt service
17. Employees of XYZ tell you exactly when services will be performed Empathy
18. XYZ gives you personal attention
19. Employees of XYZ understand your specific needs
20. XYZ has operating hours convenient to all its customers
21. XYZ gives you individual attention
22. XYZ has your best interest at heart

Chapter seventeen
Determinants of Tourist Spending

Vinod B. Agarwal and Gilbert R. Yochum
*Department of Economics, Old Dominion University, 49th Street/Hampton Blvd,
Norfolk, VA 23529-0221, USA*

Introduction

Travel and tourism is the USA's third largest retail industry, after automotive dealers and food stores. In 1996, this industry generated an estimated $473 billion in
expenditures: $64 billion in federal, state and local tax revenues; $116 billion in
payroll; and $6.6 million in direct jobs. The industry created an estimated 8.9 mil-
lion jobs indirectly and provided more than 684,000 executive-level positions. The
industry was the nation's leading services export. International visitors, numbering
46.3 million, spent approximately $90 billion and created a surplus of $26 billion
as international visitors spent more money in the USA than Americans spent
abroad (Travel Industry Association of America, 1996b). However, very little is
known about determinants of spending by visitors.

The Travel Industry Association of America (1996a), utilizing the US Travel
Data Center's National Travel Survey, reports on general patterns of travel behaviour, socio-economic and demographic characteristics of travellers, and tourist
spending patterns. This study, like its predecessors, demonstrated that travelling
households differ from total US households in key aspects, regardless of ethnic
heritage. Specifically, travelling households are more likely to have a head of
household who is older, has completed college, has higher household income and
is married. The study, however, makes no attempt to identify the determinants of
tourist spending.

Church (1969a, b) states that even though travel is an important income-pro-
ducing activity, available statistics on travel expenditures are inadequate. He proposes a model using volume and characteristics of travel to compute approximate
aggregate travel expenditures. Qui and Zhang (1995), Di Matteo and Di Matteo
(1993), and Lee *et al.* (1996) attempt to estimate determinants of travel expenditures utilizing aggregate time-series data for international travel. They all conclude
that *per capita* income and exchange rates are significant in explaining tourist
expenditures. Godbey and Graefe (1991), utilizing a cross-section sample of tourists

attending university-level football games, find a strong negative relationship between repeat attendance and per game expenditures. Davies and Mangan (1992) investigate the effect of income on hotels and holiday expenditures. Utilizing the UK's Family Expenditure Survey Data for 1988, the authors find that such expenditures are income-elastic. Further, the elasticity varies across income groups, being very high for low income groups, and lower but elastic for higher income groups. Mack *et al.* (1977) developed a model for *per capita* daily visitor expenditures (PCDVE) of US visitors to Hawaii for 1974. PCDVE is hypothesized to be a function of length of stay, income, education, party size, age, repeat visitors, etc. They find that higher income visitors spend more, education levels do not matter, length of stay varies inversely with spending, repeat visitors spend the same as first-time visitors, and married visitors spend significantly less.

The objective of this paper is to investigate major determinants of expenditures incurred by tourists when they are away from home for at least one night. This paper will employ survey data from a particular destination point over a defined 'tourist season' and investigate major factors that may determine tourist spending.

Data

This chapter focuses on overnight visitors to Virginia Beach, an Atlantic Coast beach resort, during the summer of 1997. The City has been commissioning visitor surveys every year for over 10 years. The surveys are administered by professional interviewers from a local private marketing research firm. Interviewers are assigned a series of city-blocks along the ocean front and instructed for the proper random selection of interviewees within each block. The interviewers typically walk in an imaginary diagonal across the beach (sand) from one block to another and carry a table of selected random digits to select the interviewees, i.e. the interviewer counted persons while walking along the diagonal until meeting the person in their count who coincided with the number read from the random digit card. This individual was then interviewed. Similar sampling procedures were used when visitors were interviewed on the boardwalk and first street along the beach (Atlantic Avenue), both of which are parallel to the ocean front. These surveys provide information on tourist party characteristics, plans, activities and vacation patterns, as well as the socio-demographic and economic status of visitors. A copy of the survey questionnaire used on the beach, boardwalk and Atlantic Avenue is provided in Exhibit 17.1.

During the summer of 1997 (June–August), 1200 interviews were conducted on the beach, boardwalk, and Atlantic Avenue area in three separate intervals spread across the summer (600 interviews on the sand; 300 each on the boardwalk and Atlantic Avenue). Interviews were conducted from June 6 to June 23; July 10 to July 27; and August 1 to August 19.

Surveys were conducted by six professional interviewers, and the respondents were not given any incentives for their cooperation. All interviewers had their name tags properly displayed on uniforms provided by the survey firm. Before they approached visitors for surveys, they stated, 'Hello! I'm doing a little survey for the City of Virginia Beach......' and proceeded with the survey. The survey response rate was approximately 75%. The survey response varied from about 97% on the sand to about 50% on Atlantic Avenue.

Of the 1200 surveys, 82 could not be used for this paper due to missing or incomplete information on some of the key variables used in the modelling precess. The sample was further restricted to only those visitors who came to Virginia Beach for a vacation. Those who were visiting Virginia Beach to attend a convention or for business purposes, or who simply stopped over but were on a longer vacation trip, were excluded from the analysis. Thus this paper is based on 985 surveys or observations.

Table 17.1 shows selected characteristics of 985 overnight visitors. Overnight visitors to Virginia Beach have an average income of $60,421; they spend on average $1,058 during their visit; they stay for 4.2 nights; have 3.7 people in their party; are accompanied by one child; and have an average age of the head of the visiting party of 38 years. Sixty eight percent of visitors were married; 75% were repeat visitors; 78% made advance reservations; 24% were weekend visitors; and 56% had heard or seen an advertisement about Virginia Beach.

Table 17.1 Selected characteristics of overnight visitors surveyed

Characteristic	Value	Range
Number of visitors surveyed	985	
Average length of stay	4.22	1–14
Average party size	3.69	1–12
Average number of children	1.13	0–7
Average age	38.1 years	18–76 years
Average income	$60,421	$15,000–$135,000
Average party expenditures	$1,058.10	$100–$3,800
Average party expenditures per day	$266.25	$16–$1,000
Average expenditures per person per day	$82.86	$6–$350
Percentage married	66.8%	
Percentage of repeat visitors	75.2%	
Percentage making advance reservations	79.3%	
Percentage who saw or heard an advertisement about Virginia Beach	55.8%	
Percentage visiting on weekends	24.4%	

Model

The focus of this paper is to investigate determinants of expenditures of overnight visitors. To meet these objectives, the following model is proposed:

$S=f(I,A,N,P,C)$

where $S=$ expenditures incurred by the visiting party in the City of Virginia Beach; $I=$ income of the visiting party; $A=$ age of the head of the visiting party; $N=$number of nights spent in the City of Virginia Beach; $P=$size of the visiting party; $C=$ number of children in the party under 18 years of age.

It is hypothesized that an overnight visit to Virginia Beach is a normal good. Therefore, as visitor income increases, their expenditures are expected to rise. By definition, visitors staying longer in Virginia Beach are expected to spend more. Likewise as party size increases, expenditures are expected to increase. Given that children are not income earners, an increase in the number of children in the party, *ceteris paribus*, is anticipated to lead to lower expenditures relative to party size. In accord with the life-cycle hypothesis, it is expected that spending will vary across various age cohorts. Therefore the relation between spending and age is expected to be ambiguous.

Simple correlations among these variables, displayed in Table 17.2, demonstrate that total party spending is positively associated with all the variables listed above, and these correlations are statistically significant at 0.001 level or better. Correlation of total party spending is highest with length of stay, followed by party size, number of children, income of visitors and age of the head of the visiting party, respectively. Total party spending is also highly correlated with spending per day, but its correlation with spending per day per person is quite low, yet positive and significant. To a casual observer, all of the above correlations are indicative of the fact that if any one of these variables were to increase in value, we would expect total party spending to increase. Further, except for correlation of party size and number of children in the party, where the correlation coefficient is 0.77, all other correlation coefficients among other variables are less than 0.49 in absolute size. It should be noted that correlations of spending per day, with the exception of length of stay, are all positive. Correlations of spending per day per person are not significant for income and age where the coefficients are positive, but are negative and significant with length of stay, party size and number of children.

Simple correlations, however, do not permit an analysis of a change in any one of these variables, say income on party spending, when any one or more of the remaining variables also changes. To overcome this drawback, further exploration of the effect of the suggested determinants on spending is conducted with the aid of multiple regression analysis. This analysis allows for the isolation of the effect of a change in one of the spending determinants on spending, say income, when all the remaining variables included in the regression analysis are held at constant level.

Table 17.2 Correlation of variables

Variables	Total spending	Spending per day	Spending per day per person	Nights	Party	Kids	Income	Age
Total spending	1.00	0.50	0.06**	0.62	0.38	0.29	0.24	0.19
Spending per day		1.00	0.49	-0.22	0.39	0.22	0.10	0.07**
Spending per day per person			1.00	-0.30	-0.48	-0.45	0.01***	0.02***
Nights				1.00	0.09	0.11	0.16	0.14
Party					1.00	0.77	0.06**	0.07**
Kids						1.00	0.11	0.11
Income							1.00	0.20
Age								1.00

**Significant at 10% level or better; ***insignificant even at 25% level.

In addition to the above variables, additional independent variables are added to control for potential qualitative effects. Two dummy variables, *July* and *August*, are included to control for differences in spending which could be due to seasonal variation in tourist demand and capacity constraints in accommodations. A dummy variable, *Gender*, is created to test if female spending behaviour is different from that of men. *Rsvation*, is used to control for possible market variation in accommodation prices among walk-in and advance-reservation visitors. *Wkend* is a dummy variable which accounts for historically higher weekend lodging prices. Finally, three additional dummy variables are created to represent lodging arrangements of the visiting party: *Hotel, Camp,* and *Condo.* The full model is shown below:

S=f(I, A, N, P, C, July, August, Gender, Rsvation, Wkend, Hotel, Camp, Condo)

where *S*= expenditures incurred by the visiting party in the City of Virginia Beach; *I*= income of the visiting party; *A*= age of the head of the visiting party; *N*=number of nights spent in the City of Virginia Beach; *P*= party size of the visiting party; *C*= number of children in the party under 18 years of age; *July*=1 if the month of visit is July, =0 otherwise; *August*=1 if the month of visit is August, =0 otherwise; *Gender*=1 if the head of visiting party is a male, =0 otherwise; *Rsvation*=1 if the visiting party had an advance reservation, =0 otherwise; *Wkend*=1 if the visiting party comes on a weekend, = 0 otherwise; *Hotel*=1 if the visiting party is staying in a hotel/motel, = 0 otherwise; *Camp*=1 if the visiting party is staying in a campground, = 0 otherwise; *Condo*=1 if the visiting party is staying in a cottage or condominium or apartment; =0 otherwise.

The dummy variable categories excluded from the model are: June visitor parties, parties headed by a male, those without reservations, parties visiting for more than a weekend, and those staying with friends or family while visiting Virginia Beach. A visiting party is the reference point for the empirical specification of the model and for inferences to be drawn the model's results.

Empirical Results

The model is estimated with a multiplicative or a log-linear form. This estimating format has an advantage over a linear specification in that coefficients of the quantitative variables are interpretable as elasticities. Linear specifications of the model yielded very similar results. Three different dependent variables, and therefore three different model specifications, are used as measures of tourist spending: total party expenditure, party expenditure per day, and expenditure per day per person in Virginia Beach. The results for total party expenditure are presented in Table 17.3. This regression model explains 72.92% of the variation in total party expenditures; an excellent fit for cross-sectional data. Results are also reported in this and other tables for a truncated model where a variable representing number of children and some of the qualitative variables are omitted.

Table 17.3 Results for total party expenditures

Independent variable	Full model		Truncated model	
	Parameter estimate	Beta estimate	Parameter estimate	Beta estimate
Constant	3.644 (21.515)*		3.810 (24.809)*	
Income	0.110 (4.610)*	0.08	0.108 (4.530)*	0.08
Age	0.052 (1.332)	0.02	0.056 (1.427)	0.03
Nights	0.744 (28.636)*	0.62	0.781 (36.621)*	0.66
Party size	0.461 (13.224)*	0.32	0.397 (16.000)*	0.28
Number of children	−0.009 (−3.301)*	−0.08	–	–
July	0.100 (3.453)*	0.07	–	–
August	0.076 (2.626)*	0.05	–	–
Gender	0.033 (1.378)	0.02	–	–
Reservation	0.040 (1.281)	0.02	–	–
Weekend	−0.084 (−2.539)*	−0.05	–	–
Hotel	0.950 (20.672)*	0.57	0.936 (20.376)*	0.56
Campground	0.273 (3.865)*	0.08	0.271 (3.880)*	0.08
Cottage/Condo/ Apartment	0.914 (15.386)*	0.39	0.890 (15.124)*	0.38
Adjusted R^2	0.7292		0.7184	

*Significant at 0.01 level or better.

Among the quantitative variables, age is the only variable which is not statistically significant. All other quantitative variables are significant at the 1% level or better. The estimated model indicates that, other things being equal, an increase in visiting party income of 10% will result in a total party spending increase of 1.1%. Likewise, if party size increases by 10%, party spending increases by 4.61%. A 10% increase in length of stay leads to a 7.44% increase in total party spending. Both nights and party size exhibit average elasticities of less than one and are subject to diminishing returns with respect to party expenditures. As expected, the coefficient on number of children is negative. Therefore, *ceteris paribus*, as the number of children in a party increases, party spending decreases or, if two visiting parties have the same party size and one of these parties has more children, then the party with more children spends less.

With respect to the qualitative variables, the reference party is a visiting party whose head is a male, comes to Virginia Beach in June, does not have reservations, is not here only for the weekend, and is staying with friends or family. The estimated coefficients on July and August are positive, about the same in size, and significant, implying that if a visiting party came to Virginia Beach in July or August, rather than in June, party spending would be higher. This result was expected since the tourist summer season does not really begin until the middle of June when most schools are closed.

The coefficients associated with *Hotel*, *Camp* and *Condo* are all statistically significant, and the size of the coefficient is highest for hotels and lowest for campgrounds. The results imply that parties staying in hotels spend the most and those who stay with friends and family, as might reasonably be expected, spend the least. The weekend variable is negative and significant. The coefficients associated with gender and reservation are not statistically significant, implying that whether the head of the visiting party is a male or female, and whether the visiting party had made an advanced reservation, *ceteris paribus*, does not affect total party spending. Beta coefficients are also reported in Table 17.3. These coefficients show that number of nights, staying in hotels, staying in cottages etc., and party size, respectively, are most important variables affecting total spending.

The results for the two alternative specifications of the dependent variable, expenditures per day and expenditures per day per person, are shown in Tables 17.4 and 17.5, respectively.

With respect to party expenditures per day, the results obtained demonstrate a lower adjusted R^2, 0.4753, still a good fit for cross-sectional data. The signs and significance of quantitative variables presented above are quite similar. In terms of qualitative variables and their results, there are two changes. Firstly, the coefficient on gender is positive as before but is now statistically significant at the 10% level. This result seems to imply that male heads of visiting party are likely to spend more. Secondly, the coefficient on weekend is now positive and significant, a reversal from the results discussed above. This result implies that party expenditure per day is likely to be more for those who visit Virginia beach only for the weekend, an expected result since the hotel rates are likely to be higher on the weekends.

Table 17.4 Results for party expenditures per day

Independent variable	Full model		Truncated model	
	Parameter estimate	Beta estimate	Parameter estimate	Beta estimate
Constant	3.499 (19.784)*		3.780 (23.522)*	
Income	0.076 (3.066)*	0.08	0.074 (2.977)*	0.07
Age	0.045 (1.083)	0.03	0.016 (0.393)	0.01
Party size	0.471 (12.892)*	0.43	0.375 (14.419)*	0.35
Number of children	-0.010 (-3.329)*	-0.11	–	–
July	0.084 (2.764)*	0.08	–	–
August	0.080 (2.646)*	0.07	–	–
Gender	0.046 (1.859)**	0.04	–	–
Reservation	-0.047 (-1.506)	-0.04	–	–
Weekend	0.085 (2.841)*	0.07	–	–
Hotel	0.953 (19.778)*	0.75	0.986 (20.526)*	0.77
Campground	0.205 (2.770)*	0.08	0.256 (3.484)*	0.10
Cottage/Condo/ Apartment	0.837 (13.565)*	0.47	0.852 (13.797)*	0.48
Adjusted R^2	0.4753		0.4578	

*Significant at 0.01 level or better; **significant at 0.1 level or better.

Table 17.5 Results for expenditures per person per day

Independent variable	Full model		Truncated model	
	Parameter estimate	Beta estimate	Parameter estimate	Beta estimate
Constant	2.633 (14.357)*		3.486 (17.181)*	
Income	0.083 (3.068)*	0.08	0.031 (1.009)	0.03
Age	0.091 (2.008)**	0.05	-0.025 (-0.474)	-0.01
Number of children	-0.040 (-16.975)*	-0.43	-	-
July	0.072 (2.148)**	0.06	-	-
August	0.061 (1.820)**	0.05	-	-
Gender	0.050 (1.824)**	0.04	-	-
Reservation	-0.088 (-2.571)*	-0.06	-	-
Weekend	0.081 (2.477)*	0.06	-	-
Hotel	0.896 (16.930)*	0.66	0.878 (14.573)*	0.65
Campground	0.103 (1.280)	0.04	0.080 (0.862)	0.03
Cottage/Condo/ Apartment	0.700 (10.384)*	0.37	0.626 (8.143)*	0.33
Adjusted R^2	0.4383		0.2448	

*Significant at 0.01 level or better; **significant at 0.1 level or better.

The results for party expenditures per person per day are very similar to party expenditures per day. The model has an adjusted R^2 equalling 0.4383, as demonstrated in Table 17.5, still representing a good fit for a cross-sectional data. The signs and significance of quantitative variables presented above are quite similar, with the exception of coefficient on age where it is positive and significant at the 10% level. In terms of qualitative variables and their results, there is only one change. The coefficient on reservation is negative as before, but is now statistically significant. This result implies that expenditures per person per day are likely to be lower for those who had advance reservations.

The above three models were also tested with the inclusion of a variable representing squared income, i.e. a quadratic form. The coefficient on squared income was insignificant for all three specifications. Realizing high correlation between party size and number of children, the first two models were estimated without including party size. The results obtained show that coefficient on number of children indeed became positive and significant. Respondents in surveys conducted on sand were also asked a question about whether they had requested information on Virginia Beach prior to their arrival. We included a dummy variable in all three models in an attempt to estimate the impact of requesting information on spending. Inclusion of this variable reduced the sample size from 985 to 503. However, this variable was found to be insignificant.

Conclusions

This paper demonstrates that for overnight visitors visiting Virginia Beach during summer 1997, the major determinants of expenditures are visitor's income, length of stay, party size, and number of children in the party. Spending also varies significantly depending on where visitors stay. Visitors staying in hotels/motels spend the most while those who stay with friends or family spend the least.

In terms of spending elasticities, the results indicate that, at least in the case of Virginia Beach, there are diminishing returns to progressively longer stays and to additional party members. The incremental decline in spending, on a per unit basis, is larger with respect to party size than for nights stayed. Regardless of the unit spending definition, the income elasticity of spending is relatively low. This suggests that marketing campaigns directed at higher income households, even if successful, will not result in proportionally greater visitor spending.

References

Church, D.E. (1969a) A proposed model for estimating and analyzing travel expenditures – Part I. *Journal of Travel Research* 8, 1–6.

Church, D.E. (1969b) A proposed model for estimating and analyzing travel expenditures – Part II. *Journal of Travel Research* 8, 11–15.

Davies, B. and Mangan, J. (1992) Family expenditures on hotel and holidays. *Annals of Tourism Research* 19, 691–699.

Di Matteo, L. and Di Matteo, R. (1993) The determinants of expenditures by Canadian visitors to the United States. *Journal of Travel Research* 31, 34–42.

Godbey, G. and Graefe, A. (1991) Repeat tourism, play, and monetary spending. *Annals of Tourism Research* 18, 213–225.

Lee, C.-K., Var, T. and Blaine, T.W. (1996) Determinants of inbound tourist expenditures. *Annals of Tourism Research* 23, 527–542.

Mack, J., Moncur, J. and Yonamine, D. (1977) Determinants of visitor expenditures and visitor lengths of stay: a cross-section analysis of us visitors to Hawaii. *Journal of Travel Research* 15, 5–8.

Qui, H. and Zhang, J. (1995) Determinants of tourist arrivals and expenditures in Canada. *Journal of Travel Research* 34, 43–49.

Travel Industry Association of America (1996a) *The Minority Traveler*. Washington, D.C.: TIAA.

Travel Industry Association of America (1996b) *Tourism Works for America – Report, December 1996*. Washington, D.C.: TIAA.

Exhibit 17.1: 1997 Virginia Beach Overnight Visitor Survey

The following questionnaire was used when surveying Virginia Beach overnight visitors on sand. However, respondents were not asked all questions when visitors were surveyed on the boardwalk or Atlantic Avenue. Specifically, questions 4, 8, 10, 12, 17, 20 and 30 were not asked when surveys were conducted on boardwalk, and questions 4–6, 8, 10, 12, 17, 20, 26–28 and 30 were not asked when surveys were conducted on Atlantic Avenue.

Two screening questions

a)   Are you visiting Virginia Beach or do you live here?

Visitor – **Continue**   Lives here – **Switch to Non-Overnight Visitor Survey**

b)   Have you been or will you be staying overnight in Virginia Beach for at least one night?

Yes – **Continue**   No – **Switch to Non-Overnight Visitor Survey**

---

1.   How many nights are you spending here on this trip?

__nights

2.   How long ago did you start planning this trip?

__months/weeks/days

3.   Would you describe this trip to Virginia Beach as:

(Read all choices – select one)

1- A weekend trip	5- A visit to see friends or family
2- A primary vacation	6- A convention
3- A secondary vacation	7- Or a business trip?
4- A stopover on a longer trip (**Ask Q4**)	

4.   **(If stopover)** In what city & state was your main destination?

City_____ State_____

5.   While you are here in Virginia Beach, will you go to:

(Read each and pause for response)

1-Yes 2-No	Busch Gardens
1-Yes 2-No	Colonial Williamsburg
1-Yes 2-No	The Waterside in Norfolk
1-Yes 2-No	Motorworld in VA Beach in Ocean Breeze Pk
1-Yes 2-No	Wild Water Rapids in VA Beach in Ocean Breeze Pk
1-Yes 2-No	A shopping mall
1-Yes 2-No	Go fishing
1-Yes 2-No	Play tennis
1-Yes 2-No	Play 'regular' golf, not mini
1-Yes 2-No	The VA Marine Science Museum in VB
1-Yes 2-No	The Old Coast Guard Station Museum in VB
1-Yes 2-No	Nauticus in Norfolk
1-Yes 2-No	The VA Air & Space Center in Hampton
1-Yes 2-No	The Jamestown Settlement
1-Yes 2-No	The Yorktown Victory Center
1-Yes 2-No	Water Country USA in Williamsburg

6-None of these (**Do not read**)

6.   How many total times, including this trip, will you visit or have you visited Virginia Beach this summer from May through September?

_____ times

7.   Is this the first time you have EVER visited Virginia Beach?

1-Yes 2-No (**Go to Q9**)

8.   What are the two main things that initially attracted you to vacation in Virginia Beach? (**Probe**)

1)
2)

9.   Have you seen or heard any advertising for VA Beach in the past 6 months?

1-Yes 2-No

10.   Did you, or any member of your party, write or call for information on places to stay or things to do before coming to Virginia Beach?

1-Yes 2-No

11.   Are you staying in:

(Read all choices)

1-A hotel or motel	4-In friends' or relatives' homes **(Go to Q14)**
2-In a cottage **(Go to Q13)**	5-In a condo or apartment **(Go to Q13)**, or
3-At a campground **(Go to Q13)**	X-Someplace else? **(Specify)** **(Go to Q13)**

12.   (If Hotel/Motel) Would you say the cost of your hotel or motel room was:

(Read choices)

1-Very reasonable	2-Reasonable	3-Expensive	4-Very expensive

13.   Did you make reservations for your lodging before coming to Virginia Beach this time?

1-Yes 2-No

14.   On this trip, how many people, including yourself, are in your party?

___people **(If 1, Go to Q16)**

15.   And, how many of them are children under age 18?

___children

16.   During your entire visit to Virginia Beach, how much do you think your whole party will spend in the City of Virginia Beach for:

$___.00 Lodging
$___.00 Restaurants, fast food and drinks
$___.00 Entertainment, arcades, night clubs, movies & sports
$___.00 All other expenses, including groceries, car expenses, clothes & everything you bought in Virginia Beach

17.   During your entire vacation, how much total money do you think your party will spend outside of the City of Virginia Beach?

$___.00 = total for gas, airfare, food, hotel, Busch Gardens, etc.

18.   As a place to vacation, what one thing do you like best about VA Beach? (**Probe**)

19.   And what one thing do you like least? (**Probe**)

20.   How would you rate the quality of the restaurants in Virginia Beach? Is the quality:

(**Read choices**)

1-Excellent	2-Good	3-Fair	4-Poor

21.   On a scale of 1–5, with 1 being not a good place to visit and 5 being a great place to visit, how would you rate Virginia Beach?

1	2	3	4	5
Not good				Great

22.   In your opinion, how clean is the Atlantic Avenue beach area of Virginia Beach?

Extremely clean	Quite clean	Slightly clean	Not at all clean

FRENCH TRANSLATION

1-Ext 2-Qui 3-Sli 4-Not at all	*clean*	propre
1-E 2-Q 3-S 4-N	*rundown*	délabrée
1-E 2-Q 3-S 4-N	*family-oriented*	orientation familiale
1-E 2-Q 3-S 4-N	*crowded*	bondée
1-E 2-Q 3-S 4-N	*expensive*	coûteuse
1-E 2-Q 3-S 4-N	*classy*	chic
1-E 2-Q 3-S 4-N	*visually appealing*	attrayante
1-E 2-Q 3-S 4-N	*safe*	sécuritaire
1-E 2-Q 3-S 4-N	*enjoyable*	agréable

23.　　On a scale of 1–5, with 1 being no traffic difficulties and 5 being many traffic difficulties, how would you rate the traffic situation in Virginia Beach?

1	2	3	4	5
No difficulties				Many difficulties

24.　　On a scale of 1–5, with 1 being no parking difficulties and 5 being many parking difficulties, how would you rate the parking in Virginia Beach?

1	2	3	4	5
No difficulties				Many difficulties

25.　　In deciding where to go on this trip, did you choose Virginia Beach over another resort area?

1-Yes 2-No **(Go to Q27)**

26.　　Where was the other place?

_____ **(Indicate place & state)**

27.　　Would you be likely to plan a vacation to Virginia Beach because of a particular City event or festival?

1-Yes 2-No **(Go to Q29)**

28.　　(For those who would plan a trip to Virginia Beach because of a particular City event or festival...) Would you plan to visit specifically to go to:

1-Yes 2-No　　A festival geared toward families and children?
1-Yes 2-No　　A music festival with songs from the 60s, 70s and 80s?
1-Yes 2-No　　A festival centered around a race, sports event or competition?
1-Yes 2-No　　An arts festival with exhibits of painting and sculpture and things for sale?

29.   Do you think you will be vacationing in Virginia Beach again within the next 2 years?

(Don't read choices)

1-Yes **(Go to Q31)** 2-No 3-Maybe **(Go to Q31)**

30.   Why will you not come back?

FOR STATISTICAL PURPOSES ONLY:

31.   What means of transportation did you use to travel to Virginia Beach?

(Don't read choices)

1-Auto/camper/truck/motorcycle	3-Airplane **(Go to Q33)**
2-Bus **(Go to Q33)**	X-Other **(Specify)** **(Go to Q33)**

32.   **(If Auto/Camper/Truck/Motorcycle)** What route into the city did you take? Did you cross the 17-mile long Chesapeake Bay Bridge Tunnel where you pay a toll of $10?

1-Yes 2-No

33.   Did you get into this area of Virginia Beach by traveling on the Route 44 expressway, or on Route 60 Shore Drive, or some other main road?

1-Expressway/44
2-Shore Dr/Rt. 60
Other:

34.   Are you: 1-Single   2-Married   3-Divorced or widowed?

35.   Have you ever been on Atlantic Avenue or the Boardwalk after 10:00 in the evening?

1-Yes 2-No

36.   And, what is your age?

___years

37.   And, your home zip code? (extra digit is for Canada)

38.   In what state is that? (**Don't abbreviate**)

(**If Canada...**)
Prov:

81-Alb	83-Manit	85-New Fou	87-Ont	89-Que
82-Br Col	84-New Br	86-Nova S	88-Pr Ed Is	90-Sask

39.   Is this a one or two income family?

1-One 2-Two 3-Three Other:

40.   Which category number describes the occupation of the head of your household? (**Hand card**)

Occupation categories:
01 - Clerical, Cashier, Waiter
02 - Owns a business or in a profession (doctor/dentist/lawyer/CPA/etc.)
03 - Administrative, Management, Executive
04 - Professional sales
05 - Craftsperson, Laborer, Trades
06 - Farmer
07 - Military
08 - Retired
09 - Temporarily unemployed
10 - Student
11 - Teacher, Nurse, MSW, Human services
12 - Police, Fire, Mail
13 - Homemaker
Other: (**Specify**)

41.   Lastly, what letter includes your total yearly family income (in US dollars)? (**Hand card**)

A B C D E F G H I REF/DK
1 2 3 4 5 6 7 8 9 0

Income categories:
1 - $24,999 or less
2 - $25,000 to $34,999
3 - $35,000 to $44,999

4 - $45,000 to $54,999
5 - $55,000 to $64,999
6 - $65,000 to $84,999
7 - $85,000 to $104,999
8 - $105,000 to $124,999
9 - $125,000 or more
0 - Refused to say

42.   Race:

1-White   2-African American   3-Asian   4-Other

43.   Gender:

1-Male 2-Female

DATE:

TIME:

STREET INTERSECTING WHERE YOU ARE:

Beach/sand

Boardwalk

Atlantic Avenue

Chapter eighteen
Elasticities of Tourism Demand for Selected European Countries

Mary Fish and Yi Xia
Department of Economics, University of Alabama, 1405 High Forest Drive, Tuscaloosa, AL 35406, USA

Introduction

International travel is affected by a host of factors, including prices, incomes, tastes and trends, political environments and sporting events. This project studies expenditure, own-price and cross-elasticities of US international tourists to the UK, France, Germany and Italy, from 1980 to 1995.

Most cross-elasticity studies have used single-equation models (White and Harrison, 1984) to test the impact of real price changes. The AIDS model developed in the 1980s, and later refined, is applied here. The model gives the market share of each of the four most popular destinations of US travellers in Europe, based on the prices in all four countries and total US tourist average expenditures. Since few studies have used this model, we add to its limited use and provide additional tourist data on cross-elasticities.

Wise national tourism policies and marketing plans of these four countries cannot ignore these elasticities. Travellers' sensitivity to comparative real price levels and preferences for packaging alternative sites ultimately affects travellers' decisions. Whether neighbouring nations and those some distance away are competitive or complementary sites significantly affects tourist travel and expenditure levels when their prices and exchange rates vary. Jarring price level changes can decimate the gross domestic product of complementary destinations or countries that are secondary sites for vacationers. Joint promotional projects among countries with complementary relationships are mutually rewarding for all locations involved. Marketing plans, advertising campaigns for air travel, hotels and resorts, and the links among hotel chains can use complementary relationships to their mutual benefit. When countries are substitute destinations, this information becomes equally valuable in determining the potential ramifications of price increases or political disruptions in competing destinations.

We begin with a summary of previous literature pertinent to this topic. Only research data from much earlier periods, and from different countries of origin and destination, are presently available. The AIDS model is briefly presented. Data used in the study are described. The tourist demand regression results are presented and summarized, followed by the expenditure and own-price elasticity results and cross-price elasticities. We conclude with a synopsis of the results.

Literature Background

Previous research on price effects on international tourism in Western Europe, particularly the four countries investigated, and the cross-elasticities of international tourism, provides the basis for this study. Expenditure and own-price elasticities among and between tourist sites vary. The level of elasticity, according to Crouch (1994), involves the question of the price of competing destinations. Relative prices among the countries of origin and potential destinations are important. Consumer price indexes (CPIs), used in this study, are most commonly used by researchers. While some researchers prefer using a designed travellers' price index, others argue that a general consumer index is equally satisfactory (Martin and Witt, 1987). O'Hagan and Harrison (1984) cite a difference between the CPIs and tourist prices of 2% or less. There is also the question of lag time in reaction to price changes. We do not use a lag factor since European prices are readily available in the USA. Crouch (Crouch *et al.*, 1992, 1994) suggests that tourists are aware of exchange rates, but they are not as sensitive to real price levels that also allow for the rate of inflation. He suggests these two factors, exchange and inflation rates, are equally important. Crouch (1994) also stipulates that price elasticities have increased over time because of package tours' swift response to price changes and competing advertising.

Considering the income and expenditure elasticity of countries of tourist origin, Syriopoulos and Sinclair (1993) found the UK and Sweden among the stronger income- and expenditure-elastic origin countries. While US travellers were found to have low expenditure and price elasticities, French travellers had the lowest price elasticity. Differences in elasticity coefficients demonstrate that vacation locations have differentiated their tourist sites, giving them semi-monopoly power in some cases (Syriopoulos, 1993).

Although destinations are generally considered substitutes when they have similar characteristics, the assumption of complementarity may be equally realistic. Tourists often include more than one country of destination in their travel plans. Yannopoulos (1987) found that neighbouring countries may foster a complementary relationship. He also states that the tendency to visit several countries may be strengthened when the transportation cost represents a large share of the total tourist expenditure. This is more aptly applied to long-distance travel than to closer destinations. White (1985) maintains that package tours usually include countries that are close geographically. According to Anastasopoulos (1991), neighbouring countries generally have the highest relative correlation coefficients and those among distant countries usually are very low or negative.

Anastasopoulos (1991) concludes that the elasticities of substitution between countries of origin and destination are generally insignificant for long-distance travellers. For the short-distance traveller, the elasticities of substitution are significant in the majority of cases. Destinations may show wide ranges of substitutability and complementarity. Elasticity effects may differ with unique or particular origins and destinations (Syriopoulos and Sinclair, 1993). Price changes affecting travel to dominant countries such as the UK, France and Germany may have a strong effect on smaller countries, while prices in smaller countries may not affect the numbers of travellers to major destinations such as the USA and Western European countries (White, 1985).

Using demand equations to estimate expenditures and price elasticities of the demand for travel, White (1985) found that the US and Western European travellers presented a variety of elasticities. Travellers showed high price substitutions between France and the UK as well as between France and Germany. Other Northern European destinations were complementary to France and substitutes for the UK (White, 1985). White's (1985) study also indicated that Greece and Portugal, Spain and Portugal, and Italy and Turkey were substitute destinations, whereas he found complementarities occurring between Greece and Italy, Spain and Turkey, Spain and Italy, and Portugal and Italy for most origins. Italian tourism competes with tourism in the north-east Mediterranean sub-region (Yannopoulos, 1987). Like most researchers on this topic, White (1985) recognizes the limitations of this type of study. For example, select countries may represent airline debarkation points, i.e. London and Paris for US international travellers. Thus airline prices among competitive destinations could affect several countries on the European continent.

Stone's (1954) seminal paper estimated a system of demand equations derived explicitly from consumer theory. From this research, several important models have been proposed, such as the Rotterdam model (Theil, 1965, 1976; Barten, 1969) and the translog model (Christensen *et al.*, 1970). The homogeneity and symmetry restrictions of demand theory have been extensively estimated in these latter models. Early research on the estimation of travel demand includes that by Gray (1970), Artus (1972), and Kwack (1972). Bond (1979) and Little (1980), among others, further develop their work. These studies largely relied on a single-equation estimation for individual countries which estimates changes in the levels of travellers' demand.

The single-equation methodology is extensively used in the early empirical demand analyses of tourism. However, the linear expenditure system was derived by algebraically imposing theoretical restrictions on a particular functional form. One of the most striking features of the AIDS model, from an econometric viewpoint, is that it is very close to being linear. So ordinary least squares can be used to estimate the unrestricted model. This arbitrary first-order approximation helps avoid the complicated non-linear estimation. In addition, tests for homogeneity and symmetry can be easily applied to the estimation. Syriopoulos and Sinclair

(1993) provide an excellent comparison between the single-equation models and the AIDS model used here.

The AIDS model is the extension of the Working–Leser model. In order to estimate Engel curves (income-consumption curves), Working (1943) first introduced a model used successfully by Leser (1963). The Working–Leser model relates budget shares linearly to the logarithm of total expenditures. The AIDS model has been used by O'Hagan and Harrison (1984), White (1985), and Syriopoulos and Sinclair (1993) to estimate international tourism shares.

The model

The Working-Leser model relates budget shares, w_i, linearly to the logarithm of total expenditure, x.

$$w_i = \alpha_i + \beta_i \log x \tag{1}$$

In order to use this model for time-series analysis, AIDS model choose the following function form to incorporate the effects of price.

$$\log e(u, p) = a(p) + ub(p) \tag{2}$$

Where $a(b)$ and $b(p)$ are functions of prices and can be choose

$$a(p) = a_0 + \sum_k a_k \log p_k + \frac{1}{2} \sum_k \sum_l \gamma_{kl}^* \log p_k \log p_l \tag{3}$$

$$b(p) = \beta_0 \prod p_k^{\beta k}$$

It is obvious $e(u,p)$ will be linear, homogeneous, concave function in p

$$\sum_{k=1}^n a_k = 1, \sum_k \gamma_{kl}^* = \sum_l \gamma_{kl}^* = \sum_{k=1}^n \beta_k = 0 \tag{4}$$

The $a(p)$ and $b(p)$ are substituted into equation (2), the budget shares w_i, can be derived from $\dfrac{\partial \log c(u, p)}{\partial \log p_i} = w_i$, which gives, after substitution for u, AIDS model.

$$w_i = \alpha_i + \sum_j \gamma_{ij} \log p_j + \beta_i \log \frac{x}{p} + \mu_i \tag{5}$$

Where P is priced index defined as

$$\log P = \alpha_0 + \sum \alpha_k \log p_k + \frac{1}{2} \sum_k \sum_l \gamma_{kl} \log p_k \log p_l \tag{6}$$

Where $\gamma_{ij} = \frac{1}{2}(\gamma_{ij}^* + \gamma_{ji}^*) = \gamma_{ji}$

In this model, w_i is the percentage share of country i in US tourist expenditure in the four destinations, P_i is the price facing US tourists in country i, x is the per US tourist expenditure in the countries included, and n indicates the number of countries.

Because of the severity of the multicollinearity, it is convenient to replace the P with P^*.

Whe $P^* = \prod_{i=1}^{n} p_i^{w_i}$ so the P^* is the geometric mean of the individual prices.

Estimation method

Because the price variable differs across equations and the disturbance may well be correlated across equations, estimation can use Zellners' generalized least squares method for seemingly unrelated regression (SUR).

Price elasticities

In the AIDS model, the expenditure elasticities ε_i can be calculated from

$$\varepsilon_i = \frac{\beta_i}{w_i} + 1$$

The uncompensated own price elasticities ε_{ii} are given by

$$\varepsilon_{ii} \left(\frac{\gamma_{ii}}{w_i} \right) - b_i - 1$$

The uncompensated cross-price elasticities ε_{ij} are given by

$$\varepsilon_{ij} = \left(\frac{\gamma_{ij}}{w_i} \right) - b_i \left(\frac{w_j}{w_i} \right)$$

The compensated own-price elasticities ε_{ii}^{*} and cross-elasticities ε_{ij}^{*}, are

$$\varepsilon_{ii}^{*} = \varepsilon_{ii} + w_i n_i = \left(\frac{\gamma_{ii}}{w_i} \right) + w_i - 1$$

$$\varepsilon_{ij}^{*} = \varepsilon_{ij} + w_j n_i = \left(\frac{\gamma_{ij}}{w_i} \right) + w_j$$

Data Analysis

The decision-making process followed by international travellers is frequently divided into three steps. Firstly, the decision to spend money, often a given amount, on a trip for business or pleasure or a combination of both. Although the price, aggregate tourism expenditure, and price/expenditure elasticities are the key factors in our AIDS model, some other dummy variables and time trends can also be used to explain the travel demand. However, it was observed that the inclusion of these variables failed to improve the results (Syriopoulos and Sinclair, 1993), and we did not incorporate these elements into our model. The second step is to make the decision as to the region of the globe to visit, and the third, the decision regarding the specific location of the trip or solidification of travel plans. Choices that are heavily based on price differentials among destinations can be estimated. At this point, economists can begin dealing with data that are available on expenditures and own-price and cross-elasticities.

The regression results of this study are based on US annual data for select sites for 1980–1995. They represent the most popular European countries for US visitors. The data for tourism expenditures in UK, Germany, France and Italy are obtained from the appropriate issues of the *Survey of Current Business*. While it is difficult to exclude the possibility of errors in the sampling procedures used to collect these data, Gray (1966) suggests that there is no consistent bias in these samples. We adjust these expenditures by the relevant CPIs that are demonstrated to be good proxies for tourism prices. *International Financial Statistics* provide the data for the CPIs and exchange rates.

Gronau (1970) suggests that estimations of the cost of international transportation pose considerable data problems. Crouch (1994) mentions that the seasonal variations among fares and the alternative types of transportation, as well as class of travel, present data handicaps. This study, as with most work of this type, does not include international transportation costs. In addition, although business and vacation travellers have different objectives, they are not separated in this study. The recent work by Dwyer et al. (1998) represents a breakthrough by differentiating journey purpose.

The estimation results consist of two parts. Firstly, since the independent variables are identical in all equations for each European tourist country, ordinary least squares are used to estimate the unrestricted system of equations. Secondly, the AIDS model consists of writing a set of single equation as one linear equation system. If we allow contemporaneous correlation between the error terms across equations, so that the ith error term in the ith equation is correlated with the ith error term is the jth equation, the variance–covariance matrix of xxx will not be diagonal. When we impose all of the necessary constraints across the equations, generally large gains in efficiency are observed with the Zellner estimator (Zellner, 1962). The symmetry-restricted system of equations was estimated by a two-step (iterative) feasible general least-squares procedure where the disturbance covariance matrix is singular, and then the Zellner technique where the restricted general least-squares estimator is allowed to iterate to convergence. As for autocorrelation, we adopt the same correlation coefficient for all equations. In the estimations, we account for a number of restrictions, namely homogeneity of degree one and cross-equation symmetry. Through imposing the homogeneity restriction on the unrestricted model and re-estimating the system, the homogeneity condition can be tested, using the F-test.

The US tourist demand regression results are summarized in Table 18.1. The US travel expenditures in each of the destinations varied between 22 and 28% of the total US tourist spending in the four destinations. The UK and France both received about 28%, while Germany and Italy were lower at 22 to 23%. In all cases the F-test, determining the significance of the regression equation for individual countries, was significant at the 5% level or less. The t-test, a comparison of the destination means, was also significant at the 5% level or less in all cases. The Durbin–Watson tests were calculated to determine whether the least-square residuals are autocorrelated.

Expenditure elasticities

The restricted expenditure elasticities, shown in Table 18.2, indicate that the tourism products of the four countries present unique features, for example, the expenditure elasticity for US tourists to Germany and Italy is estimated to be 1.882 and 1.237, and the expenditure elasticity for the UK and France is 0.846 and 0.249. Thus, should total US travel expenditures increase, a journey to Germany and Italy would get a larger share of the expenditure than the UK and France. So of these destinations, Germany and Italy are luxury sites. The UK's and France's expenditure elasticities are normal but do not increase proportionately. So the share of the travel expenditures in the latter group of destinations are not expected to increase as total expenditures increase. These results differ from those of White (1985). However, none of the group can be classified as an inferior location because all expenditure elasticities are positive.

M. Fish and Y. Xia

Table 18.1 US tourist demand regression result

Destination (j)	Intercept α_j	β_j	Price coefficient				Adjusted R^2	Expenditure mean	F-test	Durbin–Watson test
			γ_{i1}	γ_{i2}	γ_{i3}	γ_{i4}				
UK (1j)	−0.345	−0.042	0.208	0.0002	0.392	−0.294	0.781	0.2753	12.397	1.63
t-test	(−1.57)	(−0.90)	(0.86)	(0.02)	(1.80)	(−2.62)				
France (2j)	−0.497	−0.206	0.151	−0.136	0.211	−0.018	0.751	0.2750	10.661	2.45
t-test	(−1.16)	(−2.26)	0.32	(−1.18)	0.50	0.08				
Germany (3j)	0.568	0.195	−0.279	0.130	0.193	−0.034	0.713	0.2208	8.949	2.16
t-test	1.49	2.39	(−0.66)	1.26	(0.51)	(−0.17)				
Italy (4j)	1.274	0.054	−0.081	0.005	−0.796	−0.347	0.704	0.2289	8.596	1.78
t-test	3.38	0.67	(−0.20)	0.05	(−2.13)	1.80				

All *t*-tests are significant at 5% or less.
All *F*-tests are significant at 5% or less.
R^2, goodness of fit, shows little variation.
DW statistics are acceptable.

Table 18.2 US expenditure and price elasticity

Country	Restricted expenditure elasticity	Own price	
		Uncompensated	Compensated
UK	0.846	−0.202	−0.469
France	0.249	−1.289	−1.220
Germany	1.882	−0.322	−0.407
Italy	1.237	−2.569	−0.286

Own-price elasticities

The tourists' reactions to effective price changes, or own-price elasticities, vary for given destinations as depicted in Table 18.2. The uncompensated and compensated effective own-price elasticities from the constrained models, as expected, are negative in all cases No site appears to carry the élitest appeal that a positive elasticity would indicate. We concentrate on the results of the uncompensated data because, as indicated by Syriopoulos and Sinclair (1993), the data are more relevant for policy considerations as they pertain to changes in total US tourist expenditures. For US travellers the uncompensated own-price elasticity for Italy is the most elastic (−2.569), followed by France (−1.289). An increase in travel to Italy and France would be deterred by an increase in their prices. Decisions to travel to Germany and the UK appear to show little sensitivity to real price levels. The UK has an uncompensated price elasticity of −0.202 and Germany of −0.322. Several implications are feasible. This may indicate that the UK and Germany have differentiated their travel sites for Americans. However, these low coefficients may be related to the UK and Germany being primary sites, with France and Italy being secondary destinations

The compensated own-price elasticities assume no change in real tourist expenditures. Thus these coefficients indicate the potential change in travellers' choices owing to price changes in each of the four countries. The compensated elasticities are somewhat comparable to the uncompensated figures. However, a striking difference is found in Italy's own-price coefficient which drops to −0.286. A possible explanation is that more travellers are now regarding the site as a potential primary or secondary destination provided the price is right.

Cross-elasticities

Table 18.3 indicates the competition and complementarity among tourist destinations. The uncompensated cross-price and compensated elasticities appear to be relatively comparable, with one or the other figure being somewhat higher or lower. Only the Italian data show three sign reversals. A positive coefficient indicates the presence of competition and a negative sign a complementary relationship between markets. The country cross-price elasticities vary from a complementary elasticity between Germany and Italy of −3.5300, to a competitive coefficient of 1.4591 between Germany and the UK.

Table 18.3 US destination cross-price elasticity

Destination	UK		France		Germany		Italy	
	Uncomp.	Comp.	Uncomp.	Comp.	Uncomp.	Comp.	Uncomp.	Comp.
UK			0.0488	0.2814	1.04591	1.6458	-1.0696	0.8407
France	0.7572	0.8258			0.9329	0.9879	0.1055	0.1626
Germany	-1.5052	-0.9870	0.3445	0.8620	-3.5300	-3.2570	-0.3557	0.0761
Italy	-0.4184	-0.0779	-0.0439	0.2962				

Using the uncompensated cross-price elasticity as the basis of analysis again because it allows for a growth in expenditures, several patterns are suggested. Travellers from the US may view the UK, Germany and Italy as complementary destinations, but France appears to be a substitute for travel to the UK. US travellers to France look at the UK as a slightly competitive destination, and Germany more so. Visits to the UK and France are substituted by US travellers when prices increase in Germany. The impact on the UK, however, is somewhat greater than on France. Italy is a complementary market for travellers to Germany with a strong cross-elasticity of −3.5300. Italy appears to hold a somewhat complementary relationship with Germany and the UK. This suggests that US travellers to Italy increase as visitors to the UK and to some extent Germany increase.

Again the uncompensated and compensated cross-price elasticities are relatively similar, with the presence of competition or complementarity remaining the same. The exception is Italy. With the compensated elasticities, France's slight complementarity slips to a low degree of competition with Italy; and Italy's complementary relationship with the UK becomes competitive, as does Germany's, but to a lesser degree. It appears that Italy is re-aligning its travel position among European destinations, firstly, by distinguishing itself as a site that is highly sensitive to its pricing structure (its choice as a destination is the most sensitive of the four sites), and secondly, as Italy in the compensated model was competitive with the UK, but shifts to a complementary relationship. The change in coefficient type and size is clearly recognizable. Two processes could be occurring. Italy now may be packaged with trips to Germany and the UK. This also is substantiated by Italy's highly sensitive uncompensated own-price as well as its relatively sensitive expenditure elasticity for increase travel from the US. Another explanation is that as US visitors make return trips to Europe, they expand their choices to new sites. The visitors' profiles change as their travel experiences expand, and their past choices may not be repeated.

Figure 18.1 gives an interesting picture of the symmetry between the cross-elasticities of the four countries studied. Although the expenditures and own-price coefficients differ in strength, the type of market, except in two cases, is similar among the four destinations. Using the uncompensated coefficients, the UK and Italy have complementary relationships with each other, as do Italy and Germany. The UK and France, and Germany and France, are competitors. Only with the UK and Germany, and France and Italy, is the relationship asymmetrical. The UK complements Germany, but Germany is a competitive destination for the UK. Travel to France complements Italy, but the latter competes with France. This suggests that if US visitors to the UK increase, there is a good chance that visitors to Germany will increase, but if visitors to Germany increase, the UK may not experience an increase in travellers. An increase in visitors to France may also increase visitors to Italy, but if the initial destination increase is Italy, France's visitors probably will not increase.

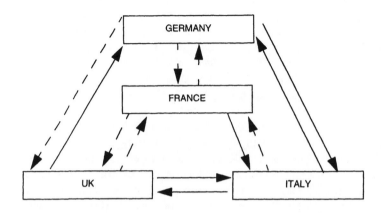

Figure 18.1 Cross-elasticities. Dashed arrows, competitive relation; straight arrows, complementary relation.

General Comments

Cross-elasticities have been determined in the past using a variety of statistical and econometric methods. The locations and times of travel have varied. Few data are available for comparison purposes. This study adds to the database available on cross-elasticities among selected Western European countries and the UK for US travellers. We use a relatively well established econometric model, AIDS. Its contributions and limitations compared to the single-equation approaches are well documented in the literature.

A review of our own-price elasticities and cross-price elasticities with the research of Syriopoulos and Sinclair (1993), White (1985), and O'Hagan and Harrison (1984) indicates that our estimates are relatively comparable in most cases. The restricted expenditure elasticities are normal for the UK and France, but suggest that Germany and Italy may be luxury sites. The uncompensated and compensated own-price elasticities are relatively low, with the exception of Italy's high uncompensated elasticity. Only Italy appears to have changed its relative position over the years. Italy indicates an increasing sensitivity to price as well as development of an inclusive role in the US tourist markets in Europe, either due to the expansion of tourists' outlooks and/or its inclusion in tour packages.

The cross-elasticities suggest that the US travellers to the UK regard Italy as a complementary destination. France and Germany compete, as do the UK and France. These results are similar to White's (1985) conclusions. The UK complements Germany, but the relationship is asymmetrical as it is between France and

Italy: the former is complementary and the latter is competitive. Our study substantiates the suggestions of Syriopoulos (1993) and Yann (1991), that elasticities vary among origins and destinations, and cross-elasticities among locations may be asymmetrical.

References

Anastasopoulos, P. (1984) Interdependencies in international travel: the role of relative prices, a case study of the Mediterranean region. Dissertation, Graduate Faculty of Political and Social Science of the New School for Social Research.

Anastasopoulos, P. (1991) Demand for travel. *Annals of Tourism Research* 18, 663–665.

Artus, J.R. (1972) An econometric analysis of international travel. *IMF Staff Papers* 19, 579–613.

Barten, A.P. (1969) Maximum likelihood estimation of a complete system of demand equations. *European Economic Review* Fall, 7–73.

Bond, M.E. (1979) The world trade model: invisibles. *IMF Staff Papers* 26, 257–333.

Christensen, L., Jorgenson, D. and Lau, L. (1970) Transcendental logarithmic utility functions. *American Economic Review* 65, 367–383.

Crouch, G.I. (1994) The study of international tourism demand: a review of findings. *Journal of Travel Research* 33, 12–23.

Crouch, G.I., Schultz, L. and Valerio, P. (1992) Marketing international tourism to Australia: a regression analysis. *Tourism Management* 13, 196–208.

Deaton, A. and Muellbauer, J. (1980) An almost ideal demand system. *American Economic Review* 70, 312–326.

Dwyer, L., Forsyth, P. and Rao, P. (1998) Tourism price competitiveness and journey purpose. Paper presented at the 29th Annual TTRA Conference, Forth Worth, Texas.

Gray, H.P. (1966) The demand for international travel by the United States and Canada. *International Economic Review* 7, 83–92.

Gray, H.P. (1970) *International Travel – International Trade*. Heath: Lexington.

Gronau, R. (1970) *The Value of Time Passenger Transportation: The Demand for Air Travel*. New York: National Bureau of Economic Research.

International Financial Statistics (selected issues). International Monetary Fund.

Jorgenson, D. and Lau, L. (1975) The structure of consumer preference. *Annals of Economic Sociological Measurement* 4, 49–101.

Kwack, S. (1972) Effects of income and prices on travel spending abroad. *International Economic Review* 13, 245–256.

Leser, C.E.V. (1963) Forms of Engel functions. *Econometrica* 31, 694–703.

Little, J.S. (1980) International travel in the US balance of payments. *New England Economic Review* May, 42–45.

Martin, C.A. and Witt, S.F. (1987) Tourism demand forecasting models: choice of appropriate variable to represent tourists' cost of living. *Tourism Management* 8, 233–246.

O'Hagan, J.W. and Harrison, M.J. (1984) Market shares of US tourist expenditure in Europe: an econometric analysis. *Applied Economics* 6, 919–931.

Rosensweig, J.A. (1988) Elasticities of substitution in Caribbean tourism. *Journal of Development Economics* 29, 89–100.

Smeral, E. (1988) Tourism demand economic theory and econometrics: an integrated approach. *Journal of Trade Research* 16, 38–43.

Stone, J.R.N. (1954) Linear expenditure systems and demand analysis: an application to the pattern of British demand. *Economic Journal* 64, 511–527.

Survey of Current Business (selected issues). US Department of Commerce.

Syriopoulos, T.C. and Sinclair, M.T. (1993) An econometric study of tourism demand: the AIDS model of US and European tourism in Mediterranean countries. *Applied Economics* 25, 1541–1552.

Theil, H. (1965) The information approach to demand analysis. *Econometrica* 33, 67–87.

Theil, H. (1976) *Theory and Measurement of Consumer Demand*, Vols 1 and 2. Amsterdam: North-Holland.

Waggle, D. and Fish, M. (1998) International tourism cross elasticities: the case of Hong Kong, the People's Republic of China and the Republic of China. *Annals of Tourism Research* (in press).

White, K.J. (1985) An international travel demand model: US travel to Western Europe. *Annals of Tourism Research* 12, 529–545.

Working, H. (1943) Statistical laws of family expenditure. *Journal of the American Statistical Association* 38, 43–56.

Yannopoulos, G.N. (1987) Intra-regional shifts in tourism growth in the Mediterranean area. *Travel and Tourism Analyst* November, 15–24.

Zellner, A. (1962) An efficient method of estimating seemingly unrelated regressions and tests for aggregation bias. *Journal of the American Statistical Association* 57, 348–368.

Chapter nineteen
The Pacific Heritage Tourism Interpretation 'Sham'

Gary Russell and Craig Walters
*School of Hotel and Restaurant Studies, Auckland Institute of Technology,
Private Bag 92006, Auckland 1020, New Zealand*

Introduction

The Pacific cultures are rich in their association with the environment through the landscape which is interwoven within their spiritual beliefs. The cultural lifestyle of the Pacific people is closely integrated within the heritage tourism resources of the region they live. Cultural patterns include customs, ceremonies, lifestyles and religious beliefs and practices, which are associated with the dependence they have upon the environment. The interface between the economic value of heritage resources and the Pacific cultural lifestyle places significant pressure on the social problems which can manifest when external government policies impact on traditional ways of Pacific communities.

The context of the decision-making process of the indigenous people in a community and the conflicting value structure between different ethnic groups makes this research important in terms of what constitutes sustainable management of an indigenous heritage tourism resource with strong interwoven cultural values. Many Pacific cultural customs have a strong spiritual significance for the people of the Pacific, but these are often at odds with western conservation and natural resource management policies. Western sustainable management practices can conflict with indigenous sustainable cultural practices. For example, customary harvesting of birds such as the native wood pigeon is a traditional event celebrated by some Maori; however; like many of New Zealand's native flora and fauna, the wood pigeon is a protected species on the brink of declining towards endangered species status. Many government-led conservation policies, backed by scientific evidence, attempt to override traditional systems followed by Pacific cultures.

Pacific indigenous conservation systems rely on traditional rights, tribal boundary laws, self-regulation, consensus, and spiritual concepts such as *rahui* and *tapu*. There is little provision within the current governing bodies to recognize these cultural concepts within the western conservation systems, and what there is may appear to be tokenistic in nature. The need is for more indigenous representation on authority bodies for greater cultural input and consultation throughout the decision-making policy process. However, this will still not allow for the provision of a full consensus approach. Western methods of heritage resource development tend towards the scientific approach. This model is not particularly valued in the cultural context of indigenous Pacific peoples. Government authorities formalize findings in legal policy where the structure of decision-making results in decisions being won or lost. Such procedures best suit an adversary method of decision-making, as in a court of law, when it comes to policy planning of heritage resources. The present structure looks at having separate sets of solutions based on a cultural approach; the need, however, is for a common problem to be addressed in partnership. This involves mutual respect and an allowance for control and ownership over resources (*Rangatiratanga*), which means that local people can make decisions on what they know best. The end result works toward an outcome or solution that is owned collectively. The need is for policy setting to be articulated in a manner which uses localized indigenous cultural processes rather than adopted western laws and values from a national governing framework. This paper examines two specific situations of heritage tourism resource use involving Pacific indigenous peoples: the New Zealand Maori, and the Fijian people of West Viti Levu. The dominance of tourism within Fiji's economy has led to the indigenous community accepting many of the western cultural values and norms within the management and development of their heritage resource. The Maori have retained a cultural link to traditional lifestyle, more by accident than design, as only in recent times has tourism started to make a significant impact over the heritage resources of the Maori.

A Maori case study for sustainable values in heritage tourism

Maori society consists of *iwi*, *whanau* and *hapu*, who view the natural environment (air, land and sea) as sacred ancestors or *Atua*, as well as simply providing for their economic well-being. In contrast, western society sees natural resources as commodities to which monetary value is assigned.

The Treaty of Waitangi recognizes Maori as the *Tangata whenua* and allows for and encourages biculturalism within government structures. In specific terms with respect to the Maori sociocultural and economic circumstances, the Treaty of Waitangi provides a legislative framework for resolving the injustices brought about by British colonialization involving issues of land ownership and retrieval, compensation for losses, and maintenance of resources. The process of reconciliation is being managed through the Waitangi Tribunal which is responsible for dispute settlement and resolution of past grievances by accounting for the interests and values of the *Tangata whenua* – the Maori people. The Maori claims to heritage resource ownership are wide-ranging and complicated by European lease systems, and will involve a number of solutions. The claims being resolved today have resulted in the return of tribal land with financial compensation for loss of interest. This has opened up the opportunity for Maori-owned tourism enterprise which can provide a unique cultural experience for tourists. According to the late Sir James Henare

> 'My own thoughts regarding the Treaty of Waitangi is that it is a sacred treasure. It was made so when the *Rangatira* signed it with a representation of their personal *moko*...they were *tohunga* because they were *kaitiaki*' (Henare, 1987, p.155).

The Treaty of Waitangi was a covenant in which the promises and conditions acquired a sacred trust of respect. To the Maori the signing of the Treaty was an act of symbolic spiritual and temporal leadership. Maori society had no written law so the spoken word was frequently entwined with Maori spirituality. The transformation from an oral society to a literate society within the short span of a century upset many of the values on which the society had relied. The general introduction of English law displaced the administration of Maori customary law by the traditional *iwi* authorities. This interpretation of English law into Maori life could hardly be expected to be effective. However, *Aotearoa* society still encompasses English legal procedural systems as part of the birthright of New Zealanders, and has suspended the customary law of the *iwi* which reflects Maori cultural norms. Over the past 160-odd years this has developed into varying degrees of conflict and criticism of the present legislative process. Moana Jackson has stated that '...the present system is not just inadequate for Maori, in many instances it is also biased against them.' (Jackson, 1988, p. 106).

Maori law was created by the wisdom, values and beliefs of past generations which bounded the people to their *tupuna* who created existence. The importance of *whakapapa* supports the cultural belief which values the needs of the *whanau* or community above those of the individual, leading to many decision-making areas being part of a group process. A call is made for a Maori justice system enabling the establishment of policies congruent with the customs and norms of Maori society. Indigenous New Zealanders have a legitimate right to preserve and practise their culture, and it is therefore implicit that Maori values and beliefs must be incorporated within the current policy-planning process, a change most important within the context of heritage resources being developed for tourism.

The Maori heritage product

The Maori cultural dimension is one of the most distinctive aspects of *Aotearoa*. The success of the Te Maori exhibition overseas shows the impact Maori culture can have in building an image of *Aotearoa* internationally. Tourists may have little conception of Maori culture, but they do want to find out more. The Auckland museum singing and dance presentation is very popular with visitors and indicates what can be achieved to bring Maori culture to tourists within a heritage complex. However, direct Maori participation in tourism has been mostly in the form of background entertainment for a European-owned tourism operation aimed at the mass tourism market. The response by Maori to active participation has been to run *marae*-based visits and overnight stays. This has brought charges of commoditization of the culture and corruption of Maori values with respect to heritage, as it differs from the European policy. The concept of property ownership in Maori society is based around extended family units (*hapu*) with specific property rights over specific boundaries. The ability to work effectively within these *hapu* and *iwi* structures is essential to any project development involving Maori control and ownership.

The problem over time has been the unwillingness of the crown to recognize Maori sovereignty over heritage resources. Statutory rights and heritage protection orders have been placed on many heritage resources, but Maori re-assertion of their sovereign rights has seen a resurgence in opposition to crown policy. Maori scepticism concerning European methods and laws is based on historical mistakes due to ignorance by Europeans of Maori spiritual links. As past grievances continue, much of *Aotearoa*'s land resources will be returned to the Maori to provide opportunities for the development of potentially valuable heritage tourism resources. In doing so, traditional concepts involving concepts of *kawa* and *tikanga* of the *Tangata whenua* will be observed. Maori conflict management is part of the ceremonial art form which is valued as a process of public scrutiny. The Waitangi Tribunal has been overturning past decisions which demonstrated a colonized view of history. The difficulty that the Maori face is in ridding themselves of a stereotypical decision-making process. Decision-making relating to heritage resources should be based on the recognition of Maori ownership of the resource and Maori participation at all stages of the policy, planning and information delivery processes. To do otherwise will misrepresent the product and undermine the culture. *Iwi* interpretation and guidance is the best way to yield the most beneficial results for the future developers of heritage resources as tourism attractions. This will open up the opportunity to identify what constitutes specifically Maori cultural tourism in relation to the tourism industry's definition of heritage tourism.

Maori Research Study

Methodology

This research was an exploratory study using in-depth personal interviews with open-ended questions and response categories using the 'utiles' ranking frame. A second follow-up study using a mail survey questionnaire was conducted with heritage tourism operators selected randomly. This approach was considered the most appropriate given the sensitive nature of the topic and in the context of the information required, which involved resolving conflicting issues in some situations. Of the respondents, 60% of tourism operators were involved in heritage tourism, but only 50% of that group actively promoted the tourist product as being heritage tourism.

Findings

A literature review of Maori tourism found that only in very recent years has research specifically related to Maori culture and heritage tourism been undertaken and published. Many of these were exploratory research papers, and the importance of Maori customs within the wider frame of the heritage tourism concept is only today being given significant acknowledgement. In fact, the understanding of the political process to which indigenous cultures have been subjected has only recently been recognized as having a touristic implication (Ryan, 1997, p. 258). Chris Ryan goes on to state that to understand the relationship between Maori and tourism requires a contextual understanding of the nature of Maori norms, and the political and social framework within which they operate, as well as simply describing the nature of Maori involvement in tourism at a business level. Hall (1996) and Zeppel (1997) have also researched the field of Maori and tourism, and their interaction. Today, with the focus on tourism as a job and a business opportunity for Maori, and with the settlement of many claims, funds are now available for Maori to exploit opportunities within the cultural and heritage tourism markets. Already many successful Maori-owned and -controlled enterprises are operating in New Zealand because of the settlement of Treaty of Waitangi claims. Barber (1993) noted that more and more Maori business was focusing on tourism and in fact was moving into the service sector as a business opportunity. In contrast, Deloitte Ross Tohmatsu's (1991) study of small tourism operators actually classified Maori cultural tourism in the 'other attraction' category, although there were eight specific attraction fields. This indicates the lack of significance accorded to Maori-developed heritage tourism by the New Zealand tourism industry sector as recently as the early 1990s.

The heritage tourism resource survey was used to assess the profile of Maori cultural tourism within the tourism industry. No distinction was found by operators between the terms cultural and heritage tourism, with operators using them interchangeably in their conceptualizing of a tourism product. The results were conflicting in terms of the interpretation of Maori heritage tourism has by both tourism industry operators and tourists.

A broad understanding of cultural and heritage tourism was introduced in the marketing strategy of the tourism industry, but it did not represent an important component within tour activity even though it was listed among promotional material. There was an element of being seen to be culturally proactive within the community about Maori cultural tourism, but effective strategies were not implemented. This supports the heritage tourism definition survey finding that although Maori cultural tourism is acknowledged by the industry in general, it is not the main component when it comes to tour activities. Tour operators focus on the entertainment aspects of the Maori culture as interpreted in the dancing and singing which present a stereotypical romanticizing of Maori culture. What is not offered is the background and stories which personify the natural features of the landscape, and which are deeply rooted in Maori spirituality and patently illustrated in the symbolic carvings of a traditional *wharenui* or meeting house. This relationship to the environment is a very potent spiritual force embodied in many *taonga*, and economic exploitation of such a heritage resource requires immense *mana* from those involved in the future decision-making process.

In order of priority, the tourism operators who promote heritage tourism used the brochure format as the main form of advertising, with personal selling the second most important element of marketing the product. Print media through selected newspapers and magazines provide the other form of communication of the heritage tourism product. *Marae*-based activities were the most promoted interest, followed by visits to heritage museums and tours of specific heritage land features. Concerts also had a place within the promoted activities. Highlighting the reliance on joint venture operations, 86% of the tourism operators promoted the tourist activities cooperatively with the heritage resource-owner/guardian.

Promotional efforts by tourism operators were directed to the key international markets of Australia, USA, Hong Kong, Germany and Japan, in order of importance. This matched the proportion of visitor statistics for that year; however, the USA and Hong Kong were disproportionate to the visitor rankings order, with the USA coming fourth and Hong Kong seventh when it came to visitor numbers. The tourism operators stated that sites associated with heritage tourism were first of what tourists wanted to visit, buildings were second, and heritage/cultural performances were third.

A cross-tabulation of the findings assisted in providing a guide to the setting of open-ended interview questions. Tourism operators agreed that heritage tourism was a growth area, however the Maori cultural element was not seen as an important factor in promoting this development of heritage tourism. The taking of ownership by Maori of their heritage resources was interpreted as a negative impact on the heritage tourist industry by the tourism operators. Only 25% of travel agents involved themselves in promoting heritage tourism, while 80% of tour operators stated that visitors want a heritage tourism experience. Only 50% of the secondary tourism attraction-providers promoted heritage tourism from a Maori cultural perspective, although 70% of them were involved in heritage tourism directly related to Maori activities.

Several barriers were identified that were seen to pose a threat to continued development of the heritage tourism resource. These were Maori rights over heritage resources which come under Treaty of Waitangi claims, and tour operator reluctance in promoting heritage sites and currently operating or using activities and resources which had any associated claims pending. The majority of tourism operators (80%) promote Maori heritage tourism as part of a bigger package; however, it is not seen as a critical element in their package and operators are apt to alter the package to suit the circumstances. Almost two-thirds of the tour operators (60%) saw future problems in maintaining Maori heritage tourism within their package as more Maori-owned enterprises took control of their heritage resources. Maori heritage tourism activity was presented from a western perspective, and only offered as a token experience of visual display, not as an interpretative experience. The settling of Treaty of Waitangi claims has seen innovative Maori-controlled schemes offering genuine *marae* visits and stays where aspects of both traditional and contemporary Maori culture are lived by the visitors. This is a unique experience, and through having total control of the planning process Maori have been able to use their heritage resources in a manner consistent with their ideals of a Maori heritage tourism development.

Future predictions

As Maori take control of resources that have the potential to yield substantial economic returns, tourism is seen as a valid opportunity to enable controlled and sustainable use of those resources. This has seen steady growth in the number of Maori tourism operators within the industry. This taking of proprietorship of heritage resources by Maori has slowly led to a movement away from the entertainment value of Maori culture towards a more participative role for visitors involved in aspects of Maori etiquette as a cultural tourism experience. This interpretative experience has meant a more substantive development, as such authenticity is more accepted and valued by the Maori community, thus creating a momentum for the development of a sustainable heritage tourism. This form of economic independence through sustainable tourism is more readily endorsed by the Maori community and augers well for the future utilization and development of Maori heritage resources for tourism purposes.

The essential factor in retaining a sustainable Maori cultural experience is to ensure that the integrity of the cultural tourism product is maintained. This entails a decision-making process based on Maori values so that a sustainable, realistic cultural experience is delivered within a commercially viable context of economic return and community benefit. The real test for a sustainable Maori heritage tourism industry will be in ensuring there is no exclusion or hostility amongst those who have a stake in the heritage tourism resource development. The Aotearoa Maori Tourism Federation says that it wants to ensure that ownership, and thus control, of Maori heritage tourism is retained by the people, and that integrity is kept through the development of standards. Their task force report on Maori tourism states that Maori tourism development must support the revival and maintenance of the culture and the society, and ensure that the definition and use of Maori culture in the tourism industry is firmly placed in responsible Maori hands (Maori Tourism Task Force Report, 1987). In essence, when a visitor asks a question about Maori culture and history, it must be a Maori who answers. The Maori people must be part of the plan so as to get part of the action. Maori must decide how much of their culture is for sale and which protocols and rituals should remain sacred. In summary, Hall (1996), Zeppel (1997) agree that policies and strategies relating to Maori art and culture will be sustainable only if they recognize the ownership of the product and their involvement in the policy-planning process.

Fijian Case Study

This research study was undertaken for the Fiji Visitor Bureau (FVB) for the west coast region on the main island of Viti Levu. Fiji has been the most important tourist destination in the South Pacific for over 30 years, and tourism was Fiji's number one economic earner of foreign exchange for that period. The survey sought to assess what importance the indigenous Fijian people place on tourism in terms of its economic, cultural and social impact on their community life. It attempted to determine the role Fijians see for themselves in the development of their own heritage tourism resources. Fiji is composed of three distinctive cultural societies: western Fijians of Melanesian extraction; eastern Fijians of Polynesian origin; and Fijian Indians who were imported as indentured labour to work the sugarcane fields at the turn of the century. As an ex-British colony, British law, values, political institutions and religion dominate many facets of Fijian lifestyle.

There are strong differing views and opinions among the ethnic groups of Fiji, so in any study it is important to distinguish between the different cultural respondents. This survey took place in the western coastal region of Viti Levu which is the main tourism destination, and focused on the indigenous Melanesian Fijians, the original proprietors of the land. Due to the patriarchal nature of Melanesian Fijian society, only a few women were prepared to be interviewed. All but one of the 65 respondents agreed that the local community benefited from tourism. All the respondents were directly employed in the tourism industry. The benefits were perceived to be not only economic, but also from the new skills learnt, qualifications gained, and foreign awareness as they met people from all over the world. Respondents attributed improvements in the infrastructure of roads, electricity, water and waste disposal services to a direct result of tourism. A majority felt that tourism maintained the strength and enthusiasm of the Fijian cultural traditions and ceremonies; however, it was recognized that much of this was in an entertainment context. The negative aspect most commented on was the influence of tourists' behaviour on the young Fijian people, shown in a lack of respect for Fijian values and protocol. The Fijians felt the young were becoming too westernized in their outlook and lifestyle, and that many traditions would be lost. Local Fijian attitudes to the impact of tourism on the environment were equal, with 50% seeing a positive influence in protecting the environment, such as the establishment of marine reserves which preserve marine biodiversity; the other 50% saw the general pollution and damage to the coral reefs and unprotected marine ecosystems. Most agreed that the more tourists who come, the greater the impact will be on the environment. With respect to policy decision-making processes, 92% felt that there should be more Fijians at a management level to effect a more genuine Fijian cultural claim to the development of tourism heritage resources. This attitude was held because it was considered that Fijian people knew their own culture better and should therefore be capable of providing a better heritage tourist product. The opposing question of respondents' attitudes to foreign investment found that 65% felt that foreign ownership was good for Fiji, although 30%

believed more Fijians should own the investment to retain the profits in Fiji. The most notable factor was the growing resentment towards the subservient jobs that are offered to local people – most want to see more middle and upper management positions go to local Fijian people. Presently there is only one Fijian who manages a resort in Fiji. This resentment is growing, and places the sustainable nature of Fiji as a tourist destination in doubt, as evidenced by recent violence towards tourists at some resorts over land rights and access difficulties. Fijian hospitality and friendliness is rated by respondents as a major reason why people visit Fiji. The problem of local resentment towards visitors is compounded as 90% of Fijians want more growth in visitor numbers purely because of the economic gain through foreign exchange and employment.

Future predictions

The 1987 coup came about because indigenous Fijian people were being deprived of the right to govern their own country and were losing control over their lands and economic rights, due to the domination of the economy by Fijian Indians and offshore interests. This study aimed to re-evaluate the region, assessing what changes have occurred since the coup to re-establish the rights of the indigenous people of Fiji. An earlier study by Plange (1992) noted that 48% of native Fijians felt their lifestyles had changed as a direct result of tourism. In terms of impact, 50% believed the effects on the Fijian lifestyle had been negative. These same questions were replicated in this study, and it was found that 50% felt that their lifestyle had not improved with tourism. Plange, in his conclusions, used a phrase from the locals –'cultural trivialisation to quench consumer demands' (Plange, 1992).

Conclusions

The need is for more emphasis on a community-based planning model in future developments in Pacific indigenous tourism. Development plans must be preceded by community impact research to assess the attitudes and perceptions of local people, so that any problems can be identified. The Fijian community have shown concerns over the lack of cultural and spiritual respect for the customs of the Fijian people with regard to their cultural values and norms. These concerns are based on western beliefs, as 70% of the local Fijians in the study are Methodist and have adopted a western spiritual focus which is based on adherence to western law. This explains why in Fiji many of the heritage resource developments have occurred without the indigenous protest seen in many other societies. They understand a need to protect their heritage values, but it maybe too late to change the situation to ensure the sustainable heritage resources are retained. Their own heritage lifestyle is intertwined too closely with the western values incorporated in their society today. The Maori still have an opportunity for sustainable heritage tourism due to a less-developed tourism sector that has not primarily focused on cultural heritage tourism, and because Maori are reclaiming control and owner-ship over their heritage resources.

References

Aotearoa Maori Tourism Federation (1994) *Position Paper: The Protection of Cultural and Intellectual Property Rights of Maori within the Tourism Industry.* New Zealand: Aotearoa Maori Tourism Federation.

Barber, D. (1993) *Maori: the corporate warrior. Tourism Management,* vol. 14 (June), 33-37.

Deloitte Ross Tohmatsu (1991) Survey highlights marketing gap. *Accountants Journal,* vol. 47 (February), 94-96.

Hall, C.M. (1996) Tourism and the Maori of Aotearoa, New Zealand. In: R. Butler and T. Hinch (eds) *Tourism and Indigenous Peoples.* London: Thomson Business Press, pp. 155-175.

Henare, J. (1987). Hui, TeTi Marae, Wellington

Jackson. M. (1988) *The Maori Justice System: He Whaipaanga Hou – A New Perspective,* Part 2. Wgtn.-Dunmore Press Ltd, Palmerston, North New Zealand

Ryan, C. (1997) Maori and tourism. *Journal of Sustainable Tourism* 5, 257-278.

Zeppel, H. (1997) Maori tourism in New Zealand. *Tourism Management* 18, 475-478.

Appendix: Glossary of Maori Terms

Aotearoa	Land of the Long White Cloud – Maori name for New Zealand
Hapu	extended family or sub-tribe
Hui	meeting
Iwi	tribe
Kaitiaki	guardian
Kawa	ways, customs
Mana	strength, authority, status
Marae	meeting place
Rahui	secular
Rangatiratanga	right of self-determination, Maori sovereignty
Tangata whenua	Maori, people of the land
Taonga	scared treasures
Tapu	sacred
Tikanga	protocol, etiquette
Tupuna	ancestors
Whakapapa	genealogy
Whanau	family
Wharenui	meeting house on *marae*

Chapter twenty
Applying Theories of Program Evaluation to Implemented Government Tourism Marketing Strategies

Arch G. Woodside
Freeman School of Business, Tulane University, New Orleans, Louisiana 70118, USA

Marcia Y. Sakai ·
University of Hawaii, Hilo, 200 West Kawili Steet, Hilo, Hawaii 96720-4091, USA

Introduction

A meta-evaluation is an assessment of evaluation practices. Meta-evaluations include assessments of validity and usefulness of two or more studies focused on the same issues. Every performance audit is grounded explicitly or implicitly in one or more theories of program evaluation. A deep understanding of alternative theories of program evaluation is helpful to gain clarity about sound auditing practices. We outline a meta-evaluation of seven government audits on the efficiency and effectiveness of tourism departments and programs. The seven tourism-marketing performance audits are program evaluations for: Missouri, North Carolina, Tennessee, Minnesota, Australia, and two for Hawaii. The majority of these audits are negative performance assessments. Similarly, although these audits are more useful than none at all, the central conclusion of the meta-evaluation is that most of these audit reports are inadequate assessments. These audits are too limited in the issues examined; not grounded well in relevant evaluation theory and practice; and fail to include recommendations that, if implemented, would result in substantial increases in performance. We describe specific recommendations on how to achieve effective performance audits of government tourism marketing departments and programs, as well as how to achieve effective tourism marketing programs. To help such integration, we include an extensive introduction to the main theories of program evaluation.

Introduction to Meta-Evaluation

In 1969 New York established the first state auditing and evaluation unit. A total
of 61 such government departments exist in the USA – at least one in each of the
50 state legislatures (Brooks, 1997). Each of these auditing offices is assigned by
the state legislature with the responsibility for conducting financial audits and performance audits of government departments and their specific programs. The
mandate of these auditing offices is to provide answers to questions, including the
following issues:

- is the audited department spending funds legally and properly in accordance
  with its legislative mandate, are the department's accounting and internal
  control systems adequate, are the department's financial statements accurate?
- is the department managing its operations efficiently?
- is the department achieving substantial impact in effectively accomplishing
  its goals?

Thus the auditing work done for state legislative branches includes two major categories of audits: financial audits and performance audits. Some state audit man-
uals distinguish between program, operations, and management audits (e.g.
Anon., 1994). For example, 'a *program audit* focuses on how effectively a set of
activities achieves objectives. A program audit can stand-alone or be combined
with an operations audit. An *operations audit* focuses on the efficiency and economy with which an agency conducts its operations. In Hawaii the term *management audit* is used often to refer to an audit that combines aspects of program and
operations audit. A management audit examines the effectiveness of a program or
the efficiency of an agency in implementing the program or both' (Anon., 1994,
pp. 1–2). In this chapter we use 'management audit' and 'performance audit'
interchangeably.

The term 'meta-evaluation' was created by Scriven (1969) to mean an evaluation of evaluations. We conducted a meta-evaluation on the performance audits
of tourism-marketing programs completed for the states of Tennessee (Anon.,
1995), Missouri (Anon., 1996), North Carolina (Anon., 1989), Minnesota (Anon.,
1985), Hawaii (Anon., 1987, 1993a), and Australia (Anon., 1993b). These performance audits address two central issues: (i) how well are the government tourism marketing programs being managed? and (ii) how effectively are the actions
of the state tourism offices contributing to their goals?

Our meta-evaluation resulted in two main conclusions. Firstly, the tourism-
marketing performance audits spotlight serious problems in the performances of
government tourism marketing programs. Secondly, the audits themselves have
major shortcomings: for example, they fail to include comprehensive reporting on
topics relevant in performance auditing. With one exception (i.e. Hawaii – Anon.,
1987), the audit reports are not grounded in relevant theory and empirical literature on best practices. Consequently, the recommendations in the reports are too

limited in scope – while beneficial, implementation of the recommendations is unlikely to have a major impact on increasing the effectiveness of state government-sponsored tourism-marketing programs.

Meta-Evaluation Objectives

Meta-evaluations have three central objectives.

Firstly, meta-evaluations are syntheses of the findings and inferences of research on performance – both on the managing of programs and on the effectiveness of achieving goals of programs. Thus meta-evaluations enlighten; they help increase our knowledge and insight about what works well and poorly in managing programs.

Secondly, meta-evaluations are reports on the validity and usefulness of evaluation methods. Meta-evaluations include guidance in the methods useful to apply for evaluating.

Thirdly, meta-evaluations may provide strong inferences on the impact, payback and repercussions of enacting specific decisions. Consequently, the findings in meta-evaluations help to justify and increase the confidence of legislative members and program managers in design and implementation of specific decisions. This third objective meets the instrumental use criterion for evaluations described by Cook (1997): 'Would those who pay for evaluation be satisfied if it created enlightenment but did not feed more directly into specific decisions? I'm not sure they would'. Related to a travel decision, Campbell (1969) provides a detailed meta-evaluation that fulfils this third objective in summarizing multiple studies on the impacts (e.g. reduction in the number of deaths) of the legislated requirement to wear safety helmets by motorcyclists.

We adopt these three objectives – enlightenment, method usefulness, and instrumental use – in preparing this report. Thus presenting bad news is not our focus; our focus is on increasing useful 'sensemaking' (Weick, 1995) and reducing 'knowing what isn't so' (Gilovich, 1991) in evaluations. Sensemaking is creating, examining and revising plausible explanations of events that have occurred; sensemaking is always retrospective: 'People can know what they are doing only after they have done it' (Weick, 1995, p. 24). Auditing is one category of sensemaking.

In the second section we present a brief review of the theory-related literature on performance audits and evaluation research. Based on the conclusions drawn from the literature review, the third section offers propositions for planning and implementing a meta-evaluation of performance audits. The fourth section describes the method for collecting and analysing performance audits of state tourism-marketing programs. The following sections present the findings from a meta-evaluation of the state performance audits, and the last section provides conclusions and implications for research and practice on performance auditing of tourism-marketing programs, as well as effective strategies for managing such programs. Five golden rules are emphasized for effective performance auditing of tourism-marketing programs.

Performance Audits and Evaluation Research

The US Office of the Comptroller General defines performance auditing as an objective and systematic examination of evidence for the purpose of providing an independent assessment of the performance of a government organization, program, activity, or function in order to provide information to improve public accountability and facilitate decision-making by parties with responsibilities to oversee or initiate corrective action. An audit is 'inherently retrospective, concerned with detection of errors past – whereas many evaluative techniques can be applied retrospectively, concurrently, or prospectively' (Pollitt and Summa, 1997, p. 89).

While additional differences between audits and evaluations have been described (see Pollitt and Summa, 1997), the Association of Governmental Accountants emphasizes: 'Policy makers [want] reliable facts and sound, independent professional judgment, and they care little about ... terminology. They use terms like performance auditing and program evaluation interchangeably. Their greatest concern is that they get answers to their most pressing questions about the performance of government programs and agencies' (AGA Task Force Report 1993, p. 13, quoted from Brooks, 1997, p. 115). Thus, although recognizing that some differences exist, we use the terms 'performance auditing' and 'program evaluation' interchangeably.

Importance of program evaluation theory

What are the key issues related to theories of performance auditing? In the case of government evaluations of state tourism-marketing programs, we believe the key issues include the following points: (i) recognition of the importance of theory in program evaluation; (ii) learning the existing alternative theories of program evaluation; and (iii) adopting a multiple-perspective approach to program evaluation-use of multiple theories as foundations for tourism-marketing program evaluations.

Shadish *et al.* (1991, p. 20) emphasize that 'It is ... a serious mistake to overlook the importance of theory in program evaluation'. Theory is defined as a set of assumptions used for sensemaking (i.e. a 'mental model' description of some topic, see Senge, 1990). 'Theory connotes a body of knowledge that organizes, categorizes, describes, predicts, explains, and otherwise aids in understanding and controlling a topic' (Shadish *et al.*, 1991, p. 30).

> 'Without its unique theories, program evaluation would be just a set of loosely conglomerated researchers with principal allegiances to diverse disciplines, seeking to apply social science methods to studying social programs. Program evaluation is more than this, more than applied methodology. Program evaluators are slowly developing a unique body of knowledge that differentiates evaluation from other specialities while corroborating its standing among them' (Shadish *et al.*, 1991, p. 31)

The fundamental reason theory is important for program evaluation is that the assumptions in the theory used are the rationale for the focus and method applied for the evaluation. All performance audits are based on implicit or explicit program evaluation theory. Program evaluation theory answers the questions of whether or not the sponsored program should achieve outcomes that would not have occurred without the program, and if the program should be judged by whether or not certain policies are implemented.

For the seven performance audits of government tourism-marketing programs examined in this report, we find little explication of program evaluation theory selected for use, and we find a poor match to features found in 'good theory for social program evaluation' (see Shadish *et al.*, 1991, ch. 2). The majority of these reports do not explicitly address the issues of program evaluation theory, beyond making a general statement early in the audits. Here is an example of one such statement:

> 'The objectives of the audit were to review the department's legislative mandate and the extent to which the department has carried out that mandate efficiently and effectively and to make recommendations that might result in more efficient and effective accomplishment of the department's legislative mandates ... The audit was conducted in accordance with generally accepted government auditing standards and includes (1) review of applicable statues, regulations, policies, and procedures; (2) examination of document files, contracts, data, and reports, including information compiled by the US Travel Data Center; (3) interviews with a contracted vendor, directors of regional tourist associations, and staff of the Departments of Tourist Development, Transportation, Health, and Environment and Conservation; and (4) site visits to the 12 welcome centers.' (Anon., 1995, pp. i–ii.)

These statements fail to display knowledge and understanding of alternative theories of program evaluation, and fail to indicate features of good program evaluation theory. Steps toward good program evaluation theory include detailed, explicit statements regarding the objectives and methods applied in a performance audit, including the auditor's view on what constitutes a high-quality evaluation of a tourism-marketing program.

For example, do the auditors agree with the views of Stake *et al.* (1997) that 'Programs designed to contribute to improvement in social well-being are to some degree meritorious just by existing'? Or do the auditors embrace Scriven's theory that a program's merit should be judged by the impact of its outcomes in comparison to other programs and written standards (evaluation checklists, see Scriven, 1995). Stake *et al.* (1997) make clear that these views can not be held simultaneously: '...we object to Michael Scriven's claim that the basic logic of evaluation is criterial [*sic*] and standards-based'.

Because of such disagreements among both program evaluation theorists and practitioners, describing a detailed, explicit statement of the theory of program evaluation being used by a performance audit team is a valuable step. Without such a detailed and explicit statement, the different stakeholders affected by the audit are likely to assume different meanings for concept words such as 'efficient' and 'effective'.

Fundamental issues in development of program evaluation theory

Related to program evaluation, fundamental issues of theory development and use include the following questions.

- Social programming: what are the important problems this program addresses? Can the program be improved? Is this program worth improving? If not, what is worth doing (including the basic issue of whether a state government should be involved at all in tourism marketing; see Bonham and Mak, 1996)?
- Knowledge use: how can I make sure my results get used quickly to help this program?
- Valuing: is this a good program? By which notion of 'good'? What justifies this conclusion?
- Knowledge construction: how do I know the my information is accurate? What counts as a confident answer? What causes that confidence?
- Evaluation practice: given my limited skills, time and resources, and given the seemingly unlimited possibilities, how can I narrow my options to do a feasible evaluation? What is my role-educator, methodological expert, and/or judge-of program worth? What questions should I ask, and what methods should I use? (adapted from Shadish *et al.* 1991, p. 35)

Several well-formed alternative theories of evaluation have different-and often opposing answers to these five issues. The details of these theories cannot be covered in depth here; however, we briefly describe the main assumptions held by a leading proponent of each theory.

To create a learning aid, we oversimplify these theories using two dimensions: valuing results versus valuing activity; and logical (post)positivism versus relativism (see Fig. 20.1). The specific placement of theorists in Fig. 20.1 is arbitrary to some extent, but does reflect the kernel assumptions of the cited theorists. The kernel theoretical propositions of each theorist are described below.

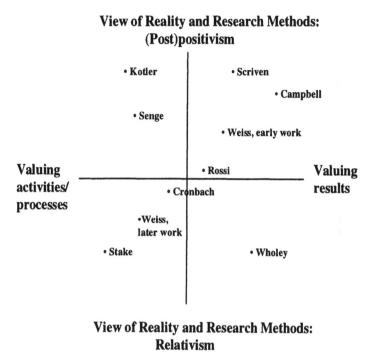

View of Reality and Research Methods:
(Post)positivism

• Kotler   • Scriven

• Campbell

• Senge

• Weiss, early work

Valuing   • Rossi   **Valuing**
activities/   • Cronbach   **results**
processes

•Weiss,
later work

• Stake   • Wholey

View of Reality and Research Methods:
Relativism

Figure 20.1 Classifying theories of program evaluation.

The two dimensions found in Fig. 20.1 address the issues (i) what should be valued in program evaluation, and (ii) what method should be used for doing evaluations? Valuing results is performance auditing built on the proposition that a (state tourism marketing) program should achieve certain outcomes that would not have occurred from other programs – including having no program. Valuing activities/processes is performance auditing built on the proposition that a program should include activities or processes specified by one or more program stakeholder groups; these activities/processes may or may not result in desirable outcomes. (Post)positivism in performance auditing builds on the proposition that one reality does exist related to performance, and that (i) multiple accounts/perspectives of this reality are data that should be collected, including quasi- and non-experimental data, for valid measurement of this one reality (the post-positivist view), or (ii) the scientific method, including test and control groups with high internal validity, should be used to measure performance (positivist view). Relativism builds on the proposition that no one reality exists – therefore data on multiple perspectives should be collected and used as indicators of performance.

Post-positivism and focusing on valuing goal-free effects: Scriven

Firstly, the body of work by Scriven (e.g. 1967, 1974, 1986, 1995) focuses on both valuing effects resulting from the program implemented, and judging the organization/processes performed. He defines evaluation as the science of valuing: 'Bad is bad and good is good, and it is the job of evaluators to decide which is which' (Scriven, 1986). Scriven believes the evaluator's ultimate task is to try very hard to condense the mass of data collected into one work: good or bad. 'Sometimes this really is impossible, but all too often the failure to do so is simply a cop-out disguised as, or rationalized as, objectivity' (Scriven, 1971, p. 53). Scriven coined the identical concepts 'goal-free' and 'needs-referenced' evaluations. 'The evaluator's job,' according to Scriven, 'is to locate any and all program effects, intended or not, that might help solve social problems. Goals are a poor source of such effects. Goals are often vaguely worded to muster political support, and rarely reflect side effects that are difficult to predict' (quoted by Shadish *et al.*, 1991, p. 80).

Scriven is a post-positivist. He rejects positivistic ideas that reality is directly perceived without mediating theories and without perceptual distortion, that scientific constructs should be operationalized directly in observables, and that empirical facts are the sole arbiter of valid scientific knowledge (Shadish *et al.*, 1991). Scriven argues that reality is independent of the observer, and it is possible to describe reality objectively. He does encourage the use of positivist research methods (e.g. experiments with test and control groups) to measure program impact; however, he stresses that practical constraints often limit the use of positivist research methods.

Note that in Fig. 20.1, Scriven is plotted right of centre, toward valuing results. Scriven (1974, p. 16) himself provides the reason, 'One way or another, it must be shown that the effects reported could not reasonably be attributed to something other than the treatment or product. No way of doing this compares well with the fully controlled experiment, and ingenuity can expand its use into most situations.' Scriven also believes in valuing activities/processes: he has developed an eighteen-point 'key evaluation checklist' that includes measuring functions and processes done (Scriven, 1980, pp. 113–116).

Scriven also advocates the use of multiple methods and observers to reach convergence for learning facts about objective reality. He acknowledges that no single scientist ever observes reality completely and undistorted; everyone observes through biased perceptual filters. Consequently, according to Scriven, using multiple perspectives and methods helps construct a more complete and accurate view of objective reality than can be accomplished by applying any one research method. He calls this view 'perspectivism', and differentiates the view from relativism: 'Perspectivism accommodates the need for multiple accounts of reality as perceptives from which we build up a true [objective] picture, not as a set of true pictures of different and inconsistent realities' (Scriven 1983, p. 255). The original concept of 'triangulation' (Denzin, 1984) is applied perspectivism: the use of multiple methods and observers to validate information about objective reality.

Positivism: true and quasi-experimentation for valuing results

Positivism focuses on achieving unbiased valuation of results of an implemented program. Positivism includes the assumptions (i) that an objective reality exists, and (ii) that we can measure accurately the effects of changing an independent variable (such as expenditures levels of a marketing program or alternative advertising campaigns) on the levels of dependent variables (such as the number of inquiries, visits, length of stay, and total visitor party expenditures).

First fully developed by Fisher (1949), the purest form of positivism is the application of the 'true experiment', that is, the use of treatment groups and control groups with random assignment of subjects among the groups to achieve 'internal validity', a term coined by Campbell. 'Random assignment promotes internal validity because it falsifies many competing interpretations (Popper, 1968) – threats to internal validity – that could plausibly have caused an observed relationship *even if the treatment had never taken place*' (Shadish *et al.*, 1991, p. 126, italics in original). Campbell and Stanley (1963) identify nine threats to internal validity in a true experiment. 'Their explication is one of Campbell's major contributions to social science and to evaluation' (Shadish *et al.*, 1991, p. 126).

Quasi-experiments (Campbell, 1969; Cook and Campbell, 1979) are novel research designs that rule out threats to internal validity when true experiments are not used. Quasi-experiments often include measuring the occurrence of a target variable (such as requests for a catalogue, visits, length of stay, expenditures) when the program implemented to cause the target variable is absent. Thus, many quasi-experimental designs fill the need to measure impact by measuring a target variable when a program is present and absent. Campbell's (1969) 'Reforms as Experiments' is probably the best-known quasi-experiment.

Contrary to popular belief, true experiments to measure the impact of a program are used often for measuring the effect (i.e. impact) of marketing and advertising programs (Banks, 1965; Caples, 1974; Woodside, 1996). Exhibit 1 presents an example of a true experiment applied to examine the effectiveness of a government tourism marketing program. The data summarized in Exhibit 1 are fictitious because no such study exists in the literature on tourism advertising.

Almost all government tourism advertisements include an offer for free literature (e.g. a 'visitors' information guide [VIG]'). The ads are created in part to gain inquiries, that is, requests, for this free literature. A VIG is an example of 'linkage advertising' (Rapp and Collins, 1987). Such linkage advertising offers provide a mechanism for advertisers to identify 'qualified prospects', that is, people displaying an interest in buying the advertised product. Marketers sometimes use lists of such qualified prospects for additional unique marketing programs to convert qualified prospects into product buyers (Rapp and Collins, 1994).

Hundreds of such true experiments have been done in industries other than government tourism-marketing programs (Caples, 1974), but surprisingly none has been reported in the travel and tourism literature (Woodside, 1990). In relation to testing the impacts of advertising campaigns, the costs of such experiments are relatively small – most likely less than 3% of the total advertising budget. Rather than using true experiments or well-designed quasi-experiments, the evaluation of the impacts of government tourism-advertising programs has used one-group conversion studies almost exclusively. These conversion studies use no non-exposed, randomly assigned group. Thus such studies cannot answer the basic issue: did the advertising program increase the number of visitors and dollar expenditures versus what would have occurred without the advertising campaign? Such one-group conversion studies are useful for comparing the conversion rates and average dollar expenditures of different groups exposed to different government tourism-advertising campaigns (e.g. Woodside and Motes, 1981) and competing advertising media (e.g. Woodside and Soni, 1990), but such studies do not address the more basic issue of whether the advertising program caused results that would not otherwise have been experienced.

Even though highly critical of both the activities and results of marketing programs, none of the seven performance-audit reports includes mention of the lack of high-quality research designs to measure advertising impacts. These performance audits do not include indications of knowledge of the core assumptions of positivism as a theory of program evaluation.

Shift away from positivism toward valuing activities and relativism methods: Weiss

Note in Fig. 20.1 that Weiss appears in two positions. 'Weiss (e.g. 1972) initially tried to use traditional experimental methods in evaluation, but the political and organizational problems she encountered in doing so sensitized her to the need to consider such problems more realistically' (Shadish *et al.*, 1991, p. 183). In her later work on evaluation theory, she perceived evaluation as a political activity in a political context; she decided that evaluation is more useful if it suggests feasible action or challenges current policy.

> 'I would like to see evaluation research devote a much larger share of its energies to tracing the life course of a program: the structure set up for its implementation, the motivations and attitudes of its staff, the recruitment of participants, the delivery of services, and the ways in which services and schedules and expectations change over time, the response of participants and their views of the meaning of the program in their lives.' (Weiss, 1987, p. 45)

Note that, unlike Scriven and Campbell, Weiss is more of a descriptive theorist than a prescriptive theorist of valuing. She advocates evaluations that report how stakeholders, such as program administrators, value their activities to assess whether or not changes are warranted/possible in policy decisions. Weiss's primary goal for evaluations is the enlightenment of stakeholder groups – in thinking about issues, defining problems, and gaining new ideas and perspectives.

Partnering with program management to achieve performance goals: Wholey

Note that Wholey is located in the bottom right quadrant of Fig. 20.1. While in principle endorsing the view that an objective reality exists and results can be measured using positivistic tools, Wholey (1977, p. 51) observes, 'Practically, however, we must settle for substantially less in virtually all federal programs. An assumption is considered "testable" if there exist test comparisons that the manager/intended user would consider adequate indication that observed effects were attributable to program activities.'

Wholey's theory of program evaluation includes working closely with program managers. He writes, 'Evaluators and other analysts should place priority on management-oriented evaluation activities designed to facilitate achievement of demonstrable improvements in government management, performance, and results' (Wholey, 1983, p. 30). Wholey and his colleagues advocate reporting by the evaluator to the program managers about progress and results at all steps in the evaluation. 'Final reports and exit briefings ought not be the places where significant findings are revealed for the first time. Evaluators should continually be sharing their insights, findings, and conclusions with staff, managers, and policy-makers' (Bellavita *et al.*, 1986, p. 291).

From an examination of the seven audits described below, government auditors completing performance audits of their governments' tourism-marketing programs follow Wholey's assumptions regarding valuing results using relativistic methods. However, the work and reports by the auditors do not follow Wholey's views on partnering with program management. The state auditors in the USA did not follow Wholey's recommendation of providing ongoing reports of findings during the audit processes – the reports are confrontational in tone, an emotional state that Wholey avoids in his auditing work.

Evaluating activities and using relativistic methods: Stake

'Stake advocates that case study methodologies be used to improve local practice' (Shadish *et al.*, 1991, p. 271). Stake's theory of program evaluation is closer to Weiss's enlightenment approach than to Wholey's partnering views. Unlike Wholey, Stake does not emphasize concerns by legislators, although he describes such concerns in his evaluations.

Stake's empirical work concentrates on evaluation of education programs. His theory of program evaluation includes the beliefs that evaluations should increase practitioner understanding and allow the practitioners (i.e. program managers) to solve any problems uncovered by the evaluation. Major concerns for Stake include (i) how can evaluations be made to facilitate their use, and (ii) how can evaluation reports be made credible? He argues that credible reports are more likely to be used than reports believed to be false, and that case studies are the best way to produce credible reports (Stake and Easley, 1978; Stake *et al.*, 1997).

Consequently, Stake is a strong advocate of the use of case-study methods. These methods include the use of interviews, observation, examination of documents and records, unobtrusive measures, and investigative journalism, resulting in a case report that is complex, holistic, and involves many variables not easily unconfounded. These written cases are informal, narrative, with verbatim quotations, illustrations, allusions, and metaphors.

Stake distinguishes between a preordinate evaluation and a responsive evaluation. 'Many evaluation plans are more "preordinate", emphasizing (1) statement of goals, (2) use of objective tests, (3) standards held by program personnel, and (4) research-type reports' (Stake, 1980, p. 76). He advocates the use of 'responsive evaluation' in place of preordinate evaluation. A program evaluation is responsive evaluation '(1) if it orients directly to program activities rather than to program intents, (2) if it responds to audience requirements for information, and (3) if the different value-perspectives of the people at hand are referred to in reporting the success and failure of the program' (Stake, 1980, p. 77).

Our meta-evaluation of the seven performance audits of tourism-marketing programs indicates that they do not match closely with the core propositions of Stake's theory of program evaluation: these audits do not include rich, detailed case studies of the programs examined; they do not include a relativist perspective of reality. Although triangulation methods are the primary research methods used in these seven audits, the auditors use triangulation to achieve convergence rather than divergence.

Objective reality and valuing activities: Kotler

Kotler's work on marketing audits (Kotler et al., 1977, 1989; Kotler, 1997) may be viewed accurately as a post-positivist theory of program evaluation similar to Scriven's (1983, 1995) contributions: both Kotler and Scriven imply an objective reality exists and can be best learned using multiple research methods (i.e. triangulation to achieve convergence). However, Kotler focuses much more than Scriven on valuing activities rather than results. Thus, note the placement of Kotler in the upper left quadrant of Fig. 20.1.

Kotler (1997, p. 777) defines a marketing audit to mean 'a comprehensive, systematic, independent, and periodic examination of a company's – or business units' [or, policy program such as government tourism-marketing programs] – marketing environment, objectives, strategies, and activities with a view to determining problem areas and opportunities and recommending a plan of action to improve the company's marketing performance.' He reports, '... most experts agree that self-audits lack objectivity and independence ... the best audits are likely to come from outside consultants who have the necessary objectivity, broad experience in a number of industries, some familiarity with the industry being audited, and the undivided time and attention to give to the audit' (Kotler, 1997, p. 777).

He continues, 'The cardinal rule in marketing auditing is: Don't rely solely on the company's managers for data and opinion. Customers, dealers [i.e. firms carrying manufacturers' product lines], and other outside groups must also be interviewed. Many companies do not really know how their customers and dealers see them, nor do they fully understand customer needs and value judgments' (Kotler, 1997, p. 779). Similar to Scriven's 'key evaluation checklist', Kotler provides check-lists, rating forms and open-ended questionnaires useful for the marketing audit he describes (Kotler, 1997, pp. 776-782). Kotler's 'components of a marketing audit' open-ended questionnaire focuses on evaluating the behaviour of markets, customers [or clients], competitors, distribution and dealers, facilitators and marketing firms, and the public. Kotler's audit form includes questions relating to valuing how well the executives of the audited organization are scanning the organization's stakeholders (e.g. markets, industry, customers and competitors), planning decisions, implementing these decisions, and assessing profitability and costs.

In our meta-evaluation, none of the seven performance-audit reports indicated use of checklists, rating forms, or open-ended questionnaires for valuing the scanning, planning, or implementing activities of the programs evaluated. The seven audits exhibit little evidence of systematic performance auditing for valuing the full range of management functions, as proposed by Kotler (1997).

Systems thinking and systems dynamics modelling as a theory of program evaluation: Senge

While Senge (1990) and other systems researchers (e.g. Hall *et al.*, 1994) do not refer to program evaluation, their work clearly relates to valuing activities and outcomes of programs as systems. Similar to Wholey (1983), Senge does not suggest program evaluation to find fault. But Senge goes farther than Wholey, 'In mastering systems thinking, we give up the assumption that there must be an individual, or individual agent, responsible. The feedback perspective suggests *that everyone shares responsibility for problems generated by a system*' (italics in original: Senge, 1990, p. 78). Senge recommends developing a useful microworld (i.e. simplified representative view of the events and flows of relationships) of actual systems; he views everything in life as a system. A systems-dynamic modelling is an advanced form of creating microworlds (Hall, 1983). The view that customer behaviour influences the behaviour of program managers and program manager behaviour influences the behaviour of customers is the circular linkage included in a systems theory of program evaluation. Developing long-term relationship marketing programs with customers, including an interactive database-marketing strategy with multiple contacts over several years, is a systems view of program valuing.

Note that Senge is located in a positivistic, valuing activity position in Fig. 20.1. However, systems researchers never advocate one reality as optimal; they advocate modelling the activity relationships among variables in a system and measuring the impacts of inputs and outcomes for each variable over time – using objectively viewed indicators for each variable. Hall provides useful examples of such systems evaluation work (Hall, 1983, Hall *et al.*, 1994).

A systems-thinking approach to tourism-marketing program evaluation includes identifying the participants, their activities, and the relationships among events occurring in implementing the program. Core assumptions in such systems-modelling work include the following propositions:

- all events are both causes and outcomes of other events
- several feedback loops among two or more participants and events occur in the implementation of the program
- participants in managing and operating a tourism-marketing program have incomplete mental models of how the program functions – the human mind can not comprehend clearly the substantial complexities and nuances in a system
- the longer, indirect paths in systems often have a total impact opposite of the effect of shorter, more direct paths
- the principal objective of performance auditing of the program is to create useful systems models of the program and to test improvements in program outcomes via simulating the running of the program.

A program-evaluation case study by Hall and Menzies (1983) illustrates the detail in systems performance auditing. They describe a performance audit using micro-systems modelling of a leisure-sports organization – a curling club in Winnipeg, Canada.

The propositions in a systems theory of program evaluation receive no specific attention among the seven performance audits reviewed in the meta-evaluation of government tourism-marketing programs. For example, none of the performance audits includes evaluations concerning the lack of database marketing behaviour for building long-term relationships with inquirers – inquirers responding to government offers of free travel information (e.g. visitor information guides). Because of the advances in the efficiency and effectiveness in database-marketing programs and in system dynamics modelling (e.g. *ALPHA/Sim*: Anon., 1998), applications of systems thinking in performance auditing of government tourism-marketing programs are likely to occur – given that government performance auditors receive training in applications of database marketing and systems dynamics modelling.

Comprehensive theories of program evaluation: Cronbach and Rossi

Two comprehensive theories of program evaluation are positioned in central locations in Fig. 20.1. These locations identify the contributions to program evaluation theory made by Lee Cronbach and Peter Rossi. Both Cronbach's and Rossi's views have much in common: they both advocate the use of multiple methods including positivistic and relativistic research methods. They both believe that no single paradigm (i.e. set of assumptions representing a mental model) for knowledge construction has sufficient empirical or theoretical support to dominate the field. Both want evaluators to study program description, causation, explanation and generalization, sometimes including all of them in the same study, albeit with different priorities depending on circumstances (Shadish *et al.*, 1991, p. 318).

The proposition that dependable knowledge is contingent on multiple conditionals captures Cronbach's belief about objective reality. Rather than seeking a general estimate of objective reality, Cronbach seeks to reduce uncertainty and increase understanding of the complexities of relationships in given local contexts. Such complex, dependable, explanatory knowledge requires evaluators to place more weight on interpretive (relativistic), thick-descriptive methods rather than on methods traditionally espoused in social sciences – positivistic research methods, such as experimentation.

Cronbach *et al.* (1980) in *Toward Reform of Program Evaluation* make some highly perceptive observations about program administration and decision-making in general:

'... rarely are decisions made rather than slipped into; rarely is there a single decision maker; rarely do data about optimal decisions take precedence over politics; rarely do all stakeholders give the project the same attention and meaning as evaluators; rarely is a report ready on time; rarely are decisions made on particular days; and rarely are evaluation results used to modify programs in ways that instrumentally link the modifications to the evaluation. Cronbach and his co-authors depict a world of politics and administration that undercuts the rational model and its image of clear command and optimal decision making.' (Shadish *et al.*, 1991, p. 335)

This view of sensemaking matches well with the later work on sensemaking by Weick (1979, 1995). Weick views most decision-making as following behaviour rather than preceding behaviour. He asks, 'How can I know what I value until I see where I walk [what I've done]? People make sense of their actions, their walking, and their talking. If they are forced to walk the talk, this may heighten accountability, but it also is likely to heighten caution and inertia and reduce risk taking and innovation'. (Weick, 1995, p. 183)

Consequently, Cronbach believes that evaluations must be crafted to the political system as it is rather than to an abstract model of how it should be. He suggests that it is unwise to focus on whether or not a project has 'attained its goals' (Cronbach *et al.*, 1980, p. 5). For Cronbach, evaluation is a pluralist enterprise. Evaluations should contribute to enlightened discussions of alternative paths for social action, clarifying important issues of concern to the policy-shaping community (Shadish *et al.*, 1991, p. 338). Evaluators as educators and as knowledge resources reflect Cronbach's views of program evaluation.

Rossi's theory of program evaluation recognizes three kinds of studies by evaluators: (i) analysis related to the conceptualization and design of interventions (e.g. government social programs, such as tourism-marketing programs), (ii) monitoring of program implementation, and (iii) assessment of program utility (i.e. worth). Related to government tourism-marketing programs, the first kind of study would include asking the following question: what type of marketer–customer relationship should state government design and how should state government go about implementing such a design? Only one government audit, the *Evaluation of the Australian Tourist Commission's Marketing Impact* (Anon., 1993b), comes close to raising this issue.

Related to the program monitoring – the second issue – Rossi believes that 'Program monitoring information is often as important or more important than information on program impact' (Rossi and Freeman, 1985, p. 144). He suggests that evaluators can help by monitoring '(1) whether or not the program is reaching the appropriate target population, and (2) whether or not the delivery of services is consistent with the program design specifications' (Rossi and Freeman, 1985, p. 139). Regarding program utility, Rossi and Freeman (1985, p. 40) state, 'Unless programs have a demonstrable impact, it is hard to defend their implementation and continuation'. Going much further than other evaluation theorists, Rossi and Freeman devote a chapter to cost–benefit analysis.

Note in Fig. 20.1 that Rossi is positioned above the mid-point on the (post) positivistic–relativistic dimension. This positioning is based in part on his view that 'Assessing impact in ways that are scientifically plausible and that yield relatively precise estimates of net effects requires data that are quantifiable and systematically and uniformly collected' (Rossi and Freeman, 1985, p. 224). Rossi's theory of program impact measurement includes measuring effects in the absence of the program:

'Adequate construction of a control group is usually central to impact assessment. Such groups should consist of multiple units comparable to the treatment group [group exposed to the tourism-marketing program] in composition, experiences, and dispositions. The preferred option is use of randomized controls, something that is often more feasible with innovations than established programs. When randomization is not feasible, other options are (from most to least preferred): matched controls, statistically compared controls ... Rossi also advises increasing the precision of impact evaluations by adding multiple pre- and postmeasures and using large sample sizes.' (Shadish *et al.*, 1991, p. 403)

Rossi also believes that assessing how well program innovations are implemented is crucial. 'The components of the delivery system must be explicated and criteria of performance developed and measured' (Rossi and Freeman, 1985, p. 77). 'This [measuring] includes assessment of the target problem and population; service implementation; qualifications and competencies of the staff; mechanisms for recruiting targets; means for optimizing access to the intervention, including location and physical characteristics of service delivery sites [e.g. visitor information guides; websites; interstate visitor welcome centres]; and referral and follow-up' (Chen and Rossi, 1983; quoted from Shadish *et al.*, 1991, p. 401).

Conclusions

The seven performance-audit reports do not include mention of alternative theories or methods for program evaluation. They all report using a triangulation of methods, including interviews, document analysis, and site visits. Although not stated formally, the goal of using multiple methods to ensure divergent viewpoint data is not implied in these reports. Rather, the two objectives for using a triangulation of research methods in most of these reports include (i) uncovering major problems in the actions and outcomes of operating the government tourism-marketing program, and (ii) achieving convergence for presenting a Scriven-type summary view of the one, objective, reality of program activities and performance outcomes (i.e. 'good' or 'bad').

For example, the 'Audit Highlights', the first page in the Tennessee performance audit of the Department of Tourist Development (Anon., 1995), addresses one activity found to be a problem by the auditors. 'The Cost-Effectiveness of Using State Personnel Instead of Outside Contractors Should Be Analyzed' (all capitals in the original, Anon., 1995). Similarly, the 1994–1995 performance audit of Missouri's Department of Economic Development, Division of Tourism reports, 'Our review was made in accordance with applicable generally accepted government auditing standards and included such procedures as we considered necessary in the circumstances. In this regard, we reviewed the division's revenues, expenditures, contracts, and other pertinent procedures and documents, and interviewed division personnel' (Anon., 1996).

The central theme of the Missouri audit report is on reporting improper activities and bad performance. The report includes written responses to these findings by the Missouri Division of Tourism. The North Carolina 1989 audit report of the Division of Travel and Tourism has the same theme: 'In reviewing the activities of the division we found that the division had failed to answer 93,221 reader service inquiries during the first part of 1988' (Anon., 1989, p. 2). Note that this quote comes from the Executive Summary of the North Carolina State Auditor report. Although less adversarial, the 1985 Minnesota audit of tourism programs of the Department of Energy and Economic Development (DEED) focuses on identifying shortcomings in activities of the program – including DEED's lack of assessment of the return on investment of its tourism-marketing programs (Anon., 1985).

With the exception of the audit report for Australia's tourism-marketing program, the performance-audit reports do not include a comprehensive coverage of the activities and results of government tourism-marketing programs. Again, with the exception of the Australian audit, the audits do not attempt to identify best practices in assessing performance of tourism-marketing programs. The audits do not describe other possible theories of program evaluation as foundations for performance auditing. The audits include only brief mentions of the theoretical grounding in accounting for the audits.

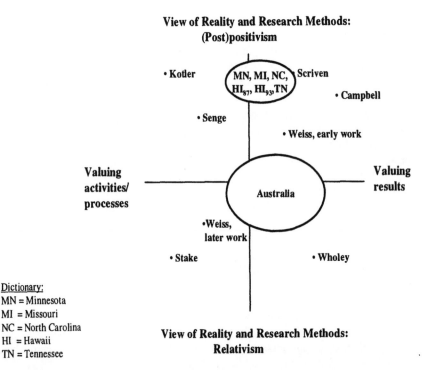

View of Reality and Research Methods:
(Post)positivism

Dictionary:
MN = Minnesota
MI = Missouri
NC = North Carolina
HI = Hawaii
TN = Tennessee

View of Reality and Research Methods:
Relativism

Figure 20.2 Classifying performance audits of government tourism-marketing programs by two dimensions of program evaluation theory. MN, Minnesota; MI, Missouri; NC, North Carolina; HI, Hawaii; TN, Tennessee.

We conclude that the substantial majority of performance audits of government tourism-marketing programs are summarized accurately as post-positivistic and are oriented towards valuing both activities and results. Related to the theories of program evaluation described earlier, these audit reports most closely follow the assumptions of Scriven's theory of program evaluation. Figure 20.2 shows a summary of our meta-evaluations of the theories in use for the seven performance audits.

Notably, the only performance audit that was compiled jointly with an audit department and the department managing the tourism-marketing program is Australia's audit, compiled by The Department of Finance, Department of Arts, Sport, the Environment, Tourism and Territories and the Australian Tourist Commission (Anon., 1993b, cover page). The executive summary of the Australian performance audit states, 'This is the first comprehensive evaluation of the Australian Tourist Commission's (ATC) marketing and promotional activities' (Anon., 1993b, p. 1).

The performance-audit partnering of departments and the attempt to achieve a comprehensive program evaluation are examples of the evidence we used to locate the Australian audit among the theoretical assumptions of Wholey, Weiss's later work, and Cronbach (see Fig. 20.2). However, several findings in the Australian audit report support the conclusion that the Australian auditors assume an objective reality exists; the Australian report uses triangulation to achieve convergence, as well as divergence. The Australian audit report is the only one among the seven analysed that includes references to tourism-marketing impact studies done by other governments. Thus the theory of program evaluation covers Rossi's assumptions and recommendations for estimating objective reality.

References

Anon. (1985) *Economic Development.* St Paul, Minnesota: Program Evaluation Division, Office of the Legislative Auditor, State of Minnesota.

Anon. (1987) *Management Audit of the Hawaii Visitors Bureau and the State's Tourism Program*, Report Number 87-14. Honolulu: Legislative Auditor, State of Hawaii.

Anon. (1989) *Performance Audit: Department of Commerce, Division of Travel and Tourism and North Carolina Film Office.* Raleigh, North Carolina: Office of the State Auditor.

Anon. (1993a) *Management and Financial Audit of the Hawaii Visitors Bureau,* Report Number 93-25. Honolulu: The Auditor, State of Hawaii.

Anon. (1993b) *Evaluation of the Australian Tourist Commission's Marketing Impact.* Sydney: Australian Tourist Commission.

Anon. (1994) *Manual of Guides (1994).* Honolulu: The Auditor, State of Hawaii.

Anon. (1995) *Performance Audit: Department of Tourist Development.* Nashville, Tennessee: State of Tennessee, Comptroller of the Treasury, Department of Audit, Division of State Audit.

Anon. (1996) *Special Review of the Department of Economic Development, Division of Tourism,* Report No. 96-86. Jefferson City, Missouri: Offices of the State Auditor of Missouri.

Anon. (1998) *ALPHA/Sim.* Burlington, Massachusetts: Alphatech, Inc.

Banks, S. (1965) *Experimentation in Marketing.* New York: McGraw-Hill.

Bellavita, C., Wholey, J.S. and Abramson, M.A. (1986) Performance-oriented evaluation: prospects for the future. In: J.S. Wholey, M.A. Abramson and C. Bellavita (eds) *Performance and Credibility: Developing Excellence in Public and Nonprofit Organizations.* Lexington, Massachusetts: Lexington Press.

Binter, M.J., Booms, B.H. and Mohr, L.A. (1994) Critical service encounters: the employee's view. *Journal of Marketing* 58, 95–106.

Bonham, C. and Mak, J. (1996) Private versus public financing of state destination promotion. *Journal of Travel Research* 35, 3–10.

Brooks, R.A. (1997) Evaluation and auditing in state legislature. In: E. Chelimsky and W.R. Shadish (eds) *Evaluation for the 21st Century: A Handbook.* Thousand Oaks, California: Sage, pp. 109–120.

Campbell, D.T. (1969) Reforms as experiments. *American Psychologist* 24, 409–429.

Campbell, D.T. and Stanley, J.C. (1963) *Experimental and Quasi-Experimental Designs for Research.* Chicago: Rand McNally.

Caples, J. (1974) *Tested Advertising Methods,* 4th edn. Englewood Cliffs, New Jersey: Prentice-Hall.

Chen, H. and Rossi, P.H. (1983) Evaluating with sense: the theory-driven approach. *Evaluation Review* 7, 283–302.

Cook, T.D. (1997) Lessons learned in evaluation over the past 25 years. In: E. Chelimsky and W.R. Shadish (eds) *Evaluation for the 21st Century.* Thousand Oaks, California: Sage.

Cook, T.D. and Campbell, D.T. (1979) *Quasi-Experimentation.* Boston: Houghton Mifflin.

Cronbach, L.J., Ambron, S.R., Dornbusch, S.M., Hess, R.D., Hornki, R.C., Phillips, D.C., Walker, D.F. and Weiner, S.S. (1980) *Toward Reform of Program Evaluation.* San Francisco: Jossey-Bass.

Denzin, N.K. (1984) *The Research Act.* Englewood Cliffs, New Jersey: Prentice-Hall.

Fisher, R.A. (1949) *The Design of Experiments,* 5th edn. New York: Hafner.

Gilovich, T. (1991) *How We Know What Isn't So.* New York: Free Press.

Hall, R.I. (1983) The natural logic of management policy making: its implications for the survival of an organization. *Management Science* 30, 905–927.

Hall, R.I. and Menzies, W.B. (1983) A corporate system model of a sports club: using simulation as an aid to policymaking in a crisis. *Management Science* 29, 52–64.

Hall, R.I., Aitchison, P.W. and Kocay, W.L. (1994) Causal policy maps of managers: formal methods for elicitation and analysis. *System Dynamics Review* 10, 337–360.

Kotler, P. (1997) *Marketing Management,* 9th edn. Upper Saddle River, New Jersey: Prentice-Hall.

Kotler, P., Gregor, W.T. and Rodgers, W.H. (1977) The marketing audit comes of age. *Sloan Management Review* 18, 25–43.

Kotler, P., Gregor, W.T. and Rodgers, W.H. (1989) Retrospective commentary. *Sloan Management Review* 30, 59–62.

Pollitt, C. and Summa, H. (1997) Performance auditing. In E. Chelimsky and W.R. Shadish (eds) *Evaluation for the 21st Century: A Handbook.* Thousand Oaks, California: Sage.

Rapp, S. and Collins, T. (1987) *Maxi-marketing.* New York: McGraw-Hill.

Rapp, S. and Collins, T. (1994) *Beyond Maxi-marketing.* New York: McGraw-Hill.

Rossi, P.H. and Freeman, H.E. (1985) *Evaluation: A Systematic Approach,* 3rd edn. Beverly Hills, California: Sage.

Scriven, M.S. (1967) *The Methodology of Evaluation.* AERA Monograph Series on Curriculum Evaluation, No. 1. Chicago: Rand, McNally.

Scriven, M. (1969) An introduction to meta-evaluation. *Education Product Report* 2, 36–38.

Scriven, M. (1971) Evaluating education programs. In: F.G. Caro (ed.) *Readings in Evaluation Research.* New York: Sage, pp. 49–53.

Scriven, M.S. (1974) Evaluation perspectives and procedures. In: J.W. Popham (ed.) *Evaluation in Education: Current Application.* Berkeley, California: McCutchan, pp. 3–93.

Scriven, M.S. (1980) *The Logic of Evaluation.* Inverness, California: Edgepress.

Scriven, M.S. (1983) Evaluation ideologies. In: G.F. Madaus, M. Scriven and D.L. Stufflebeam (eds) *Evaluation Models: Viewpoints on Educational and Human Services.* Boston: Kluwer-Nijhoff, pp. 229–260.

Scriven, M. (1986) New frontiers of evaluation. *Evaluation Practice* 7, 7–44.

Scriven, M.S. (1995) The logic of evaluation and evaluation practice. In: D.M. Fournier (ed.) *Reasoning in Evaluation: Inferential Links and Leaps*. San Francisco: Jossey-Bass, pp. 49–70.

Senge, P. (1990) *The Fifth Discipline*. New York: Doubleday.

Shadish Jr, W.R., Cook, T.D. and Leviton, L.C. (1991) *Foundations of Program Evaluation*. Newbury Park: Sage.

Stake, R.E. (1980) Program evaluation, particularly responsive evaluation. In: W.B. Dockrell and D. Hamilton (eds) *Rethinking Educational Research*. London: Hodder & Stoughton.

Stake, R.E. and Easley, J.A. (1978) *Case Studies in Science Education*. Champaign, Illinois: University of Illinois, Center for Instructional Research and Curriculum Evaluation.

Stake, R., Migotsky, C., Davis, R., Cisneros, E.J., DePaul, G., Dunbar Jr, C., Farmer, R., Feltovich, J., Johnson, E., Williams, B., Zurita, M. and Chaves, I. (1997) The evolving syntheses of program value. *Evaluation Practice* 18, 89–103.

Weick, K.E. (1979) *The Social Psychology of Organizing*. New York: McGraw-Hill.

Weick, K.E. (1995) *Sensemaking in Organizations*. Thousand Oaks, California: Sage.

Weiss, C.H. (1972) *Evaluation Research: Methods for Assessing Program Effectiveness*. Englewood Cliffs, New Jersey: Prentice-Hall.

Weiss, C.H. (1987) Evaluation social programs: what have we learned? *Society* 25, 40–45.

Wholey, J.S. (1977) Evaluability assessment. In: L. Rutman (ed.) *Evaluation Research Methods: A Basic Guide*. Beverly Hills, California: Sage.

Wholey, J.S. (1983) *Evaluation and Effective Public Management*. Boston: Little, Brown.

Woodside, A.G. (1990) Measuring advertising effectiveness in destination marketing strategies. *Journal of Travel Research* 29, 3–8.

Woodside, A.G. (1996) *Measuring the Effectiveness of Image and Linkage Advertising*. Westport, Connecticut: Quorum Books.

Woodside, A.G. and Motes, W.H. (1981) Sensitivities of market segments to separate advertising strategies. *Journal of Marketing* 45, 63–73.

Woodside, A.G. and Soni, P.K. (1990) Performance analysis of advertising in competing media vehicles. *Journal of Advertising Research* 30, 53–66.

Index

Note: page numbers in **bold** text refer to figures, those in *italic* refer to tables